What the world's leading author of business best-sellers is saying about The One Page Business Plan®...

"The One Page Business Plan is an out-and-out winner. Period.

It makes great sense to me as a so-called *business thinker*. But the acid test was applying it to a start-up I co-founded. We spent several days drafting our one pager — and have been editing it ever since. It is a powerful, living document; the very nature of which has led us to important new insights.

The One Page Business Plan = the proverbial better mouse trap!"

— Tom Peters

author of
In Search of Excellence,
Thriving on Chaos,
Liberation Management,
The Pursuit of Wow!,
and *The Circle of Innovation*

WARNING — DISCLAIMER

This book was designed to provide information in regard to the subject matter covered. It is not the purpose of this manual to reprint all of the information available to the author/publisher, but to complement, amplify and supplement other sources.

Use of The One Page Business Plan℠ does not in any way guarantee the success of an idea or organization, nor does it ensure that financing will be made available. When legal or expert assistance is required, the services of a competent professional should be sought.

The author/publisher shall have neither liability nor responsibility to any person or entity with respect to any loss or damage caused, or alleged to be caused, directly or indirectly by the information contained in this book.

If you do not wish to be bound by the above, you may return this book to the publisher for a full refund.

THE ONE PAGE BUSINESS PLAN WITH CD ROM

Published by:

The One Page Business Plan® Company

1798 Fifth Street
Berkeley, CA 94710
Phone: (510) 705-8400
Fax: (510) 705-8403
e-mail: jhoran@onepagebusinessplan.com
www.onepagebusinessplan.com

9th Printing 2005, Third Edition with CD ROM

Library of Congress Catalog Card Number: 97-92653

ISBN 1-891315-07-2

Book design by Designwise™
Edited by Rebecca Salome Shaw, Entrepreneurial Authors
Printed in the United States of America

The One Page Business Plan®

Start with a vision, build a company!

by

Jim Horan

Berkekey, California

What Others Are Saying

The One Page Business Plan® takes a complex process and makes it simple!

"I've had a number of business plans, but none of them were effective. Having all the essentials of our plan on one page helped get me and my partners on track!"

Norman Kurtin, Design Media, Inc.

"The friendly visual graphics, and the no-nonsense approach to business planning got me over my reluctance to write a business plan. This process got me to think out of the box and to create my dream business! Now I have a great plan and it's working."

Kendall Moalem, Kendall Moalem Design

"My board of advisors applauded my one page business plan. They finally understood my business and are contributing important advice because they have a written plan to review."

Nicole Lazzaro, President, XEODesign, Inc.

"I was too busy developing plans for clients to complete my own, but a one page business plan of key words and short phrases seemed so easy and "doable" that I wrote one immediately!"

Diane Weinsheimer, The Marketing Manager

"I have been writing the same goals and visions for my business over and over. What I wrote in March, I wrote in June, and again in September. After I heard Jim speak, I wrote my one page plan. I now choose my opportunities more wisely and waste less time because I have my plan in place."

Linda Pollock, Professional Organizer

"The One Page Business Plan is the business owner's Cliff Notes."

Fred DaMert, Chairman, DaMert Company

"This is an innovative, fresh approach to business planning. If all loan applicants would provide us with clear, concise summaries of their business plan, a banker's life would be a lot easier."

Jim Ryan, Chairman, Bank of Walnut Creek, California

"As a banker, I love The One Page Business Plan. I know the potential business owner is serious, committed and professional. This is truly a breakthrough in business planning!"

Jerry Ricketts, Vice President, Scotts Valley Bank

"The One Page Business Plan truly helps the prospective entrepreneur or existing business owner get focused and clear on one page. When they are clear on one page, they have a much better chance for success!"

Greg Garrett, Program Manager, One Stop Capital Shop

"It's easy for a stockbroker to get wrapped up in the market and lose perspective that you are in business for yourself. In order to be successful for the long run, one must have a plan and The One Page Business Plan is a great tool."

Ralph Miljanich, Vice President, Dean Witter Reynolds, Inc.

"It's wonderful that someone finally came up with a business plan for independent professionals. It de-mystifies business planning so that the average business professional can actually write a business plan that makes sense!"

Rebecca Salome Shaw, Entrepreneurial Authors

"The One Page Business Plan revolutionizes business planning! It cuts the fluff and the filler and gets right to the point. This is a powerful tool for businesses of all sizes!"

Roger McAniff, Sage Consulting

This book is dedicated to the
family, friends, and the extended
community that supports and
nurtures entrepreneurs.

Without their love and support,
many entrepreneurs would not be able to
make their dreams come true.

Introducing

The One Page Business Plan®

Colorado Garden Window Company

2006 Business Plan Summary

vision

Become recognized as the leader in designing and manufacturing custom and replacement garden windows and skylights.

Vision

How do you visualize your company in the future?

mission

Bring light, air and the beauty of nature into homes through creative windows!

Mission

Why does this business exist?

objectives

Achieve 2006 sales of $17 million with $1.5 million in pretax profits.
Grow garden window division at 8% per year and achieve $5.3 million in 2006.
Expand skylight/custom window product lines; grow sales to $7.5 million in 2006.
Implement profit improvement programs & reduce product cost to 38%.
Reduce distribution costs to 4% of sales thru facility consolidation & technology.
Reduce inventory levels to 3.3 months by August 31st.
Achieve 98% ontime delivery with 98% order accuracy in 1st quarter.

Objectives

What accomplishments must this business achieve within one year to be successful?

strategies

Focus on new upscale home developments & baby-boomer remodeling trends.
Build Colorado Garden Window into nationally-recognized brand name.
Become vendor-of-choice by maintaining inventory of standard window sizes.
Control quality by manufacturing in-house.
Increase capacity by minimizing duplicate products & increasing mfg. efficiencies.
Centralize distribution into one location; reducing costs, improving service.

Strategies

How will this business be built and managed over time?

plans

Introduce new Scenic Garden Windows at SF Products Show (March 2006).
Hire new sales rep by April; focus on Signature Homes in Denver and Provo.
Implement new MRP software by July 31st to achieve inventory reduction.
Complete skylight product rationalization program by Aug. 15th.
Phase in new packaging design beginning March 31st.
Complete employee benefit program redesign by Sept. 30th.

Plans

What specific projects and actions will be taken this year to achieve the objectives?

Author's Note

"You must simplify.

You must make the complex simple, then you must make it work."

— I.M. Pei
Master Architect

There is a new breed of business owner in the marketplace today. These business owners are either starting up new businesses or reinventing established businesses. These individuals are intensely passionate and strategic. They are very competitive and heartfull. They care about people, the environment, and their communities. They do not run their businesses casually. They are professional entrepreneurs.

There is also another type of entrepreneur, the accidental entrepreneur. These individuals are finding themselves considering self-employment for the first time in their lives. Many have experienced firsthand the downsizing of corporate America and are now ready to act on their own business ideas.

I know the accidental entrepreneur very well, I happen to be one. I came kicking and screaming into the world of entrepreneurship in 1990 after spending 17 years in Fortune 500 companies as a senior financial executive. In 1990, I began a search for my next career. I found myself self-employed, as a business and financial advisor, drawn to working with entrepreneurs and independent business owners.

Today, Rent.a.CFO℠ is a broad-based consulting practice serving both professional and accidental entrepreneurs. Client companies are in a wide range of industries including specialty gifts, home improvement, professional services, and food products.

All these companies share similar issues. Business is complex, resources are limited, and time is of the essence. There is no room for big mistakes. Business owners can't know it all and can't do it all by themselves. Therefore, other people will become involved in the business. That means employees, independent contractors, investors, and potentially partners. Additionally, your business may require the use of "other people's money." Other people and "other people's money" necessitate having a written business plan. It's no longer optional.

The One Page Business Plan® was inspired by my work with entrepreneurs. These individuals like to think fast and move fast, and the concept of a traditional business plan was out of the question. An innovative, fresh approach to business planning was required, and the One Page Business Plan® was born.

The One Page Business Plan℠ is designed to act as a catalyst for your ideas. It's a powerful tool for building and managing a business in the 21st century. It's short, it's concise, and it delivers your plan quickly and effectively. There can be no question as to where you are going when it's in writing. Start with your vision, build a company.

— Jim Horan

How to Use This Book

The primary purpose of this book is to help you get your business plan onto paper. It has been carefully crafted to capture the business plan that is in your head.

Carry this book with you, write in it, use it as a container for capturing your thoughts as they occur. If you have multiple businesses, buy a book for each one.

It's not necessary to do all the exercises in this book. If you can write your One Page Business Plan® by reviewing the samples — skip the exercises. They are there to help guide you through the process if you need help.

This book does not look like the typical business planning book — it isn't intended to. The exercises and examples are meant to stimulate you. The graphics and images are meant to guide you. If they look playful, be playful and explore. If they look analytical, be analytical and focused. The examples and samples are from real business plans. They are meant to show you how powerful a few words or a well-constructed phrase can be.

Not all people think or work the same way. Some are auditory; others respond visually; some need to write. Some do their best thinking alone, silently. Others do their best thinking out loud. This book has been designed to accommodate all of these different styles.

Do not underestimate the power of the questions in this book that appear simple! They are simple by design. That's so you will understand them. If you do not get an "aha" from them, have somebody ask you the questions. Important insights may begin to flow.

This book is divided into seven sections with the focus on the five elements of The One Page Business Plan® You can start anywhere. It's OK to jump around!

There are five types of exercises in the book. They are clearly marked and identified at the top of each page. Each type of exercise is designed to achieve a specific purpose:

- **Brainstorming**— generate new ideas by considering provocative questions
- **Research**— gather information from external sources
- **Focusing**— process of prioritizing ideas and concepts
- **Summarizing**— condensing, final prioritizing, editing
- **Feedback**— solicit objective feedback from trusted advisors

There are many different ways to use and interact with this book. Exercises can be done:

- by oneself
- with a planning partner (one business owner working with another business owner)
- as a management team
- as a group — feedback exercise (one business owner receiving input from several business owners or professionals)
- by a group of entrepreneurs or business owners for brainstorming business planning concepts, ideas, strategies
- with a professional business consultant

Some final thoughts...

There is no right, wrong, or perfect business plan. Your business will always be evolving. So will your plan. It will also get better with time. Remember, it is not necessary to do all the exercises in this book nor is it desirable to do it all by yourself. Use this book as a catalyst. When you think you are finished, stop. If you get stuck, put it aside for a few days or a week. Come back to it when the ideas start to flow. Take your time and enjoy the journey.

How to Use the CD

The Entrepreneur's Toolkit CD contains additional tools to make the creation of your business plan simple and easy.

The interactive exercises, forms and templates from the book are available on Microsoft Word® for those who prefer to use word processing software.

Need help estimating or budgeting your sales? The Sales Calculators on this CD are easy to use.

Budgeting? We have simplified budgeting to a single page.

Ready to track results? Use The One Page Performance Scorecards.

CD also contains ten (10) Bonus Tools and fifteen (15) additional sample plans!

MACINTOSH USERS:

Please refer to page 98 of this book for secific instructions for your Macintosh computer!

What's on your CD:

Interactive Exercises & Templates

Included on the CD are 22 exercises from the book*. The file names on the CD relate to the specific pages in the book so they are easy to find.

Most of the forms, templates and exercises have text boxes that you can type directly into.

Powerful Sales Calculators

Contained in your CD Toolkit are three (3) Sales Calculators* that allow you to perform multiple "what-if sales scenarios". You don't need to be a CPA, MBA, or Marketing Guru to get a sense of what your sales might look like in 1, 3, or 5 years.

Each Sales Calculator has one or more colorful, easy-to-read graphs to help you visualize the growth of your business in addition to seeing the actual numbers. This is a great tool for entrepreneurs who have been intimated by the "numbers" associated with business!

Also included with the Sales Calculators is a Sales Budgeting System that helps you create a Sales Budget by Month for up to seven products, services, product lines or business units.

* Requires Microsoft Word® and/or Excel®

One Page Budget Worksheet

Every business needs a budget; especially small ones! Start the process by using one of the Sales Calculators to determine your sales by month, when finished enter the sales into the budget worksheet. Next, estimate your expenses by month referring to your Action Plans to ensure you have accounted for all of the expenses necessary to implement your plan. Fine tune sales and/or expenses until you are satisfied with the results.

One Page Performance Scorecards

The disciplined tracking of your results and progress is critical for achieving the Objectives in your One Page Business Plan. We encourage you to create a Scorecard for each of your Objectives and update them monthly.

Even More Sample Plans

Included are an additional fifteen One Page Business Plans® that can be accessed with Microsoft Word®.

... and 10 Bonus Tools

Your CD Toolkit contains 10 bonus tools, templates and techniques that we have created and used in working with thousands of entrepreneurs in workshops around the world.
These tools are simple and easy to use!

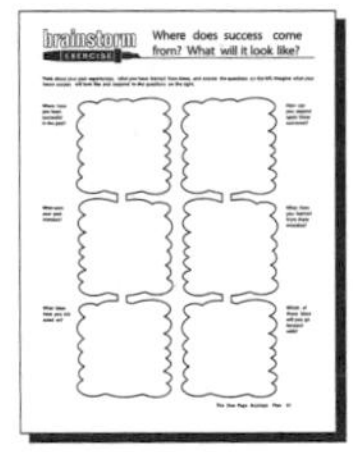

Interactive Exercises, Forms and Templates

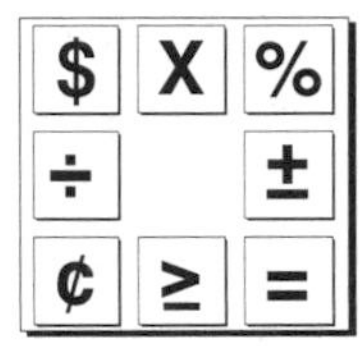

Sales Calculators

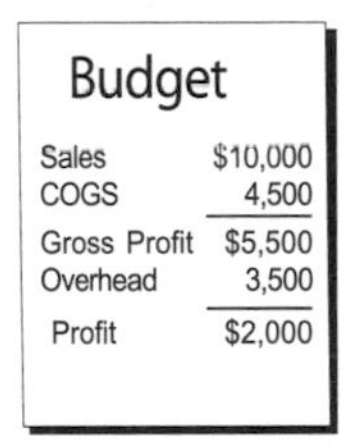

One Page Budget Worksheet

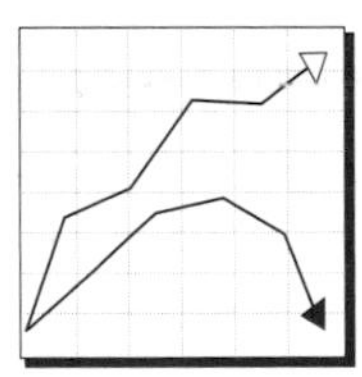

Performance Scorecards

Extra Sample Plans

Contents

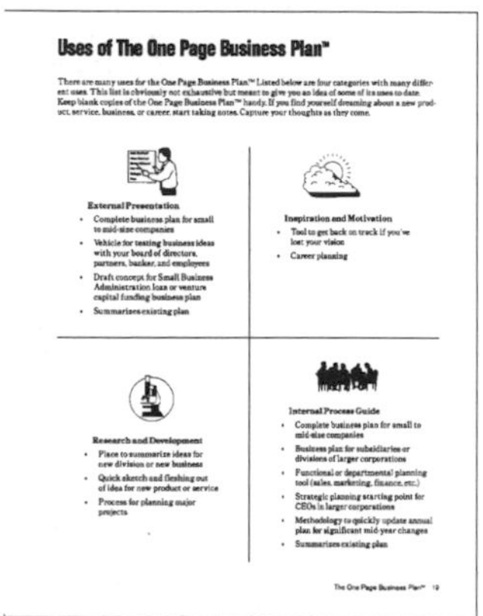
Uses of The One Page Business Plan™

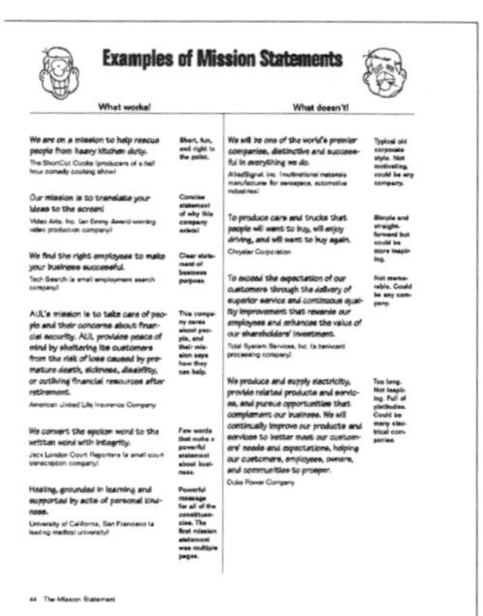
Examples of Mission Statements

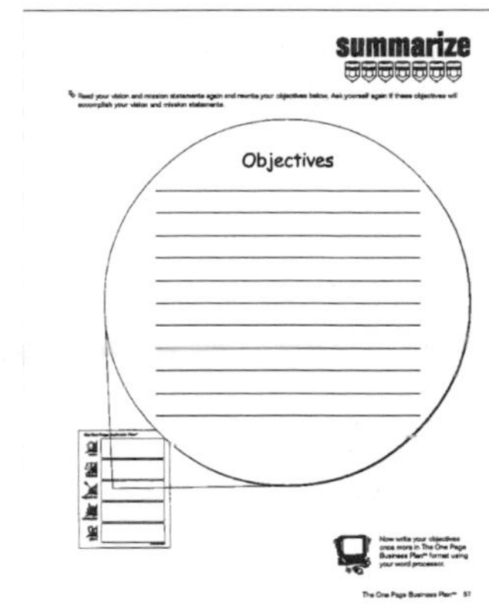

59 The Strategies

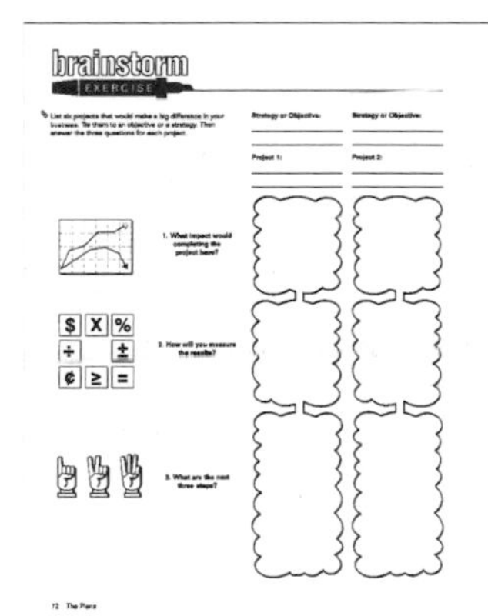

71 The Plans

79 You Did It!

Business Plan Myths

- All business plans are in writing.
- They must be long to be good.
- Their primary purpose is to obtain financing.
- It's easier for others to do business plans.
- You can and should do it all by yourself.
- It takes six months, a significant amount of the owner's and key staff members' time, and expensive consultants.
- If completed, it will sit unused on a bookshelf.
- My business is too small; business plans are for big businesses.
- I know where I'm taking my business, I do not need a written business plan.
- I can just pay to have a consultant write it for me, and that will be good enough.

Let's dispel the myths.

Introduction

The One Page Business Plan®

Visionaries are the keepers of the dreams.

Entrepreneurs take risks and make the dreams real.

The community nurtures and supports creative businesses.

Every business owner has a business plan. Meet a business owner at a party and most likely you will hear the majority of that plan within 30 minutes. Of course they will boast about their latest product success, and moan about employees, customers, and partner problems. If you listen, you'll also hear them freely describe their vision, objectives, strategies, and their plans.

Business plans don't have to be long to be good. A single page can contain all of the essential elements you need to tell your employees, board of directors, potential partners, or banker where you are taking your business and how you are going to get there. This book is going to show you how to do that.

The most important reason to have a business plan is to clarify your thinking, regardless of the size of your company. Is it possible to have too much clarity or focus? How much of your time and your business resources are wasted on projects that detract from your primary mission? What could you accomplish if everyone in your organization really knew what you were trying to do? To have a business plan is to be clear about where you are taking your business. When you're clear, and it's in writing, others will know and understand your vision and how you plan to get there.

Extensive business plans are required by those people and organizations who have money that you want. They have specific requirements that must be met or you will not get their money. This book is not about those business plans, but can greatly simplify their preparation. If you can get focused and clear on one page, you can then turn each short phrase into a paragraph, a full page, a chapter, etc. It is always easy to expand, it's much more difficult to focus and simplify. Mark Twain once said, "give me three weeks and I'll write you a short letter."

It doesn't have to take six months of agonizing meetings, pounds of written documents, endless spreadsheets, and complicated flowcharts to produce a meaningful business plan. It also does not take an army of expensive consultants. A few well-constructed phrases and short sentences can say a lot. The examples in this book will demonstrate that for you.

"The most important reason to have a business plan is to clarify your thinking, regardless of the size of your company."

You and your team know your business, inside and out. You know your industry — the major trends. You talk with your competitors and suppliers regularly. You read the newspaper, and trade journals, and maybe even surf the net a little. You also share your dreams with your close friends, associates, and family. You have everything you need to draft the plan in your head. You could draft it this morning and have a meaningful discussion with someone you trust this afternoon. If you want to bring in a consultant to help, great! Give them a copy of your draft and interview them. If they have valuable insights, hire them and have them help you refine it.

Business planning concepts are not difficult. You already understand all of them. You dream about your business, you set goals, and you work throughout the year in an organized manner to make it all happen. You probably would like to do it with less stress and better results. That's why the concept of a one page plan sounds good to you.

Why must you have a written plan? You know where you are going. But without a written plan, it's always subject to change. Every time you talk about it, it will be different. Put it in writing and everyone sees the same thing.

If writing a business plan still seems too big of a task, even after reading this book, get another business owner to commit to doing his or her plan at the same time. It's kind of like going to the health club with a friend. Get a planning partner, commit to a process, and set some deadlines. Serve as coach and cheerleader to your planning partner. It works. I know because I got writer's block when I attempted to write my own. A fellow entrepreneur gently but firmly guided and challenged me through the process. I did the same for him.

A business plan brings out the best and worst in most business professionals. It facilitates creative and analytical thinking, problem solving, communications, interfunctional sharing, and teamwork. It generates hope and enthusiasm about the future. It also brings out procrastination, frustration, differences of opinions, and possibly anger. It is not a benign process. But when done well, the process is very valuable and has its own sense of satisfaction. Your business will be stronger.

Uses of The One Page Business Plan®

There are many uses for the One Page Business Plan.® Listed below are four categories with many different uses. This list is obviously not exhaustive but meant to give you an idea of some of its uses to date. Keep blank copies of the One Page Business Plan® handy. If you find yourself dreaming about a new product, service, business, or career, start taking notes. Capture your thoughts as they come.

External Presentation

- Complete business plan for small to mid-size companies
- Vehicle for testing business ideas with your board of directors, partners, banker, and employees
- Draft concept for Small Business Administration loan or venture capital funding business plan
- Summarizes existing plan

Inspiration and Motivation

- Tool to get back on track if you've lost your vision
- Career planning

Research and Development

- Place to summarize ideas for new division or new business
- Quick sketch and fleshing out of idea for new product or service
- Process for planning major projects

Internal Process Guide

- Complete business plan for small to mid-size companies
- Business plan for subsidiaries or divisions of larger corporations
- Functional or departmental planning tool (sales, marketing, finance, etc.)
- Strategic planning starting point for CEOs in larger corporations
- Methodology to quickly update annual plan for significant mid-year changes
- Summarizes existing plan

— Thomas Moore
Care of the Soul and Soulmates

The Power and Magic of Writing

"Writing allows others to participate in your dream and give you feedback."

There is magic in the written word! Especially when they're your words about an idea that you have been thinking and talking about for sometime. Somehow the process of writing initiates the transformation from idea to reality. It also does many other wonderful things.

Things get clearer when you write. Of course at first the process can feel very awkward, and the results seem poor and anything but clear. But given time and patience, the process results in a connection of the mind with the reality of the paper. Thoughts begin to develop into images. Images turn into key words and short phrases. An outline begins to emerge, and the clarity builds.

If you stick with your writing, you also get focused. In the beginning, you'll have many ideas, more than you can ever implement. But the process of capturing them on paper results in a conscious and unconscious ranking and prioritization. I believe it is important to capture as many of your thoughts regarding your product, service, or business as possible without critiquing them. The natural process of writing will keep the best and strongest of your ideas. Your vision and mission will become more concise through this evolutionary process, resulting in a focused approach.

Writing allows others to participate in your dream and give you feedback. Writing provides a consistent forum, whereas in conversation the context changes each time you speak. Allowing others to participate and help support your idea to its next step is crucial to your overall success. The lone ranger mentality is no longer necessary nor effective.

The written word also produces a contract with yourself that results in immediate action. Haven't you found that if you make up a grocery list and leave it at home you almost always remember everything on the list? Many users of The One Page Business Plan® report that as soon as they begin to write their action items — some of which they have been thinking about for years — they start to take action on them. *I think it's magic!*

1. Architects visualize the details of a new building and produce a simple sketch to see how it might look.

2. Songwriters mentally hear a new melody and then test it out on a piano to see how it will sound.

3. Movie producers imagine the setting of their next picture and produce storyboards to help them produce a more complete image of their story.

Modeling the New Idea

"...business owners need a way to test their ideas without having to put their cash or business at high risk."

Architects, songwriters, movie producers, and inventors make models in some shape or form so they can see their ideas in a more visual, concrete manner. This process is one of the early steps that makes an idea something real and tangible. Models are a technique to help with the visualization of ideas.

As creators of businesses, we need a methodology for exploring our business ideas. It's too difficult, expensive, and nonproductive to produce working models or samples for every potential idea that comes our way. Market research is also very expensive and is generally reserved for our very best ideas. Complicated products with long lead times, requiring expensive raw materials and manufacturing facilities, obviously cannot be produced and tested like a new melody on the piano. And yet business owners need a way to test their ideas without having to put their cash or business at high risk.

Most individuals in business check out their ideas in conversation with trusted associates, consultants, friends, and relatives. But conversation is fluid, flexible, and frequently informal. Also we may not deliver the same message and details to everyone; hence the response we receive may be affected by the way we presented our thoughts. A melody played from written music will sound similar regardless of the piano it's played on. Unfortunately the spoken word is subject to much greater ambiguity when delivered.

Business people do however have the written word to describe their thoughts and ideas. The written word allows the sharing of our ideas with others in a consistent, clear fashion. The business plan is, in effect, our modeling tool. It provides the sketch, the vision, the road map for our ideas. In many ways, it's just like the composer's first few chords; the musician gets to hear it and so do others. The business plan works the same way. You get to see your ideas in writing and so do others.

INTERVIEW exercise

Ask your planning partner or a fellow business owner to interview you with the questions below. Tape the session so both of you can take notes from the recorder afterwards. Then write each person's notes below. ⌛ 30 minutes

Describe your business. Where are you going with it? What will it look like in five years?

What market need will your company's product or service fulfill? Why are you in this business? What's your passion?

What would you like to celebrate this year? What would you like to celebrate this time, next year?

What has made your business successful to date? What will make your business successful over time?

What business-building projects are on your to-do list? What have you been procrastinating on that you know would make a difference in your business?

Why The One Page Business Plan® Works

Business plans don't have to be complex and cumbersome. The One Page Business Plan® is meant to be simple and to help you get focused quickly.

Simplicity

The One Page Business Plan® is effective because it takes a complex subject and makes it simple. It's easy to read and understand. If you are the writer, you will know when you are finished because you have effectively covered all of the important elements of your business plan.

Focus

The One Page Business Plan® works because it focuses on what's important. There is no room for fluff or filler. The use of key words and short phrases tells your reader that only the essence is being presented for review. The fact that this business plan is only one page communicates that the investment in reading is limited.

Readily Understandable

The five elements of the One Page Business Plan® are readily understandable. As you read each section, the business plan element telegraphs the kind of information being presented. You know the vision statement is going to be expansive and idealistic. You expect the mission statement to be powerful and customer oriented. Objectives should be realistic and measurable. Strategies are well thought out, and plans are action oriented.

Versatility

The One Page Business Plan® works because it's a tool for communication. If you are the owner of a business, this one page document can be an important tool for communicating to your existing or prospective employees, partners, shareholders, investors, or banker the kind of company you are building and how you plan to build it.

Consistency

It's an effective communication tool because you send the same message to every person you give it to — unlike the spoken word, which may change every time you speak. Additionally, with the written word, you have chosen your words carefully and you are communicating only the most important elements of your business plan.

Flexibility

The One Page Business Plan® works because it's easy to change and update with your latest thinking. An important thought in the morning can be in your plan that afternoon. Capturing those "moments of clarity" quickly and in a useful manner will preserve them for further review, consideration, and possible action.

So what's the benefit of having a one page plan? It's your plan, your ideas, in your words. It's a reference point for any significant business or financial decision you may be considering. It's simple, concise, and it's you. Bankers, investors, and potential partners can have a complete overview of your business at a glance. Attach your budget and you're ready for a meaningful discussion about your business.

Building a Business Is a Journey . . .

The business plan is your map!

"Had you considered that Queen Isabella of Spain was one of the most powerful and important venture capitalists of all time?"

Building a business is a journey, it always has been. Marco Polo, Christopher Columbus, and Ferdinand Magellan were all great adventurers who took extended journeys. These journeys were explorations into the unknown parts of the world seeking new lands, exotic spices, fame, and fortune. These explorers were also businessmen and many of them had venture capitalists. Had you considered that Queen Isabella of Spain was one of the most powerful and important venture capitalists of all time?

Great journeys start with a vision. The vision is the dream. It describes what the journey is about and what you hope to find or create. Columbus's vision was to reach the Indies by sailing west.

All great journeys also have a mission. The mission describes the purpose for the trip. Columbus wanted to prove the world was round. Queen Isabella's mission was different. She wanted the riches and the power that conquering the new lands would bring.

Journeys have specific goals or objectives that drive certain behavior. John F. Kennedy wanted to have a man on the moon by the end of the 1960s. This goal focused many people's energy into specific actions to achieve this deadline. That's the purpose of a well-defined objective; it produces meaningful action.

Strategies set the direction. They are the road signs. They help to keep you on target so that you ultimately achieve your destination. Great strategies remain constant over the entire journey; Columbus kept heading west and it worked! Establish clear strategies for building and growing your business and stick to them.

Successful journeys have a plan. The plan details the important actions that must be taken to make the venture a success.

Wherever you are, today is the starting point. Develop a business plan that guides the building of your business. Use your business plan as a map to keep you on track to your destination.

A Vision Statement That Works:

To build Phoenix Electronic Controls, Inc. into the premier industrial process control company in the Southwest.

Within five years grow PEC, Inc. to $20 million in revenues by expanding its role from a manufacturing representative business to a value-added company offering complete engineering, field service, and integration engineering services.

The Vision Statement

How do you visualize your business?

"The Vision Statement should describe your idea in a manner that captures the passion of the idea."

The vision section of The One Page Business Plan® is very important. It's the place where you get to describe your vision, your way! Vision statements should be expansive and idealistic. They should stimulate thinking, communicate passion, and paint a very graphic picture of the business you want. Great vision statements are fun to read. When written well, they can trigger emotional and sensory reactions. If perchance you are looking for investors, a great vision statement is essential.

There is another important reason to create a large vision. When you describe your vision in an expanded manner, you are inviting others to help you see possibilities you might not see. I believe vision statements are all about exploration, creating possibilities, and asking "what if" and "why not."

You can hardly exaggerate your vision statement. Go ahead and write a wildly optimistic, no limits, maybe even outrageous, vision statement. Ask your friends and associates to push you to think "way out of the box." Then live with what you wrote for a while. Don't rush into the editing process. It may just turn out that you decide to build something more exciting than you originally believed possible.

Don't sanitize your vision statement. Keep it full of passion. This is your opportunity to describe your dream. This section of the business plan is not the place to be analytical. If you describe a limited vision, one that is dull and boring, how can you expect to be excited about your business? And if you aren't excited, how can you expect to be successful? If you don't capture the passion you feel, others will have difficulty getting interested in your project. In fact, investors typically say that the dream is almost always worth more than the reality.

The key to capturing your vision is to be free flowing and not to restrict the flow of any thoughts. Capture all thoughts that come to your mind and use powerful adjectives to describe all the characteristics. Be sure to include the personal elements of your vision, as this is the source of your passion that will carry you through the difficult and frustrating times.

Your vision has evolved over time and will continue to change. Don't allow future ideas to impede your writing today. Describe your vision as you see it now!

brainstorm EXERCISE

Your Vision...

As you think about the questions on these two pages, write down any words or short phrases that come to mind in the "idea balloons" below.

WHAT?

Products or services? or both? How many?

Company Image: What will this company be known for?

Owner's Role: What is your role? How will you spend your time?

WHERE?

Business: Local, regional, national or international?

Customers: Where are they? What cities, states, countries?

Business Operations: Headquarters, sales offices, manufacturing, etc.?

WHO?

Customers: Who are they? (most businesses have several types of customers)

Strategic Alliances: Who can you partner with?

Advisors: Who can provide professional and strategic advice and help you grow this business properly?

Creating the Company You Want

Don't worry about answering all of the questions; just try to capture your immediate thoughts.

WHEN?

Start-up: When will this business be operational?

Facilities: When will office/ manufacturing/distribution space be required?

Systems: When must they be selected, tested, and operational?

WHY?

Owner: Why am I creating this business?

Customers: Why will they buy these products or services?

Investors/Bankers: Why will they invest/loan money to this business?

HOW?

Financing: How will this business be financed?

Culture: How do you want to interact with employees, suppliers, customers?

Personal Beliefs: How will your personal beliefs about business impact this business?

INTERVIEW exercise

This exercise helps you envision the kind of company you want (and don't want) in terms of products and services, customers, and the work environment. Sometimes, it's easier to answer the questions on the right first. Have your planning partner lead you through this exercise.

What's the product or service?

Describe three characteristics of your product or service:

Describe three things your product or service WON'T DO:

Who's the customer?

Describe three characteristics of your BEST current or potential clients or customers:

Describe three characteristics of clients or customers you would be better off NOT SERVING:

What's the business environment?

Describe three characteristics of successful businesses you admire and WOULD like to emulate:

Describe three characteristics of businesses you WOULD NOT like to emulate:

Crafting Your Vision Statement

focus EXERCISE

STEP 1: Create a vision statement by filling in the blanks below. Have another person read it back to you.

Vision Statement (first draft)

Within the next ________ **years, grow** ______________________________ **into**
company name

a successful ☐ local ☐ regional ☐ national ☐ international ______________________________
type or description of business

providing ______________________________
description of products and/or services

to ______________________________.
describe your customers

STEP 2: Rewrite the vision statement above, modifying it using your own words:

____

____

____

____

____

____

STEP 3: Now write a wildly optimistic, no limits, outrageous vision statement!

Examples of Vision Statements ....

Vision statements are individualized and stylistic. Here are 11 statements written by small to mid-sized business owners, with comments about what works well for each:

Sounds intriguing and innovative. Playful and yet stimulating. It's a large vision but very believable.

Create a network of Creativity Cafes around the world that are live and cyberspace networking salons featuring educational entertainment and electronic cyber theater. A fun place where people gather for play and work; where creative people, using the marriage of art and state-of-the-art technology learn from each other and have a forum for showcasing their work.

Creativity Cafe™ (www.creativity.com)

Narrative style. Personal, yet professional.

McAniff Consulting envisions a business that does excellent consulting work with small to medium clients in the Northwest and large companies nationally. The consulting work will emphasize the integration of the three "P"s of Planning, Process, and Performance to achieve excellent business results. My vision is to share office space and interact with other management consulting professionals to develop a successful practice.

McAniff Consulting

Reflects owners' personal style and commitment to change and values. Business concept well defined.

To create an innovative global consulting and training firm to support the emergence of a new paradigm in business using the Core Group Process as its foundation.

Guiding Principles:

- Experience joy! Create a satisfying and fulfilling experience for all of us.
- Model the processes that are the foundation of this business within the business.

PeopleAssets (Innovative Consulting and Training Services for Tomorrow's Business)

Offers a lot of information about the company. Includes elements of mission statement. States what is important to owners.

GeoCentral is a Napa-based company that is known globally for its:

- Commitment to sharing earth's finest treasures by offering innovative products and services that showcase the richness and diversity of nature.
- Contribution for educating and promoting people's connection to this planet.
- Customer orientation, quality products, personal service, and retail earnings opportunity.

Locally, GeoCentral is known for its beautiful, open, artistic offices, motivated employees, and community contributions.

GeoCentral (www.geocentral.com)

Very clear description of business. Appeals with humor.

To produce a weekly, wacky fun food show for national syndication where we take the everyday job of cooking and dish out some super easy, low-fat recipes and top it off with ladles of laughs. We want to become known as the Joan Rivers of cooking.

The ShortCut Cooks...

Personal with important statement of key elements.

California Knits is a creative, soul-filled enterprise that provides:

- vibrant, unique, comfortable clothing as art for women.
- custom design capabilities for individual clients.
- training and mentoring of the next generation of machine knit artists.

California Knits

Concise. Important statements regarding location, products, and customers.

Build a successful local business furniture company that specializes in providing competitively priced furniture with superior service to companies with 10 to 50 employees.

Custom Business Interiors

Clear description of business. Product described very elegantly, yet friendly and inviting to use.

To manufacture and distribute nationally, incredibly delicious crepes, ready to serve instantly, for any occasion, from the most elegant to the most informal.

Crepes dianne

Concise. Solid definition of business.

In Northern California, become the premiere full home service company and the leading industrial and municipal sewer/pipeline maintenance company.

Sanact Inc. (dba Roto Rooter) (www.sanact.com)

Concise, clear, and powerful!

To have Design Media become recognized as the world leader in web-based training and educational delivery systems.

Design Media (www.designmedia.com)

Short and powerful. Makes you want to know more.

To become recognized as the world leader in toys and games that entertain and educate.

DaMert Company (www.damert.com)

.... **That Work!**

FEEDBACK exercise

↳ Take a few days to reflect on the three vision statements you wrote on page 33. Then share them with a couple of friends or associates. Use this page to take notes and incorporate their feedback into your vision statement.
⌛ 60 minutes, 30 minutes per person.

First Person Feedback

Second Person Feedback

Note here key words and phrases from above or other sources you would like to use in your own vision statement:

summarize

Rewrite your vision statement below. Use your own style to describe your vision and choose words that are comfortable and meaningful to you.

Vision Statement

Now rewrite the vision statement one more time in The One Page Business Plan® format using your word processor.

A Mission Statement That Works:

DaMert Company's mission is to create FUTURE CLASSIC products that capture...the wonders of the world around us, the magic of our imagination, the spark of innovation within each of us, and the mysteries of the future.

DaMert Company
(an international toy and gift company)

The Mission Statement

Why does this business exist?

Mission Statements always answer the question, "Why will customers buy this product or service?"

The mission statement describes the purpose for which your product, service, or business exists. Great mission statements are short and memorable. They communicate in just a few words the company's focus and what is being provided to customers. They always answer the question, "Why will customers buy this product or service?"

There is a current trend towards making mission statements very clear and focused. Often just a few words can truly describe a company's essence. For example, — Nike's *Just Do It*, Tandem Computer's *Total Reliability, No Limits*, or FEDEX's *The World On Time* are powerful statements about their mission. While these examples are more typically considered tag lines or company slogans, they communicate volumes about these companies in just a few words. That's what a good mission statement should do. Your initial mission statement is likely to be multiple sentences, but try to keep it concise and powerful.

Mission statements are also about commitments and promises. Ask yourself, "What is your company committed to providing your customers or constituencies?" Under what circumstances would you refund your customer's money and apologize for not providing what was promised? What would you be willing to do to make amends with a dissatisfied customer?

The answers to these questions may help you to understand why your business exists. Consider them carefully.

Successful businesses balance meeting the needs of their customers with meeting their own needs. This balance is delicate, but it must be addressed in order for your business to succeed. Failure to define both your customer's and your needs may make the business equation out of balance. "Out of balance" can ultimately translate to "out of business" or being in a business that you don't like, want, or understand.

Mission statements are not about money. Include your financial goals in your vision statement and quantify them in the objectives, but leave them out of the mission statement. Pursuing an idea primarily to satisfy the need for money usually results in an unsatisfying business.

Mission statements must reflect the owner's passion and commitment. When the business satisfies an owner's passion for creativity, independence, or the need to serve others, there is substance and staying power in the mission. With a clear mission, you'll have the grounding necessary to see you through the tough times. If you're not well grounded, you may abandon your company when the seas get too rough.

brainstorm EXERCISE

Your Mission...

Use these questions to reflect on why your business will be successful. Capture your thoughts using key words and short phrases.

1 What is the product or service? What differentiates you from the competition?

2 Describe your ideal customers.

What's in it for the customer and you?

3 Why will customers buy this product or service? What value does this product or service provide the customer? What unique benefits does this product or service provide the customer?

4 What passion(s) are you trying to satisfy by building this business? What beliefs do you have about business that will impact this business? What is the highest good that this business can achieve? What values will drive this business? Who will benefit from this business?

INTERVIEW exercise

The interviewer writes down your answers to the questions on the left. As you ask the interviewer to restate what he/she heard you say, write your notes on the right. ⌛ 30 minutes

The Interviewer	You
Why will customers buy your company's product or service?	**Answer restated:**
What is your company committed to providing your customers?	**Answer restated:**
What can your company promise?	**Answer restated:**
What passion(s) are you trying to satisfy by building this business?	**Answer restated:**

Crafting Your Mission Statement

focus EXERCISE

Federal Express exists solely for one reason: Overnight Package Delivery.

Experiment with 1-6 key words that describe why your company exists from a customer point of view. Capture your competitive marketing edge or unique selling proposition.

1st Attempt ____

2nd Attempt ____

Does this mission support your vision?

Examples of Mission Statements

What works!

We are on a mission to help rescue people from heavy kitchen duty.

The ShortCut Cooks (producers of a half hour comedy cooking show)

Short, fun, and right to the point.

Our mission is to translate your ideas to the screen!

Video Arts, Inc. (an Emmy Award-winning video production company)

Concise statement of why this company exists!

We find the right employees to make your business successful.

Tech Search (a small employment search company)

Clear statement of business purpose.

AUL's mission is to take care of people and their concerns about financial security. AUL provides peace of mind by sheltering its customers from the risk of loss caused by premature death, sickness, disability, or outliving financial resources after retirement.

American United Life Insurance Company

This company cares about people, and their mission says how they can help.

We convert the spoken word to the written word with integrity.

Jack London Court Reporters (a small court transcription company)

Few words that make a powerful statement about business.

Healing, grounded in learning and supported by acts of personal kindness.

University of California, San Francisco (a leading medical university)

Powerful message for all of the constituencies. The first mission statement was multiple pages.

What doesn't!

We will be one of the world's premier companies, distinctive and successful in everything we do.

AlliedSignal, Inc. (multinational materials manufacturer for aerospace, automotive industries)

Typical old corporate style. Not motivating, could be any company.

To produce cars and trucks that people will want to buy, will enjoy driving, and will want to buy again.

Chrysler Corporation

Simple and straightforward but could be more inspiring.

To exceed the expectation of our customers through the delivery of superior service and continuous quality improvement that rewards our employees and enhances the value of our shareholders' investment.

Total System Services, Inc. (a bankcard processing company)

Not memorable. Could be any company.

We produce and supply electricity, provide related products and services, and pursue opportunities that complement our business. We will continually improve our products and services to better meet our customers' needs and expectations, helping our customers, employees, owners, and communities to prosper.

Duke Power Company

Too long. Not inspiring. Full of platitudes. Could be many electrical companies.

Other Mission Statements

Personally made the way you want it.
A specialty, custom craft company

The purpose of the Bay Area Entrepreneur Association is to provide: education, networking, and support for new, prospective, and experienced entrepreneurs in the San Francisco Bay Area.
Bay Area Entrepreneur Association

We help you get out of bed feeling great so that you can experience the day the way you want to.
East West Healing Arts Center

We bring authors and books together!
Cody's Books

We do for families what no one should ever have to do.
Crime Site Cleanup Company

Total Reliability.
No limits.
Tandem Computers

We move at the speed of business.
United Parcel Service

It's about communications between people... the rest is technology.
Ericsson (a global telecommunications company)

To provide color, light, and energizing beauty in comfortable, natural fiber clothing.
California Knits

Saving the last great places on earth...
The Nature Conservancy

To provide growing companies a single source for purchasing all of their office furniture from an experienced professional that understands how to create attractive, functional, flexible, and affordable office layouts.
Custom Business Interiors

Help us lose weight. Recycle bimonthly.
Sacramento Waste Management

We bring the taste of India to your home.
Bhurji Indian Grocery Store

Bring light, air and the beauty of nature into homes through creative windows!
Colorado Garden Window Company

Establish the Creativity Cafe as the *New School for the Next Millennium.* To inspire and empower the public in both cyberspace and in communities around the world by providing affordable access to technology and instruction and by creating experiences that inspire and educate us to be better human beings.
Creativity Cafe™

Helping people see better, one hour at a time.
LensCrafters

That Work!

FEEDBACK exercise

Review your mission statements on page 43 and the examples on pages 44 and 45. Is yours too long? Unclear? Refine your mission statement below and then discuss it with two people. Use their feedback to complete your final version. ⌛ 60 minutes, 30 minutes per person.

Use the examples on the preceding pages to help you refine your mission statement:

First Person Feedback

Second Person Feedback

summarize

Rewrite your mission statement below. Experiment with different adjectives and verbs. It may help to move on to another section and come back to summarize your mission statement.

Mission Statement

____

____

____

____

____

____

____

____

Now rewrite the mission statement one more time in the One Page Business Plan® format using your word processor.

Objectives That Work:

2006 Objectives for Sports Apparel Company…

Grow sales to $5.5m in 2006, $7.0m in 2007, and $9.0m in 2008.

Achieve profit before tax of $480,000 in 2006, increase to 10% of sales by 2007.

Introduce approximately 15 new products in 2006, achieving sales of $750,000.

Increase number of existing accounts with greater than $100m volume from 8 last year to 15 in 2006.

Secure two major product license agreements: NBA and NFL by 6/30/06.

Reduce shipping expense to 3% of sales, starting in 1st quarter.

Aggressively manage inventory to budgeted levels, maintain active inventory at 93%.

Reduce overtime to 3% of total manufacturing hours.

The Objectives

What are the goals? How does the business define success?

"Meaningful specifics *are those individuals who know what they want to achieve in very specific terms and have targets and time frames written down to help them get there."*

Objectives clarify what it is you are trying to accomplish in specific, measurable goals. For an objective to be effective, it needs to be a well-defined target with quantifiable elements that are measurable.

Zig Ziglar, a nationally known motivational speaker, says in order to achieve the goals that are important, you must become a *meaningful specific.* Meaningful specifics are those individuals who know what they want to achieve in very specific terms and have targets and time frames written down to help them get there. People who have vague ideas, with no target dates, never get to the finish line. Zig refers to these people as *wandering generalities.*

Whereas your vision statement is expansive and idealistic, and the mission statement short, powerful, memorable, and customer oriented, your objectives are designed to focus your resources on achieving specific results. The purpose of a well-defined objective is to cause meaningful action.

There are many types of objectives and your plan should include a wide variety. For many businesses the two most important categories will be the financial and marketing objectives. It is important, however, to tailor your objectives to cover the entire scope of your business, focusing on the goals that are most critical to your success.

Although there is no magical or precise number of objectives, The One Page Business Plan® can accommodate eight to nine different ones. If you have an objective for revenue, profitability, two or three for marketing, that leaves four or five to cover manufacturing, operations, personnel, and other important goals that are critical to your success.

Keep your objectives meaningful by making them specific and important. One of the most powerful aspects of the One Page Business Plan® is the limited amount of space. This requires prioritization and pruning to get to a list of only the most important goals.

The exercises in this section are designed to help you analyze the important objectives for your business to achieve. The exercises will focus you on past successes and failures, as these are a great source of ideas for creating goals. The examples are designed to demonstrate how to construct powerful goals.

Create objectives that can be measured and then measure the results throughout the year. Objectives are a prime tool for accountability. Stay focused and stay on track!

brainstorm EXERCISE

What accomplishments would you like to celebrate...

↳ Brainstorm three business accomplishments you would like to be celebrating at the end of this year and next year.

...this year?

...next year?

Imagine what you might say at the company celebration dinner:

CONGRATULATIONS!

"We successfully completed (____)."

"We are proud to announce the beginning of (____)."

"We no longer have to deal with (____) because we (____)."

"We increased (____) by (____)."

"We decreased (____) by (____)."

brainstorm EXERCISE

Where does success come from? What will it look like?

Think about your past experiences, what you have learned from these, and answer the questions on the left. Imagine what your future success will look like and respond to the questions on the right.

Where have you been successful in the past?

How can you expand upon these successes?

What were your past mistakes?

What have you learned from these mistakes?

What ideas have you not acted on?

Which of these ideas will you go forward with?

What targets will you aim for?

Check at least six objectives below that are critical for your success. Check as many in each category as you find to be appropriate and add your own if necessary.

Financial	Marketing and Sales	Operations	Human Resources
☐ sales	☐ image	☐ hours of operation	☐ compensation
☐ profit	☐ market share	☐ number of locations	☐ benefits
☐ gross margin	☐ number of accounts	☐ suppliers	☐ safety
☐ cash flow	☐ number of customers	☐ shipping time	☐ morale
☐ inventory	☐ number of new customers	☐ customer service	☐ environment
☐ owner compensation	☐ advertising	☐ equipment	☐ overtime
☐ debt	☐ visibility	☐ ____________	☐ use of contractors
☐ ____________	☐ literature		☐ volunteers (nonprofit)
	☐ ____________		☐ ____________

Examples of Objectives

Financial

- Increase sales to $1 million in 2006, $1.5 million in 2007.
- Increase product margin to 42%.
- Reduce cost of goods sold to 28% by purchasing in bulk containers.
- Reduce number of days in receivables from 48 to 35 by 6/30.
- Reduce interest expense by 20% by renegotiating long-term notes.

Marketing and Sales

- Introduce 4 new products in 2nd qtr; 6 in 3rd qtr; 2006 incremental sales $500,000.
- Launch new account incentive program in 3rd qtr; goal 50 new accounts generating $20k per month.
- Improve sales per employee to $120k per quarter by May 31st.
- Obtain one major new account per quarter generating $150,000 per year.

Operations

- Achieve billable time of 75%.
- Expand order entry access to 24 hours per day effective 6/30.
- Ship 98% of orders the same day and 100% of orders within 3 days.
- Produce and ship all special orders within 5 working days.
- Consolidate from 5 warehouses to 2 by 6/30; achieve annual savings of $500,000.
- Reduce customer service labor costs per order by 5% by 3/31/06.

Human Resources

- Hire general manager by 6/15.
- Reduce turnover to 3%; implement job rotation program by 1/1.
- Reissue updated employee handbook by 6/30.
- Develop scholarship program for employees' children by 9/1.

focus EXERCISE

Use the examples of objectives below to help you decide which types of objectives are most important.

R & D	Manufacturing	Personal	Other
☐ new products	☐ production units/cost	☐ role/involvement	☐ environment
☐ introduction dates	☐ capacity	☐ compensation	☐ investors
☐ functionality	☐ quality	☐ creative needs	☐ bankers
☐ image	☐ dual sourcing	☐ retirement	☐ suppliers
☐ environmental	☐ safety	☐ education	☐ government
☐ design capabilities	☐ labor efficiency	☐ personal growth	☐ community
☐ product improvements	☐ downtime	☐ charitable contributions	☐ ______
☐ ______	☐ inventory level	☐ public speaking	☐ ______
	☐ ______	☐ ______	

Examples of Objectives

R & D

- Complete clinical study #124 by 2/15.
- Develop prototypes for marketing samples by 1/15.
- Complete exploratory work on project *top cat* by 4/15; report available for management review 5/15.
- Decrease microbiology sample test costs to $1.50 per sample by 8/15.
- Automate laboratory documentation procedures by 6/15.

Manufacturing

- Produce 1.3 million units in 2006.
- Expand our packaging line to 2 million unit capacity by 12/31.
- Reduce production labor to 8% of sales by 12/31.
- Develop dual sources for household and hair care products by 8/15.
- Significantly improve plant safety; target no loss time accidents.
- Improve manufacturing yield to 98%; achieve savings of $450,000.

Personal

- Commit to working no more than 50 hours per week; play on most weekends.
- Increase vacation to 3 weeks.
- Read one book per month.
- Exercise at least twice a week.
- Lose 20 pounds by yr end; 5 pounds per quarter.
- Relandscape backyard.

Other

- Host community business luncheon in 4th quarter.
- Create five-year plan by 6/30 and begin investigating new sources of capital funding.
- Complete buy/sell agreement with partners; begin business succession planning.
- Commit 10 hours per quarter to community service projects.

focus EXERCISE

What does this business need to accomplish?

Review the objective ideas you checked on the previous two pages. Choose four of them and answer the questions for each.

Type of objective:	Describe the activity required:	What will happen and when?	What is the financial impact?
1 Type of objective:			
2 Type of objective:			
3 Type of objective:			
4 Type of objective:			
EXAMPLE Type of objective: R&D	Develop/introduce new products	A book 6/30; A tape 7/31	Sales of $10,000 in 3rd qtr; $20,000 in 4th qtr

Crafting Meaningful Objectives

focus EXERCISE

Now rewrite the objectives on the left into sentences or phrases combining your responses in the four columns. The first two objectives will always be sales revenue and profitability.

sales revenue objective:

profitability objective:

1

2

3

4

Will meeting these objectives accomplish your vision and mission?

example:

Introduce a book by 6/30 and an audio tape by 7/31, resulting in 2006 sales of $30,000.

Examples of Objectives

What works!		What doesn't!	
Increase sales 25% to $4 million in 2006; $5 million in 2007, & $6.3 million in 2008.	Specific, measurable.	Develop a sustainable business; minimize peaks and valleys.	Not specific. No way to measure.
Obtain "Oracle Named Account Status" by July 2006; SunMicro key acct status by year end. Bob Smith.	Measurable, easily understood, accountability assigned!	Develop strategic marketing alliances with key partners.	Not specific. Which partners and when to achieve what?
Introduce new hair care line, 1st quarter, estimated 2006 sales of $250,000; skin care line 3rd quarter, estimated 2006 sales of $100,000.	Measurable, specific, financial impact known.	Develop and introduce new products to grow business.	Vague. Needs type of products, how many, and financial impact.
Improve overall product margin to 40% by reducing discounts on low volume accounts to 3%; enforce minimum new product margin target of 45%.	States goal and how it will be achieved.	Improve profitability and cash flow to support business growth.	Needs to be quantified.
Reduce overtime to maximum of 3%; introduce 401k by June 30th; implement recognition program by Sept. 30th.	Says how morale issue is going to be tackled and when.	Improve employee morale.	No way to measure. No statement of work to be done.
Reduce inventory to $950,000 by 9/30/06; maintain raw materials @ 1.5 months; finished goods @ 2 months.	Clear, measurable goals.	Reduce inventory levels.	Doesn't state the desired result. Might cause other problems.

summarize

Read your vision and mission statements again and rewrite your objectives below. Ask yourself again if these objectives will accomplish your vision and mission statements.

Objectives

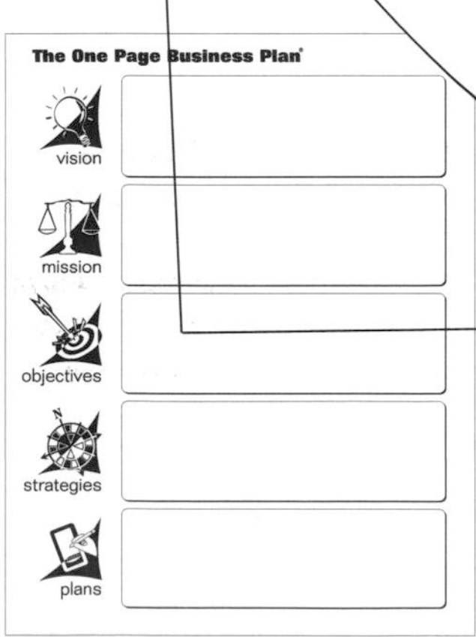

Now write your objectives once more in The One Page Business Plan® format using your word processor.

Strategies for the 21st Century...

Price isn't everything

Lots of customers will pay extra for a helpful, well-trained staff. Ask Nordstrom.

Attract the very best employees and give them a stake in the business

Give rank-and-file employees a vested interest in how a company performs. Intel does.

Think fast

Particularly in the high-tech world, move and evolve quickly. Learn from Netscape.

Superior Execution

A well-executed plan for a simple product will beat a poor implementation of a great product everyday.

Be visible, be a resource

Write articles, newsletters, books, web pages. Speak to any group that will hear you. Volunteer your time and expertise whenever you can.

Don't try to do it all

Specialize in what you do best. Contract or forget the rest.

The Strategies

How to Grow and Manage the Business

Strategies set the direction, philosophy, values, and methodology for building and managing your company. Strategies also establish guidelines and boundaries for evaluating important business decisions. Following a predefined set of strategies is critical to keeping a business on track.

"Following a predefined set of strategies is critical to keeping a business on track."

One way of understanding strategies is to think of them as "industry practices." Every industry has its leaders, its followers, and its rebels, and each has an approach for capturing market share. Pay attention to the successful businesses in your industry and you can learn important lessons. Miss an important lesson and your business may not even get off the ground.

Strategies are not secret. In fact they are common knowledge and openly shared in every industry. Pick up any industry's publication and you will know precisely what the industry's leaders have to say about the opportunities and how to capitalize on them. These leaders will also share their current problems and their solutions. This is critical information for building and managing your business.

In most industries there are four to six core strategies that the successful businesses follow. These core strategies are easy to understand, remain relatively constant over time, are used by market leaders, and result in growth and profitability.

Great strategy statements can be broad and yet create tremendous focus. When you have the right strategies for your business, they will probably last for several years with minor changes. A significant breakthrough in your industry, or a significant change in your business, can of course cause you to revisit your strategies.

A properly constructed set of strategies will define your business and keep it focused. For example, a CPA whose vision is to build a local practice would be significantly off track to accept international clients who would take him out of the country on extended trips. An upscale boutique targeting high-income clientele would not be wise to locate right next door to a K-Mart. A labor-intensive product with low margins should probably not be made in New York City.

Strategies must address both internal and external influences that are affecting or may affect your business. External strategies capitalize on opportunities to grow the company or overcome outside threats. Internal strategies address issues related to the business's strengths and weaknesses in the areas of culture, capabilities, efficiency, and profitability.

Strategies provide the answer to the question: "What will make this business successful over time?"

brainstorm EXERCISE

Key Elements to Building Your Business

Check the boxes that represent those topics *critical* to growing and operating your business. Refer to your objectives while making your selections. Feel free to add to the list.

☐ Market Presence	☐ Product Uniqueness	☐ Company Image	☐ Location
☐ Employees	☐ Technical Knowledge	☐ Reputation	☐ Visibility
☐ Distribution Channel	☐ Trademarks/Patents	☐ Key Customers	☐ Number of Accounts
☐ Referrals	☐ Customer Service	☐ Quality	☐ Technology/Equipment
☐ Partners	☐ Board of Advisors	☐ Other People's Skills	☐ Family Support/Money
☐ Shared Support Services	☐ Time Management	☐ Capital	☐ Strategic Alliances
☐ Product Cost	☐ Cash Flow	☐ Trade Industry Acceptance	

☐ ____________________

☐ ____________________

Decide Which Strategies Are Appropriate for Your Business

Finding appropriate strategies for your business is not difficult. Much information is readily available to you for free or at minimal cost. Selecting strategies you can utilize is also not difficult.

Where do you find strategies specific to your business? Trade journals, local business newspapers, and national business magazines are great places to start. These publications are filled with current articles on industry trends in the critical areas of marketing, finance, and operations. They are usually short, concise, and written by industry experts. They describe the problems and opportunities with which the industry is struggling and the solutions that businesses are implementing. A review of the contents for the last few issues will certainly give you a solid perspective on what's important in your industry and how the leading edge companies are planning their futures.

If you are starting a business, you'll have access to some important information that you will want to seriously consider before proceeding. Also, if this is a new business, and it requires funding, you can be sure the lender will want to know how you are planning to address these issues.

Other people that know your business can be very helpful in identifying and selecting strategies. Your banker, CPA, attorney, vendors, and employees have a lot of insight into your business. Ask them for their thoughts.

RESEARCH
exercise

Opportunities and Threats

Review the last three issues of your industry's trade association journal and answer the questions below.

What opportunities exist?

How can we capitalize on them?

What threats exist?

How can we minimize the threats or turn the threats into opportunities?

Examples of Industry Issues

pricing	environment	economic	the public
customers	market	technology	taxes
suppliers	competition	media	import/export regulations
cost reduction	government		

focus EXERCISE

Who are your customers?

List and describe up to three categories of your **BEST CUSTOMERS**.

Use the words below to help brainstorm your customer descriptions:

age
sex
income
occupation
education
language
family size
countries
regions
size of cities
social class
lifestyle
personality
purchase frequency
purpose of purchase
brand loyalty
habits
hobbies

Use the following words to help brainstorm how you will promote and sell to your customers:

workshops
associations
newspapers
direct mail
outplacement agencies
referrals
partnerships
Internet
local retailers
television
radio
telemarketing
magazines
speaking
government agencies
trade journals

1

2

3

How will you promote and sell to them?

Where/how do these customers buy your products now? Where/how will they buy them in the future?

How do you plan to **PROMOTE** your products or services to these three categories of customers?

brainstorm EXERCISE

What's working in your company?

It's just as important to know what works in your company as what doesn't. Use the keywords list at the bottom to help you brainstorm if you get stuck. (For established companies only.)

What currently works well in my company?

How can we improve?

What doesn't work well?

How do we solve the problems?

management	employee benefits	flexibility	customer service
employees	overtime	yields	safety
business practices	internal controls	expense control	profit margin
facilities	product quality	communication	morale
	manufacturing capacity	inventory management	

Critical Issues Examination

focus EXERCISE

Select three critical issues that are limiting your company's growth, profitability, or effectiveness. This exercise helps you differentiate between symptoms and root causes so that you can see more clearly what needs to happen to achieve a permanent and effective change. (For established businesses only.)

List 3 issues or symptoms:	What is the root cause of this?	What needs to change?	How will results be measured?
EXAMPLE Back orders are excessive!	No sales forecast, and capacity is too low	Develop monthly sales forecast by product and expand packaging	Track output per week vs. planned output; monitor back orders daily

focus EXERCISE

How do we get from here to there?

What has made your company successful or limited its growth to date? How will you build on the successes and overcome the current limitations to achieve your vision?

	Current Business*	Vision
Success Factors		
Limiting Factors		

*Current business could be your business or industry

Crafting Meaningful Strategies

focus EXERCISE

From the focus exercise on the previous page, select up to five areas that are critical to building your company. Draft a strategy statement for each one below.

1

2

3

4

5

Do these strategies describe:

How the business will be built and managed?

How we will capitalize on market opportunities?

How we will solve our business's critical problems?

Examples of Strategies

What works!		What doesn't!	
Position company for strategic acquisition in 2006; build brands, identity, management team, and profits.	Sets the direction with the big picture and exit strategy.	Make money, limit investment in business and employees, think about retirement at age 65.	Everything is wrong with this strategy.
Sell total solutions, not time, not parts.	Selling value, not time. Allows for much higher margins.	Employees: hire at the lowest possible wages, perform important functions ourselves.	Great employees are worth their weight in gold.
Employees: hire the best, have them just before we need them, retain them thru job satisfaction and equity participation.	Always need good people. Have a people strategy.	Ideal client: anyone who will buy our products and services.	It's impossible to be everything to everyone. Specialize.
Control expenses and growth; self-capitalize/bank finance company; achieve sales and profit plans.	Build a strong company with good internal controls.	Product: whatever is hot this year, we will sell.	Followers rarely have the volume or margin the leaders do. Invest in R&D.
Focus on web-based training and communications products with delivery via Internet, Intranet, CD-ROM.	Defined set of products. Clear and understandable.	Increase prices to maintain margins.	Might work in the short run. Competitors will find a way to do it better for less.
Aim high with minimum project size of $300,000.	Sets lower limits.	Project size: all projects.	Not all clients or projects are profitable. Refer low-margin projects to your competitors.

summarize

Use this summary to refine your strategies by writing them below. Check each strategy for the following characteristics: easy to understand, constant over time, used by market leaders, and results in growth and profitability.

Strategies

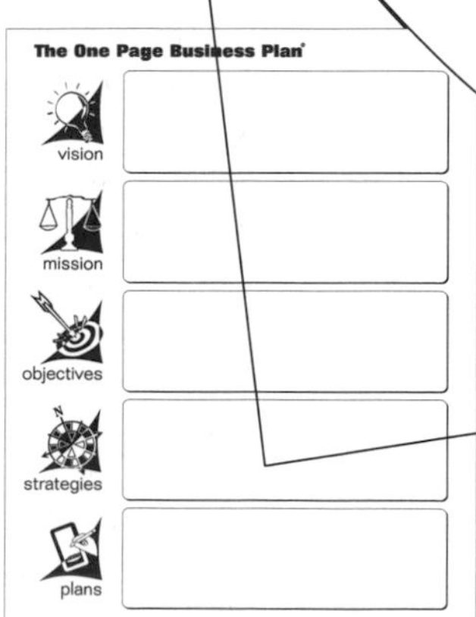

Now write your strategies once more in The One Page Business Plan® format using your word processor.

Strategies, objectives, and plans interrelate with each other:

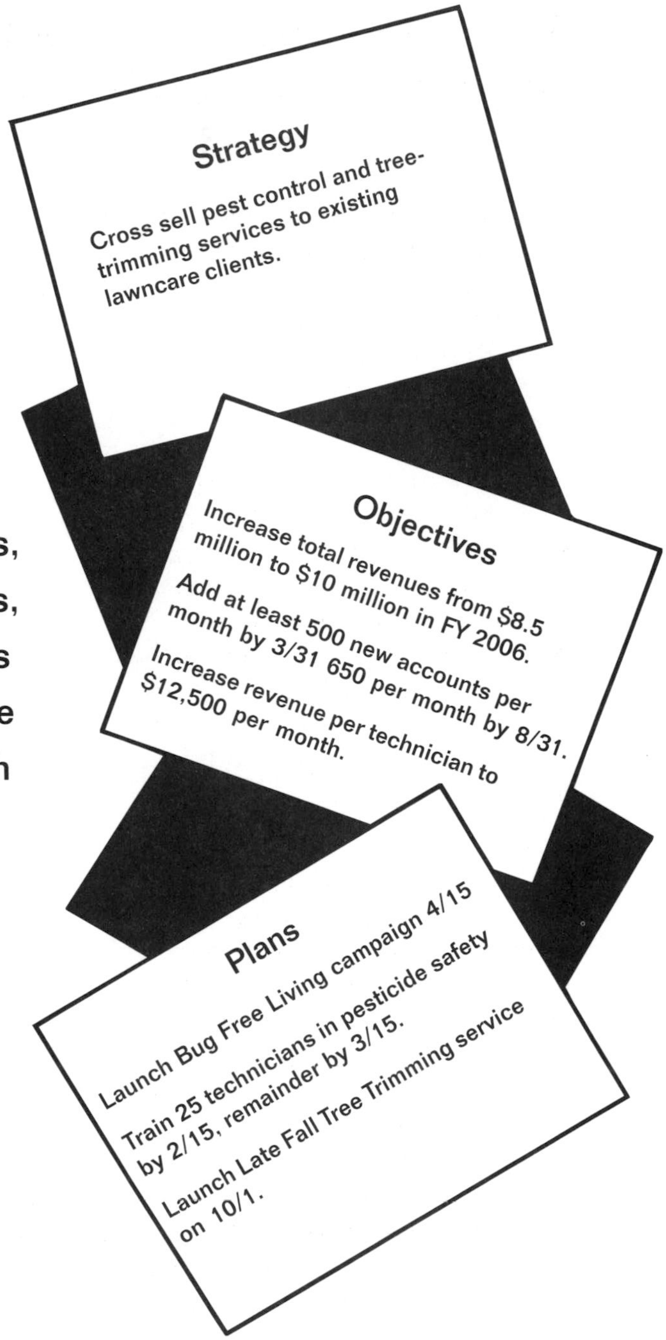

The Plans

What specific actions will the business implement to achieve its goals?

"It's not enough to talk about it... you must say how and why!"

— *Inc. Magazine* March 1995 comment on business planning

Plans are the specific actions the business must implement to achieve the objectives. Plan or action items should be important, significant, and contribute to the growth of your business. Each plan or action item is, in effect, a project.

Ideally, each plan statement should directly relate to an objective and a strategy. Plans should be action oriented, should specify specific tasks, and should have deadlines. If your business has employees, independent contractors, or utilizes outside resources to complete tasks, the ideal plan statement will identify who is responsible for performing each function.

Most business owners or prospective business owners have a to-do list a mile long. They struggle not with what needs to be done, but how to get it all done. The One Page Business Plan® is designed to keep you and your business focused on the important, but not necessarily urgent, business tasks. Steven Covey in *First Things First* writes about how easy it is to focus on the most important tasks every day and never get to the things that will really grow your business. By having your business-building action list clearly defined, and delegated appropriately, it becomes possible to complete the tasks that will build your business.

The exercises in this section are designed to guide you in the development and prioritization of your action plans and in relating them to specific objectives and or strategies. The exercises suggest that you prepare estimates of the financial or operational impact of each of these projects and determine in advance how you will measure the results. This process provides both an objective framework for selecting the projects with the highest benefit or payback and a method for postauditing the results.

In preparing your plans, estimate the cost and time frame for each project. Transfer this information into your budget worksheets, calculate the impact of your to-do list on your cash flow. I've learned that if you don't know what your projects will cost, it's quite likely you will not have enough cash to fund them. A project with no cash is like a car with no gas — it's not going very far.

Make your plans carefully. Execute them on time, within budget, and with excellence. Measure their impact routinely.

brainstorm EXERCISE

List six projects that would make a big difference in your business. Tie them to an objective or a strategy. Then answer the three questions for each project.

Strategy or Objective:

____

____

Project 1:

____

____

Strategy or Objective:

____

____

Project 2:

____

____

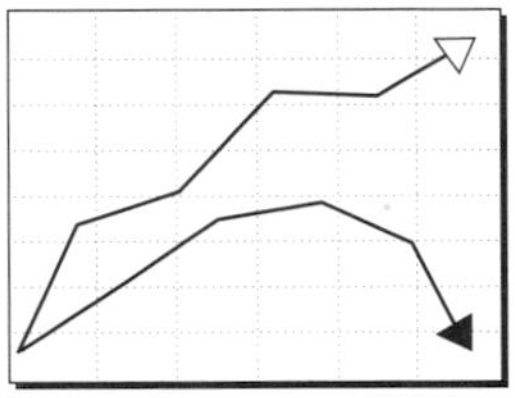

1. What impact would completing the project have?

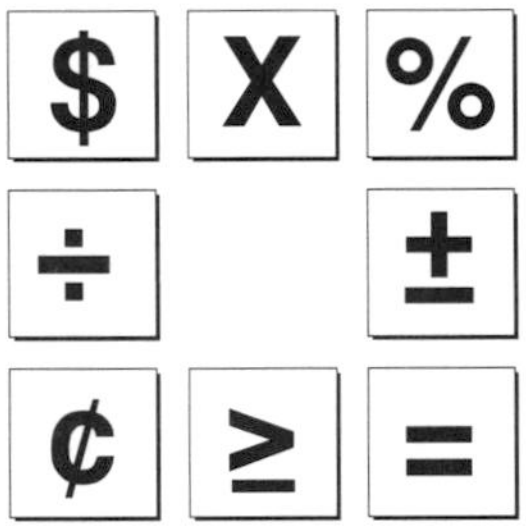

2. How will you measure the results?

3. What are the next three steps?

Business-Building Projects

Strategy or Objective: ______________________

Project 3: ______________________

Strategy or Objective: ______________________

Project 4: ______________________

Strategy or Objective: ______________________

Project 5: ______________________

Strategy or Objective: ______________________

Project 6: ______________________

focus EXERCISE

Integrating Objectives, Strategies, and Plans

Choose five projects from the preceding two pages and complete the chart below.

Objective or Strategy	Project to be Completed	Person Responsible	Completion Date
Plan 1			
Plan 2			
Plan 3			
Plan 4			
Plan 5			
EXAMPLE			
Increase sales volume 10% in 2006	Introduce new skin care line	M. Jones	6/30/06

Crafting Meaningful Plans

focus EXERCISE

Now rewrite the plans on the left into sentences or phrases, combining your responses in the four columns.

1

2

3

4

5

example:

Complete new skin care line and have ready for September 6th convention; M. Jones project team leader

Examples of Plans

What works!		What doesn't!	
Attend NY trade show in June; LA in September; and Chicago in October.	Identifies specific activity with dates.	Write annual employee reviews for R. Smith and B. Jones by 2/28.	Important activity but not a task that builds the business.
Complete phase III network design by 7/31. Utilize Berkeley Software, Inc. for QA review.	States work to be completed with completion date; identifies vendor.	Complete February financials by 3/15.	Routine activity; this is not a strategic business activity.
Overhaul skin care emulsion equipment during June shutdown.	Concise statement of time frame.	Implement new business practices.	Not specific; no dates and no accountability.
Hire route salesman for Sacramento territory in fourth quarter.	Specific position; some leeway for completion.	Hire approximately six new employees.	All new hires should be identified by position and approximate hire dates.
R. Smith to complete grant for handicap access upgrade by February 28.	Clear accountability and responsibility.	Develop committees for fundraising.	When? Who is responsible?
Redo tax seminar marketing brochures in 2nd quarter. Bob Jones to lead team.	Specific with accountability.	Increase all prices during this year.	Not specific; should identify specific products. Percent increase should agree with budget assumptions.
Move to new Pleasanton facility October 15th.	Simple statement; allows others to plan accordingly.		

summarize

Use this summary to refine your plans by writing them below.

Plans

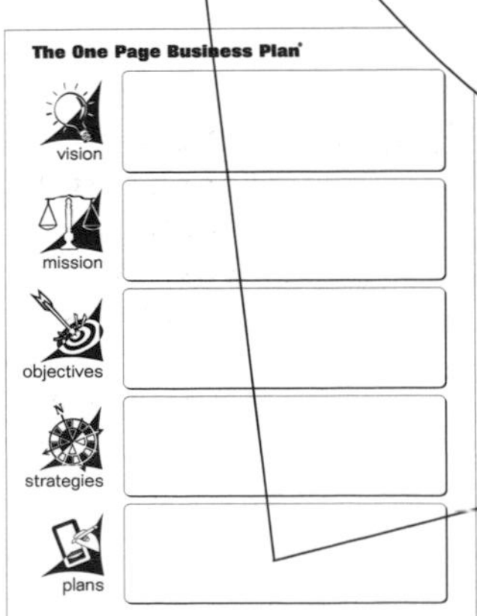

Now write your plans once more in The One Page Business Plan® format using your word processor.

"He who chooses the beginning of a road chooses the place it leads to. It is the means that determine the end."

— Harry Emerson Fosdick

You Did It! Congratulations! Your plan is now in writing. You are feeling a major sense of accomplishment. Go ahead and celebrate. This was hard work. Having your plan, in your words, on one page is a powerful business tool.

At this time you should have a final draft of your One Page Business Plan® in your word processor. Step back and review it. How does it look to you? If you are like most people, parts of your plan feel very tight and others still need some work. That's normal and OK. As you have learned by now, this process is iterative. Use the checklist on the following page to help make any minor editing changes that are necessary and you are ready to start sharing the complete plan. This is polishing; do not do a major rewrite at this time.

Now that you have your plan in a final draft form, it's time to put it to work.

You clarified and organized your thoughts into a concise business plan. Now others can respond to your plan.

Polishing Checklist

Overall Review

- Do the key words and short phrases describe the essence of your plan?
- Does your vision feel big, expansive, and exciting?
- Is your mission statement powerful?
- Are your objectives specific and measurable?
- Do your strategies state how you are going to build and manage this business over time?
- Are your plans action oriented and will they accomplish this year's objectives?

Order and Abbreviation
(*Edit objectives, strategies, and plan statements to one line*)

- Eliminate all unnecessary words and phrases.
- Abbreviate words when necessary.
- Use symbols like "&" in lieu of "and" to save space.
- Use "k" or "m" for thousands, "M" for millions.
- Communicate the importance and priority of objectives, strategies, and plans by placing the most important ones first in each section.

Creative Considerations
(*especially with layout of vision and mission statements)*

- Split sentences into multi-lines.
- Center text.
- Use bullets to make key points stand out.
- Double space to accent.
- Highlight key phrases in italics.

Strengthening Exercises

- Draft and edit vision, mission and strategy until they are enduring statements that resonate with you, your partners, your management team, and key employees.
- Refine objectives and plan statements until they are very specific, measurable, and define clear accountability.
- Drop low-priority items; remember "less can produce more."
- Ask others for their comments.

Putting the Plan into Action

Putting the plan into action is the most important step because the actions deliver the results you wanted when you started this process. For most entrepreneurs, this is easy. You are action oriented and can't wait to get started. Now is the time to put the plan to work. A few guidelines or suggestions for uses of the plan are summarized below:

Use it to talk with your banker about financing.
Most bankers who have reviewed The One Page Business Plan® have found it to be an excellent tool for understanding both the business and the plans. It won't always lead to a loan being approved, and does not complete all the steps of the loan process, but it is an excellent start. Sharing your plan with your banker will get you useful feedback and lead to improved banker relations.

Discuss your plan with investors.
Your completed One Page Business Plan® is an excellent tool for focusing discussions with present or potential investors. The plan shows what you intend to do and how you will make it happen. Combined with your enthusiasm and commitment, the plan will be a significant aid in getting investors and keeping them happy.

Convert the plan into budgets.
Putting the plan into action usually requires quantifying the plans and objectives and getting the resources into place to support implementation. This is the process of budgeting. For many of my clients, this means going through the process of First Time Budgeting. Don't be afraid of it! Budgets help define the resources we need and provide the measures that allow us to know we are on track. If you need help in budgeting, get it. This is an important part of your path to success.

Manage the implementation.
Planning is a vital first step toward success but not the last step. Implementing the plan and making it work is the vital next step. More companies fail because of *Failure To Implement* than for any other reason. Managing the implementation is the process of using the goals, plans, measures, and other tools that we have defined and making sure that the actions take place and are in line with the defined strategies, objectives, and plans. Everyone must be held accountable for meeting their goals. Frequent reviews and continuous monitoring of results will help move you toward the defined goals. *Failure To Implement* is not acceptable and must be dealt with immediately.

External Presentation

- Complete business plan for small to mid-size companies
- Vehicle for testing business ideas with your board of directors, partners, banker, and employees
- Draft concept for Small Business Administration loan or venture capital funding business plan
- Summarizes existing plan

Inspiration and Motivation

- Tool to get back on track if you've lost your vision
- Career planning

R&D

- Place to summarize ideas for new division or new business
- Quick sketch and fleshing out of idea for new product or service
- Process for planning major projects

Internal Process Guide

- Complete business plan for small to mid-size companies
- Business plan for subsidiaries or divisions of larger corporations
- Functional or departmental planning tool (sales, marketing, finance, etc.)
- Strategic planning starting point for CEOs in larger corporations
- Methodology to quickly update annual plan for significant mid-year changes
- Summarizes existing plan

Keep the plan with you.

Update it with new thoughts.

Share it with people you trust and whose opinions you value.

Measure your progress at least quarterly.

Prepare a budget to match the plan.

Make a copy for everyone.
Have them post it on the wall of their office. Plans need to be communicated and understood to help drive the necessary decisions and actions that will lead to success. Certainly, all your managers and employees should have a copy of your plan. Others you may want to share it with could include your advisors, bankers, accountants, suppliers, key customers, and key community members. Share it with anyone who could help your business succeed. Remember that communities support entrepreneurs, but they must first know about you to support you.

Review your plan at team and company meetings.
Get some energy going around it. Implementing the plan means paying attention to it. Don't let it sit on a shelf. Your One Page Business Plan® is a working document that will work for you if you continually use it to remind your team and your employees about where you are going and how you will get there.

Use it as a decision-making tool.
Managers make decisions on the fly every day. The One Page Business Plan® is the guide they should use to make those decisions. Does the proposed action support where the company is going? How would we decide on this item based on the plan? The strategies, objectives, and plans are very clear guides on where resources should be used and what the priorities should be. The vision and mission are more general guides that help determine the overall direction and the values and principles that apply. The plan as a whole is the prime decision making document that should be checked when key business decision are made.

Useful plans drive decisions and actions and get everyone working toward the same goals. Decisions and actions that help implement the plan are positive and support the success of the company. Decisions and actions that go in different directions significantly reduce the probable success of the business. We plan in order to focus our actions and decisions to achieve the desired results. Words which sum up The One Page Business Plan® process are:

Focus → Action → Results

The plan provides the focus, and then we implement through actions guided by the plan. The planned actions lead to the results. When in doubt at this point, act. Sometimes try several actions, monitor the results quickly and carefully, and then decide on the best course of action to continue.

One Page Business Plan® Samples

As you modify your plan over time, use the following pages of sample plans to give you ideas for refining your content or design.

PeopleAssets

Innovative Consulting and Training Services for Tomorrow's Businesses

vision

Within the next 3 years, grow CGP into a $3 million national consulting firm specializing in creative leadership development programs for Fortune 100 companies.

mission

We help companies develop effective leaders!

objectives

- Increase revenue to $1.8 million in FY 2006
- Increase gross margin to 54% from 31% by 12/31/06.
- Earn a pretax profit of $450,000 for FY 2006.
- By 12/31/06 establish a client base of at least 10 companies.

strategies

- Leverage CGP's worldwide identity as entree into business consulting.
- Build company awareness by networking at executive level.
- Create simple, easily-produced materials from existing CGP products.
- Use first clients to define product offering/build momentum.
- Use a train the trainer approach to maximize reach in larger clients.
- Create product ranges so that any business can afford a system.

plans

- Develop a written marketing plan by 2/16/06.
- Trademark Core Group Process by 4/4/06.
- Publish 4 quarterly newsletters; send to the first 1500 prospects by 3/15.
- Deliver 5 workshops by 6/30; and another 4 by Q3.
- Create high quality company brochure by 7/1/06
- Create 4 mini-books on personnel management techniques by 12/31.

Z - TEC, Inc.

vision

Within the next three years build Z-TEC International into a $50 million enterprise software solutions company specializing in integrated work-flow management solutions for large industrial process firms.

mission

Streamline the flow of work...in large industrial production facilities!

objectives

- Grow 2006 Revenue 20% to at least $27 Million.
- Achieve 2006 Profit before Interest & Taxes of $3.5 Million.
- Complete at least 8 new installations; yield fees of $6 million.
- Obtain 16 new clients w/ average project size of $500,000.
- Reduce accounts receivables from 63 days to 40 days by April 30th
- Migrate at least 20 existing clients to web-product by Sept. 30th.
- Reduce employee turnover from 25% to less than 10% by Q4.

strategies

- Growth: 50% each yr by developing new clients & migration of existing clients.
- Reputation:Product leadership & reputation from existing client referrals.
- Partners:Align w/industry leaders, partner for mktg & new products.
- Competitive Position:Optimize user-based pricing & modular system for flexibility.
- Products:Configure more than customize, business rules vs. custom programs.
- R&D:Work-flow solutions, open systems, multiple environments, object oriented.
- Resources: have people & systems resources in place before they are needed.
- Aligned team, know the plan, sense of urgency, responsibility/accountability.
- Use Employee Incentives to share rewards, create excitement & have Fun.

plans

- Implement financial reporting system at project/dept level by May 31st.
- Establish Software Forum for sharing project mgt & tech. issues by June 30.
- Measure progress against the business plan and allow for quarterly updates.
- Develop Sales & Marketing Resource Plan by 3rd quarter 2006.
- Develop partner strategies w/ Oracle, Sun Micro, IBM. by Oct. 31st.
- Implement Professional Skills Programs in Nov.; Mgt Development in Dec.
- Complete sales showroom remodel by Aug. 15th.
- Implement contractor peakwork load program by Sept. 15th.
- Upgrade internal systems including server, network, workstations by Dec. 31.

A high-tech company

All-Right Engineering, Inc.

VISION:

Develop economically viable solution to 6782 printer memory error problem.

MISSION:

Reduce the incidence of printer fatal error messages.

OBJECTIVES:

Achieve .0000032 per thousand memory errors per average test cycle by 9/1/06.
Keep cost of upgrade to $1.53 per shipped unit.
Operate within budget of $356,000.00

STRATEGIES:

Use 3 teams of 2 engineers plus 2 outside consultants.
Concentrate on fixing current design rather that replacing it with another.
Hold weekly progress meeting with team to review progress against plan/budget.
Use outside consultants on as needed basis for new laser technologies.

PLANS:

Establish teams by 3/1.
Identify and qualify 2 outside consultants by 3/1; finalize contracts by 3/1.
Complete problem assessment by 5/31.
Propose an engineering solution by 6/30
Complete prototypes by 7/31
Complete product trials by 8/30.
Document final product specs by 9/30.
Complete installation of modified production equipment by 11/30.

A management-consulting firm

Synergen Associates, Inc.

Management Team Development Process

Vision

Within the next 12 months, evolve the existing management team into a vital growing force that:

- Fuels the growth of the company by seeing and being a part of the larger vision.
- Builds on its own energy and successes; learns from its failures/shortfalls.
- Expands capacity to contribute to the overall management of the company.
- Develops an espirit de corps that is supportive of the individual, the team, and the company.
- Design work style/culture that is adaptable/flexible to move quickly to meet customers needs.

Mission

Build a management team that builds the business.

Objectives

- Improve quality of decision making (measurement to be determined).
- Decrease amount of time to achieve management buy-in on key projects (measurement TBD).
- Reduce average time in management meetings from 25 hours/month to 12.
- Reduce average work week for management from 60 hours to 45 hours.
- Increase internal promotion ratio from 5% to 25%.
- Decrease management turnover from 20% a year to 5%.

Strategies

- Evolve the management team over time; do not go for immediate, but temporary fixes.
- Encourage growth/participation; do not push team faster than they can grow.
- Transfer skills from president to mgt. staff; provide training and coaching as required.
- Allow for small errors, learn from all mistakes, and celebrate the successes
- Minimize fanfare about the process; let team respond to positive, subtle changes.

Plans

- Implement business planning and budgeting process starting on November 2nd.
- Design and implement financial reporting system at Level 2 by Jan. 31st.
- Implement monthly business review sessions starting 2/24.
- Utilize CGC Consulting Group to facilitate quarterly development meetings starting Mar. 15th.
- Implement new managers training program in June; New supervisors training in August.
- Complete development of new employee orientation web-based learning module by 9/30.

Management Development

Bay Area Entrepreneur Association...
the Association for Self-Employment Success!

VISION

Build BAEA into a nationally recognized micro-enterprise organization with an extensive greater San Francisco Bay Area network of entrepreneurial support groups providing nationally recognized products, programs and services to entrepreneurs, small-business owners and partner organizations.

MISSION

The mission of the Bay Area Entrepreneur Association is to positively impact the community by creating viable businesses and successful entrepreneurial leaders through networking, support and connection to resources.

OBJECTIVES

- Increase total revenues from $125,00 to $350,000 in FY2006
- Increase membership from 500 to 750 by December 31st.
- Launch 4 networks by June 30th; 6 additional networks by Dec. 31st.
- Generate $35,000 from entrepreneurial programs, events and products in FY 2006.
- Conduct 24 workshops/programs generate $18,000 in gross profit.
- Conduct 4 Corporate Connection programs with 400 attendees; generate $8,000 profit.
- Increase low-income/minority memberships from 50 to 100 by Sept. 30th.
- Award 10 scholarships totaling $10,000 in FY 2006.

STRATEGIES

- Use public relations and media to share successes, educate, recruit and fund BAEA.
- Market and sell BAEA endorsed products and services nationally.
- Collaborate with natl micro-enterprise org. in national awareness programs and funding.
- Establish BAEA center to create long-term community presence & financial asset base.
- Attract/retain low-income entrepreneurs by offering scholarships funded by corp. sponsors.
- Utilize multi-lingual/cultural programs to attract minority entrepreneurs.
- Package successful BAEA programs & products to sell to other micro-enterprise organizations.
- Use technology to manage growth, streamline operations, deliver programs, & sell products.

PLANS

- Complete funding plan by March 15th. Raise $100,000 by June 30th.
- Hire executive director by May 15th.
- Expand board of directors from 5 to 9 by August 31st.
- Develop BAEA product and service marketing plan by Sept. 15th.
- Develop 2-year network expansion plan by October 31st.
- Launch sales/marketing plan of One Page Business Plan by Nov. 15th.
- Collect /write 20 success stories by Aug. 1st. Implement public relations plan by Nov.1st.

A nonprofit association

California Knits

2006 Business Plan

Vision

California Knits is a creative, soul-filled enterprise that provides:

- vibrant, unique, comfortable clothing as art for women.
- custom design capabilities for individual clients.
- training and mentoring of the next generation of machine knit artists.

Mission

To provide color, light, and energizing beauty
in comfortable, natural fiber clothing,

Objectives

- 2006 Revenue $150,000.
- Achieve profit margin of 50% by holding production labor to 18%.
- Increase active store count to 20, an increase of 30% over 2006.
- Outsource 50% of production by 4th quarter.
- Add three new designs; 2 ready-to-wear, 1 gallery collectible.
- Attend at least six trade/trunk shows in 2006; yielding sales of $40,000

Strategies

- Produce gallery quality garments to attract high-end consumers, galleries, & collectors.
- Design products w/ multiple price points; attract attention w/ gallery quality garments, but have affordable products available at $150 - $200 price point.
- Build network & professional relationships w/in fashion & garment industry.
- Outsource ready-to-wear lines, reserve personal time to create one-of-a-kind garments.
- Develop professional team for production and operation of business.
- Cultivate relationships with upscale clients for referrals and shows.
- Explore avenues to entertainment industry for costume and personal clients.

Plans

- Develop budget and plans for capital needs for business 4/06.
- Complete 2 ready-to-wear designs for show in Aspen in April.
- Contact six (list attached) fashion magazines; present portfolio for publication.
- Submit 10 applications (list attached) for retail and wholesale craft fairs (2/06).
- Attend three trunk shows: New York, June; Santa Fe, August, Carmel, October.
- Continue to send garments to consignment galleries where advantageous.
- Complete redesign of display booths for fairs by March 15th.
- Hire interns or apprentices for in-house production, maintenance, office work (2/06).

A specialty manufacturing company

Phoenix Electronic Controls, Inc. — Business Plan

VISION

To build Phoenix Electronic Controls, Inc. into the premier industrial process control company in the Southwest by expanding its role from a manufacturing rep. company to a valued-added rep. company offering complete engineering, field service, and integration engineering services.

MISSION

PEC's mission is to help its clients control their processes
and
to provide an effective marketing, sales, service, and distribution channel for its manufacturers.

OBJECTIVES

Grow business 20% & achieve total sales revenues of $8 million in 2006.
Secure at least $500,000 in muni contracts in 2nd Qtr.
Land at least 8 system projects at a minimum of $100,000 each in 2006.
Increase gross margin from 14.8% to 15.5%.
Achieve net profit of $300,000, an increase of 50% over last year.
Increase sales per employee from $500,000 to $600,000.
Reduce Accounts Receivables from 58 days to 40 days by June 30.

STRATEGIES

Sell total solutions, not parts.
Build value-added services capability: engineering, service, eng. integration services.
Expand market geographically into Nevada and Colorado.
Aggressively target muni market & large scale processing manufacturers.
Increase margins by selling bundled parts & service; make cust. support a profit center.
Increase outside sales force effectiveness by strengthening sales support function.
Control expenses & growth, self-capitalize/bank finance, achieve sales & profit plans.
Develop autonomous, self-directed & controlled management team.
Share growth & prosperity w/ employees through incentive & equity participation.

PLANS

Complete 2006 business plan & budgets.
Write business plan for Tucson muni contract - 1st Qtr.
Develop marketing program for major systems sales - 1st Qtr.
Organize & staff sales territories; reduce discounts from 5% to 4% - Jan. 06.
Hire Tech Support Mgr. & Service Group Mgr. in 1st Qtr.
Purchase Colorado company or develop plan to expand w/ internal resources - 1st Qtr.
Develop incentive comp. programs for sales support & key employees - 1st Qtr.
Host two user seminars for key clients: April & Sept.

A distribution / manufacturing representative company

Custom Business Interiors

2006 Business Plan

Vision

Build a successful business furniture company that specializies in providing competitively priced furniture with superior service to companies with 10 to 50 employees.

Mission

To provide growing companies a single source for purchasing all of their office furniture and equipment from an experienced professional that understands how to create attractive, functionable, flexible, and affordable office layouts.

Objectives

- Generate sales of $500,000 and profits of $100,000 in 2006.
- Increase gross margin from 28% to 35%.
- Increase # of orders at $10,000 level to 50% of business.
- Conduct 15 "workspace efficiency" workshops for small businesses.
- Limit personal work time to 40 hrs; will hire assistant in Feb.

Strategies

- Build reputation for excellent service; become the Nordstrom of office furniture.
- Focus on growth companies in Contra Costa, Alameda, and Solano counties.
- Target market to financial institutions, insurance & computer companies.
- Keep competitive price advantage by keeping overhead low.
- Sell via catalogs and not invest in showrooms or inventory.

Plans

- Complete revised marketing brochure & mail to existing clients Jan. 31st.
- Complete research on two new suppliers by June 06; annouce in Aug.
- Add PC-based design and layout software in May; announce in Aug.
- Redesign ACT! database by April to simplify direct mail process.
- Notify network by Jan. 15th regarding hiring plans for assistant.

A business-to-business product / service company

E Management Book

VISION

Become nationally known author, publisher, and consultant
serving entreprenuers and independent business owners.

~

- Consult primarily in SF Bay Area; approximately 30% of my time.
- Create products (books, tapes, CD's) for the entrepreneurial market (25%).
- Speak extensively regionally, building to national recognition.

MISSION

Simplify the business of business for entrepreneurs.

~

Create professional business tools,
for entrepreneurs that build strong businesses.

OBJECTIVES

Complete E Management book by 6/27; print 500 cc's in July.
Publish article in Inc. Magazine by 12/31/06; Yield 50 inquiries.
Sell 2,000 books in 2006.
First Fortune 1000 client in 2006, yielding consulting revenues of $50k.
One national convention speaking engagement in 2006; 6 in 2007.
Ten registered/certified E Mgt. practitioners by 12/31/06.
Complete E Mgt. audio tape by 8/31/06; annual sales of $50,000.
Complete Breakthrough Business book w/R. Miller by 12/31/06; 1st year sales $25K.

STRATEGIES

Collaborate to complete; can't do this by myself...Always keep it simple!
Use network/personal contacts to create opports to speak, get reviews, articles published.
Self-publish to start, prove marketability, seek national publisher.
Continue to turn consulting processes into products; products into programs.
Create products & programs for others to sell that serve the entrepreneurial market.
Seek endorsements/approval/intros/quotes from noted authors, CEOs, SBA.
Build brand & corporate identity.
Exit strategy: sell to major publisher or business training company in 5 - 7 yrs.

PLANS

Develop publicity & marketing plan by 7/31.
Develop E Management practitioners program by 7/31.
Contract w/ Audio Design Productions for audio tape production 4/06.
Submit articles to Inc, Entrepreneur, Home Base Business for Dec. publication.
Complete mailing to 250 trade associations by 10/06 for speaking engagements.
Schedule 4 meetings w/R. Miller to complete 2nd book; 9/15 & 30, 10/15 & 10/31.

A business plan for a product

Would you like to share your One Page Business Plan® with others?

Show us how well this process worked for you by sending us a copy of your One Page Business Plan®. Please be sure to include your name, phone number and your responses to the survey on the following page.

The One Page Business Plan® Company

The One Page Business Plan Company
1798 Fifth Street
Berkeley, CA 94710

Phone:
(510) 705-8400

Fax:
(510) 705-8403

jhoran@onepagebusinessplan.com
www.onepagebusinessplan.com

We want your feedback!

We appreciate the opportunity to act upon your feedback. Please take a minute to answer the questions below and fax to **510-705-8403**.

How easy was each section to understand and complete?
1 = very easy 5 = somewhat difficult

	1	2	3	4	5
The Vision Statement	❐	❐	❐	❐	❐
The Mission Statement	❐	❐	❐	❐	❐
The Objectives	❐	❐	❐	❐	❐
The Strategies	❐	❐	❐	❐	❐
The Plans	❐	❐	❐	❐	❐

Who are you?

- ❐ Entrepreneur (with an existing business)
- ❐ Entrepreneur (starting your first business)
- ❐ Corporation or corporate division
- ❐ Nonprofit organization
- ❐ ______________________

How long did it take to complete your One Page Business Plan®?

How have you used or how do you plan to use your One Page Business Plan®?

How did you hear about The One Page Business Plan® and where did you purchase it?

What success have you experienced as a result of learning about or using The One Page Business Plan®?

Do you have any suggestions or other comments?

____

____

____

THANK YOU!

If you would like to receive literature from The One Page Business Plan Company, please complete the information below:

NAME ______________________ COMPANY NAME ______________________

ADDRESS ______________________ CITY, STATE AND ZIP ______________________

PHONE ______________________ FAX ______________________ E-MAIL ______________________

The One Page Business Plan® Company

If you would like additional information on products or services, please contact The One Page Business Plan® Company:

The One Page Business Plan Company
1798 Fifth Street
Berkeley, CA 94710

Phone:
(510) 705-8400

Fax:
(510) 705-8403

jhoran@onepagebusinessplan.com
www.onepagebusinessplan.com

CALL 1-800-852-4890 TO ORDER TODAY FOR ONLY $34.95

NAME ____________________ COMPANY NAME ____________________

ADDRESS ____________________ CITY, STATE AND ZIP ____________________

PHONE ____________ FAX ____________ E-MAIL ____________

☐ Put me on your list to receive the latest updates on *One Page Business Plan*® products and services.

Credit Card Payments Only

Call **1-800-852-4890** or fax your order to **707-838-2220**

☐ VISA ☐ MasterCard ☐ American Express ☐ Discover

SIGNATURE ____________________ EXPIRATION DATE ____________

FOR PAYMENTS BY CHECK, PLEASE MAIL TO RAYNE FULFILLMENT, P.O. BOX 726, WINDSOR, CA 95492

# OF BOOKS	PRICE EACH	TOTAL
	$31.05	
Add 8.25% sales tax for California deliveries		
Add $4.50 S&H for the first book and $1.00 for each additional book		
Total amount due		

CALL 1-800-852-4890 TO ORDER TODAY FOR ONLY $34.95

NAME ____________________ COMPANY NAME ____________________

ADDRESS ____________________ CITY, STATE AND ZIP ____________________

PHONE ____________ FAX ____________ E-MAIL ____________

☐ Put me on your list to receive the latest updates on *One Page Business Plan*® products and services.

Credit Card Payments Only

Call **1-800-852-4890** or fax your order to **707-838-2220**

☐ VISA ☐ MasterCard ☐ American Express ☐ Discover

SIGNATURE ____________________ EXPIRATION DATE ____________

FOR PAYMENTS BY CHECK, PLEASE MAIL TO RAYNE FULFILLMENT, P.O. BOX 726, WINDSOR, CA 95492

# OF BOOKS	PRICE EACH	TOTAL
	$34.95	
Add 8.25% sales tax for California deliveries		
Add $4.50 S&H for the first book and $1.00 for each additional book		
Total amount due		

The One Page Business Plan® Company

If you would like additional information on products or services, please contact The One Page Business Plan® Company:

The One Page Business Plan Company
1798 Fifth Street
Berkeley, CA 94710

Phone:
(510) 705-8400

Fax:
(510) 705-8403

jhoran@onepagebusinessplan.com
www.onepagebusinessplan.com

The One Page Business Plan® Company

Workshops and TeleClasses

The One Business Page Plan® is available to your company or organization as a workshop, annual retreat, teleclass or complete planning program. Experienced facilitators will tailor the presentation to meet your needs.

All classes and programs are hands-on working sessions designed to teach participants how to write a clear, concise, understandable business plan, on a single page, in the quickest and simplest way possible.

Enterprise Planning Software

This innovative system uniquely links The One Page Business Plan® with an Executive Dashboard and a Simplified Project Tracking System that can be used in a variety of companies from small professional service firms to international corporations.

The system requires no IT support and can be learned in 30 minutes. Interested? The One Page Planning and Performance System is rapidly becoming the planning system of choice for CEOs and business owners.

Professional Certification

We are interested in partnering with experienced business, government, and not-for-profit consultants and coaches. If your firm provides strategic planning and/or performance management consulting services, The One Page Business Plan® may be a profitable addition to your toolkit.

Coaches and consultants who successfully complete the training and certification programs will be licensed to market and deliver One Page Business Plan® products and services.

The One Page Business Plan® Company
1798 Fifth Street
Berkeley, CA 94710
Phone: (510) 705-8400
Fax: (510) 705-8403
jhoran@onepagebusinessplan.com
www.onepagebusinessplan.com

The Entrepreneur's CD Toolkit
How Install and Use the CD

Installation Instructions:
Simply load the CD into your CD drive. It contains an automatic installer that will create a directory on your hard drive called Entrepreneur's Toolkit located in your My Documents Folder.

This CD-ROM is NOT a stand-alone software program and requires the use of Microsoft Word® and/or Excel® to use the templates, forms and spreadsheets. If for some reason the auto-installer does not work:

1) Double-click on My Computer,
2) Double-click the icon for the CD-ROM
3) Double-click on setup.exe to launch the Auto-Installer.

How to Use Entrepreneur's Toolkit
Click on Toolkit icon on Desktop to open Windows Explorer directory. Directory will contain the following folders:

1. Forms and Templates
2. Sales Calculators
3. Budget Worksheets
4. Scorecards
5. Sample Plans
6. Bonus Tools

Open any Directory with a double-click. Select desired Word® document or Excel® spreadsheet.

CAUTION:
Immediately after opening any of the files we encourage you to save the file with a new name using the "SAVE AS" command in order to preserve the original content of the file.

No Technical Support
This CD is provided without technical or software support. Please refer to your Microsoft Word® or Excel® User Manuals for questions related to the use of these software programs.

System Requirements:
Windows 95/98/NT/2000/XP
Macintosh OS 9.1 or higher
Microsoft Word® and Excel®
CD/ROM drive
7MB available disk space on hard drive

Special Note to Macintosh Users:
For a Macintosh compatible version of The Entrepreneur's CD Toolkit visit:
www.onepagebusinessplan.com/mac
and enter the password: 75plan57

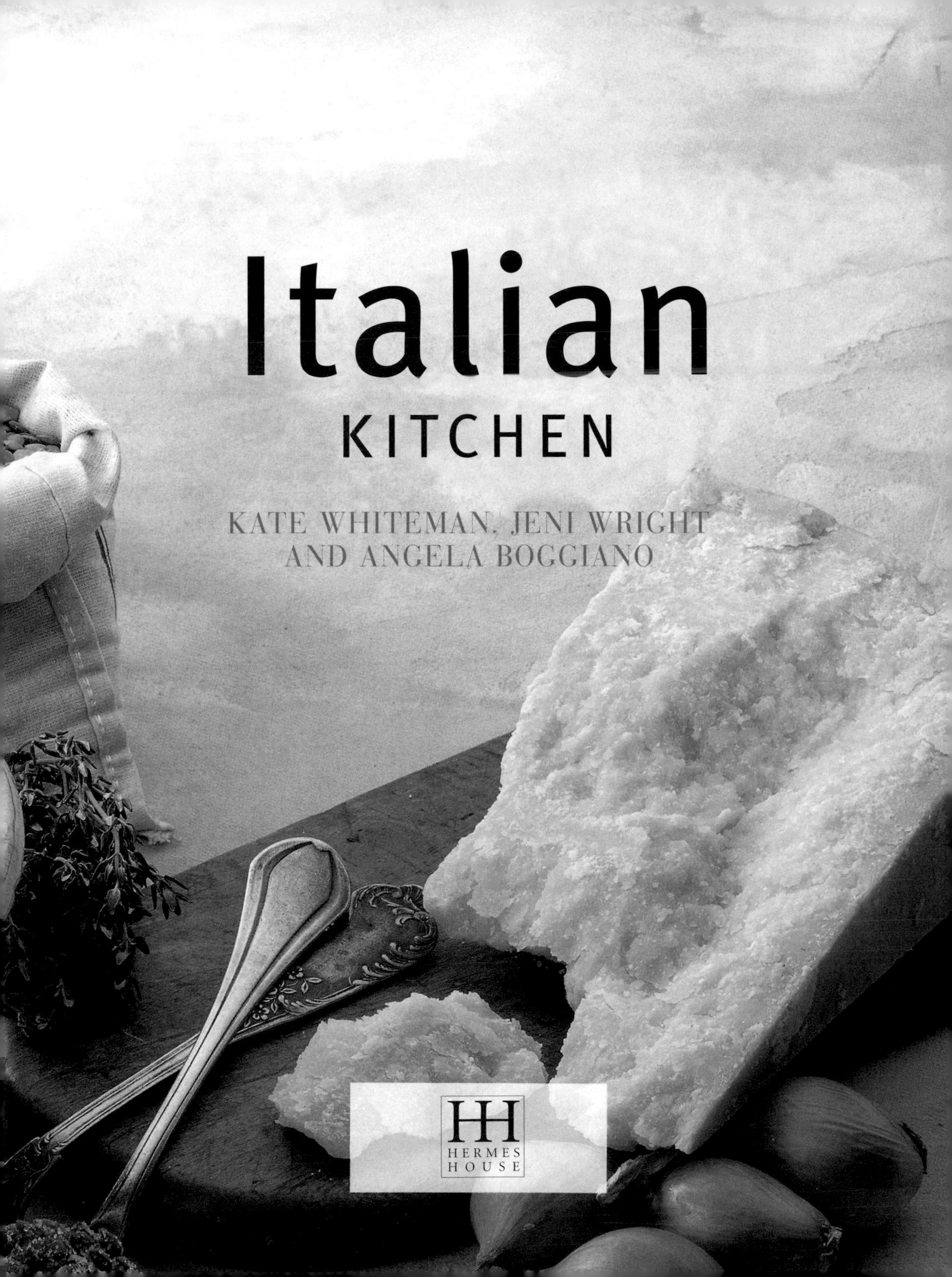

Italian
KITCHEN

KATE WHITEMAN, JENI WRIGHT
AND ANGELA BOGGIANO

HH
HERMES
HOUSE

This edition published in 2001 by Hermes House

Published in the USA by Hermes House
Anness Publishing Inc.
27 West 20th Street
New York
NY 10011

Hermes House is an imprint of Anness Publishing Inc.

Publisher: Joanna Lorenz
Senior Editor: Linda Fraser
Photographers: William Adams-Lingwood and Janine Hosegood (cut-outs)
Home Economist: Lucy McKelvie, assisted by Sophie Wheeler
Stylist: Marian Price
Designer: Sian Keogh
Illustrator: Lucinda Ganderton
Production Controller: Don Campaniello

Also published as *The Italian Ingredients Cookbook and The Italian Kitchen Bible*

Printed and bound in China

1 3 5 7 9 10 8 6 4 2

NOTES

Standard spoon and cup measures are level.
Large eggs are used unless otherwise stated.

Contents

Introduction

Italian cooking reflects the fact that the country was unified only in 1861. Until then, each region produced its own characteristic cuisine, relying exclusively on ingredients that could be gathered, cultivated or reared locally. Nowadays, of course, regional produce can be easily transported all over the country, but Italians still prefer to base their cooking on local ingredients, because they regard quality and freshness as more important than diversity and innovation. So the most flavorful sun–ripened tomatoes, eggplants and bell peppers are still found in the south, the freshest seafood is available along the coast, the finest hams come from the area where the pigs are raised, and so on. *La cucina italiana* remains distinctly regional; northern Italian cooking, for example, incorporates ingredients that are simply never found in the recipes of Sicily and Naples, and vice-versa. In the dairy-farming north, butter is used in place of the olive oil so prevalent in the south; bread and polenta are eaten instead of pasta. The only unifying feature is the insistence on high quality ingredients. Good food has always been essential to the Italian way of life. *La cucina italiana* is one of the oldest cooking cultures in the world, dating back to the Ancient Greeks and perhaps even earlier. The Romans adored food and

THIS ITALIAN BUTCHER'S SHOP (BELOW) NOT ONLY SELLS THE LOCAL *CINGHIALE* (WILD BOAR), BUT ALSO CURED MEATS, CHEESES AND OTHER ESSENTIAL COOKING INGREDIENTS.

often ate and drank to excess; it was they who really laid the foundations of Italian and European cuisine. The early Romans were peasant farmers who ate only the simple, rustic foods they could produce, such as grain, cheeses and olives. For them, meat was an unheard-of luxury; animals were bred to work in the fields and were too precious to eat. Trading links with other parts of the world, however, encouraged Roman farmers to cultivate new vegetables and fruits and, of course, grapes, while their trade in salt and exotic spices enabled them to preserve and pickle all kinds of meat, game and fish. Food became a near-obsession and ever more elaborate dishes were devised to be served at the decadent and orgiastic banquets for which the Romans were famed. The decline and fall of the Roman Empire led inevitably to a deterioration in the quality of cooking and a return to simple, basic foods. For centuries, regional cuisine reverted to its original uncomplicated style. With the Renaissance, however, came great wealth and a new interest in elaborate food. Once again, rich families strove to outdo each other with lavish banquets where courses of rich, extravagant foods were served—truffles, song–birds, game, desserts dripping with honey and spices—all washed down with vast quantities of wine. The poor, of course, continued to subsist on the simple foods they

OLIVES (TOP) GROWING IN GROVES ALONGSIDE GRAPE VINES ON AN UMBRIAN HILLSIDE, AND A SELECTION OF CURED SAUSAGES AND AIR-DRIED PROSCIUTTO (ABOVE) ARE JUST TWO OF THE VAST ARRAY OF TRADITIONAL ITALIAN INGREDIENTS THAT ARE NOW EXPORTED AROUND THE WORLD.

ITALIAN COOKS INSIST ON HIGH-QUALITY COOKING INGREDIENTS, AND EVEN LOCAL DELICATESSENS (RIGHT) ARE PACKED FULL OF FRESH AND PRESERVED INGREDIENTS AND OTHER FOODS—FRUITY CAKES AND CRISP COOKIES, SUCH AS *PANFORTE* AND *CANTUCCI*, DRIED *FAGIOLI* (BEANS), FLAVORFUL OLIVE OILS AND VINEGARS, *PROSCIUTTO CRUDO* (CURED HAMS), TRADITIONAL CHEESES, SUCH AS PARMIGIANO REGGIANO, PICKLES AND PRESERVES, MARINATED OLIVES, CANNED TOMATOES AND BOTTLED SAUCES.

THE SUN-DRENCHED SOUTHERN REGIONS OF ITALY PROVIDE ESSENTIAL PANTRY INGREDIENTS, SUCH AS FULL-FLAVORED GREEN AND BLACK OLIVES AND DELICIOUS SUN-DRIED TOMATOES.

had always eaten, but the wealthier middle classes developed a taste for fine foods and created their own bourgeois dishes. The finer features of Italian cooking even reached the French, when Catherine de' Medici went to Paris to marry the future Henri II, taking fifty of her own cooks with her. They introduced new ingredients and cooking techniques to France and in return learned the art of French cuisine. In those regions of Italy that border France, you can still find reciprocal influences of French classical cooking but, generally speaking, Italians do not like elaborately sauced dishes, preferring to let the natural flavors of their raw ingredients speak for themselves.

The essence of Italian cooking today is simplicity. The Italian way of cooking fish is a good example of this. In coastal areas, freshly caught fish is most often simply grilled over hot coals, then served with nothing more than a splash of extra virgin olive oil, a wedge of lemon and freshly ground black pepper. Recipes such as *carpaccio di tonno*, in which the fish is so delicious raw that cooking seems unnecessary, and *branzino al forno*, where the delicate flavor of fennel is used to complement rather than obscure the fresh taste of the fish, are typically simple, as is *grigliata di calamari*, squid grilled with chilies to reflect its robust character.

Italians learn to appreciate good food when they are young children, and eating is one of the major pleasures of the day, no matter what the day of the week or time of the year. Witness an Italian family gathered around the Sunday lunch table in a local restaurant, and consider how the Italian menu of *antipasto* followed by pasta, rice or gnocchi, then fish, meat and vegetables served in sequence is devised so that each can be savored separately—both the food and the occasion are to be enjoyed as long as possible. The first course, or *antipasto*, is a unique feature. In restaurants, this can be a vast array of different dishes, both hot and cold, from which diners can choose as few or as many as they wish. At home with the family, it is more likely to be a slice or two of *salame* or *prosciutto crudo* with fresh figs or melon, if these are in season. But no matter how humble or grand the setting or the occasion, the *antipasto* is always visually tempting. Colorful dishes such as *bruschetta casalinga* and *peperoni arrostiti con pesto*, are typical in this way.

The variety and diversity of the Italian ingredients available at supermarkets and delicatessens will surely inspire you to concoct any number of delicious meals, from a simple dish of pasta to a full-blown four-course dinner. A plate of *antipasto* followed by pasta or risotto flavored with seasonal ingredients, then simply-cooked meat or fish and finally a local cheese and fruit makes a veritable feast. You could prepare a different meal along these lines every day of the year and almost never repeat the same combination. If you visit Italy, avail yourself of the wonderful local ingredients to prepare a menu full of the flavors of the region. Every area has its own special delights that make cooking a real pleasure.

Fresh ingredients are highly prized by Italian cooks and are often sold at the local outdoor markets: Dozens of *carciofi* (artichokes) are tied ready for transport to a local market (below), and an outdoor stall is piled high with a typically wide selection of high-quality fresh herbs and salad greens, vegetables and fruits (bottom).

Negroni

The Ingredients

Italian cooks have traditionally relied on local ingredients—whatever could be gathered, cultivated or reared locally. Today, our supermarkets and delicatessens are full of these flavorful, good-quality ingredients. This comprehensive guide provides essential information on the huge range of Italian foods and shows you how to prepare and cook them.

Pasta

If there is one ingredient that sums up the essence of Italian cooking, it must surely be pasta, that wonderfully simple and nutritious staple that can be formed into an almost infinite variety of shapes and sizes. In Italy, pasta is an essential part of every full meal and does not constitute a meal on its own. Il primo, *as the pasta course is called, is eaten between the* antipasto *(appetizer) and* il secondo *(the main course). Sometimes small pasta shapes are served in soup as* pasta in brodo. *There are two basic types of pasta,* pastasciutta *(dried) and* pasta fresca *(fresh).*

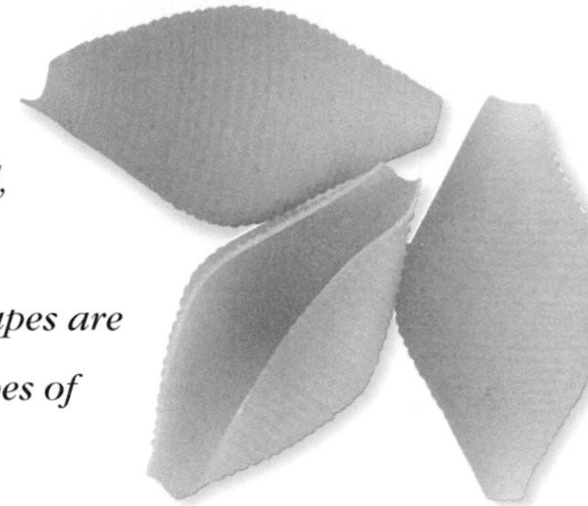

Today pasta is almost always factory-made. The dough is made from hard durum wheat, which produces an elastic dough, ideal for shaping into literally hundreds of different forms, from long, thin spaghetti to elaborate spirals and frilly, bow-shaped *farfalle*. Basic pasta dough is made only from durum wheat and water, although it is sometimes enriched with eggs (*pasta all'uovo*), which add an attractive yellow tinge, or colored and flavored with ingredients such as spinach (*pasta verde*) or squid ink (*pasta nera*). These traditional flavorings are more successful than modern gimmicky creations such as chocolate-flavored pasta. (Most Italians would throw up their hands in horror at this unauthentic folly.) Dried pasta has a nutty flavor and should always retain a firm texture when cooked. It is generally used for thinner-textured, more robust sauces.

Fresh pasta is usually made by hand, using superfine plain white flour enriched with eggs. Unlike dried pasta dough, it can be easily kneaded and is very malleable. Fresh pasta is often wrapped around a stuffing of meat, fish, vegetables or cheese to make ravioli, tortelli or cappelletti, or layered with sauce and meat or vegetables, as in lasagne.

Commercially made fresh pasta is made with durum wheat, water and eggs. The dough is harder than that used for handmade pasta, but it can be easily kneaded by machine. The flavor and texture of all fresh pasta is very delicate, so it is best suited to more creamy sauces.

History

The argument about the origins of pasta will probably rage on forever; the Chinese claim that they were the first to discover the art of noodle-making and that pasta was brought to Italy by Marco Polo. The Italians, of course, claim it as their own invention. Historians tell us that the Romans and probably even the Ancient Greeks used to eat pasta. Certainly the climate of southern Italy was ideally suited to growing durum wheat, so this theory is quite likely, but the popularity of pasta really spread in the fourteenth century, when bakeries in southern Italy started to sell pasta as an alternative to bread.

Then, as now, pasta was the traditional *primo* of the south, although in the poorest areas it constituted a complete meal. Its popularity filtered up to the north of Italy, and by the nineteenth century huge factories had been set up to mass-produce vast quantities of pasta, which quickly became an integral part of all Italian cooking.

Buying and Storing

Always buy dried pasta made from Italian durum wheat. Even after the package has been opened, dried pasta will keep for weeks in an airtight container. Handmade fresh pasta will keep only for a couple of days, but it can be successfully frozen. Machine-made fresh pasta is pasteurized and vacuum-packed, so it will keep in the refrigerator for up to two weeks and can be frozen for up to six months. When buying colored and flavored pasta, make sure that it has been made with natural ingredients.

Cooking Pasta

Allow about 3 oz pasta per serving as a first course. All pasta must be cooked in a large saucepan filled with plenty of salted, fast-boiling water.

For long shapes like spaghetti, drop one end of the pasta into the water and, as it softens, push it down gently until it bends in the middle and is completely immersed.

Cooking times vary according to the type, size and shape of the pasta, but, as a general rule, filled pasta takes about 12 minutes, dried pasta needs 8–10 minutes and fresh pasta only 2–3 minutes. All pasta should be cooked al dente, *so that it is still resistant to the bite. Always test pasta for doneness just before you think it should be ready; it can easily overcook. To stop the cooking, take the pan off the heat and run a little cold water into it, then drain the pasta.*

Preparing Fresh Pasta

1 Allow 1 egg to $3^{1}/_{2}$ oz superfine plain flour. Sift the flour and a pinch of salt into a mound on a clean work surface and make a well. Break the eggs into the well and gradually work in the flour until completely combined.

2 Knead the dough with floured hands for at least 15 minutes, until it is very smooth, firm and elastic. (If you are short on time or energy, you can do this in a food processor.)

3 Chill the dough for 20 minutes, then roll it to the required thickness and cut it into your desired shape. (You can buy a specially shaped rolling-pin to make the squares for filled pasta.) A pasta machine will make this process much easier. Let the pasta dry for at least 1 hour before cooking it.

Pasta Varieties

Pasta shapes can be divided roughly into four categories: long strands and ribbons, flat, short and filled.

The best-known long variety is spaghetti, which comes in a thinner version, spaghettini, and the flatter *linguine*, which means "little tongues." *Bucatini* are thicker and hollow—perfect for trapping sauces in the cavity. Ribbon pasta is wider than the strands: Fettuccine, *trenette* and tagliatelle all fall into this category. Dried tagliatelle is usually sold folded into nests, which unravel during cooking. A mixture of white and green noodles is known as *paglia e fieno* (straw and hay). Pappardelle are the widest ribbon pasta; they are often served with *sugo alla lepre* (hare sauce). The thinnest pasta strands are vermicelli (little worms) and ultra-fine *capelli d'angelo* (angel's hair).

In Italy, flat fresh pasta is often called *maccheroni*, not to be confused with the short tubes with which we are familiar. Lasagne and cannelloni are larger flat rectangles, used for layering or rolling around a filling; dried cannelloni are already formed into wide tubes. Layered pasta dishes such as this are cooked *al forno* (baked). Fillings for fresh pasta squares include meat, pumpkin, artichokes, ricotta and spinach, seafood, chicken and rabbit. There are dozens of names for filled pasta, but the only difference lies in the shape and size. Ravioli are square, tortelli are usually round, while tortellini and *anolini* are ring-shaped.

As for pasta shapes, the list is almost endless and the names wonderfully descriptive. There are *maltagliati* (badly cut), *orecchiette* (little ears) and *cappellacci* (bad hats), while from the natural world come penne (quills), *conchiglie* (little shells), *farfalle* (butterflies) and *lumache* (snails).

When choosing the appropriate pasta shape for the sauce, there are no hard and fast rules, but long, thin pasta is best for olive-oil-based and delicate seafood sauces. Short pasta shapes with wide openings (such as *conchiglie* and penne) will trap meaty or spicy sauces, as will spirals and curls. Almost any pasta is suitable for tomato sauce.

Tonnarelli al nero
Flavored and colored with squid ink

Spinach fettuccine

Bavette
Flavored with porcini *(ceps)*

Plain fettuccine

Paglia e fieno

Long Pasta

Fresh tagliatelle *Flavored with squid ink*

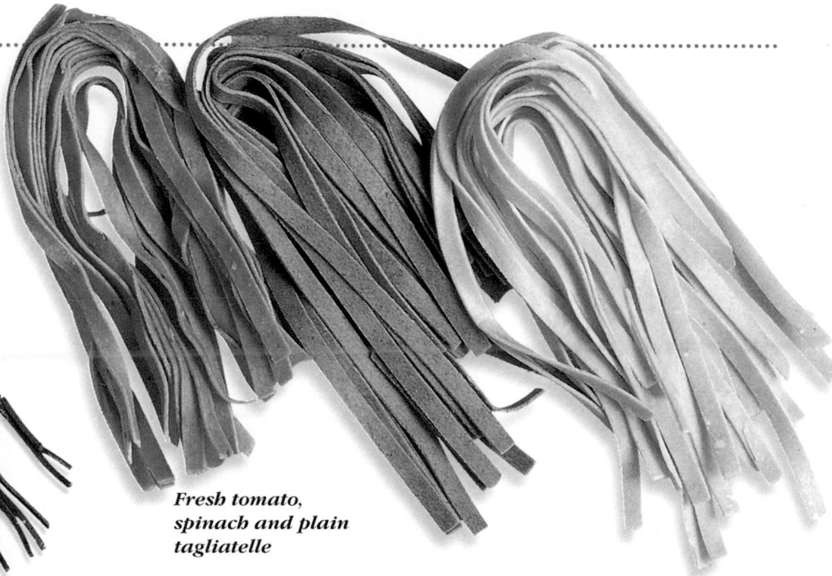

Fresh tomato, spinach and plain tagliatelle

Fresh spaghetti

Fresh paglia e fieno

Fresh tagliolini

Long Pasta

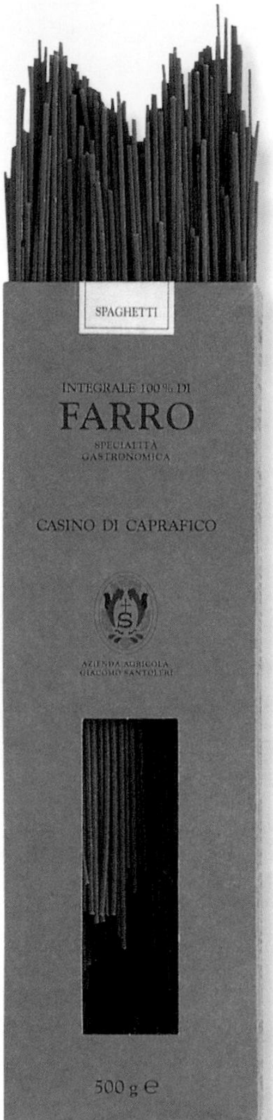

Farro spaghetti

Long, plain spaghetti
In Italy, still sold in the traditional blue paper roll

Spaghetti tricolori
Mixed plain, spinach and tomato spaghetti

Long, plain spaghetti

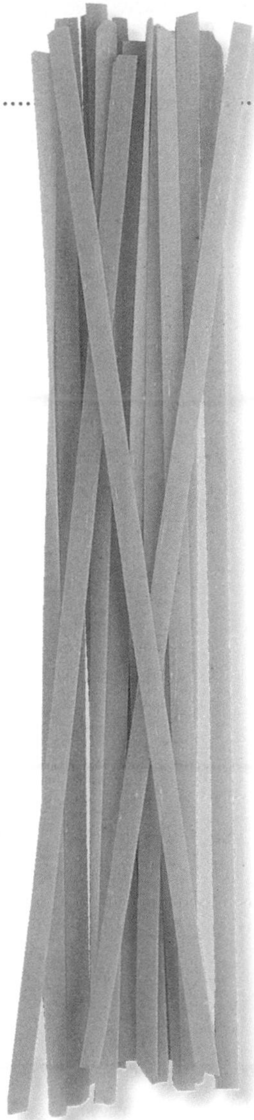

Fettuccelle

Linguine

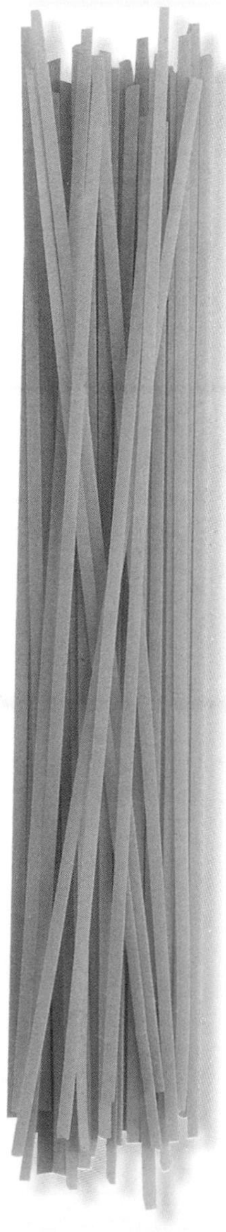

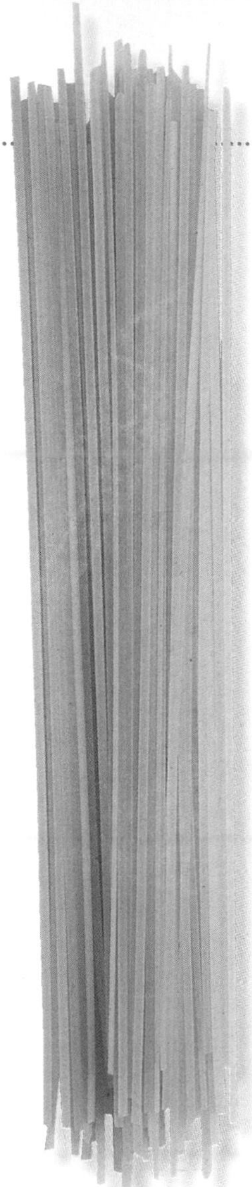

Linguinette

Plain tagliatelle

Tagliatelle
Flavored with squid ink

Mushroom-flavored tagliatelle

Spinach tagliatelle

Long Pasta

Vermicelli

Bucatini

Ziti

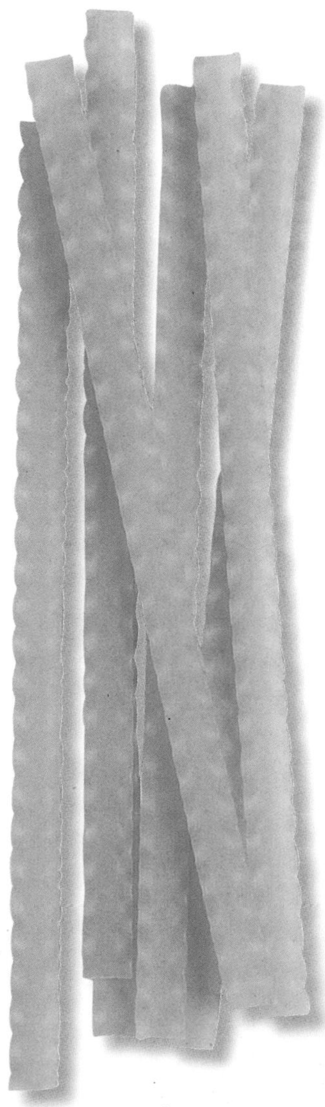

Lasagnette

Angel's hair pasta

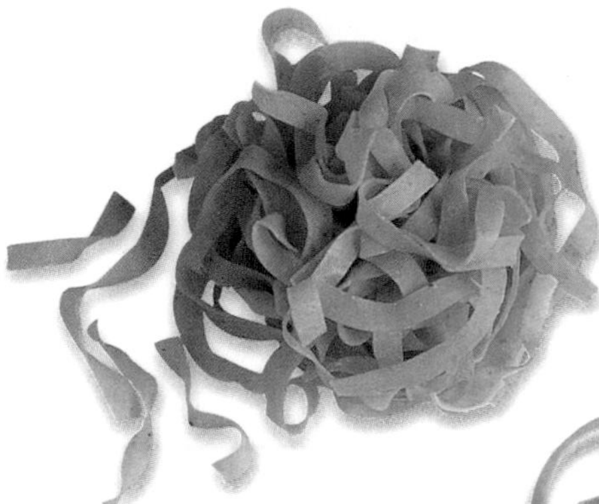

Chili-flavored tagliatelle

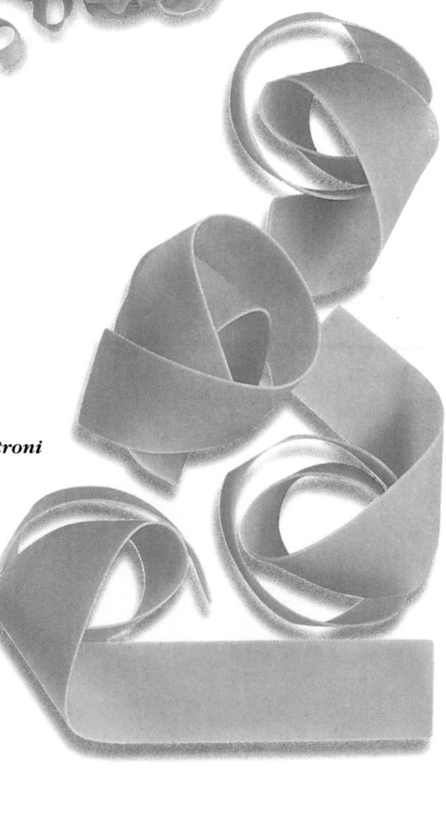

Nastroni

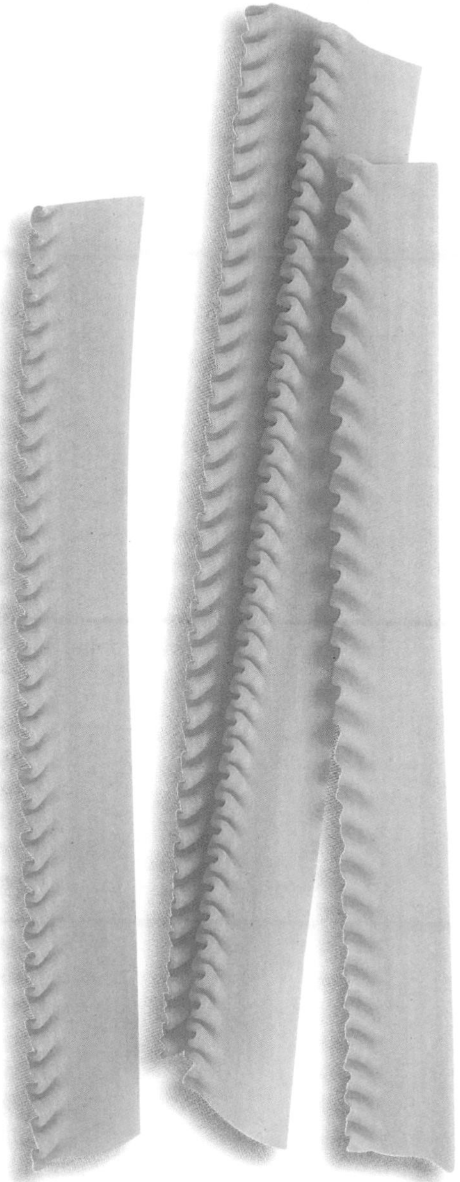

Pappardelle

Short Pasta

Tomato and spinach orecchiette

Farfalle

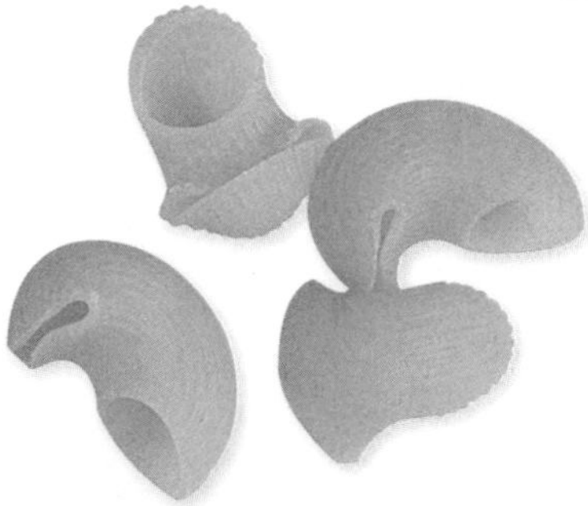

Pipe rigate

Chili-flavored fusilli

Gigli del Gargano

Plain and spinach farfalle

Pepper- and spinach-flavored fusilli

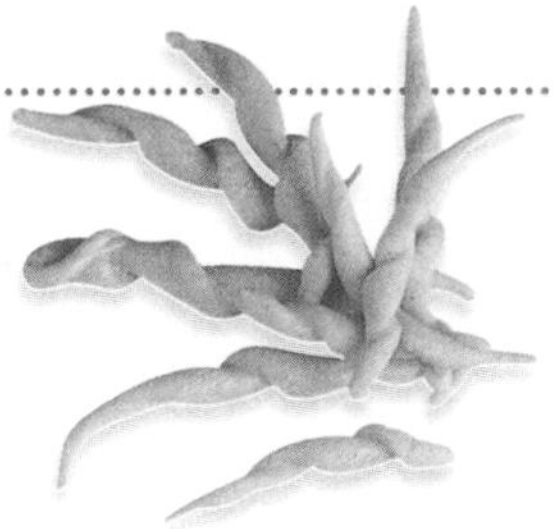

Trofie

Plain pasta shells

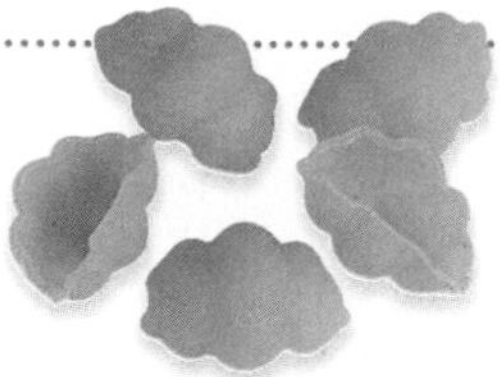

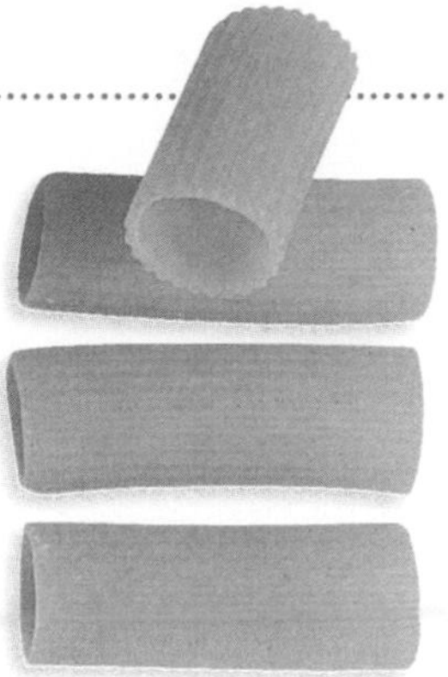

Rigatoni

Conchiglie rigate paglia e fieno

Fusillata casereccia

Lumaconi rigati

Conchiglie rigate

Large lumache rigate

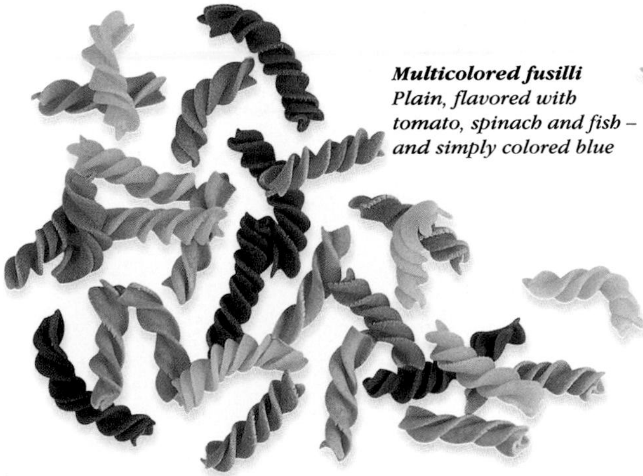

Multicolored fusilli
Plain, flavored with tomato, spinach and fish – and simply colored blue

Large conchiglie

Short Pasta

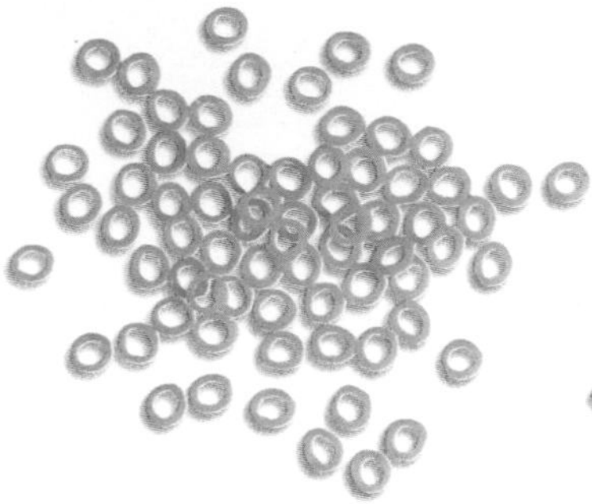

Anellini

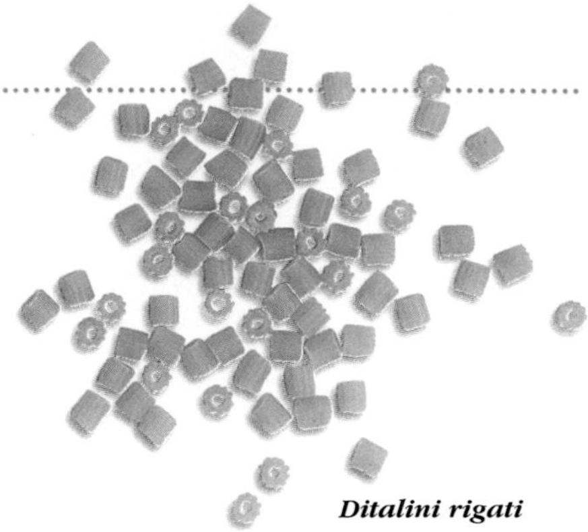

Ditalini rigati

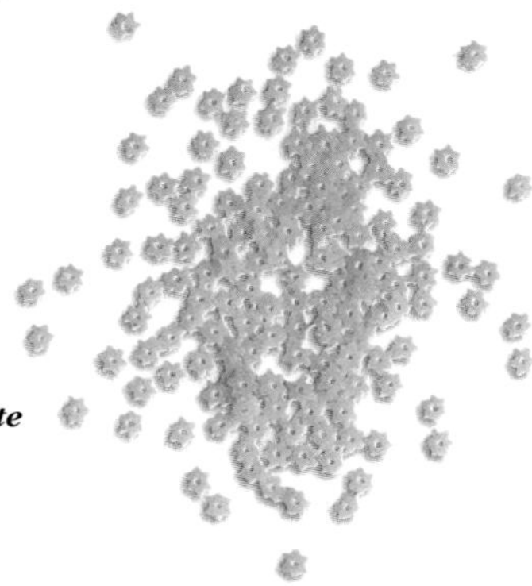

Stellette

Pennette rigate

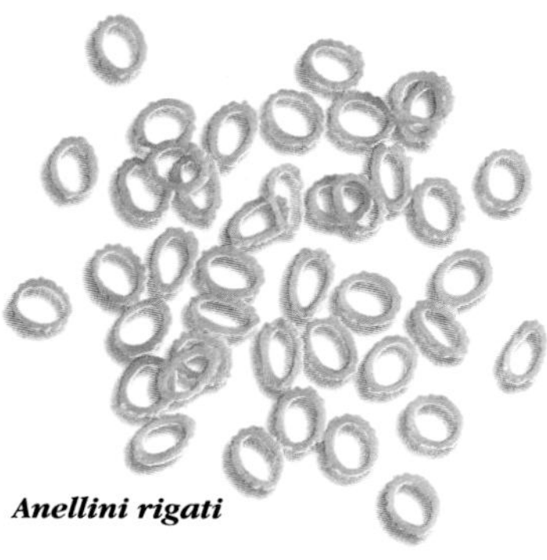

Anellini rigati

Fresh macheroni rigati

Gremiti

Penne

Penne rigate
Flavored with squid ink

Penne rigate
Flavored with chili

Penne rigate

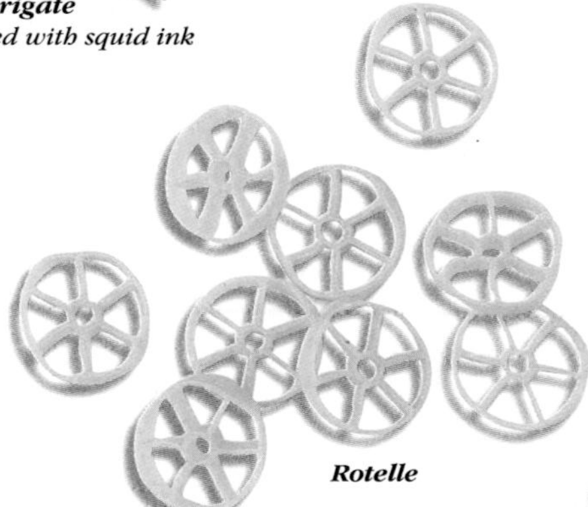

Rotelle

Cappelletti tricolori

Penne rigate
Flavored with spinach

Flat Pasta

Lasagne

Spinach lasagne

Fresh lasagne

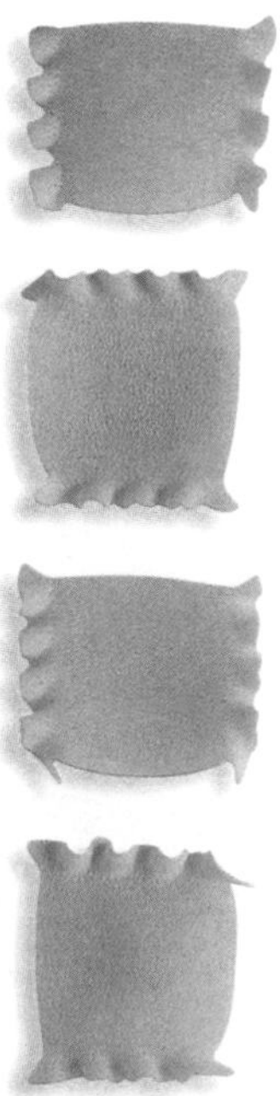

Tacconi

Filled Pasta

Tortellini

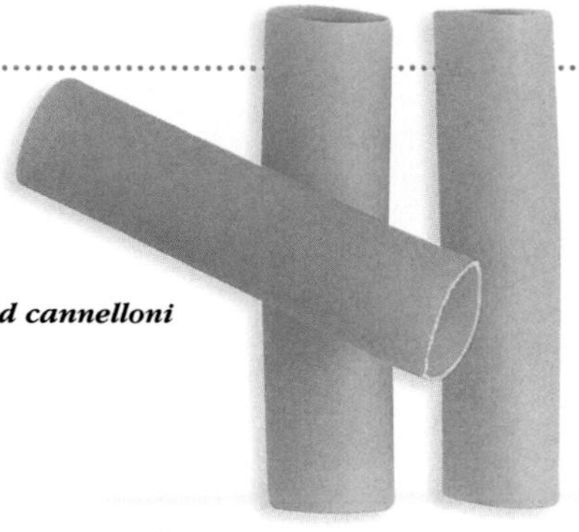

Dried cannelloni

Fresh ravioli

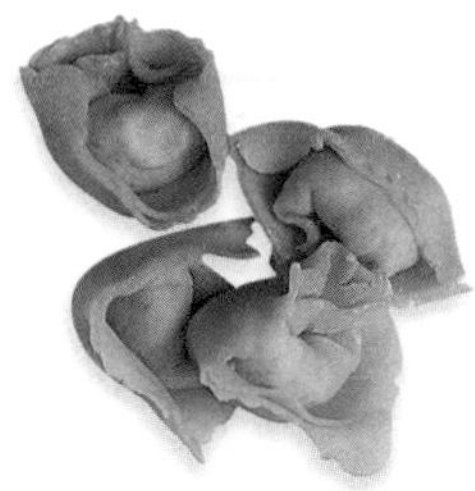

Fresh tortelli

Cappelletti
Filled with sun-dried tomatoes

Cappelletti fantasia
These multicolored cappelletti are bought ready for filling and cooking

Fresh filled cannelloni

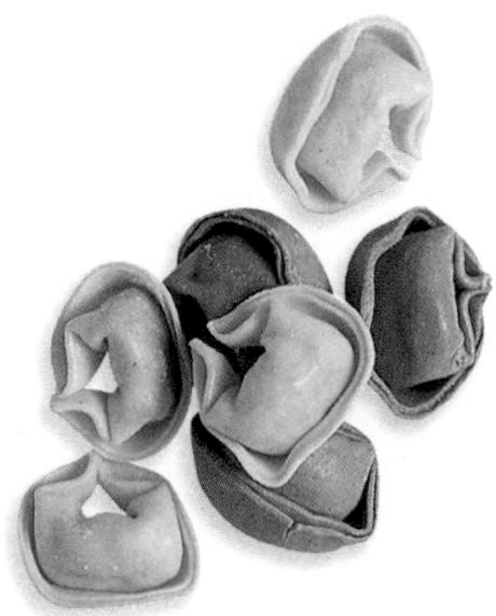

Tortelli
Plain and flavored with spinach

Gnocchi

Gnocchi fall into a different category from other pasta, being more like small dumplings. They can be made with semolina (milled durum wheat), flour, potatoes or ricotta and spinach and may be shaped like elongated shells, ovals, cylinders or flat discs, or roughly shredded into *strozzapreti* (priest-stranglers); store-bought gnocchi are usually ridged ovals. However they are made, gnocchi should be extremely light and almost melt in the mouth.

Culinary Uses

Gnocchi can be served like any pasta, as a first course, in clear soup or occasionally as an accompaniment to the main course. Almost any pasta sauce is suitable for serving with gnocchi; they are particularly good with a creamy Gorgonzola sauce, or they can be served simply, drizzled with olive oil and dredged with freshly grated Parmesan.

Buying and Storing

Gnocchi are usually sold loose at better supermarkets. They are quite filling, so a small portion is enough for a first course; allow 4 oz per serving. They will keep in a ziplock bag in the refrigerator for two or three days. Homemade gnocchi dough will also keep for a couple of days before cooking.

Cooking Gnocchi

With the exception of oven-baked gnocchi alla romana, *all other types of gnocchi should be poached in a saucepan of lightly salted, barely simmering water.*

Drop the gnocchi into the water in batches and cook for about 5 minutes; they will rise to the surface when they are done. Scoop out the cooked gnocchi with a slotted spoon and transfer to a plate: keep them warm while you cook the rest.

Fresh plain gnocchi

Fresh potato gnocchi

Gnocchi di patate

The best-known type of gnocchi are those from northern Italy made with potatoes and a little flour. To make 4 servings, peel $1^1/_4$ lb floury potatoes and boil until very tender. Drain and mash until smooth, then mix in 1 large egg and season with salt and pepper. Add $3^1/_2$–4 oz flour, a little at a time, stirring well with a wooden spoon until you have a smooth, sticky dough that forms a ball on the spoon (you may not need all the flour). Turn out the dough onto a floured surface and knead for about 3 minutes, until soft and smooth. Cut the dough into 6 equal pieces and, with floured hands, roll these into sausage shapes about $^3/_4$ in in diameter. Slice the dough into $^3/_4$-in discs. Hold a fork in your left hand and press the discs against the tines just hard enough to make ridges, then flip them downward off the fork so that they curl up into elongated shell shapes. Poach them as above.

Fresh spinach and ricotta gnocchi

Spinach and ricotta gnocchi

These attractive green gnocchi originated in Tuscany where, confusingly, they were known as ravioli. For 4 servings, you need:

12 oz cooked spinach, well drained and finely chopped
1 container (8 oz) ricotta, mashed until smooth
2 eggs
1 cup freshly grated Parmesan
3 tbsp flour
5 tbsp butter, melted
salt, pepper and nutmeg

1 Put the spinach, ricotta and seasoning in a saucepan and cook gently, stirring continuously, for 5 minutes. Off the heat, beat in the eggs, 3 tbsp of the Parmesan and the flour. Chill the mixture for at least 4 hours. Lightly shape into small rounds and roll them in a very little flour. Poach them as described, left.

2 Preheat the oven to 350°F. Pour a little melted butter into a serving dish and put in the cooked gnocchi. Sprinkle with some of the remaining Parmesan and place in the oven.

3 Add the rest of the gnocchi as they are cooked and cover them with melted butter and Parmesan. Put the dish in the oven for another 5 minutes before serving.

Fresh gnocchi made with semolina

Gnocchi alla romana

These substantial gnocchi from Lazio are made with semolina milled from durum wheat.
For 4–6 servings, you need:

4 cups milk
8 oz semolina
1 cup freshly grated Parmesan
2 eggs, plus an extra yolk, lightly beaten
5 tbsp butter
salt, pepper and nutmeg

1 Bring the milk to a boil, season with salt, pepper and nutmeg, then add the semolina in a steady stream, whisking for about 15 minutes, until the mixture is very thick. Off the heat, stir in half the Parmesan and the beaten eggs.

2 Pour the mixture into a greased baking tray to a thickness of about $^1/_2$ in, or spread it over a dampened work surface. Let cool completely, then cut out $1^1/_4$ in discs with a plain or fluted cookie cutter.

3 Preheat the oven to 350°F. Layer the semolina discs in a buttered baking dish, dotting each layer with flakes of butter and a sprinkling of grated Parmesan, finishing with the cheese. Bake the gnocchi for about 15 minutes, until browned on top.

Spinach and Parmesan gnocchi

Rice, Grains & Beans

Almost as important as pasta in Italian cooking are rice, polenta and beans, which all appear as primi piatti *(first courses) in various guises. Like all basically agricultural countries, Italy relied heavily on these protein-rich ingredients when luxuries such as meat were in short supply, and a host of wholesome and delicious recipes were developed using these modest ingredients.*

Riso (Rice)

Italy produces more rice and a greater variety of rice than any other country in Europe. Most of it is grown in the Po Valley in Piedmont, where conditions are perfect for cultivating the short-grain Carnaroli, Arborio and *Vialone Nano* rice, which make the best risotto. Italian rice is classified by size, ranging from the shortest, roundest *ordinario* (used for puddings) to *semifino* (for soups and salads), then *fino* and finally the longer grains of the finest risotto rice, *superfino*. *Superfino* rice swells to at least three times its original size during cooking, enabling it to absorb all the cooking liquid while still retaining its shape and firm *al dente* texture combined with a creamy smoothness.

History

The Saracens first introduced rice to Italy as long ago as the eleventh century (some believe even earlier), but it only became popular in the sixteenth century, when it began to be cultivated on a large scale in the Po Valley. Traditionally, rice has played a much greater part in the cooking of northern Italy than in the south, particularly in the Veneto, where the famous dish of *risi e bisi* (Venetian dialect for "rice and peas") opened the banquet served every year by the Doges to honor their patron Saint Mark.

Superfino Carnaroli rice **(left and above)**
This short-grained variety is one of the finest Italian rices. Its ability to absorb liquid and cook to a creamy smoothness while still retaining its shape makes it perfect for risotto

Arborio rice

Superfino Arborio rice

Vialone Nano rice

Preparing Risotto

The most famous of all Italian rice dishes is risotto, which was invented in Milan in the sixteenth century. A good risotto can be made only with superfine rice. All risotti are basically prepared in the same way, although they can be flavored with an almost endless variety of ingredients. The rice is coated in butter or oil, then simmering stock is added, one ladleful at a time, and the rice is stirred over low heat until all the liquid has been completely absorbed.

Only then is more stock added, and the risotto is cooked in this way for about 20 minutes, until the rice is tender and creamy. The final touch is called mantecatura; *off the heat, a pat of butter or a couple of spoons of olive oil and some freshly grated Parmesan are stirred into the risotto to make it more creamy.*

Leftover risotto can be rolled into balls enclosing a piece of mozzarella, coated in fine bread crumbs and deep-fried to make supplì al telefono *or the Sicilian equivalent,* arancini.

Riso (Rice)

Rice is often used in Italian soups; it combines well with almost all vegetables and makes a substantial addition to minestrone. Baked rice dishes are also popular. Cooked rice is layered in a buttered ovenproof dish with meatballs, vegetables or poultry and cheese, then topped with bread crumbs and baked until the top is crispy and brown. The Italians never serve main dishes on a bed of rice, but prefer to serve plain boiled rice on its own with plenty of butter and cheese stirred in.

Buying and Storing

Buy only special superfine risotto rice for use in Italian cooking. Shorter grain *semifino* is best for soups, and *ordinario* for puddings (try *riso nero*, a rice pudding topped with melted chocolate). Once you have opened the package, reseal it tightly; you can then keep the rice in a dry place for several months.

Semifino rice

Brown semifino rice

Supplì al telefono

These rice croquettes contain mozzarella, which, when cooked, melts into strings that resemble "telephone wires." For 4 servings, you will need:

2 eggs, lightly beaten
8 oz cold, cooked risotto
6 oz prosciutto, cut into ½-in dice
4 oz mozzarella, cut into ½-in dice
fine dried bread crumbs, for coating
oil, for deep-frying
salt and freshly ground black pepper

1 Mix the eggs into the cold risotto and season to taste with plenty of salt and pepper.

2 Form the rice mixture into balls about the size of a small orange and make a hollow in each one. Fill this with a cube of ham and one of cheese, then roll each ball in your hand to enclose the ham and cheese completely, adding a little more rice if necessary.

3 Spread out the bread crumbs on a shallow tray or plate and roll the rice balls in the bread crumbs to coat them lightly.

4 Heat the oil in a deep, heavy pan and deep-fry the rice balls in batches for 3–5 minutes, until golden brown. Drain on paper towels and keep warm while you cook the remainder. Serve piping hot.

Farro

Cook's Tip

When cooking rice, a good rule of thumb is: The better the rice, the longer the cooking time required, so ordinario *will need only 10–12 minutes' cooking compared with up to 20 minutes for* superfino.

This is the Tuscan name for spelt, a hard brown wheat with pointed grains, which is rarely used in other parts of Italy. *Farro* is much harder than other wheat and therefore takes longer to process and cook, but it will grow even in poor soil. In Tuscany it is used to make *gran farro*, a delicious and nourishing soup, which is served as a first course instead of pasta.

Culinary Uses

Farro is used mainly as an ingredient for soups, but in remoter country areas of Italy it is sometimes used to make bread.

Cook's Tip

Farro *is a very hard grain and must be boiled for up to 3 hours to make it digestible before adding to other recipes. It can also be simply cooked and served with olive oil and freshly ground black pepper.*

Ordinario rice

Farro

Gran farro

This Tuscan soup is often served as a first course instead of pasta. For 4 servings, you will need:

8 oz dried borlotti or cannellini beans, soaked overnight, then drained
1 onion, chopped
2 garlic cloves, chopped
4 oz finely chopped *pancetta*
4 sage leaves
a pinch of chopped fresh oregano
3 tbsp olive oil
8 oz chopped fresh tomatoes
5 oz prepared *farro*
salt, freshly ground black pepper and grated nutmeg

1 Cook the beans in fresh water until tender (reserve the cooking water). Put the beans through a vegetable mill. Gently cook the onion, garlic, *pancetta* and herbs in the olive oil until pale golden brown. Add the tomatoes, season with salt, pepper and nutmeg, then simmer for 10 minutes.

2 Add the bean purée and enough of the cooking water to make a thick soup. Stir in the *farro* and simmer for 45 minutes, adding more water if the soup becomes too thick. Serve with some extra virgin olive oil to trickle into it.

Polenta

For centuries, polenta has been a staple food of the north of Italy, particularly around Friuli and the Veneto. This grainy yellow flour is a type of cornmeal made from ground maize, which is cooked into a kind of porridge with a wide variety of uses. Polenta is sometimes branded according to the type of maize from which it is made. *Granturco* and *Fioretto* are the two most common types.

In Italy, polenta is available ground to various degrees of coarseness to suit different dishes, but there are two main types—coarse and fine. Coarse polenta has a more interesting texture but takes longer to cook.

Grilled or Fried Polenta

Pour the cooked polenta onto a wooden board and spread it to a thickness of about 1 in. Let cool and harden, then cut into squares.

Fry in hot vegetable oil until crunchy and golden, then drain on paper towels or grill until golden brown on both sides.

To make a pasticciata *(layered baked dish) of polenta, cut the cold polenta horizontally into* ½*-in slices and layer it in a buttered baking dish with your chosen sauce, mushrooms, cheeses, etc. Bake for about 15 minutes, until the top is lightly browned.*

History

The Romans made a savory porridge they called *puls* using *farro*, a kind of spelt, and the tradition continued in northern Italy, where gruels were prepared from local cereals such as buckwheat, barley and oats. Maize or corn was only introduced into Italy from the New World in the seventeenth century; soon it was being grown in all the northeastern regions, where cornmeal overtook all other types of grain in popularity, because it combined so well with the local dairy products. Traditionally, polenta was cooked in a *paiolo*, a special copper pot which hung in the fireplace; here, it was stirred for at least an hour, to be served for breakfast, lunch or dinner (sometimes all three).

Culinary Uses

Polenta is extraordinarily versatile and can be used for any number of recipes, ranging from rustic to highly sophisticated. Although it is most often served as a first course, it can also be used as a vegetable dish or main course and even made into cookies and cakes. Plain boiled polenta can be served on its own, or enriched with butter and cheese to make a very satisfying dish. It goes wonderfully well with all meats, sausages and game, helping to cut the richness and mop up the sauce. It can be cooled and cut into squares, then fried, grilled or baked and served with a topping or filling of mushrooms, meat, vegetables or cheese. Fried or grilled squares of polenta form the basis of *crostini*, which are served as an *antipasto*.

Fine polenta

BUYING AND STORING

It is possible to buy quick-cooking polenta, which can be prepared in only 5 minutes. However, if you can spare the 20 minutes or so that it takes to cook traditional polenta, it is best to buy this for its superior texture and flavor. Whether you choose coarse or fine meal is a matter of personal preference; for soft polenta or sweet dishes, fine-ground is better, while coarse-ground meal is better for frying. Once you have opened the bag, put the remaining polenta in an airtight container; it will keep for at least a month.

Coarse polenta

SWEET POLENTA FRITTERS

Polenta can be used to make sweet as well as savory dishes. To make enough fritters to serve four, combine 3 cups milk, 6 tbsp superfine sugar and a pinch of salt in a saucepan and bring to a boil. Add 5 oz polenta in a steady stream, stirring constantly for 20 minutes. Off the heat, stir in 2 tbsp butter, 3 egg yolks and the grated rind of 1 lemon and continue to stir for 1 minute. Spread out the polenta on a dampened baking sheet to a thickness of ½ in. When cold, cut into rectangles or diamonds. Coat lightly with fine dry bread crumbs, then deep-fry in hot oil until golden. Drain on paper towels and dust with confectioners' sugar before serving.

COOK'S TIP

Polenta can be cooked in water, stock or a mixture of water and milk. Whichever liquid you use, cook the polenta very slowly and steadily so that it does not become lumpy. Allow ½ cup polenta meal per person.

Recipe for Basic Polenta

To make a basic polenta for 4–6 people, bring 6 cups salted water or stock to a boil.

Gradually add 2 cups polenta in a steady stream, stirring continuously with a wooden spoon. Continue cooking, stirring constantly, until the polenta comes away from the sides of the saucepan. This will take 20–30 minutes (5 minutes for quick-cooking polenta).

One alternative, foolproof (though unauthentic) method is to put the polenta meal into a saucepan, add salt, then stir in the cold water, bring the mixture slowly to a boil and simmer gently for about 20 minutes, stirring occasionally.

Another is to cook the polenta on the stove for 5 minutes, then finish cooking it in the oven for an hour.

Pour the cooked polenta into a serving dish, season with pepper and stir in abundant quantities of butter and a strong-flavored cheese—Parmesan, Fontina, Bel Paese and Gorgonzola are all delicious with piping hot polenta.

Beans

Fagioli (beans)

Beans are another staple of Tuscan cooking; indeed, the Tuscans are sometimes nicknamed "the bean-eaters," although beans are eaten all over Italy. The most popular varieties include the pretty red-and-cream speckled borlotti, the small white cannellini (a kind of kidney bean), the larger *toscanelli* and *fagioli coll'occhio* (black-eyed beans). All these are eaten as hearty stews, with pasta and in soups, and cannellini are often served as a side dish simply anointed with extra virgin olive oil. *Ceci* (chickpeas) and *fave* (fava beans) are also popular.

History

Beans were a staple of the Roman and Greek diet, and several recipes for bean stews survive from that period. Many of the beans were brought to Italy from the Middle East, but some, such as *fave*, were indigenous and were used as ritual offerings to the dead at Roman funerals. Beans have always been a popular peasant food, but, during the Renaissance, Catherine de Medici attempted to refine Italian cuisine, and beans fell out of favor with the nobility and sophisticated urban dwellers. Thanks to their highly nutritious and economical qualities, however, beans and legumes have once again become an important element in Italian cooking.

Culinary Uses

Beans can be made into any number of nutritious soups and stews, or served as the basis of a substantial salad such as *tonno e fagioli* (tuna and beans). One popular Tuscan dish is *fagioli all'uccelletto* (beans cooked like little birds). Cooked cannellini beans are combined with chopped garlic, fresh sage leaves and tomatoes and simmered for about 15 minutes, until tender and fragrant. This dish is delicious served with coarse country sausages.

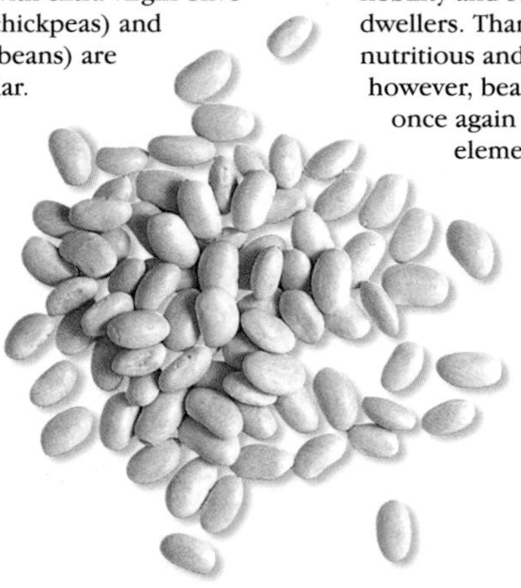

Dried cannellini beans

Dried red borlotti beans

Dried borlotti beans

Dried cannellini beans

Buying and Storing

During the summer and early autumn in Italy, you may find fresh beans, sometimes still in the pod. Borlotti beans come in an attractive speckled pod, cannellini in a slim yellowish pod. The pods represent a high proportion of the weight, so allow at least 12 oz per serving. Most beans, however, are sold dried. Try to buy these at a store with a quick turnover, or they may become shriveled and very hard. Prepackaged beans will have a "best before" date on the package. Loose beans will keep for several weeks in a cool, dry place, but are at their best soon after purchase.

If you don't have the time to prepare dried beans, canned varieties make an acceptable substitute, but you cannot control the texture and they are sometimes too mushy. They are, however, fine for recipes that call for puréed beans. Bear in mind, though, that they are an expensive alternative to dried beans.

Canned borlotti beans

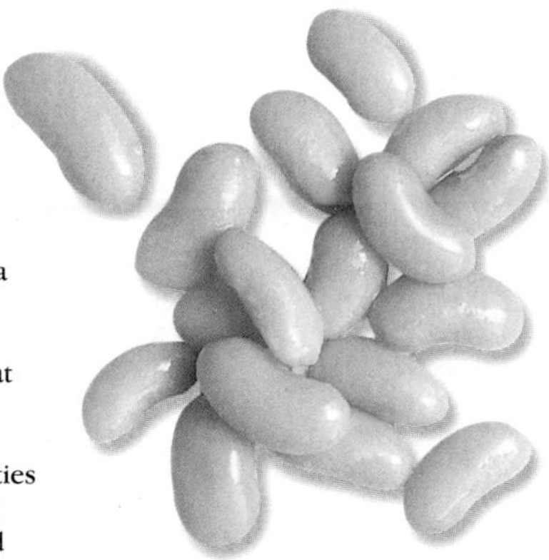

Canned beans

Canned black-eyed beans

Canned cannellini beans

Cooking Beans

All dried beans should be soaked for about 8 hours in cold water or 4 hours in boiling water before cooking (this is not necessary for fresh beans). Discard the soaking water before cooking the beans.

Cook the beans in plenty of unsalted boiling water. Boil briskly for 10 minutes (this is essential to kill off the toxins, which may cause severe stomachaches), then simmer for 1–2 hours, depending on the size and freshness of the beans.

You can add whatever flavorings you wish to the cooking liquid, but never add salt or any acidic ingredients, such as tomatoes or vinegar, until the beans are cooked, or they will never become tender however long you cook them. To make a hearty stew, after the initial boiling, the beans can be mixed with pancetta, *garlic and herbs and cooked very slowly in the oven.*

Pulses

Fave (broad beans)

Broad beans are nicest eaten fresh from the fat green pod in late spring and early summer when they are very small and tender with a bittersweet flavour. They are particularly popular in the area around Rome, where they are eaten raw with *prosciutto crudo*, salami or Pecorino. Later in the season, they should be cooked and skinned (hold the hot beans under cold running water; the skin will slip off quite easily). Cooked *fave* have a milder flavour than raw and are excellent with ham and *pancetta*. When buying fresh *fave* in the pod, allow about 350 g/12 oz per person; it may seem a lot, but the pods themselves are comparatively heavy, so a lot goes only a little way. Dried *fave* should be soaked, and the skins removed before cooking. They are used for soups and stews and need about 45 minutes' cooking.

Chick-peas
These round golden pulses can be bought dried (above), or canned and ready to use (left)

Broad beans
Dried fave *need to be soaked overnight before cooking*

Ceci (chick-peas)

These round golden pulses are shaped rather like hazelnuts and have a distinctive, nutty flavour. They are the oldest of all known pulses and, though not indigenous to Italy, have become very popular in Italian country cooking.

CULINARY USES

Chick-peas are cooked and used in the same way as haricot beans and are an essential ingredient of *tuoni e lampo* (thunder and lightning), a sustaining dish of pasta and chick-peas served with tomato sauce and Parmesan. They can also be served cold, dressed with lemon juice, chopped fresh herbs and olive oil, to make a substantial salad.

Broad beans
The canned beans (right) are ready to use

COOK'S TIP

Chick-peas can be very hard, so it is best to soak them for at least 12 hours, then cook them in plenty of boiling water for up to 2 hours.

Lenticchie (lentils)

Although lentils grow in pods, they are always sold podded and dried. Italian lentils are the small brown variety, which are grown in the area around Umbria; they do not break up during cooking and are often mixed with small pasta shapes or rice for a contrast of flavours and textures. They make the perfect bed for cooked sausage, such as zampone or cotechino, and are delicious served cold dressed with olive oil. The ultimate Italian pulse feast must surely be *imbrecciata*, a nutritious and sustaining soup from Umbria made with chick-peas, haricot beans and lentils.

Brown lentils
These are available in different sizes, large (below) and small (above)

COOK'S TIP

Lentils will absorb the flavours of whatever aromatics they are cooked with, so add any appropriate herbs or spices to the cooking liquid.

Cheeses

Italy has an even greater variety of cheeses than France, ranging from fresh, mild creations, such as mozzarella, to aged, hard cheeses with a very mature flavor, such as Parmesan. All types of milk are used, including sheep's, goat's and buffalo's, which produces the best mozzarella, and some cheeses are made from a mixture of milks. As in France, the Italians eat their cheese after the main course, either accompanied or followed by fresh fruit. You will not, however, find the large selection of cheeses offered on a French menu; Italian restaurants serve only one or two types of cheese and rarely have a cheeseboard.

Many of the cheeses made in Italy are suitable for cooking. What would a pizza be without its delicious, stringy topping of melted mozzarella, or a pasta dish without a grating of fresh Parmesan?

History

Fresh, rindless cheeses were first introduced to Italy by the ancient Greeks, who taught the Etruscans their cheese-making skills. They in turn refined the craft, developing the first long-matured cheeses with hard rinds, which could last for many months and would travel well. Today's Parmesan and Pecorino cheeses are probably very similar to those produced 2,500 years ago.

In ancient days, the milk was left to curdle naturally before being made into cheese. The Romans discovered that rennet would speed up this process. Originally, they probably used rennet made from wild artichokes (this is still used in remoter parts of Italy), but later they began to use animal rennet. The process used to make farmhouse cheeses today has changed very little since Roman times.

Italian cheeses can be divided into four categories: hard, semi-soft, soft and fresh. Some cheeses have an enormously high fat content; others are low in fat and suitable for dieters. Many Italian cheeses are eaten at different stages of maturity; a cheese that has been matured for about a year is known as *vecchio*; after 18 months, it becomes *stravecchio* and tends to have a very powerful flavor. Almost all Italian cheeses can be eaten on their own and also used for cooking.

Hard Cheeses

Asiago

This cheese from the Veneto region develops different characteristics as it ages. The large round cheeses with reddish-brown rinds each weigh 22–55 lb. They are made from partially skimmed cow's milk and have a fat content of only 30 percent. Asiago starts life as a pale straw-colored dessert cheese, pitted with tiny holes, with a mild, almost bland flavor. After six months, the semi-matured cheese (*asiago da taglio*) develops a more piquant, saltier flavor, but can still be eaten on its own. Once it has matured for 12 to 18 months, the *stravecchio* cheese becomes grainy and sharp-tasting, resembling an inferior Grana Padano, and is really only suitable for grating and cooking.

Asiago

Parmesan

Parmesan is by far the best-known and most important of the Italian hard cheeses. There are two basic types—Parmigiano Reggiano and Grana Padano—but the former is infinitely superior.

Parmigiano Reggiano

Parmigiano Reggiano can be made only in a strictly defined zone, which lies between Parma, Modena, Reggio-Emilia, Bologna and Mantua. The farmers of this area claim that the cheese has been made there for over 2,000 years; certainly it appears to be almost identical to that produced by the Etruscans and the methods of production have scarcely changed. The milk comes only from local cows, which graze on the area's rich pastureland.

It takes about 132 gallons of milk to make one 70–80 lb wheel of Parmigiano Reggiano. The milk is partially skimmed and some of the whey from the previous day's cheese-making is added, then the mixture is carefully heated before rennet is added to encourage curdling. (The rest of the whey is fed to local pigs destined to become prosciutto) The curds are poured into wheel-shaped forms and the cheese is then aged for a minimum of two years; a really fine Parmesan may be aged for up to seven years. During this time, it is nurtured like fine wine, until it becomes pale golden with a slightly granular flaky texture and a nutty, mildly salty flavor. Authentic Parmigiano Reggiano has the word "Reggiano" stamped on the rind.

Grana Padano

This cheese is similar to Parmigiano Reggiano, but is inferior in flavor and texture. Although it is made in the same way, the milk used comes from other regions and the cheese is matured for no more than 18 months, so it does not have the crumbly texture of Reggiano and its flavor is sharper and saltier. Its grainy texture (hence the name "grana") makes it fine for grating and it can be used for cooking in the same way as Reggiano.

Culinary Uses

A really good Parmigiano Reggiano can be eaten on its own, cut into chunks or slivers; it is delicious served with ripe pears and a good red wine. But Parmesan, both Reggiano and grana, really comes into its own when used for cooking. Unlike other cheeses, it does not become stringy or rubbery when exposed to heat, so it can be grated over any number of hot dishes, from pasta, polenta and risotto to minestrone, or layered with eggplant slices or truffles and baked in the oven. Slivers of fresh Parmesan are also excellent with asparagus or in a crisp salad. Don't throw away the rind from Parmesan; use it to add extra flavor to soups and vegetable stocks.

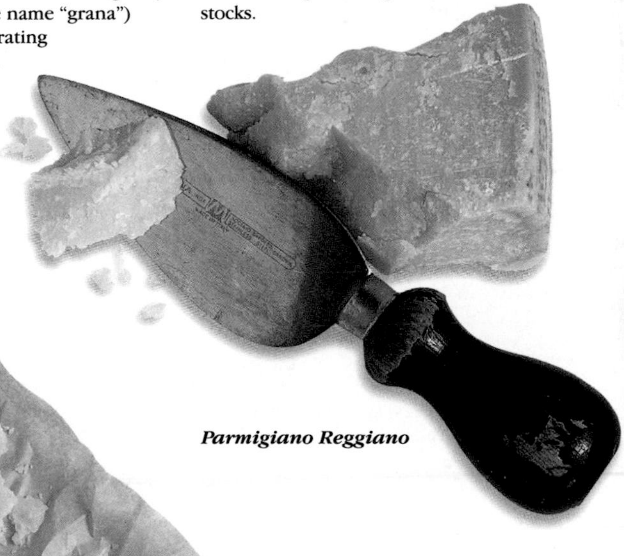

Parmigiano Reggiano

Grana Padano

Buying and Storing

If possible, buy Parmigiano Reggiano, which is easily recognizable by the imprint "Reggiano" in pinpricks on the rind. Whether you buy Reggiano or grana, always buy it in a piece cut from a whole wheel and grate it freshly when you need it; if possible, avoid pre-packed pieces and never buy ready-grated Parmesan, which is tasteless. Tightly wrapped in foil, a hunk of Parmesan will keep in the refrigerator for at least a month.

Hard Cheeses

Pecorino

All Italian cheeses made from sheep's milk are known as Pecorino, but they vary enormously in texture and flavor, from soft and mild to dry and strong. The best-known hard Pecorino cheeses are *romano* from Lazio and *sardo* from Sardinia; both are medium-fat, salty-tasting cheeses with a sharp flavor, which becomes sharper the longer the cheeses are matured. The milder *sardo* is usually aged for only a few weeks; the *romano* for up to 18 months. Hard Pecorino is a pale, creamy color with a firm granular texture with tiny holes like Parmesan. Sicilian *pecorino pepato* is studded with whole black peppercorns, which add a very piquant note.

Fresh Pecorino comes from Tuscany and is sometimes known as *caciotta.* This semi-hard cheese has a delicious mild, creamy flavor, but is not easy to find outside Italy, as it keeps for a very short time.

History

Pecorino romano is probably the oldest Italian cheese, dating back to Roman times. Then, as now, the cheeses were shaped and laid on *canestri* (rush mats, rather like hammocks) to be air-dried. Sicilian Pecorino is still called *canestro* after these rush mats.

Culinary Uses

Hard Pecorino can be grated and used exactly like Parmesan. It has a more pungent flavor, which is well suited to spicy pasta dishes, such as *penne all'arrabbiata*, but it is too strong for more delicate dishes such as risotto or creamy chicken dishes. *Caciotta* can be cubed and marinated in olive oil for about 2 hours, then served with a grinding of black pepper to make a delicious and unusual *antipasto*.

Buying and Storing

Fresh or semi-hard Pecorino should be eaten the day you buy it, but well-matured Pecorino will keep in the refrigerator for several weeks wrapped tightly in foil.

Pecorino pepato
This cheese is studded with whole black peppercorns

Pecorino sardo
A milder version that is aged for only a few weeks

Caciotta
A semi-hard cheese with a mild, creamy flavor

Provolone

A southern Italian cheese, straw-white in color with a smooth, supple texture and an oval or cylindrical shape, Provolone comes in many different sizes (some enormous) and can often be found hanging from the ceiling in Italian delicatessens. Provolone can be made from different types of milk and rennet; the strongest versions use goat rennet, which gives them a distinctively spicy flavor. In the south of Italy, buffalo milk is often used, and the cheeses are sometimes smoked to make *provolone affumicato*. The cheese is made by the *pasta filata* (layering) process, which gives it a smooth, silky texture; the curds are left to solidify, then they are cut into strips before being pressed together into a sausage shape. This is salted in brine for 6 to 12 hours, then the cheese is shaped and left to mature.

Variations on Provolone include *caciocavallo*, a smooth smoky cheese made from a mixture of cow's and goat's or sheep's milk, which develops a sharp flavor that becomes sharper as it matures. It gets its name from the way the oval cheeses are tied up in pairs and hung up to dry over a wooden pole, as though on horseback. (One false theory is that the cheese was originally made from mare's milk; another is that the cheeses were stamped with a horse, which is the symbol of Naples.) In Calabria, a version called *burrino* is made enclosing a lump of unsalted butter in the center of the cheese, so that when it is sliced, it resembles a hard-cooked egg.

Provolone burrino
There is a lump of butter buried in the center of this cheese, so that when cut it resembles a hard-cooked egg yolk

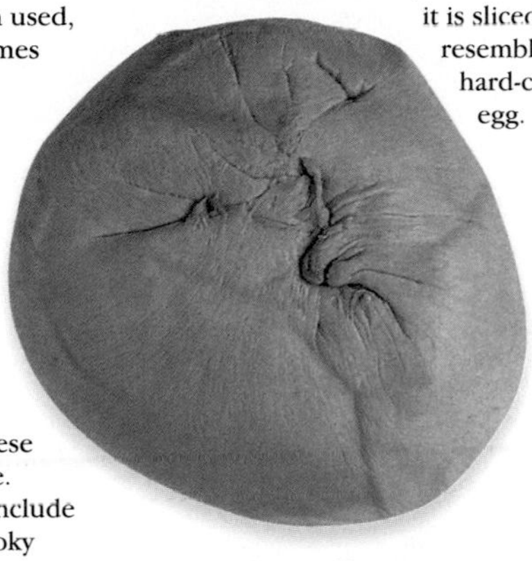

Provolone affumicato

Culinary Uses

Milder fresh Provolone can be eaten on its own or in a sandwich with mortadella or ham. Once it becomes strong, it should only be used for cooking; its stringy texture when melted makes it ideal for pizzas and pasta dishes.

Buying and Storing

Enclosed in their wax rinds, Provolone and similar cheeses will keep for months. Once they have been opened, they should be eaten within a week. Provolone can be used for cooking in the same way as Parmigiano Reggiano.

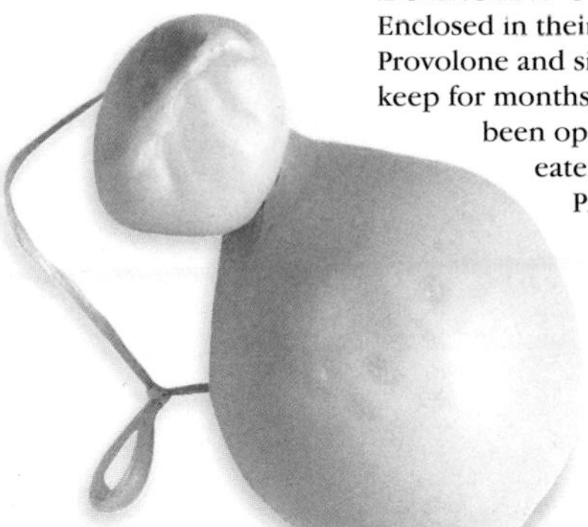

Provolone
Its stringy texture when melted makes this cheese particularly good for pizzas

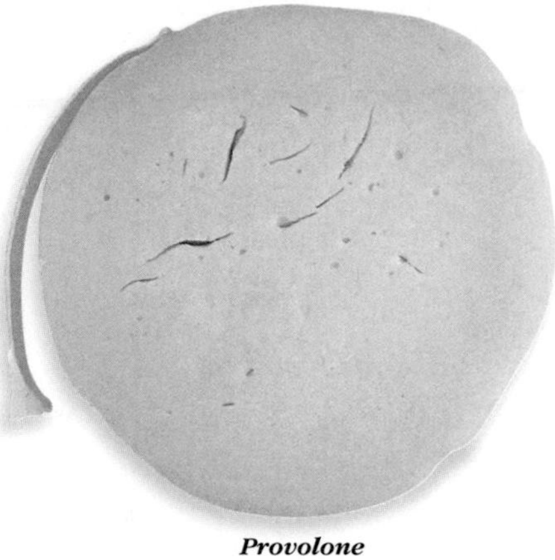

Provolone

Semi-hard Cheeses

Bel Paese

This cheese, poetically named "beautiful country," is a baby among Italian cheeses, having been created by the Galbani family from Lombardy early this century. Made from cow's milk, it contains over 50 percent fat, which makes it very creamy. It is the color of buttermilk, with a very mild flavor, and is wrapped in pale yellow wax to preserve its freshness. A whole Bel Paese weighs about $4\frac{1}{4}$ lb, but it is often sold pre-packaged in wedges.

Culinary Uses

Bel Paese can be eaten on its own; its mild creaminess makes it popular with almost everyone. It is also excellent for cooking, with a good melting quality, and can be used as a substitute for mozzarella, but because it is rather bland it will not add much flavor to a dish.

Buying and Storing

Like most cheeses, it is best to buy a wedge of Bel Paese cut from a whole cheese; pre-packaged pieces tend to be soggy and tasteless, although they are fine to use in cooking. Use freshly cut cheese as soon as possible after purchase, although wrapped in foil or plastic wrap it will keep in the refrigerator for two or three days.

Fontina

The only genuine Fontina comes from the Val d'Aosta in the Italian Alps, although there are plenty of poor imitations. True Fontina is made from the rich unpasteurized milk of Valdostana cows and has a fat content of 45 percent. Although today Fontina is produced on a large scale, the methods are strictly controlled and the cows are grazed only on alpine grass and herbs. Because it is matured for only about four months, the cheese has a mild, almost sweet, nutty flavor and a creamy texture, with tiny holes. Longer-matured Fontina develops a much fuller flavor and is best used for cooking. A whole Fontina weighs about 33–44 lb; the cheese is pale golden and the soft rind is orangey-brown. The rind of authentic Fontina has the words "Fontina dalla Val d'Aosta" inscribed in white writing.

History

Fontina has been made for at least 500 years; it is mentioned in the "dairy bible" *La Summa Lacticiniorum* of 1477. Its name probably comes from the mountain peak Fontin.

Culinary Uses

Fontina is delicious eaten on its own, and because it melts beautifully and does not become stringy, it can be used instead of mozzarella in a wide variety of dishes. It is also perfect for making a *fonduta*, the Italian equivalent of a Swiss cheese fondue.

Fontina
The sweet nutty flavor and creamy texture of this cheese makes it delicious to eat on its own

Bel Paese
This creamy, mild-flavored cheese can also be eaten on its own, and it is excellent for cooking, too

Soft Cheeses

Taleggio

A square creamy cheese from Lombardy with a fat content of almost 50 percent, Taleggio has a mild, salty-sweet flavor, which can become pungent if it is left to age for too long (it reaches maturity after only six weeks). The cheeses are dipped in brine for about 14 hours before maturing, which gives them a slightly salty tang. Each cheese with its soft edible rind weighs about $4\frac{1}{4}$ lb. If you intend to eat the rind, remove the paper from the top.

Culinary Uses

Taleggio is perfect eaten on its own as a cheese course. Like Fontina, it melts into a velvety smoothness when cooked and does not become stringy, so it can be used in any cooked dish that requires a good melting consistency.

Buying and Storing

Both Fontina and Taleggio should be eaten as soon as possible after purchase. If necessary, they can be tightly wrapped in waxed paper or plastic wrap and kept in the refrigerator for a day or two.

Taleggio
Perfect to eat on its own, Taleggio has a mild, sweet flavor

Stracchino

Stracchino is made from very creamy milk and matured for only about ten days, and never longer than two months. The smooth rindless cheese with a fat content of about 50 percent is reminiscent of Taleggio, but softer-textured and with a sweeter flavor. Robiola is a small, square Stracchino weighing about $3\frac{1}{2}$ oz. Because these cheeses are so delicate, they are wrapped in plasticized paper to preserve their freshness.

History

The name Stracchino comes from the Lombardian dialect word meaning "tired." It does not reflect on the quality of the cheeses, but merely indicates that they were traditionally made in the winter months when the cows were tired from their long trek down from the mountains to their winter quarters on the plain of Lombardy. Some farmhouse-produced Stracchini are still made only in winter, but most are now produced all year round.

Culinary Uses

Stracchino should only be eaten as a dessert cheese; it is not suitable for cooking. On Christmas Eve in Lombardy, Robiola is served as a special delicacy with the spicy candied fruit relish, *mostarda di Cremona*.

Stracchino
A soft-textured cheese with a sweet flavor

Robiola
This is a small square stracchino and is always wrapped in paper to preserve its freshness

Soft Cheeses

Gorgonzola

The proper name for this famous blue-veined cheese is Stracchino Gorgonzola, because it is made from the curds of Stracchino. Originally made only in the town of Gorgonzola, the cheese is now produced all over Lombardy.

Gorgonzola is prepared by making alternate layers of hot and cold curds. The difference in temperature causes the layers to separate, leaving air pockets in which the mold (*penicillium glaucum*) will grow. The best Gorgonzola cheeses are left until the mold forms naturally, but more commonly copper wires are inserted into the cheese to encourage the growth. The cheeses are matured from three to five months; the longer the aging, the stronger the flavor.

Gorgonzola is a very creamy cheese, the color of buttermilk, with greenish-blue veining and a fat content of 48 percent. Its flavor can range from very mild (*dolce*) to extremely powerful (*piccante*). The best-known mild version outside Italy is Dolcelatte (sweet milk), which is exceptionally creamy and delicately flavored. Another version, *torta*, consists of Gorgonzola and mascarpone arranged in alternate layers like a cake.

History

Gorgonzola has been made in the village of the same name since the 1st century AD, when the cheeses were matured in the chilly caves of the Valsassina.

Culinary Uses

Although it is usually eaten as a cheese course, Gorgonzola is also used in cooking, particularly in creamy sauces for vegetables or pasta or as a filling for pancakes and ravioli. It is delicious stirred into soft polenta, or spread on deep-fried polenta *crostini*. Surprisingly, cooking diminishes the flavor of Gorgonzola, so that it does not dominate a delicate dish.

Buying and Storing

Supermarkets sell vacuum-packed portions of Gorgonzola, which are acceptable but not nearly as good as a wedge cut from a whole, foil-wrapped cheese. If you don't like a very strong flavor, be sure to buy *gorgonzola dolce* or Dolcelatte. Wrapped in plastic wrap, the cheese will keep for several days in the refrigerator.

Dolcelatte
An exceptionally creamy, delicately flavored Gorgonzola

Torta
This striped cheese consists of layers of Gorgonzola and mascarpone

Gorgonzola
The greenish-blue veining is typical of this classic cheese

Fresh Cheeses

Caprini

These little disc-shaped goat cheeses come from southern Italy. They have a pungent flavor, which becomes even stronger as the cheeses mature. Fresh Caprini do not travel well, so you will rarely find them outside Italy, but they are available bottled in olive oil flavored with herbs and chilies.

Culinary Uses

Fresh goat's cheeses can be fried and served warm with salad leaves as an appetizer, or crumbled over pizzas to make an unusual topping. Bottled Caprini should be drained and eaten as a cheese course. If you like a spicy kick, trickle on some of the oil from the jar, but beware—it will be very piquant.

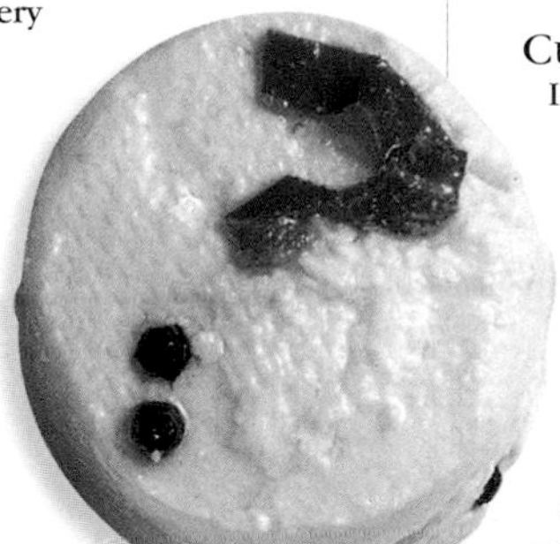

Caprini
Rarely found fresh outside Italy, these cheeses are usually found bottled in flavored olive oil

Mascarpone

This delicately flavored triple cream cheese from Lombardy is too rich to be eaten on its own (it contains 90 percent fat), but can be used in much the same way as whipped cream and has a similar texture. Mascarpone is made from the cream of curdled cow's milk. It is mildly acidulated and adds a distinctive richness to risottos and creamy pasta sauces. It takes only 24 hours to produce, so it tastes very fresh, with a unique sweetness that makes it ideal for making desserts. A new lighter version called *fiorello light* is now being produced for the health-conscious. While it is useful for those on a diet, it is nothing like the real thing.

Culinary Uses

In Italy, mascarpone is used for savory dishes as well as desserts. It makes wonderfully creamy sauces for pasta and combines well with walnuts and artichokes. Mascarpone can also enhance the texture and flavor of risottos or a white bean soup. It is most commonly used in desserts, either served with fresh berries, or as a filling for pastries. It is an essential ingredient of tiramisù and can be churned into a rich, velvety ice cream.

Buying and Storing

Delicatessens in Italy serve fresh mascarpone by the *etto* (about $3^{1}/_{2}$-oz) from large earthenware bowls, but outside Italy it is sold in 9 oz or $1^{1}/_{4}$ lb plastic tubs. Although the flavor is not as good, pre-packaged cheese will keep for a week in the refrigerator; fresh mascarpone should be eaten immediately.

> **Cook's Tip**
> *To lighten the texture of mascarpone and make it less rich, fold in some beaten egg white.*

***Mascarpone* (above and below)**
A triple cream cheese that is too rich to eat on its own, but is ideal for dessert; it is an essential ingredient in tiramisù

Fresh Cheeses

Cow's milk mozzarella
Known as fior di latte*—"flower of the milk"*

Smoked mozzarella
This cheese has a very smooth texture, a rich golden color and an interesting smoky flavor

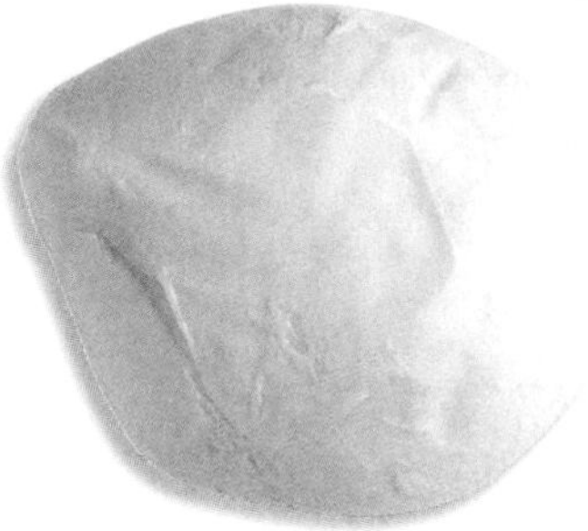

Mozzarella
The best is made from buffalo milk

Mozzarella

Italian cooking could hardly exist without mozzarella, the pure white, egg-shaped fresh cheese whose melting quality makes it perfect for so many dishes. The best mozzarella is made in the area around Naples, using water buffalo's milk. It has a moist, springy texture and a deliciously milky flavor. The cheeses are made by the *pasta filata* (layering) method, where the curds are cut into strips, then covered with boiling water. As they rise to the surface, they are torn into shreds and scrunched into egg-shaped balls each weighing about 7 oz. These are placed in light brine for 12 hours, then packed in their own whey inside a paper or plastic wrapping to keep them fresh.

Other types of mozzarella include a cow's milk version called *fior di latte* (flower of the milk) and tiny balls of cheese called *bocconcini* (little mouthfuls). Sometimes, the cheese is wound into braids called *trecce*. All these are fresh cheeses, but mozzarella can also be smoked, which gives it a golden-brown color and an interesting flavor. You will also find in supermarkets a pale yellow semi-hard mozzarella, which is sometimes sold ready-grated. This is the type used in cheap pizzas; it resembles mozzarella only in name and should be avoided.

History

No one is quite sure when water buffaloes were brought to Italy from India. They may have been introduced by the Greeks or the early Christians; certainly by the sixteenth century they had become a feature of southern Italian agricultural life. At this time, farmers began to use the buffalo milk to make mozzarella. Its popularity soon spread to the northern regions, where cheese-makers started to produce inferior versions made from cow's milk.

Culinary Uses

Fresh mozzarella is delicious served in an *insalata tricolore*, a salad in the colors of Italy, with white mozzarella, red tomatoes and fresh green basil. Smoked mozzarella is good in sandwiches or as part of an *antipasto*. When cooked, mozzarella becomes uniquely stringy, so it is perfect for topping pizzas or filling *mozzarella in carrozza* (mozzarella in a carriage), sandwiches dipped in beaten egg and deep-fried. A favorite Roman dish is *supplì al telefono*: mozzarella wrapped inside balls of cooked rice and fried until it melts to resemble telephone wires.

Buying and Storing

Cow's milk mozzarella is perfectly adequate for cooking, but for a really fine cheese buy *mozzarella di bufala*. Unopened, mozzarella will keep in the refrigerator for several days, but once the wrapping has been pierced it should be eaten as soon as possible. Opened mozzarella can be kept for a brief time in a covered bowl containing the whey from the bag or, failing that, skim milk or lightly salted water.

Mozzarella bocconcini
The name means "little mouthfuls"

Ricotta
Widely used in Italian cooking, ricotta can be combined with spinach for a ravioli filling, or used in desserts, such as cheesecake

Ricotta salata
This hard, salted version of the cheese has a compact, flaky texture and can be used as a substitute for Parmesan or Pecorino

Ricotta

Ricotta derives its name (literally "recooked") from the process of reheating the leftover whey from hard cheeses and adding a little fresh milk to make a soft white curd cheese with a rather solid yet granular consistency and a fat content of only about 20 percent. The freshly made cheeses are traditionally put into baskets to drain and take their hemispherical shape and markings from these *cestelli* (little baskets).

Commercially produced ricotta is made from cow's milk, but in rural areas sheep's or goat's milk is sometimes used.

Ricotta salata is a hard, salted version of the cheese, made from the whey of Pecorino. It has a compact, flaky texture and looks rather like a hard Pecorino.

Culinary Uses

Ricotta is widely used in Italian cooking for both savory and sweet dishes. It has an excellent texture but very little intrinsic flavor, so it makes a perfect vehicle for seasonings such as black pepper and nutmeg or chopped fresh herbs. In its best-known form, it is puréed with cooked spinach to make a classic filling for ravioli, cannelloni or lasagne, or delicious light gnocchi.

It is often used in desserts, such as baked cheesecakes, or it can be sweetened and served with fruit.

Hard *ricotta salata* can be grated and used as a lower-fat substitute for Parmesan or Pecorino.

Buying and Storing

Fresh ricotta should always be eaten the day it is bought, as it quickly develops a sour taste. Most supermarkets sell a pre-packaged version of the cheese, which stays fresh longer.

Ricotta salata is sometimes sold in pre-packaged wedges, but for a good flavor and texture you should buy it freshly cut from a whole cheese. Tightly wrapped in foil, it will keep in the refrigerator for up to a month.

Cured Meats & Sausages

Every region of Italy has its own special cured meats and sausages, each differing as widely as the regions themselves. Prosciutto crudo *and* salame *appear in every guise and often constitute an* antipasto *(appetizer) on their own.*

HISTORY

Italy was traditionally an agricultural country, so almost every rural family kept a pig and cured every part of it, from snout to tail, to provide food for the family throughout the year. In any Italian larder, a range of home-cured hams, sausages and bacon would be found hanging from the ceiling. Nowadays hundreds of different types of hams, cured meats and sausages are commercially produced, many still using the old artisanal methods. Wherever you travel in Italy, you will find regional variations on the same theme.

Most of these cured meats are served as an *antipasto* before a meal. A Tuscan *antipasto* will consist of a selection of thinly sliced *affettati* (sliced ham and *salame*), and it is sometimes served with pickled vegetables, which are designed to whet the appetite.

Prosciutto

Italy is famous for its *prosciutto crudo*, salted and air-dried ham that requires no cooking. The most famous of these hams, *prosciutto di Parma*, comes from the area around Parma, where Parmesan cheese is also made. The pigs in this region are fed partly on the whey from the cheese-making process, which makes their flesh very mild and sweet. Because they are always reared and kept in sheds and never allowed to roam outdoors, they tend to be rather fatty. Parma hams are made from the pig's hindquarters, which are lightly salted and air-dried for at least one year (and sometimes up to two). The zone of production of Parma ham is restricted by law to the area between the Taro and Baganza rivers, where the air and humidity levels are ideal for drying and curing the hams. In fact, every year thousands of ready-salted hams are sent here from neighboring regions to be dried and cured in the unique air around Parma.

Prosciutto di Parma
The most famous Italian ham comes from the area around Parma, where Parmesan is also made

Prosciutto cotto

Italy also produces a range of cooked hams, usually boiled. They can be flavored with all sorts of herbs and spices. Cooked ham is sometimes served as an *antipasto* together with raw ham, but it is more often eaten in sandwiches and snacks.

San Daniele

Some people regard these hams from the Friuli region as superior even to Parma ham. San Daniele pigs are kept outside, so their flesh is leaner, and their diet of acorns gives it a distinctive flavor. San Daniele is produced in much smaller quantities than Parma ham, which makes it even more expensive.

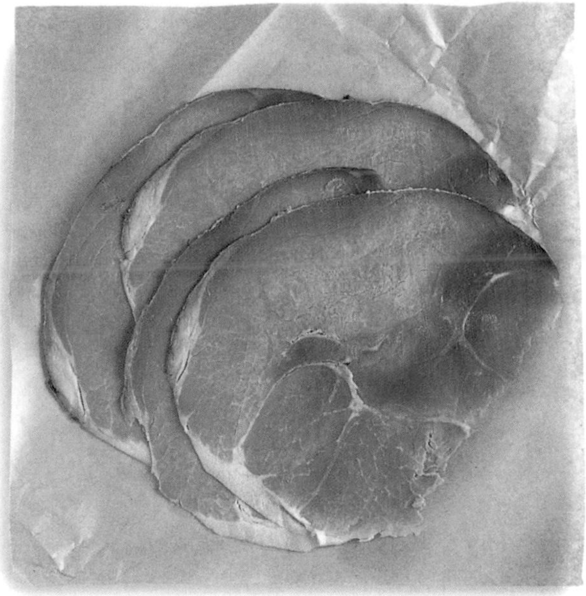

Prosciutto cotto
This cooked ham is sometimes served with sliced cured hams as an antipasto

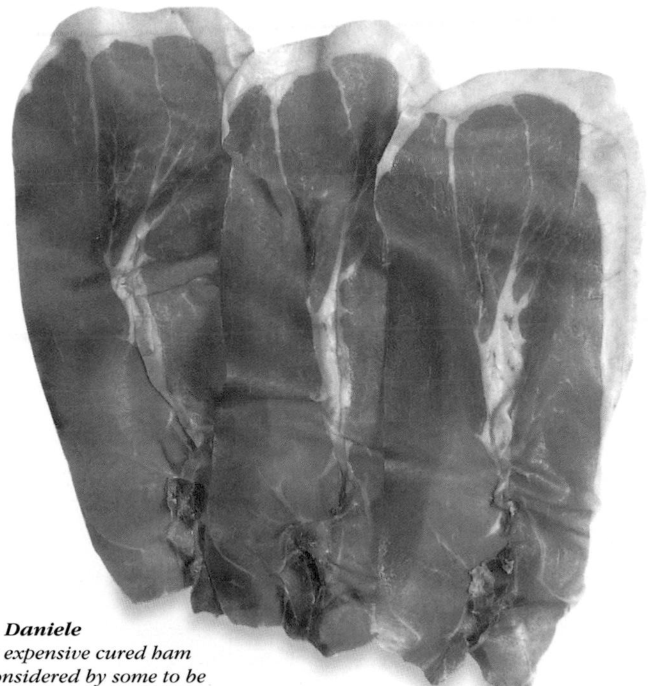

San Daniele
This expensive cured ham is considered by some to be even finer than Parma ham

Culinary Uses

Wafer-thin slices of *prosciutto crudo* are delicious served with melon or fresh figs or, when these are out of season, with little cubes of unsalted butter. If you serve bread with this ham, that too should be unsalted to counterbalance the salty-sweetness of the ham. *Prosciutto crudo* can be rolled up with thin slices of veal and sage leaves and pan-fried in butter and white wine or Marsala to make *saltimbocca alla romana*, finely chopped and added to risotti and pasta sauces, or used as a filling for ravioli.

Buying and Storing

The best part of the ham comes from the center. Avoid buying the end pieces, which are very salty and rather chewy. Because *prosciutto crudo* should be very thinly sliced, buy only what you need at any one time or it may dry out. Ideally you should eat it on the day it is bought, although it will keep in the refrigerator for up to three days.

Cured Meats

Pancetta and Lardo

Pancetta resembles unsmoked bacon, except that it is not sold sliced, but rolled up into a sausage shape. It is made from pork belly, which is cured in salt and spices to give it a mild flavor. *Lardo* is very similar (but flat) and less readily available.

CULINARY USES

Pancetta can be eaten raw as an *antipasto* (although it is very fatty), but it is usually cut into strips and cooked like bacon. It is an essential ingredient for *spaghetti alla carbonara.*

Pancetta

These round rolled slices of cured pork belly are the Italian equivalent of unsmoked bacon

Smoked pancetta

The smoked version of pancetta *is sold in thin strips rather than being rolled*

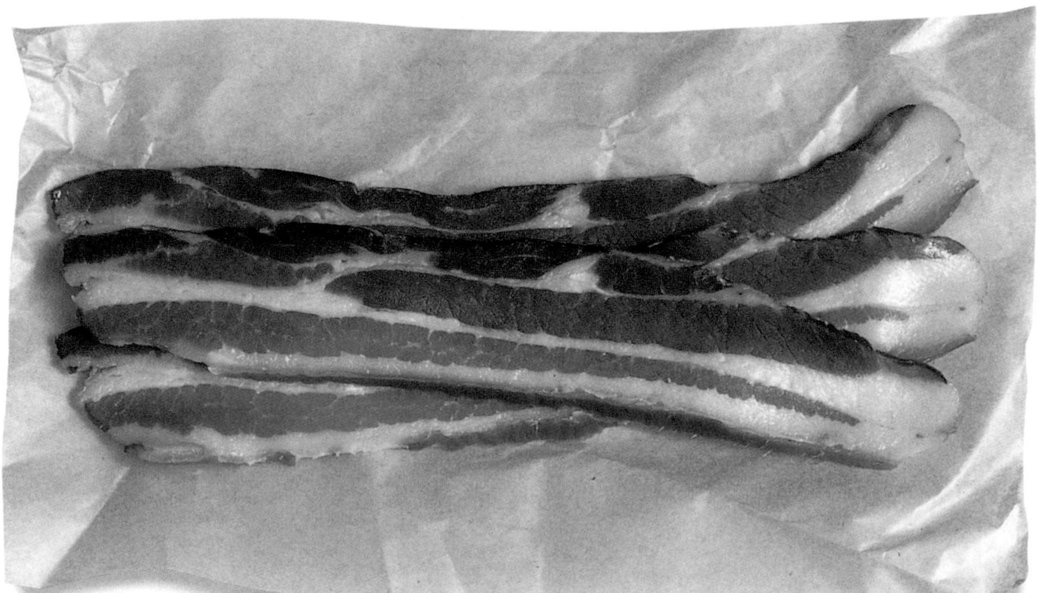

Speck

This fatty bacon is made from pork belly, which is smoke-cured over beechwood with herbs and spices, then air-dried. Sometimes it is covered with peppercorns or dried herbs, which add a distinctive flavor. It comes from the Tyrol, near the Swiss border, which explains its German-sounding name.

Culinary Uses

Speck is too fatty to be eaten raw, but it is used to add flavor to soups, stews and sauces. It is excellent cooked with fresh peas or lentils.

Buying and Storing

Italian bacon is sold by sections, not sliced. Wrapped in plastic wrap, *pancetta*, *lardo* and *speck* will keep in the refrigerator for up to one month.

Speck
A fatty ham, smoke-cured over beechwood with herbs and spices, then air-dried

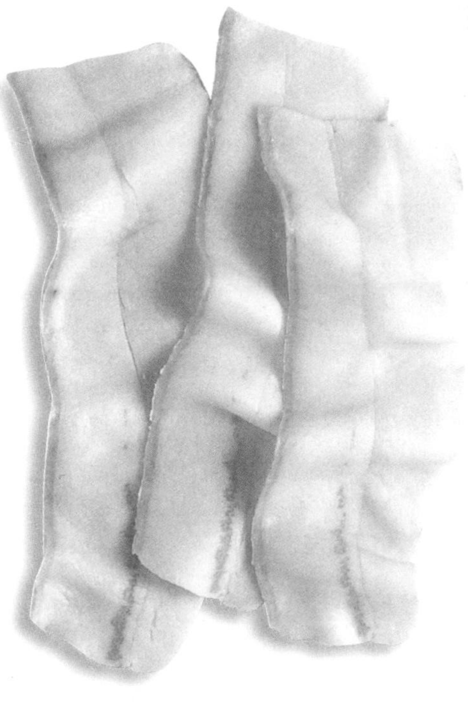

Lardo
An extremely fatty Italian bacon that is always used for cooking

Cured Meats

Bresaola

This cured raw beef is a specialty of Valtellina in Lombardy, but it is eaten and enjoyed all over Italy. It can be made from any cut of beef, but prime fillet produces the best bresaola. It is first cured in salt, then air-dried for many months before being pressed to produce an intensely dark red meat, which resembles *prosciutto crudo* in flavor, but is more delicate and less salty. Like *prosciutto crudo*, it is always sliced wafer-thin and served in small quantities, so you don't need to buy very much. Each bresaola weighs 4¼–6¼ lb, depending on the size of the original cut of beef.

Culinary Uses

Bresaola is often served as an *antipasto*, sliced very thinly and simply dressed with a drizzle of extra virgin olive oil and a sprinkling of fresh lemon juice. In Lombardy, bresaola is sometimes wrapped around a filling of soft goat cheese and then rolled up like cannelloni.

Buying and Storing

Only buy bresaola made from beef fillet. You can tell the type from the shape; that made from fillet is long with rounded edges, like the original cut of beef, while the cheaper bresaola made from other leg cuts is pressed into an oblong shape. Use it as soon as possible after slicing, preferably the same day, or it will dry out and develop an unpleasantly sharp flavor.

Bresaola
The delicate flavor of this salt-cured beef makes it perfect to serve, thinly sliced, as an antipasto

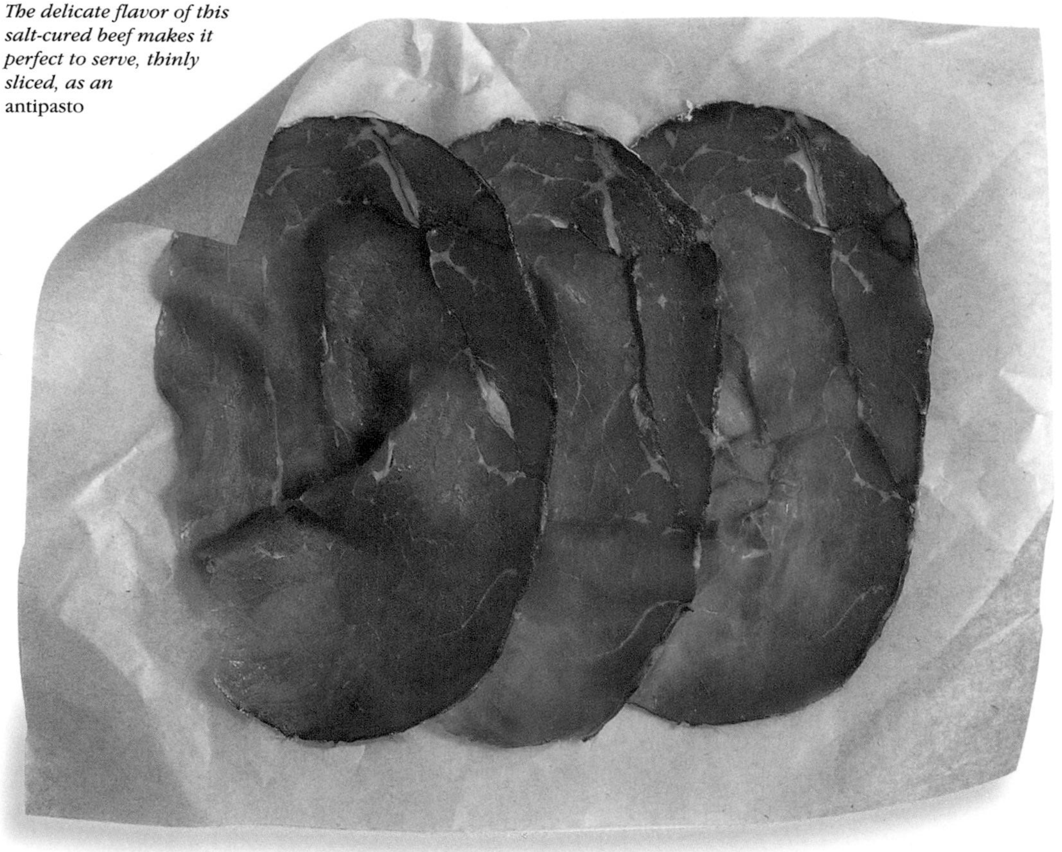

Sausages

Italy boasts almost as many different sausages as there are towns. Practically all are made with pork, although venison and wild boar sausages are popular in country areas. Most sausages and salami are factory-produced today, but many towns in Italy still have *salumerie* (sausage shops) selling homemade sausages flavored with local produce, such as wild mushrooms or herbs and spices. The most famous sausage-producing town is Bologna. Fresh sausages are made from coarsely chopped pork and contain a high proportion of fat for extra flavor. They are usually sold in links, tied together with string. Most Italian sausages, however, are cured and ready to eat.

Luganega

A specialty of northern Italy, luganega is a mild, spiced country sausage made from pork, which often contains Parmesan cheese. Sometimes known as *salsiccia a metro*, because it is sold in a long continuous rope, coiled up like a snake, and is sold by the foot or whatever length you require. It can be grilled or pan-fried with white wine and is often served on a bed of lentils or mashed potatoes. Luganega can also be cut into short lengths and stirred into a hearty risotto.

Cotechino

A large fresh pork sausage weighing about 2¼ lb, which has been lightly spiced and salted for only a few days. Cotechino is a specialty of Emilia Romagna, Lombardy and the Veneto. It takes its name from *coteca*, meaning "skin."

Cooking Cotechino

Cotechino is boiled and served hot, often as part of a bollito misto *(mixed boiled meats). Pierce the skin in several places and place the sausage in a large saucepan. Cover with cold water and bring slowly to a boil, then simmer slowly for 2–3 hours.*

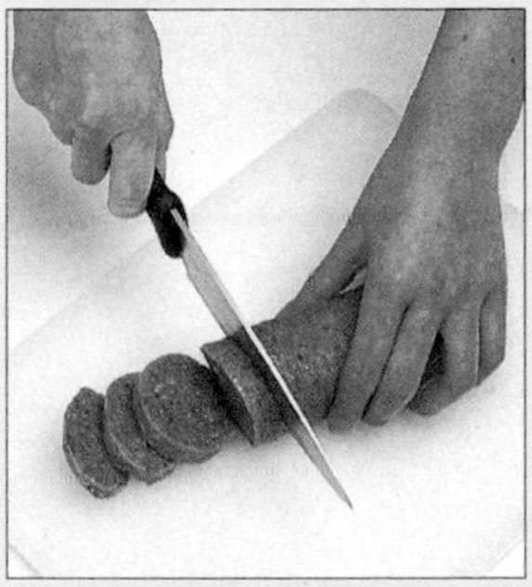

Slice the cotechino thickly and serve on a bed of cooked lentils, mashed potatoes or cannellini beans.

Luganega
This mildly spiced sausage, which is coiled up like a snake, is sold by the foot, or whatever length you require

Sausages

Coppa

This salted and dried sausage is made from neck or shoulder of pork, and the casing is made from natural skin. *Coppa* has a roughly rectangular shape and a rich deep red color. It comes from Lombardy and Emilia Romagna, although, confusingly, in Rome you will find a *coppa* that is a sort of pig's head brawn (this variety is never exported).

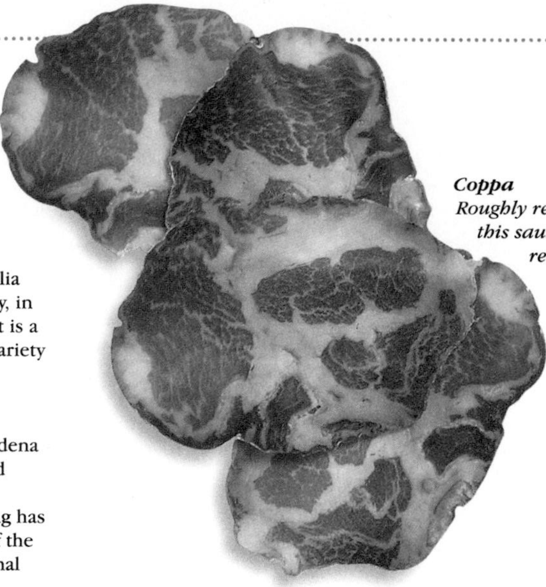

Coppa
Roughly rectangular in shape, this sausage has a rich, deep red color

Zampone

This speciality sausage from Modena is a pig's leg stuffed with minced pork shoulder and other cuts, including some skin. The stuffing has a creamy texture and the skin of the leg encloses it to retain its original shape, complete with feet. Each zampone weighs up to $4^1/_4$ lb.

Cooking Zampone

A raw zampone needs to be boiled for 2–3 hours, depending on the size, although some vacuum-packed varieties are already partially-cooked and need only to be heated through. For a fresh zampone, make a couple of slits in the skin and cook in the same way as cotechino. Zampone is traditionally sliced into rings and served with lentils or mashed potatoes. A bollito misto often contains a zampone.

Zampone
A partially-cooked zampone needs only to be heated through

Mortadella

The most famous of all the sausages from Bologna, mortadella is also the largest, often having a diameter of up to 18 in. Today it is cooked in hot-air ovens to a core temperature of 140°F, which means that it will keep for several weeks. It is considered to be the finest Italian pork sausage, with its wonderfully smooth texture, although it has a rather bland flavor. Apart from its huge size, mortadella is distinctive for its delicate, pale pink color studded with cubes of creamy white fat and sometimes pale green pistachios. It is the original bologna.

Buying

Authentic Bolognese mortadella is made only from pure pork, but cheaper varieties may contain all sorts of other ingredients, such as beef, tripe, pig's head, soy flour and artificial colorings.

Beware of mortadella that looks too violently pink and, if you are buying it sliced and pre-packaged, check the ingredients on the package before you buy.

Culinary Uses

Mortadella is usually thinly sliced and eaten cold, either in a sandwich or as part of a plate of assorted cold meats as an *antipasto*. It can also be cubed and stirred into risotto or pasta sauces just before the end of cooking, or finely chopped to make an excellent stuffing for poultry or filled pasta.

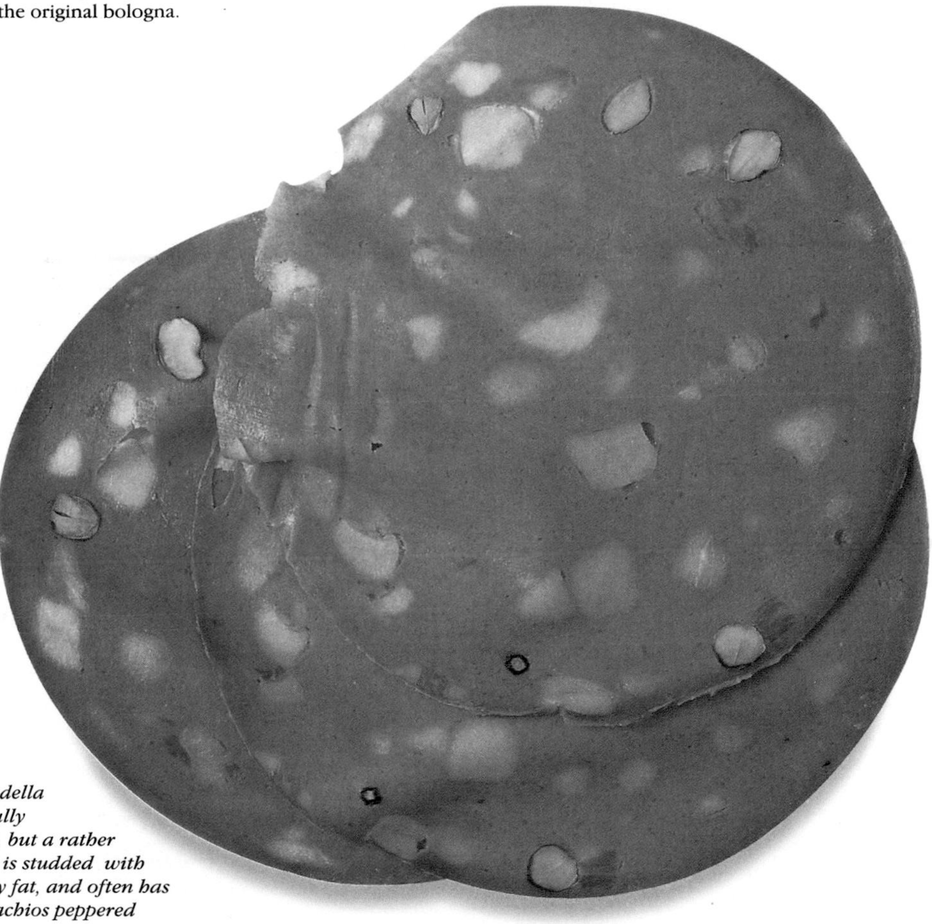

Mortadella
Considered to be the finest Italian cooked sausage, mortadella has a wonderfully smooth texture, but a rather bland flavor. It is studded with cubes of creamy fat, and often has pale green pistachios peppered through the meat

Salame

Salame

There are dozens of types of *salame*, whose texture and flavor reflect the character and traditions of the different regions of Italy. Essentially, all *salami* are made from pure pork, but the finished product varies according to the kind of meat used, the proportion of lean meat to fat, how finely it is minced, the seasonings and the period of drying and seasoning.

Salame di Felino

This soft, coarse-cut sausage comes from Felino near Parma and is regarded as one of the finest Italian *salami*. It has a very high proportion of lean pork to fat and is flavored with peppercorns, a small amount of garlic and the local white wine. Because it is only very lightly cured, it has a very delicate flavor but does not keep well. You may find it at good Italian delicatessens, where it is easily recognizable by its uneven truncheon shape, which makes it look handmade. Like its neighbor, Parma ham, *salame di Felino* is very expensive, but well worth the cost.

Salame fiorentino

This large, coarse-cut pork sausage from Tuscany is often flavored with fennel seeds and pepper, when it is known as *finocchiona*. The fennel gives it a very distinctive flavor.

Salame di Felino
One of the finest Italian salami*—this lightly cured sausage is flavored with peppercorns, garlic and white wine*

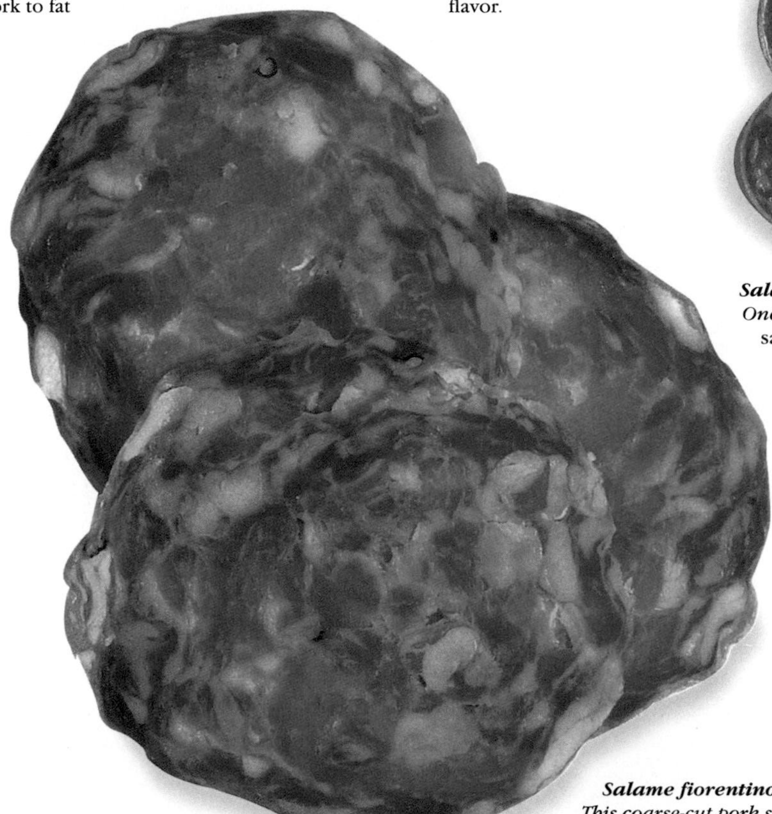

Salame fiorentino
This coarse-cut pork sausage from Tuscany is often flavored with fennel seeds and pepper

Salame milano

Probably the most commonly found of all *salami*, this Milanese sausage is made from equal quantities of finely minced pork, fat and beef, seasoned with pepper, garlic and white wine. It is deep red in color and speckled with grains of fat resembling rice. Also known as *crespone*, it is mass-produced and regarded as inferior to most other *salami*. There is also a small whole *salame milanese*, weighing about 1¼ lb, called *cacciatoro*, which is cured and matured for a much shorter time and has a more delicate flavor and softer texture.

Salame sardo

This fiery red *salame* from Sardinia is a rustic sausage flavored with red pepper. A similar sausage is *salame napoletano* from Naples, which uses a mixture of black and red pepper for a powerful kick.

Salame ungherese

Despite its name, this *salame* is manufactured in Italy, using a Hungarian recipe. It is made from very finely minced pure pork or pork and beef, and flavored with paprika, pepper, garlic and white wine. The fat is evenly spread throughout the sausage, giving it a mottled appearance.

Buying and Storing

With the exception of *salame di Felino*, almost all *salami* can be bought ready-sliced and vacuum-packed, but taste much better if they are freshly cut from a whole *salame*. A good delicatessen will slice the *salame* to the thickness you require. Ideally, it should be eaten the same day, but it will keep for three or four days in the refrigerator.

Salame ungherese
Made in Italy from a Hungarian recipe

Salame sardo
A fiery salame *flavored with red pepper*

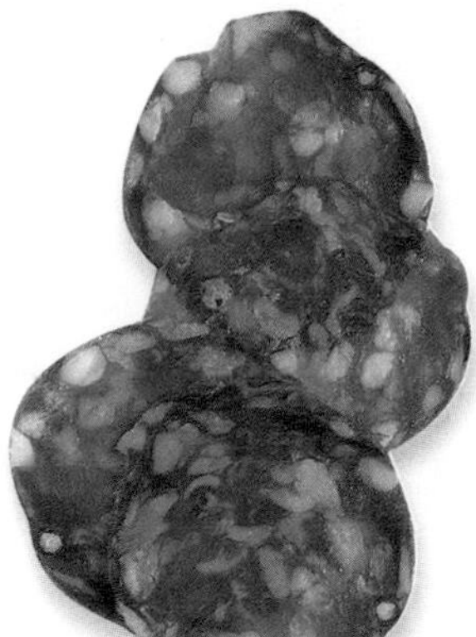

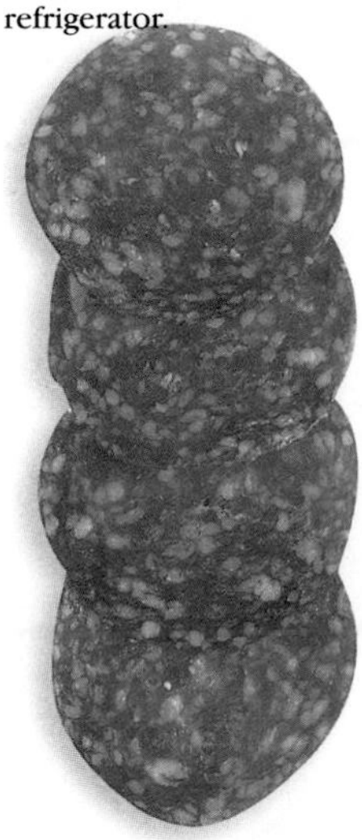

Salame milano

Salame napoletano
Similar to salame sardo, *this salame uses a mix of black and red pepper*

Cacciatoro
This small whole salame milanese *is cured and matured for only a short time*

Meat & Poultry

Until recently, meat did not figure largely in Italian cooking, which relied much more heavily on the peasant staples of pasta, bread, vegetables and, in coastal areas, fish. As the country became more prosperous, however, more people added meat to their daily diet, and now animals are farmed all over Italy to provide veal, pork, beef, lamb and goat.

Veal is a favorite meat in Italy and appears in innumerable recipes from every region. The best comes from milk-fed calves that are reared in Piedmont. The area around Rome is famous for its lamb, and spit-roasted suckling lamb and goat are popular specialties of the region. Superb beef cattle are bred in Tuscany, but the beef from other regions comes from working cattle that have reached the end of their useful lives, and is best used for stews and dishes that require long, slow cooking.

Many peasant families in Italy still own a pig, which provides pork as well as a huge variety of hams, sausages and other cured meats. Every part of the pig is eaten in one form or another, from snout to tail. Indeed, Italians never waste any edible part of their meat, so offal of all kinds is used in many dishes. A Tuscan *fritto misto* is composed of a variety of offal ranging from brains to sweetbreads and lungs, while the Milanese version also includes cockscombs—so, unless you are an offal lover, be warned if you see these dishes on a menu!

Poultry is another popular food. Factory farming does exist in Italy, but many flavorful free-range birds are still available. Chicken, guinea fowl and turkey appear in a huge variety of simple and delicious dishes and are usually filleted for quick cooking. Duck and goose make their appearance, too, often cooked with sharp fruits to counteract the richness of the meat. Many recipes use wild duck, shot by the enthusiastic (some say over-enthusiastic) hunters who abound in every region. Mercifully, the Italian habit of shooting every type of wild bird, whether edible or not, is less prevalent than it was, but hunters are lax about observing a close season for shooting, so game, both feathered and furred, seems to be available almost all year round.

Abbacchio and agnello (lamb)

Lambs are bred mainly in southern Italy, particularly in the area around Rome. They are slaughtered at different ages, resulting in distinctive flavors and textures. The youngest lamb is *abbacchio*, month-old milk-fed lamb from Lazio, whose pale pinkish flesh is meltingly tender. *Abbacchio* is usually spit-roasted whole. Spring lamb, about four months old, is often sold as *abbacchio*. It has darker flesh, which is also very tender and can be used for roasting or grilling. A leg of spring lamb weighs about 2¼–3½ lb. Older lamb (*agnello*) has a slightly stronger flavor and is suitable for roasting or stewing.

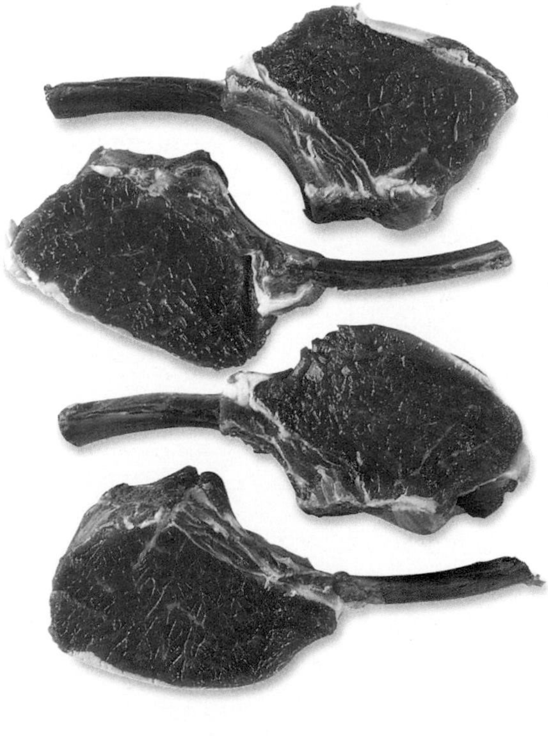

Lamb cutlets
Allow at least three small, succulent lamb cutlets like these per serving.

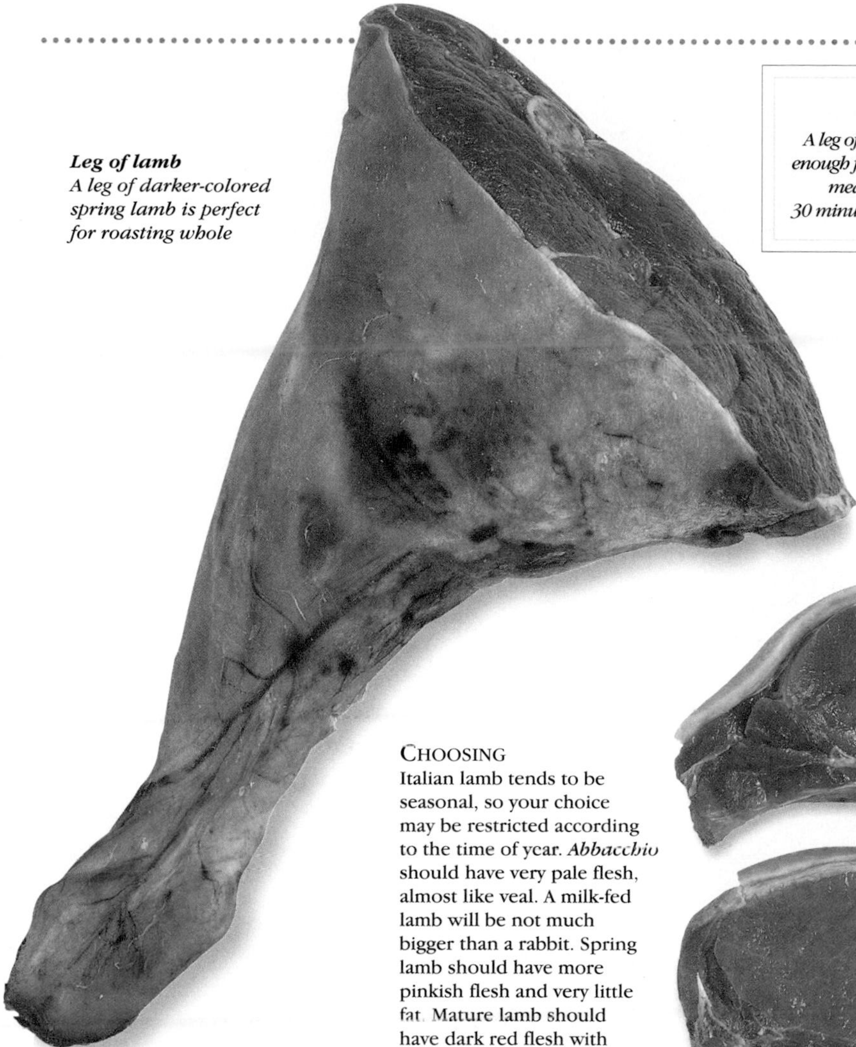

Leg of lamb
A leg of darker-colored spring lamb is perfect for roasting whole

COOK'S TIP
A leg of baby abbacchio *is only enough for two people. Roast in a medium oven for about 30 minutes, basting occasionally.*

CHOOSING
Italian lamb tends to be seasonal, so your choice may be restricted according to the time of year. *Abbacchio* should have very pale flesh, almost like veal. A milk-fed lamb will be not much bigger than a rabbit. Spring lamb should have more pinkish flesh and very little fat. Mature lamb should have dark red flesh with a layer of creamy fat on the outside.

CULINARY USES
Lamb is cooked in a variety of ways, from *al forno* (roast) to *costolette alla milanese* (fried breaded cutlets). Roast lamb is the traditional Easter dish. It is not cut into thin slices, but served in large chunks, which should be so tender that they fall off the bone. A favorite recipe for spring lamb is *agnello alla giudea* (Jewish-style lamb), braised in a delicate egg and lemon sauce.

Maiale (pork)

Most Italian pork is transformed into sausages, *salami* and hams, but fresh meat is enjoyed all over Italy, often combined with local herbs such as rosemary, fennel or sage. Different regions eat different parts of the pig; Tuscany is famous for its *arista di maiale alla fiorentina*, (loin of pork roasted with rosemary), while in Naples *il musso* (the snout) is considered a great delicacy.

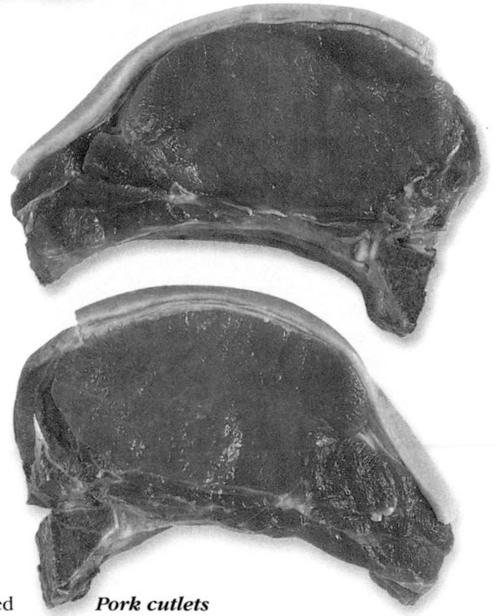

Pork cutlets
Tender chops or cutlets can be grilled or braised with herbs

CULINARY USES
Pork chops or cutlets can be grilled or braised with herbs or artichokes. Loin of pork is deliciously tender braised in milk (*arrosto di maiale al latte*), or it can be roasted with rosemary or sage.

Meat & Poultry

Manzo (beef)

Italian beef has an unjustifiably poor reputation. It is true that in agricultural areas, particularly the south, beef can be stringy and tough. This is because the cattle are working animals, not bred for the table, and are only eaten toward the end of their hard-working life. This type of beef is only suitable for long, slow-cooked country stews. In Tuscany, however, superb beef cattle from Val di Chiana produce meat that can rival any other world-renowned beef and provide the magnificent *bistecche alla fiorentina* (T-bone steaks).

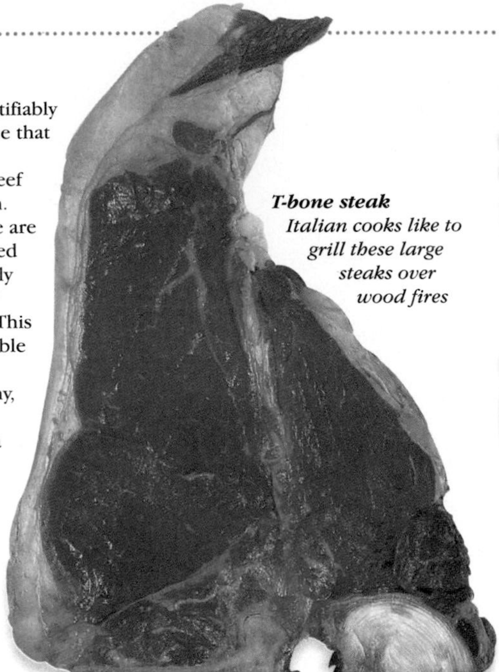

T-bone steak
Italian cooks like to grill these large steaks over wood fires

Beef olives
Thinly sliced topside rolled around a flavorful stuffing

CULINARY USES

Thick-cut T-bone steaks (*bistecche alla fiorentina*) from Val di Chiana cattle are grilled over wood fires until well-browned on the outside and very rare inside. Rump or fillet steaks are also cooked very rare and sliced on the bias as a *tagliata*. A modern creation is *carpaccio*, wafer-thin slices of raw beef marinated in olive oil and herbs and served as an *antipasto*. Thinly sliced topside is rolled around a stuffing to make *involtini* (beef olives). A favorite Italian family dish is *bollito misto*, a mixture of boiled meats and offal including beef. Leftover boiled beef can be sliced and made into a salad.

Less tender cuts of meat are usually braised, stewed or ground to be used in *ragù* (meat sauce) or *polpettone* (meat loaf).

Minced beef
Less tender cuts of beef are ground and used for ragù *(meat sauce) or* polpettone *(meat loaf)*

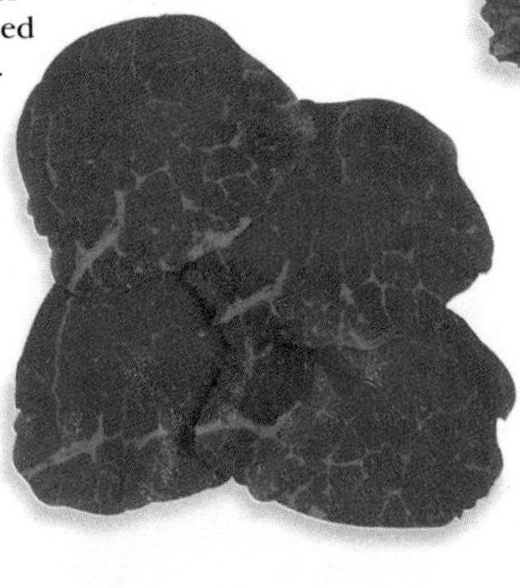

Carpaccio
These wafer-thin slices of raw beef are simply marinated in olive oil and served as an antipasto

Frattaglie (offal)

Nothing is wasted by Italian butchers, so a huge variety of offal is available. Liver is a great favorite; the finest is *fegato di vitello*, tender calf's liver, which is regarded as a luxury. Chicken livers are popular for topping *crostini* or for pasta sauces, and pork liver is a specialty of Tuscany. Butchers often sell pig's liver ready-wrapped in natural caul (*rete*), which keeps the liver tender as it cooks. Lamb's and calf's kidneys (*rognoni* or *rognoncini*), brains (*cervello*) and sweetbreads (*animelle*) are specialties of northern Italy. The latter two are similar in texture and flavor, but sweetbreads are creamier and more delicate. Every region has its own recipes for tripe (*trippa*); this almost always comes from veal calves rather than other cattle, whose tripe has a coarser texture and flavor. All parts of a veal calf are considered great delicacies. The head is used in *bollito misto* (mixed boiled meats), and the legs give substance to soups and stews. Oxtail (*coda di bue*) comes from older beef cattle.

Cooking Offal

Most offal will benefit from being soaked in milk before cooking to remove any coarseness of flavor. Some types, such as liver and brains, require very little cooking in order to preserve their delicate texture. In Venice, thinly sliced calf's liver is cooked with onions to make *fegato alla veneziana*; this is often served with grilled polenta. The Milanese version is coated in egg and bread crumbs and fried in butter. The simplest and one of the most delicious ways with liver is to sauté it quickly in butter with fresh sage. Brains and sweetbreads can be blanched, then quickly fried in butter, or pounded to a paste and made into croquettes (*crocchette*). Kidneys should be sautéed in butter, or braised with wine and onions or Marsala (*trifolati*). Pre-prepared (dressed) tripe will have been scrubbed, soaked and boiled by the butcher, but it should still be blanched for 30 minutes before cooking. Tripe can be prepared *alla fiorentina* in tomato sauce flavored with oregano or marjoram; the version from Parma (*alla parmigiana*) is fried in butter and topped with Parmesan cheese, while in Bologna, eggs are added to the mixture.

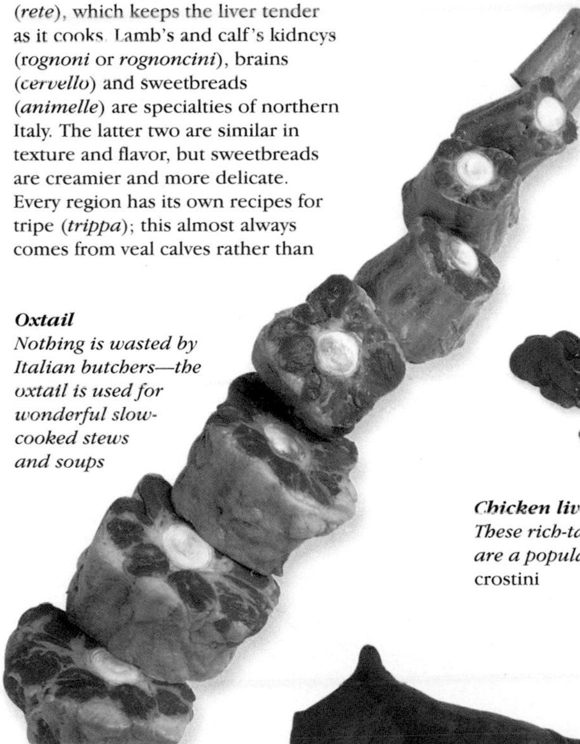

Oxtail
Nothing is wasted by Italian butchers—the oxtail is used for wonderful slow-cooked stews and soups

Chicken livers
These rich-tasting livers are a popular topping for crostini

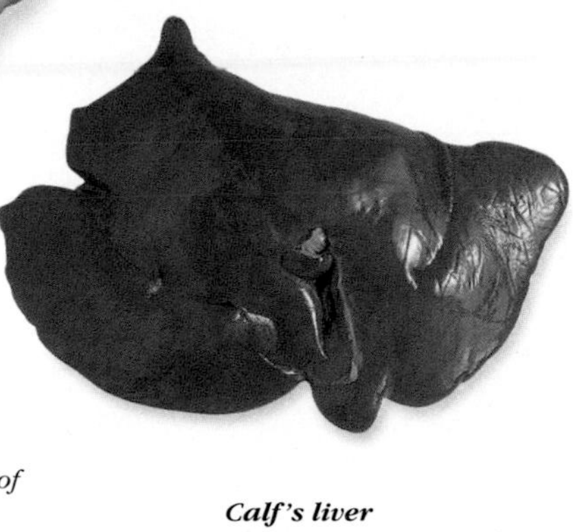

Pig's liver
This is a specialty of Tuscany

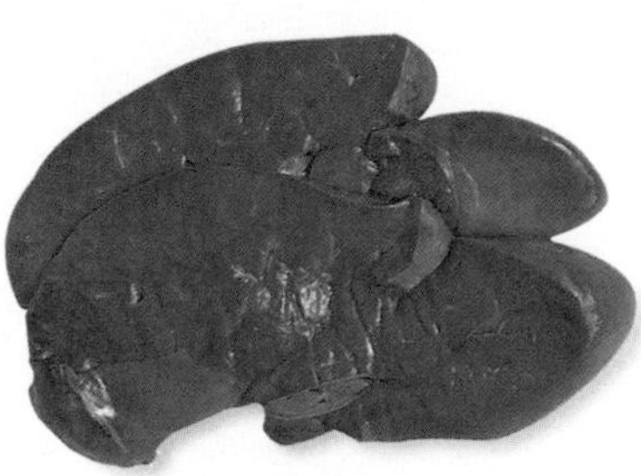

Calf's liver
Thinly sliced, this is often simply pan-fried with onions

Meat & Poultry

Vitello (veal)

Veal is the most popular meat in Italy and appears in hundreds of different recipes. Like lamb, calves are slaughtered at different ages to produce different qualities of meat. The best and most expensive veal is *vitello di latte* from Piedmont and Lombardy. The calves are fed only on milk and are slaughtered at just a few weeks old, producing extremely tender, very pale meat with no fat. Older calves, up to nine months old, are known as *vitello*. Their flesh is still tender, but darker in color than milk-fed veal. *Vitellone* is somewhere between veal and beef. It comes from bullocks aged between one and three years, who have never worked in the fields and whose flesh is therefore still quite tender and lighter in color than beef.

Culinary Uses

Young, milk-fed veal is ideal for *scaloppine* (scallops) and *piccate* (thin scallops), which need very little cooking. *Vitello* can be served as chops, cutlets or a rolled roast. The shin is cut into *osso buco* (literally "bone with a hole"), complete with bone marrow, or *stinco* (the whole shin), and braised until meltingly tender. An unusual combination that works wonderfully well is *vitello tonnato*, cold roast veal thinly sliced and coated in a rich tuna sauce. *Vitellone* should be treated like tender beef. It can be grilled, roasted or casseroled, but it is not suitable for scallops or similar cuts.

Choosing

Young veal should have very pale, slightly rosy fine-grained flesh with no trace of fat. *Vitellone* should be pinker and paler than beef, with only a faint marbling of fat, and should feel firm, not flabby. Scallops and *piccate* must be cut only from very young veal. They should be sliced across the grain so that they keep their shape and do not shrivel during cooking. If you are buying boned veal, ask the butcher to give you the bones, which make wonderful stock.

Veal scallops
These are always sliced very thinly across the grain

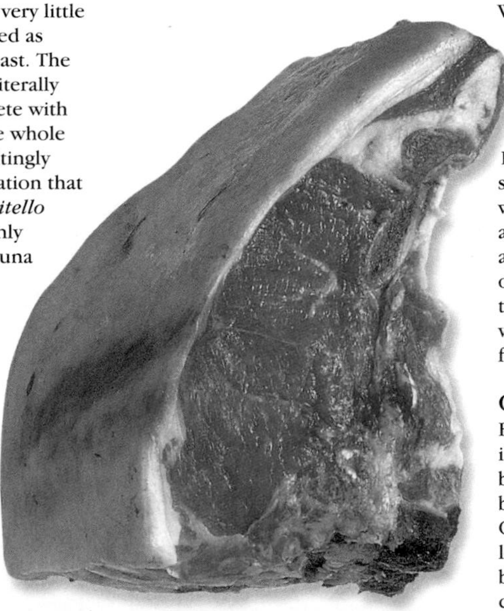

Loin of veal
Usually boned, then roasted with herbs—the bones make the most wonderful stock

Cooking Veal

Scallops should be pounded lightly, dusted with flour and fried for just a few moments on each side. The pan juices can be mixed with lemon, white wine or Marsala to make a sauce. Very thin scallops can be rolled around a stuffing and braised in tomato sauce. Thicker scallops can be coated with egg and bread crumbs alla milanese *and fried until golden, or seasoned with herbs and gently cooked with white wine.* Costolette alla valdostana *are stuffed with Fontina cheese and fried in butter. Loin of veal is usually boned and roasted with herbs, or braised in milk. Less tender cuts such as shoulder and breast are casseroled or braised.*

Cinghiale (wild boar)

Wild boar are the ancestors of domestic pigs, which used to roam in large numbers in the forests of Tuscany and Sardinia, but which are becoming increasingly rare because of widespread hunting. Baby wild boar are an enchanting sight, with light brown fur striped with horizontal black bands. The adults have coarse, brown coats and fierce-looking tusks. The flesh of a young *cinghiale* is as pale and tender as pork; older animals have very dark flesh, which is tougher but full of flavor.

Culinary Uses

Haunches of wild boar are made into hams, which are displayed in butchers' shops. Young animals can be cooked in the same way as pork. Older boar must be marinated for at least 24 hours to tenderize the meat before roasting or casseroling. The classic sweet and sour sauce, (*agrodolce*), sharpened with red wine vinegar, complements the gamey flavor of the meat.

Coniglio (rabbit) and lepre (hare)

Farmed and wild rabbits often replace chicken or veal in Italian cooking. The meat is very pale and lean and the taste is somewhere between that of good-quality farmhouse chicken and veal. Wild rabbit has a stronger flavor, which combines well with robust flavors; farmed rabbit is very tender and much more delicate.

Hare cannot be farmed, so the only animals available come from the wild. Despite the popularity of hunting in Italy, the hare population has not been totally decimated. The wily creatures, who mange to escape the gun, continue to breed. A hare weighs about twice as much as a rabbit (4¼ lb is about average). The flesh is a rich, dark brown and has a strong gamey flavor similar to that of wild rabbit.

Hare
This is always wild—the rich brown flesh has a strong gamey flavor

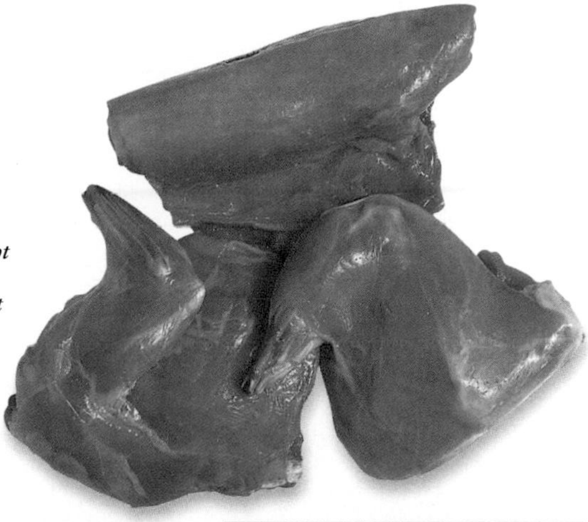

Rabbit
This can be bought either farmed or wild—wild rabbit has a stronger flavor

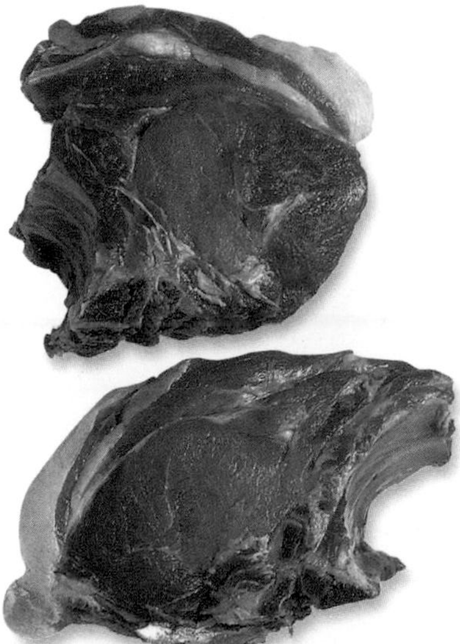

Wild boar
Chops like these can be cooked in the same way as pork

Culinary Uses

Farmed rabbit can replace chicken or turkey in almost any recipe. Wild rabbit can be stewed or braised in white wine or Marsala, or with eggplants, bacon and tomatoes. It can be roasted with root vegetables or fresh herbs. In Sicily, rabbit is often cooked with raisins and pine nuts in an *agrodolce* (sweet and sour) sauce.

Hare is generally casseroled in red wine or Marsala, cooked *in agrodolce* or made into a rich sauce for pappardelle or other wide noodles. Both rabbit and hare are often served with polenta or fried bread.

Cooking Rabbit and Hare

Wild rabbit and hare must be cut into six or eight pieces and marinated in red wine and herbs for 24 hours before cooking. If you like a sweet and sour flavor (game in agrodolce *is very popular in Italy), add plenty of red wine vinegar to the marinade. A rabbit weighing about 2¼ lb when cleaned will need about 1½ hour's braising or stewing; a hare needs about 2 hours.*

Meat & Poultry

Fagiano (pheasant)

Occasionally, in the Italian countryside, you may still catch a glimpse of a pheasant with its beautiful plumage and long tail feathers. Cock pheasants have bright, iridescent blue and green feathers, while hens are browner and less dramatic-looking. Pheasant farming is still unknown in Italy, and wild pheasants are something of a rarity, so they are regarded as a luxury. They are not hung, but are eaten almost as soon as they are shot, so their flavor is less gamey than in some other countries. Although pheasants are expensive, they are meaty birds for their size, so a cock pheasant will feed three to four people and a hen pheasant two to three.

Culinary Uses

Hen pheasants are smaller than cocks, but their meat is juicier and the flavor is finer. Young hen pheasants can be roasted with or without a stuffing, but cock birds are more suitable for casseroling. Pheasant breast can tend to be dry, so it should be well wrapped with bacon or thickly smeared with butter before roasting. A big pat of butter placed inside the cavity will help to keep the flesh moist. For special occasions, pheasants can be stuffed with candied fruits or pomegranate seeds and nuts. Pheasant breasts can be sautéed and served with a wine or balsamic vinegar sauce, but they can sometimes be rather dry.

Pheasant
Usually eaten as soon as they are shot, Italian pheasants are less gamey than in some other countries. Remember that pheasants contain lead-shot pellets, so take care not to bite down on these!

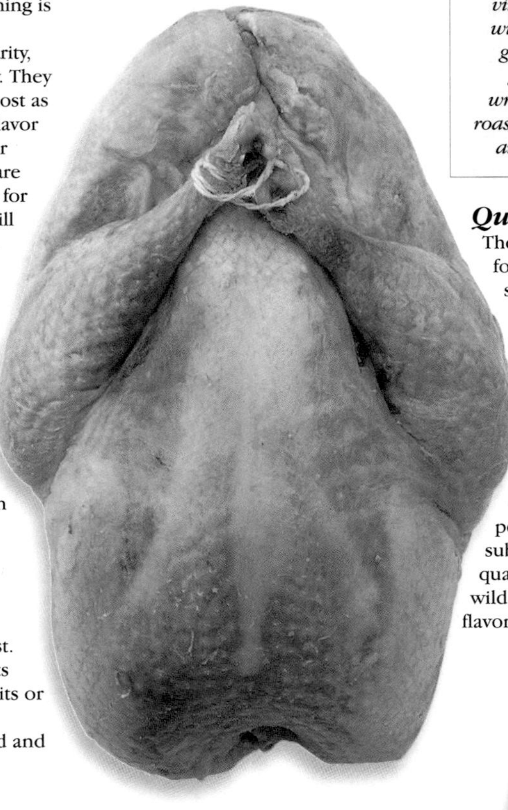

Cooking Pheasants

Unless you know for sure that a pheasant is very young, it is best to wrap the breast in fatty bacon before roasting to prevent dryness. To roast a pheasant, put a pat of butter inside the cavity, or make a stuffing, drape bacon rashers over the breast and roast at 400°F for about 40 minutes, until tender. Plain roast pheasant is often served with a risotto. Pheasant can also be pot-roasted or casseroled with wine and herbs. If you are serving cock birds, it is worth removing the lower part of the legs after cooking, as they contain hard sinews that are not pleasant to eat.

Cooking Quail

Quail should be browned in butter until golden all over, then roasted in a hot oven for about 15 minutes. Their flavor is well complemented by the fruit of the vine, so they are often served with a light sauce containing grapes or raisins soaked in grappa. They can also be wrapped in vine leaves before roasting, which keeps them moist and adds a delicious flavor.

Quaglie (quail)

These small migratory birds are found in Italy throughout the summer months. Wild quails have the reputation of being so stupid that they never run away from hunters, but stay rooted to the spot as sitting targets. As a result, they have become very rare, and most of the birds now available are farmed. They are very small (you need two to serve one person) and have a delicate, subtly gamey flavor. Farmed quails have less flavor than the wild birds and benefit from added flavorings, such as grapes.

Quail
These birds have a very delicate, gamey flavor. They are very small, and so you will need to serve two per person.

Faraona (guinea fowl)

Guinea fowl are extremely decorative birds with luxuriant gray-and-white spotted plumage. They originated in West Africa, but are now farmed all over Europe, so that although they are technically game, they are classified as poultry. They taste similar to chicken, but have a firmer texture and a more robust flavor.

Cooking Guinea Fowl

Although their abundant plumage makes them seem larger, guinea fowl are only about the size of a small spring chicken, so one bird will not feed more than three people. To roast guinea fowl, wrap the breasts with bacon slices and roast like chicken, basting frequently. A vegetable stuffing will keep the flesh moist. Guinea fowl can be substituted for chicken or turkey in any recipe.

Culinary Uses

Guinea fowl are hugely popular in Italy, where they are served in much the same ways as chicken. The flesh of an adult guinea fowl is firmer than that of a chicken, so it is best to wrap it or cover the breasts with bacon slices before roasting. The breasts are sometimes sautéed and served with the pan juices mixed with balsamic vinegar, or with a sauce of cream and Marsala. The birds can be roasted or pot-roasted whole, or cut into serving pieces and casseroled with mushrooms (wild mushrooms are especially delicious) or herbs. A favorite autumn dish in Tuscany is guinea fowl braised with chestnuts.

Guinea fowl
These popular birds can be pot-roasted, roasted or casseroled with wild mushrooms

Piccione (pigeon)

Wood pigeons have dark, gamey flesh and a robust flavor, which the Italians love. They are generally too tough to roast, but they make the most delicious casseroles. Domestic pigeons are also reared for food and you will often see large dovecotes in farmyards. Domestic birds are less likely to be tough than wild ones, but their flavor is less robust.

Wild pigeon
Italians love the rich, robust flavor of these small birds; however, they can be very tough, so cook them very slowly, either by braising or casseroling

Cooking Pigeons

Wild pigeons can be tough, so, unless you are sure that they are young, it is best to casserole them. In Tuscany, they are braised with tomatoes and olives; the classic Venetian way is to stew them with pancetta, *ox tongue and fresh green peas. If you really want to roast wild pigeons, marinate them in a red wine marinade for three days before cooking, then stuff them with a moist vegetable stuffing. Cover the breasts with fatty bacon and roast for about 20 minutes, basting with the marinade every few minutes.*

Fish & Shellfish

Italy's extensive coastal waters once teemed with a huge variety of fish and shellfish, many unique to that part of the Adriatic and Mediterranean. Sadly, pollution and over-fishing have taken their toll, and there is no longer the abundance of seafood there once was, but what remains is of excellent quality. A visit to an Italian fish market will reveal fish and shellfish of every description, some beautiful, some hideous, many unknown outside Italy. Italians like their seafood very fresh and tend to cook it simply, without elaborate sauces. Large fish are usually plainly grilled or baked and dressed with olive oil, or baked in cartoccio *(enclosed in a paper bag). Small shellfish are deep-fried for a crisp* fritto misto di mare. *Every coastal area has its own version of fish soup, which uses a mixture of local fish and constitutes a meal in itself—*cacciucco *from Livorno, cold* burrida *from Sardinia,* brodetto *from the Adriatic coast—each region claims that its version is the best.*

It is impossible to give a complete list of all the fish that you will find in Italy. Popular favorites include *coda di rospo* (monkfish), *dentice* (dentex—a white-fleshed fish found only in Italy), *sogliola* (sole) and even non-indigenous fish such as salmon.

Freshwater fish—trout, perch, carp and eels—abound in the lakes and rivers and are eaten with gusto. Eels are regarded as a particular delicacy and are cooked in many different ways, from grilling to baking, stewing and frying.

Some fish are dried, salted or preserved in oil. The most popular is tuna, which is packed in olive oil and sold by weight from huge cans. *Baccalà* is salted dried cod, which is creamed to a rich paste or made into soups and stews. Anchovies are salted, or packed in olive oil, or preserved in a sweet and sour marinade. Sardines are also very popular and are used to make a Sicilian pasta sauce.

Anchovies
Canned in olive oil (above) or salted (left)—these tiny, strong-tasting fish are used to add flavor to pasta sauces and salads

Salt cod *(baccalà)*
This dried fish is creamed to a paste or made into soups and stews

CHOOSING FRESH FISH

You can almost guarantee that any fish you buy in an Italian early morning market will be ultra-fresh, but at fishmongers and restaurants you should look for pointers. Fish should have bright, slightly bulging eyes and shiny, faintly slimy skin. Open up the gills to check that they are clear red or dark pink and prod the fish lightly to check that the flesh is springy. All fish should have only a faint, pleasant smell; you can tell a stale fish a mile off by its unpleasant odor.

Orata *(gilt-head sea bream)*

This Mediterranean fish takes its name from the crescent-shaped golden mark on its domed head and the gold spots on each cheek. It has beautiful silvery scales and slightly coarse but delicious flaky white flesh. Orate usually weigh between 1 lb 6 oz and 2¼ lb; a larger fish will serve two greedy people. Orata is best simply broiled, baked *in cartoccio* or barbecued.

Pesce spada *(swordfish)*

In Italy, you will occasionally find a whole swordfish on the fishmonger's slab. These huge Mediterranean fish, up to 15 feet long and weighing 220–1200 lb, are immediately recognizable by their long sword-like upper jaw. Because of their size, they are more usually sold cut into steaks. Their firm, close-grained, almost meaty flesh has given them a nickname of "steak of the sea."

COOKING SWORDFISH

Swordfish tends to be dry, so it should be marinated in oil and lemon juice or wine and herbs before cooking. It is excellent grilled or barbecued, or part-cooked in butter or olive oil, then baked in a sauce. Its firm texture makes it ideal for kebabs. It is plentiful in the waters around Sicily, where it is cooked with traditional Mediterranean ingredients such as tomatoes, olives, capers, raisins and pine nuts. Another popular Sicilian dish is braciole di pesce spada, *thin slices of swordfish rolled around a stuffing of bread crumbs, mozzarella and herbs and grilled. It is also delicious sliced wafer-thin, marinated in olive oil, lemon juice and herbs and served raw.*

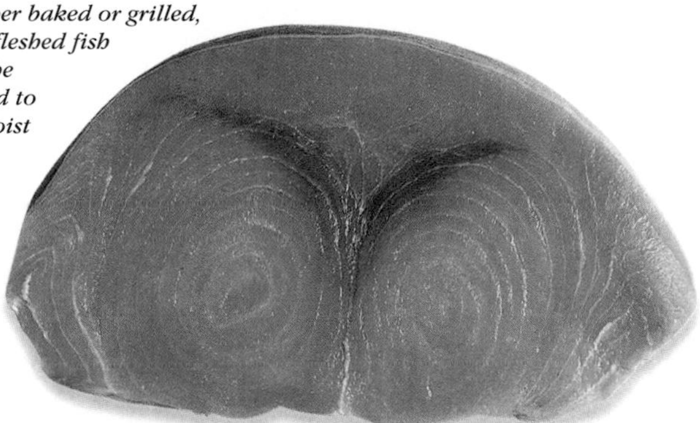

Swordfish
Often either baked or grilled, this firm-fleshed fish needs to be marinated to keep it moist during cooking

Tuna
Immensely popular throughout Italy, canned tuna in oil is either sold by weight from huge cans or bought in small cans like these

Fish

Sarde or sardelle (sardines)

Fresh sardines probably take their name from Sardinia, where they were once abundant. These small, silvery fish are still found in Mediterranean waters, where they grow to about 5 in. They are at their best in spring. Allow about four larger sardines or six smaller fish per serving. Sardines have very oily flesh and should only be eaten when extremely fresh. They can also be bought preserved in oil or salt.

Sardines
These fish are at their best in the spring

Preparing and Cooking Sardines

Sardines should be gutted before cooking. If the fishmonger has not already done this, cut the head almost through to the backbone and pull it off; the gut will come away with the head.

Sardines can be barbecued, broiled or baked alla genovese *with fresh potatoes, garlic and parsley. Their oily flesh combines well with spices and tart ingredients such as capers and olives. In Sicily they are stuffed with bread crumbs, pine nuts, raisins and anchovies and fried, then finished in the oven* (a beccaficcu). *Sardines can also be deep-fried, either plain or stuffed with mushrooms, herbs and cheese* (alla ligure) *or with chopped spinach and cream* (alla romana).

Spigola or branzino (sea bass)

The silvery sea bass, which come from Mediterranean waters, are as beautiful to look at as to eat, although their rapacious nature has earned them the nickname of "sea wolf." These slim, elegant fish are almost always sold whole and rarely weigh much more than $2\frac{1}{4}$ lb, so one fish will feed no more than two or three people. Sea bass is prized for its delicate white flesh and lack of irritating small bones. As a result, it is never cheap.

One way of bringing the price down is to farm sea bass, but the flavor of the farmed fish is not as fine as that of wild sea bass, whose predatory habits ensure that their flesh develops a full flavor. So far, farming of these wonderful fish does not seem to have caught on in Italy, where flavor is rarely compromised for cost.

Preparing and Cooking Sea Bass

Sea bass should be gutted before cooking. They have quite hard scales, which should be removed before grilling or pan-frying. Scale the fish with a de-scaler or blunt knife, working from the tail toward the head. If you are going to poach or bake sea bass, leave the scales on, as they will hold the fragile flesh together.

Sea bass has rather soft flesh, so it is best broiled, barbecued or pan-fried and dressed with a trickle of olive oil. It can be stuffed with sprigs of fresh herbs (fennel is particularly good) and baked for 20–30 minutes, depending on the size of the fish. For spigola alla livornese, *lay the fish in an ovenproof dish on a layer of rich tomato sauce, sprinkle with seasoned bread crumbs and olive oil and bake.*

Triglia (red mullet)

These small Mediterranean fish rarely weigh more than 2¼ lb. They have bright rose-colored skin and a faint golden streak along their sides. Their flesh is succulent with a distinctive, almost shrimp-like flavor, quite unlike any other fish. The liver of red mullet is regarded as a great delicacy and is not removed during cooking, which gives the mullet its nickname of "sea woodcock." Red mullet are extremely perishable and should be eaten the day they are bought. The skin should always look very bright; dullness is a sure indication that the fish is not fresh.

Preparing and Cooking Red Mullet

Larger fish should be scaled before cooking, but be warned—this is a delicate operation, as the skin is very fragile. Scaling is worth the effort, however, as it reveals the wonderful red skin in all its glory. Red mullet combines well with traditional Mediterranean flavors of olive oil, black olives, herbs, garlic, saffron and tomatoes. It can be baked, grilled or cooked in cartoccio *with powerful herbs such as rosemary or fennel. For* triglia all'italiana, *place whole red mullet on a bed of finely chopped mushrooms and onions that have been sweated until soft and mixed with fresh bread crumbs, and bake for 20–30 minutes.*

Red mullet
The flesh of these pretty fish has a distinctive almost shrimp-like flavor

Sea bass
Prized for their delicate white flesh, these slim, elegant fish are almost always sold whole

Shellfish

Italian coastal waters are host to a huge variety of shellfish and crustaceans, many with wonderfully exotic names such as *datteri di mare* (sea dates; a kind of mussel), *tartufi di mare* (sea truffles; a type of clam) and *fragolino di mare* (sea strawberry; a tiny octopus that turns bright pink when cooked). Almost all seafood is considered edible, from clams to *cannolicchi* (razor-shells), *lumache di mare* (sea snails) and *canestrelli* (small scallops). Shrimps come in all sizes and colors, from vibrant red to pale gray, while crustaceans range from bright orange crawfish to blue-black lobsters.

Cooking Squid and Cuttlefish

Small squid and cuttlefish should be cooked only briefly—just until they turn opaque—or they will become rubbery and tough.

Larger specimens need long, slow cooking to make them tender. They can be stuffed with ground fish or meat, anchovies and seasoned bread crumbs or rice, baked with tomatoes and wine sauce until tender, or cut into rings and fried in a light batter or simply dusted with seasoned flour and deep-fried. Squid and cuttlefish are also delicious stewed in their own ink; seal the mollusks in hot oil with some chopped onions and garlic, add finely chopped fresh parsley and seasoning, then cover with dry white wine and a little water and simmer gently for 15 minutes. Crush the ink sacs, mix the inky liquid with a little cold water and 2–3 tbsp flour and work into a smooth paste. Add the flour mixture to the pan and cook for another 5–10 minutes.

Squid
Large specimens such as this one need long, slow cooking to make them tender—conversely, small baby squid should be cooked very quickly or they will become tough

Calamari or totani (squid) and seppie (cuttlefish)

Despite their appearance, squid and cuttlefish are actually mollusks whose shell is located inside the body. They are indistinguishable in taste, but cuttlefish have a larger head and a wider body with stubbier tentacles. The cuttlebone, much loved by parrots, is the bone of the cuttlefish inside the body. Once this has been removed, cuttlefish are very tender. The "shell" of a squid is nothing more than a long, thin, transparent quill. Both *seppie* and *calamari* have ten tentacles.

Squid and cuttlefish are immensely popular in Italy, cut into rings and served as part of either an *insalata di mare* (seafood salad) or *fritto misto* (mixed fried fish). Their black ink is used to flavor and color risotto and fresh pasta.

Preparing and Cooking Mussels

Scrub the shells under cold running water. Pull off the "beard" protruding from the shell. Give any open mussels a sharp tap; they should close immediately. Discard any that do not, as they are probably dead.

The simplest way to cook mussels is alla marinara. *For 4 people, finely chop 1 large onion, 2 garlic cloves and 1 tbsp chopped parsley, put in a large pan with 2¼ cups white wine and simmer for 5 minutes. Add the scrubbed mussels, cover and steam, shaking the pan occasionally, for 5 minutes, or until the shells have opened. Discard any unopened mussels, sprinkle the rest with extra parsley and serve. For a richer sauce, transfer the mussels to a bowl and reduce the sauce over high heat. Pour it over the shellfish and serve.*

Preparing Squid

You can usually buy squid already cleaned, but failing that, it is easy to prepare it yourself. Hold the body in one hand and the head in the other, and pull the head gently but firmly. The soft entrails will come away cleanly. Cut off the tentacles and remove the dark ink sac from the head.

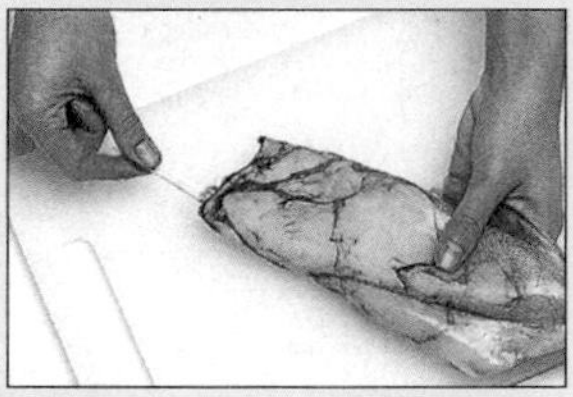

Pull out the transparent quill and rinse the body inside and out. Peel off the purplish membrane. Unless the squid are tiny enough to serve whole, cut the body into ¼ in rings and the tentacles into manageable pieces.

Polipi *(octopus)*

These are much larger than squid and have only eight tentacles. Their ink sac is not located in the head but in their liver, and the ink has a strong, pungent taste. Octopus look and taste similar to squid, but need a good deal of preparation. They must be pounded (99 times, some say) to tenderize them before they are subjected to very long, slow cooking.

If you can find very small octopus, they can be cooked in the same way as squid, but otherwise it is less trouble to substitute squid or cuttlefish.

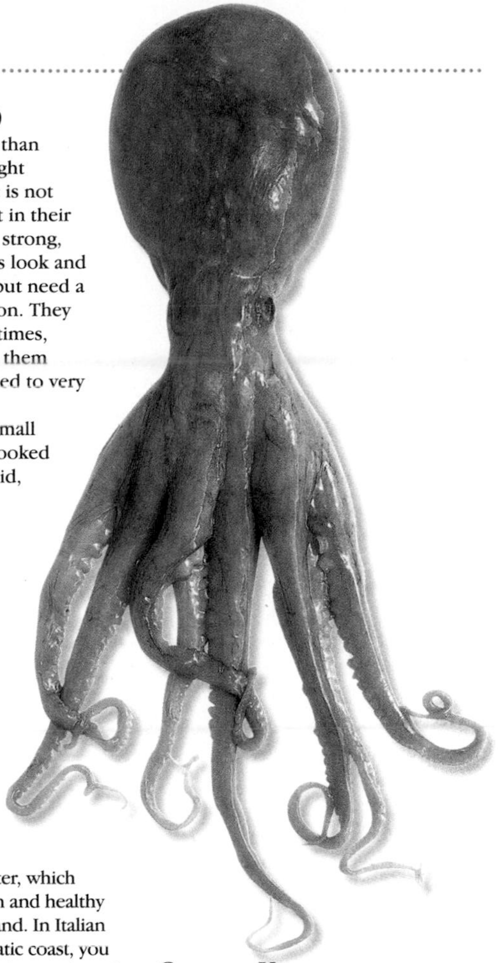

Octopus
When small, these can be cooked like squid

Cozze *(mussels)*

Mussels, with their smooth texture and sweet flavor, make an attractive addition to many pasta and fish dishes. Pollution in the Mediterranean has threatened the indigenous mussel population, so nowadays most Italian mussels are farmed by the *bouchot* method, on ropes attached to long stakes set in pure seawater, which keeps the mollusks clean and healthy and free from grit and sand. In Italian fish markets on the Adriatic coast, you may find small sweet local mussels with different names like *peoci* or *datteri di mare*. These can be prepared in the same way as other mussels.

Choosing

Mussels, sold by the litre in Italy, are very inexpensive. Because the shells constitute so much of the weight, allow at least a generous 2½ cups mussels per serving. Choose those that feel heavy for their size and discard any with broken shells. Use mussels the day they are gathered or bought.

Mussels
Steamed mussels combine well with black fettuccine or tagliatelle

Culinary Uses

Once mussels have been steamed open, they can be served with a garlicky tomato sauce, or baked on the half shell with garlic butter or a bread crumb topping. For *cozze gratinate al forno*, lay the mussels on the bottom shells in an ovenproof dish, sprinkle lavishly with bread crumbs seasoned with garlic and parsley and drizzle with olive oil. Bake for 10 minutes.

Shelled cooked mussels are combined with shrimp and squid for an *insalata di mare* (seafood salad), or used as a pizza topping, while mussels in the shell are often mixed with other seafood and pasta for dishes like *spaghetti allo scoglio* ("spaghetti of the rock").

Shellfish

Gamberetti, gamberelli and gamberoni (shrimp)

There are so many different varieties of shrimp in Italian coastal waters that it is almost impossible to recognize them all. The smallest are the *gamberetti*, small pink or brown shrimps that are usually boiled and served simply dressed with olive oil and lemon juice as part of an *antipasto*. Next in size come the *gamberelli*, pink shrimp with a delicate flavor. These are the shrimp that are most commonly used in a *fritto misto di mare* (mixed fried seafood). *Gamberi rossi* are the larger variety of shrimp, which turn bright red when they are cooked. They are highly prized for their fine, strong flavor, and are eaten plainly cooked and dipped into a bowl of *maionese* (mayonnaise). Best (and most expensive) of all are *gamberoni*, large succulent shrimp from the Adriatic, which have a superb flavor and texture. Similar to these is the *cicala*, which resembles a small flattish lobster.

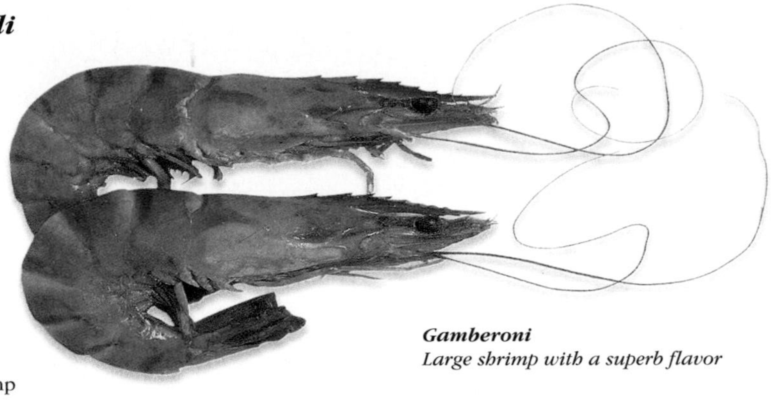

Gamberoni
Large shrimp with a superb flavor

Cooking Shrimp and Scampi

Whatever the size, all types of shrimp can be cooked briefly in boiling salted water (sea water, if possible) until they turn pink. Medium shrimp will take only 1–2 minutes, large shrimp up to 5 minutes. The robust flavor of shrimp makes them ideal for serving in a rich tomato or cream sauce or with rice. Shell them after cooking. To grill gamberoni, *rub the shells with olive oil and coarse salt and grill over charcoal or on a grilling pan, turning them frequently. When they turn opaque, slit them through the underside and open them out flat like a butterfly. Brush the underside with oil and grill until just cooked. Peeled shrimp can be pan-fried in olive oil flavored with garlic and/or chili, parsley and capers or coated in batter or egg and bread crumbs and deep-fried.*

Gamberi rossi
These large shrimp turn bright red when cooked

Preparing Shrimp and Scampi

Shrimp should be deveined before or after cooking. Pull off the heads, shell the tails and pick out the black thread-like intestine with a knife tip.

CHOOSING

Almost all the shrimp you buy in Italy are sold uncooked. They should have bright shells that feel firm; if they look limp or smell of ammonia, do not buy them.

CULINARY USES

Shrimp are extremely versatile and can be used in a wide variety of dishes. Small shrimps are served as *antipasti*, either on their own, or as a stuffing for tomatoes. They can be added to risotto and pasta dishes or seafood sauces.

Larger shrimp combine well with almost any other seafood. They are usually included in an *insalata di mare* (seafood salad) or *fritto misto di mare* (mixed fried seafood). They make a fine *antipasto* added to an *insalata russa* (Russian salad) or served with green beans dressed with extra virgin olive oil. They combine well with a spicy tomato sauce or mushrooms, and can be used for seafood casseroles. Large shrimp can be skewered or split and grilled, or boiled and served with mayonnaise or lemon.

Gamberetti
These small pink shrimps are delicious simply dressed with olive oil and lemon juice

Vongole (clams)

There are almost as many different types of clam as there are regions in Italy, ranging from tiny smooth-shelled *arselle* or *vongole* to long thin razor shells and the large Venus clams with beautiful ridged shells called *tartufi di mare* ("sea truffles"). All have a sweet flavor and a slightly chewy texture. Because they vary so much in size, it is best to ask the fishmonger how many clams you will need for a particular dish.

Clams
These smooth-shelled vongole *are often steamed and served as part of a seafood salad*

PREPARING AND COOKING CLAMS

Their habit of burying themselves in the sand makes clams rather gritty, so they should be left in fresh water for an hour or so to open up and disgorge the sand inside the shells. To open large clams, either use an oyster knife, or put them in a medium oven for a few minutes until they gape open.

Clams can be served raw like oysters, or cooked in exactly the same way as mussels (see page 70). The cooking time depends on the size of the clams; tiny specimens take only a minute or two. Steamed shelled clams are often served as part of an insalata di mare *or in a risotto. Miniature clams in their shells are stewed with olive oil, garlic and parsley and served with their juices (*in bianco*) or used in a tomato sauce (*in rosso*) for* spaghetti alle vongole, *or served on fried bread as* crostini. *Large varieties can be pan-fried with lemon and parsley, or stuffed with seasoned bread crumbs and grilled or baked.*

Vegetables

Vegetables have always played a very important role in Italian cooking, particularly in the south of the country, where meat was a luxury that few could afford. They are most often served as dishes in their own right, rather than accompaniments, and the range of imaginative vegetable recipes from all over Italy seems infinite.

White asparagus
This variety is grown under mounds of earth to retain the pale color

Green asparagus
Enjoyed by Italians, simply boiled or roasted in olive oil

One of the great joys of Italy is shopping at the markets, where an astonishing range of seasonal vegetables is on display, from asparagus, beans and *cavolo nero* from the north to eggplants, peppers and zucchini from Calabria and Sicily. In spring and summer, you will find at least ten different varieties of lettuce, and you will be overwhelmed by the aroma of freshly picked local tomatoes still on the vine. Italians almost never buy imported or out-of-season vegetables, but prefer to purchase fresh seasonal produce bursting with flavor.

Asparagi (asparagus)

Asparagus has been grown commercially in northeastern Italy for over 300 years and is still highly prized as a luxury vegetable. It has a short growing season from April to early June and is really only worth eating during this period. Both green and white asparagus are cultivated in Italy; the green variety is grown above ground so that the entire spear is bright green. They are harvested when they are about 6 in high. The fat white spears with their pale yellow tips are grown under mounds of soil to protect them from the light, and harvested almost as soon as the tips appear above the soil to retain their pale color. Both varieties have a delicious fresh grassy flavor.

Culinary Uses

In spring, Italians enjoy young asparagus spears simply boiled, steamed or roasted in olive oil and served as a *primo* (first course) with butter and freshly grated Parmesan. For an extra treat, they add a fried egg and dip the asparagus tips into the creamy yolk. When served as a vegetable accompaniment, asparagus can be crisply fried in egg and bread crumbs. The tips also make a luxury addition to risotto.

Buying and Storing

Asparagus starts to lose its flavor as soon as it has been cut, so be sure to buy only the freshest spears. The best guide is the tips, which should be firm and tight. If they are drooping and open, the asparagus is past its best. The stalks should be straight and fresh-looking, not yellowed and shriveled or very woody at the base. Allow about eight medium spears per serving as a first course and always buy spears of uniform thickness so that they cook evenly. Asparagus will keep in the vegetable compartment of the refrigerator for two or three days.

Preparing and Cooking Asparagus

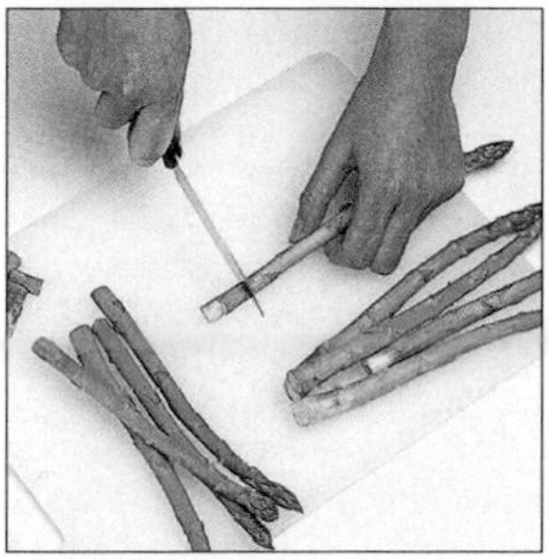

Freshly cut garden asparagus needs no trimming, but cut off at least ¾ in from the bottom of the stalks of bought spears until the exposed end looks fresh and moist. Peel the lower half with a potato peeler. (You need not do this for very thin stalks.)

Boiling asparagus can be problematic, since the stalks take longer to cook than the tips. The ideal solution is to use a special asparagus kettle, so as to immerse the stalks in boiling water while steaming the tips.

Asparagus can also be stood upright in a deep pan of boiling water, tented with foil and cooked for 5–8 minutes, until tender but still al dente. *Alternatively, steam the spears in a vegetable steamer. Serve with a drizzle of extra virgin olive oil or melted butter.*

Asparagus can also be successfully microwaved. Wash the spears and lay them in an oval dish in a single layer with the tips all pointing the same way. You need not add water. Cover tightly with plastic wrap and cook on full power for 5 minutes per 1¼ lb. If the spears are not quite done, turn them over and cook for a little longer.

To roast asparagus, heat some olive oil in a roasting pan, turn the spears in the oil, then roast in a hot oven for 5–10 minutes.

To fry, roll the spears in beaten egg and fine dried bread crumbs, then fry them a few at a time in very hot olive oil until crusty and golden. Drain on paper towel and sprinkle with sea salt.

Cardi (cardoons)

Cardoons are related to artichokes, but only the leaf-stalks are eaten. They are commercially grown in mounds of soil to keep them creamy white, but in the wild, the stalks are pale green and hairy and can grow to an enormous size. The tough outer stalks are always discarded, and only the inner stalks and hearts are eaten. Cardoons are a popular winter vegetable in Italy and can be found in the markets ready-trimmed.

Culinary Uses

Cardoons can be eaten raw as a salad, or cooked in a variety of ways—fried, puréed or boiled and served with melted butter or a rich cream and Parmesan sauce. They are traditionally used as a vegetable to dip into the hot anchovy and garlic fondue known as *bagna cauda*.

Buying and Storing

Cardoons bought at the market will have been trimmed of their outer stalks and are sold with a crown of leaves, like large heads of celery. The stalks should be plump and creamy-white and not too hairy. Wrapped in a plastic bag, they will keep in the vegetable compartment of the refrigerator for two or three days.

Preparing and Cooking Cardoons

Cut off the roots and peel the stalks with a potato peeler to remove the stringy fibers. Cut the stalks into 2½ in lengths and the hearts into wedges, and drop into acidulated water to prevent discoloration.

Blanch in boiling salted water, then simmer or fry gently in butter until tender. To serve in a sauce, put the blanched cardoons in an ovenproof dish, cover with sauce, sprinkle with grated Parmesan and broil until browned.

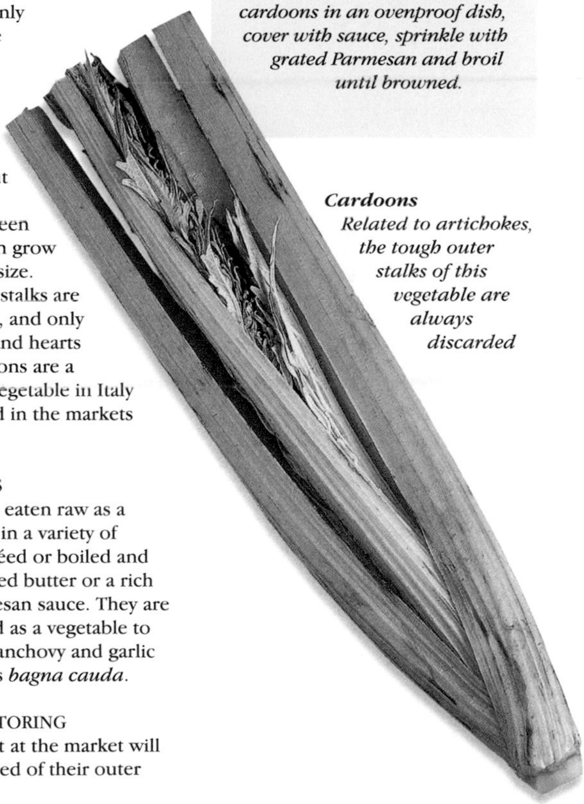

Cardoons
Related to artichokes, the tough outer stalks of this vegetable are always discarded

Vegetables

Carciofi (artichokes)

As their appearance suggests, artichokes are a type of thistle. Originating from Sicily, where they grow almost wild, they are cultivated throughout Italy and are a particular specialty of Roman cooking. The artichoke itself is actually the flower bud of the large, silvery-leaved plant. There are many different varieties, from tiny purple plants with tapered leaves, which are so tender that they can be eaten raw, to large bright or pale green globes, whose leaves are pulled off one by one and the succulent flesh at the base stripped off with your teeth.

History

Although artichokes have always grown like weeds in Sicily, they were first cultivated near Naples in the fifteenth century. Their popularity spread to Florence, where they became a favorite dish of the Medici family. They were believed to have powerful properties as an aphrodisiac and women were often forbidden to eat them!

Culinary Uses

Tiny tender artichokes can be quartered and eaten raw or braised *alla romana* with olive oil, parsley and garlic. Large specimens can be served boiled with a dressing to dip the leaves into, or stuffed with savory fillings. They can be cut into wedges, dipped in batter and deep-fried. A favorite Italian dish is the ancient Jewish recipe *carciofi alla giudea*, where the artichokes are flattened out and deep-fried twice, so that the outside is very crisp while the inside remains meltingly moist.

Buying and Storing

Artichokes are available almost all year round, but they are at their best in summer. Whichever variety you are buying, look for tightly packed leaves (open leaves indicate that they are too mature) and a very fresh color. When an artichoke is old, the tips of the leaves will turn brown. If possible, buy artichokes still attached to their stems; they will stay fresher and the peeled, cooked stems are often as delicious as the artichoke itself.

Artichokes will stay fresh for several days if you place the stalks in water like a bunch of flowers. If they have no stalks, wrap them in plastic wrap and keep in the vegetable compartment of the refrigerator for a day or two.

Preparing and Cooking Artichokes

Tiny tender artichokes can be quartered and eaten raw.

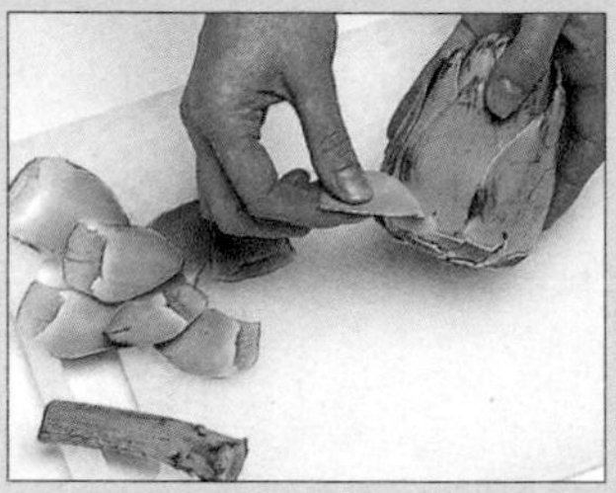

For large artichokes, snap off the stalk and pull off the tough outer leaves. Rub the cut surfaces with lemon juice to prevent discoloration and keep the prepared artichokes in a bowl of acidulated water until ready to cook.

Boil large whole artichokes for about 30 minutes, until the outer leaves can be pulled off easily.

Drain them upside-down, then pull out the center leaves and scoop out the inedible hairy choke with a spoon before serving. For stuffed artichokes, remove the choke before cooking and fill the cavity with your chosen stuffing. Braise them in olive oil and water, or invert them onto an ovenproof dish, pour on a mixture of olive oil and water, cover with foil and bake at 375°F for about 1 hour.

Very small artichokes should be quartered and boiled, braised or stewed until tender. The chokes are so soft that the artichokes can be eaten whole.

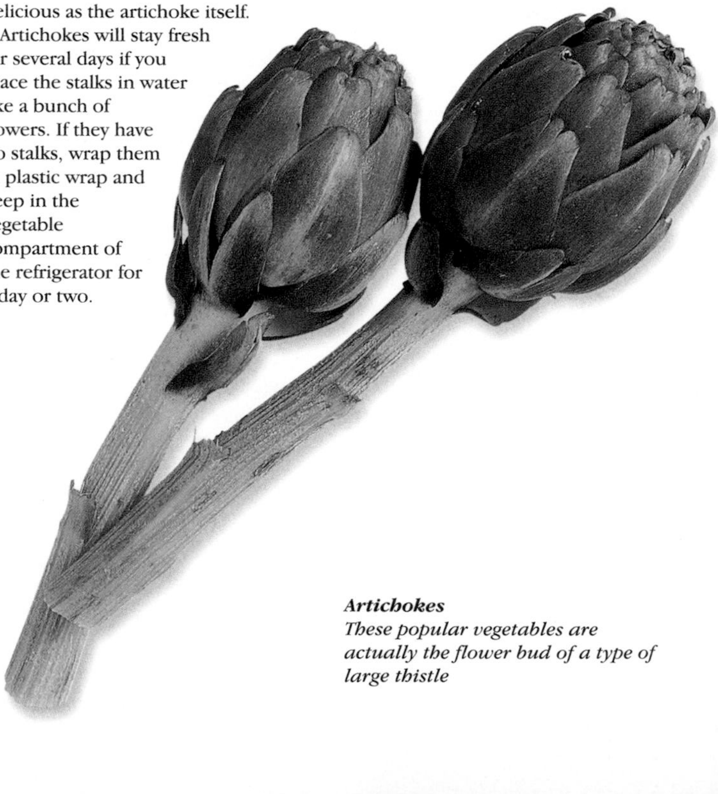

Artichokes
These popular vegetables are actually the flower bud of a type of large thistle

Cavolo (cabbage)

Cabbage is an essential ingredient of many Italian hearty winter soups. Three main types are used: *cavolo verza* (curly-leaved savoy cabbage), which is used in Milanese dishes, *cavolo cappuccio* (round white or red cabbage) and the specialty of Tuscany, *cavolo nero*, a tall leafy cabbage whose name means "black cabbage," but which is actually dark purplish green.

Culinary Uses

Italians rarely eat cabbage as a vegetable side dish, but prefer to include it in hearty soups, such as *ribollita* or minestrone, or to stuff and braise the outer leaves and serve them as a main course.

Buying and Storing

Cabbage heads should be solid and firm, with fresh, unyellowed leaves. It is best to buy them complete with their outer leaves; not only are these tasty for cooking, but they protect the hearts and give a good indication of the freshness of the cabbage. A cabbage will keep in the vegetable compartment of the refrigerator for up to a week.

Cavolo nero
The name of this tall leafy cabbage means "black cabbage"

Red and white cabbage
The red variety is often cooked gently with apples and spices to serve with rich meats, while the white variety is added to soups and stews

Savoy cabbage
This curly-leaved cabbage is used in Milanese dishes

Preparing and Cooking Cabbage

Cut off the outer leaves and stalk, cutting out a cone-shaped section of the stalk from the inside of the cabbage. To use the leaves for stuffing, blanch them in boiling water for about 3 minutes, until malleable. For soups and braised dishes, coarsely shred the cabbage and wash it well.

Cabbage can be cooked in a variety of ways. The simplest cooking method is to toss shredded cabbage in butter or olive oil until just tender. Never overcook cabbage; it should still retain some crunch.

Winter cabbages are good shredded and braised with pancetta *and garlic, while* cavolo rosso *(red cabbage) can be spiced with apples, cinnamon and cloves and stewed in a little white wine to cut the richness of pork, duck or roast goose.*

Vegetables

Cipolle (onions)

Onions are an essential part of Italian cooking. Many varieties are grown, including mild yellow onions, the stronger-flavored white onions and their baby version, which is used for pickling and sweet-and-sour onions. The best-known Italian onions are the vibrant deep red variety, which are delicious raw (in a tuna and bean salad, for example), or cooked.

Culinary Uses

The best Italian onions are grown in Piedmont, so many classic Piedmontese recipes include these versatile bulbs. Large onions can be stuffed with Fontina or ground meat and herbs, and baked. Baby white onions are traditionally cooked *in agrodolce*, a sweet-and-sour sauce of sugar and wine vinegar, and served cold as an *antipasto* or hot as a vegetable accompaniment.

Buying and Storing

You will often find young fresh onions in Italian markets. These are sold in bunches like large, bulbous scallions, complete with their leaves. They have a mild flavor and can be used for pickling or in salads. They will keep in the refrigerator for three or four days; wrap them to prevent their smell from pervading everything else in the refrigerator. Older onions have thin, almost papery skins that should be unblemished. The onions should feel firm and not be sprouting green leaves. They quickly deteriorate once cut, so it is best to buy assorted sizes, then you can use a small onion when the recipe calls for only a small amount. Stored in a dry, airy place, onions will keep for many weeks.

White onion
This variety is very strongly flavored

Red onion
This vibrant red variety is now widely available—they are delicious raw

Baby white onions
Traditionally cooked in agrodolce, *a classic Italian sweet-and-sour sauce, and served cold as an* antipasto

Yellow onions
These mild onions are best cooked gently in olive oil

Preparing and Cooking Onions

Some onions are easier to peel than others. The skins of red and yellow onions can be removed without much difficulty, but white onions may need to be plunged into boiling water for about 30 seconds to make peeling easier.

There are all sorts of old wives' remedies to prevent your eyes from watering when peeling onions. The most effective method is to hold them as far away from you as possible while you peel. For most cooked dishes, onions should be sliced or chopped, but for salads they are sliced into very thin rings.

The flavor of onions will develop in different ways, according to how you cook them. In Italian cooking, they are rarely browned, which gives them a bitter taste, but are generally sweated gently in olive oil to add a mellow flavor to a multitude of dishes.

Finocchio (fennel)

Originally a medicinal remedy for such disagreeable conditions as flatulence, fennel has become one of the most important of all Italian vegetables. Bulb or Florence fennel (so-called to distinguish it from the feathery green herb) resembles a fat white celery root and has a delicate but distinctive flavor of aniseed and a very crisp, refreshing texture.

Culinary Uses

Fennel is delicious eaten raw, dressed with a vinaigrette or as part of a mixed salad. In southern Italy, raw fennel is served with cheese as a dessert instead of fruit—an excellent aid to digesting a meal.

When cooked, the aniseed flavor becomes more subtle and the texture resembles cooked celery. Braised fennel is particularly good with white fish. Fennel can be cooked in all the same ways as celery or cardoons.

Buying and Storing

Fennel is available all year round. If possible, buy it with its topknot of feathery green fronds, which you can chop and use as an herb or garnish in any dish where you would use dill. The bulbs should feel firm and the outer layers should be crisp and white, not shriveled and yellowish. It should have a delicate, very fresh scent of aniseed and the crisp texture of green celery. Whole fennel bulbs will keep in the refrigerator for up to a week. Once cut, however, use them immediately, or the cut surfaces will discolor and the texture will soften. Allow a whole bulb per serving.

Fennel
The distinctive aniseed flavor makes this vegetable a perfect partner for white fish

Preparing and Cooking Fennel

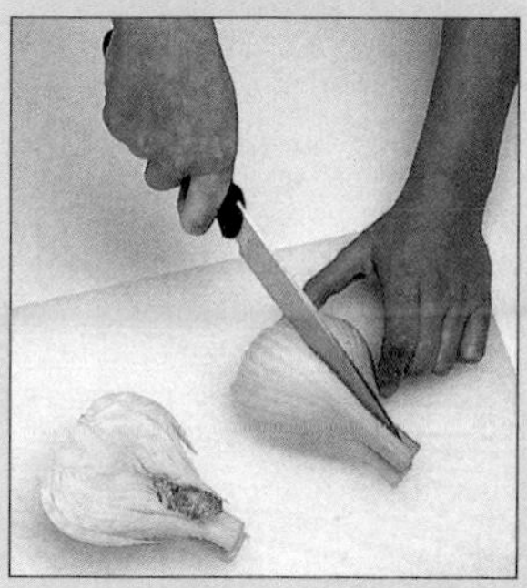

If the outer layer of the fennel bulb seems stringy, peel it with a sharp knife. Cut off the round greenish stalks protruding from the top. For salads, cut the bulb vertically into thin slices. For cooked dishes, quarter the bulb. Any trimmings can be chopped and used for soups or sauces for fish.

Fennel can be sautéed, baked or braised. For all cooked fennel recipes, blanch the quartered bulbs in a large saucepan of salted boiling water until it is just tender.

To sauté, heat about 2 tbsp butter per bulb with some chopped garlic, drain the fennel and fry it gently in the butter until very tender. To enhance the flavor, add a teaspoon of Pernod or other aniseed-flavored alcohol.

Braised fennel should be cooked in a little olive oil using a covered frying pan.

To bake fennel, lay the blanched bulbs in a buttered ovenproof dish, season, dot with butter and sprinkle a generous quantity of freshly grated Parmesan over the top. Bake at 400°F for 20–30 minutes or until the top is bubbling and golden brown.

Vegetables

Melanzane (eggplants)

The versatile eggplant plays an important role in the cooking of southern Italy and Sicily, possibly because its dense, satisfying texture makes a good substitute for meat. You will find many different eggplants in Italian markets, the two main types being the familiar deep purple elongated variety and the rotund paler mauve type, which has a thinner skin. Some are small, some huge, but they all taste similar and can be used in the same way for any recipe.

Preparing Eggplants

Some people believe that eggplants should always be sliced and salted for about 30 minutes before cooking to draw out the bitter juices; others deem this unnecessary. Salting does prevent eggplant from soaking up large quantities of oil during cooking, so it is probably worth doing.

Slice or dice the eggplants, place them in a colander, sprinkle with 1 tbsp salt per 2¼ lb. Place a dish on the eggplants and weight it down. Set aside for 30 minutes. Rinse the eggplants and dry with paper towels.

If eggplants have a very tough skin, it is best to peel them (unless you are stuffing them and need the skin as a container). Otherwise, leave the skin on, as its color will enhance the appearance of the finished dish.

Buying and Storing

Shape and size are not important when choosing eggplants; the essentials are tight, glossy skins and a fairly firm texture. Do not buy eggplants with wrinkled or damaged skins. They should feel heavy for their size; a light eggplant will probably be spongy inside and contain a lot of seeds. They will keep in the refrigerator for up to a week.

Eggplants
The familiar deep purple variety plays an important role in the cooking of southern Italy

History

Eggplant originated in Asia. They were cultivated in Europe in the Middle Ages, but only very rarely featured in Italian cooking at the time, since they were regarded with suspicion; indeed, the name *melanzane* comes from the Latin *melum insanum* (unhealthy apple). This mistrust had been overcome by the Renaissance, and eggplants began to be grown and used extensively in the south of Italy.

Culinary Uses

Eggplants are extremely versatile vegetables and add a wonderful depth of flavor to any dish in which they appear. They can be broiled, baked, stuffed, stewed and sautéed, on their own or with other ingredients, and the rich color of their skins enhances the appearance of many different Italian dishes.

Cooking Eggplants

The simplest way of cooking eggplants is to slice and fry them in a generous quantity of very hot olive oil. For a more substantial dish, coat them in light batter, then fine bread crumbs, and fry until golden brown. To bake them, halve the eggplants lengthwise, removing the calyx and stalk. Make slashes in the flesh and rub it with a cut garlic clove. Drizzle some olive oil over the top, cover with foil and bake for about 1 hour, until very soft. Season with salt and pepper and add lemon juice to taste. Probably the most famous Italian eggplant dish is melanzane alla parmigiana, *where the eggplants are layered with rich tomato sauce and Parmesan and baked. A favorite Sicilian dish,* caponata, *combines them with celery and a piquant sweet-and-sour sauce enlivened with olives and sometimes capers.*

Peperoni (bell peppers)

Generically known as capsicums, the shape of these peppers gives them the alternative name of "bell peppers." Although they come in a range of colors—green (these are unripe red peppers), red, yellow, orange and even purplish-black—all peppers have much the same sweetish flavor and crunchy texture, and are interchangeable in recipes. They are a very healthy food, being rich in Vitamin C. The locally grown peppers you will see in the markets in Italy are much larger and more misshapen than the uniformly perfect, hydroponically grown specimens but their flavor is sweet and delicious.

Culinary Uses

Each region of Italy has its own specialties using peppers. They can be used raw or lightly roasted in salads or as an *antipasto* and can be cooked in a variety of ways—roasted and dressed with olive oil or vinaigrette dressing and capers, stewed (as in *peperonata*), or stuffed and baked. Peppers have a great affinity with other Mediterranean ingredients, such as olives, capers, eggplants, tomatoes and anchovies.

Buying and Storing

Choose firm peppers with unwrinkled, shiny skins. Size does not matter unless you plan to stuff the peppers, in which case choose roundish shapes of uniform size. The skin of green peppers may be mottled with patches of orange or red; this indicates that the pepper is ripening, and as long as the pepper is unblemished, there is no reason not to buy it. Peppers can be stored in the fridge for up to two weeks.

Cooking Peppers

To make a classic Italian peperonata, *sweat sliced onions and garlic in olive oil, add sliced peppers, cover the pan and cook gently until just tender. Add an equal quantity of peeled, deseeded and chopped tomatoes, a splash of wine vinegar and seasoning and cook, uncovered, until meltingly tender. For* peperonata alla romana, *stir in some capers at the end.*

Peppers
Locally grown Italian peppers are often larger and more misshapen than the uniformly perfect varieties grown in hot-houses

Vegetables

Preparing and Cooking Peppers

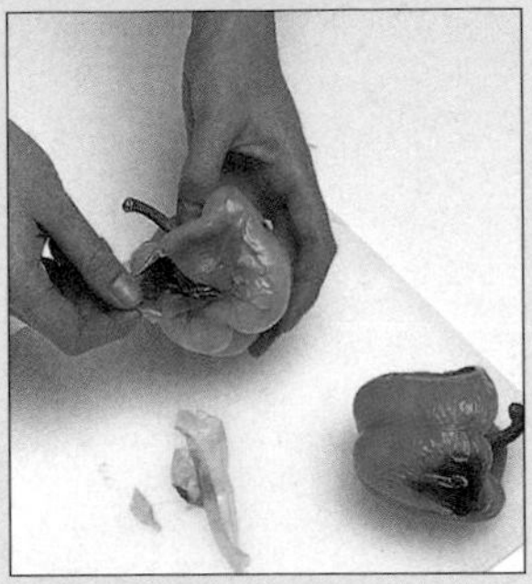

Place the peppers under a very hot broiler or hold them over a gas flame and turn them until the skin blackens and blisters. Put them in a plastic bag, seal and set aside until the peppers are cool enough to handle. The thin skin will peel off easily.

To slice peppers, halve them lengthwise, cut out the calyx and stem and pull out the core, seeds and white membranes. Cut the flesh into strips.

To stuff peppers, cut off the stalk end and remove the seeds and membranes. Fill the pepper with your chosen stuffing (rice, vegetables, meat—whatever you want) and replace the stalk end. Arrange the peppers in a shallow ovenproof dish, drizzle on some olive oil and pour in enough water to come about ¾ in up the sides of the peppers. Bake at 400°F for about 1 hour.

For baked peppers alla piemontese, *halve the peppers lengthwise and fill each with a chopped tomato, a chopped anchovy fillet and a little chopped garlic. Arrange the peppers on a baking tray, rounded side down. Drizzle on some olive oil and bake at 400°F for about 30 minutes.*

Pomodori (tomatoes)

It is impossible to imagine Italian cooking without tomatoes, which seem to be a vital ingredient in almost every recipe. But these "golden apples" were unknown in Italy until the sixteenth century, when they were brought over from Mexico. At first they were grown only in the south, but as their popularity spread, tomatoes were cultivated all over Italy and were incorporated into the cooking of every region. Italians grow an enormous variety of tomatoes, from plum tomatoes (San Marzano are the best) to ridged, pumpkin-shaped, green-tinged salad tomatoes, bright red fruits bursting with aroma and flavor, and tiny *pomodorini* (cherry tomatoes).

Culinary Uses

Tomatoes are used in so many different ways that it is hard to know where to begin. They can be eaten raw, sliced and served with a trickle of extra virgin olive oil and some torn basil leaves (basil and tomatoes have an extraordinary affinity). They are the red component of an *insalata tricolore*, partnering white mozzarella and green basil to make

Cherry tomatoes
Bright red and bursting with flavor, these tiny tomatoes can be used to add color and flavor to any dish

Plum tomatoes
San Marzano are the best variety of these smooth-skinned tomatoes

up the colors of the Italian flag. Raw ripe tomatoes can be chopped with herbs and garlic to make a fresh-tasting pasta sauce, or made into a topping for *bruschetta*.

Tomatoes can be broiled, fried, baked, stuffed, stewed and made into sauces and soups. They add color and flavor to almost any savory dish.

Buying and Storing

Tomatoes are at their best in summer, when they have ripened naturally in the sun. Choose your tomatoes according to how you wish to prepare them. Salad tomatoes should be very firm and easy to slice. The best tomatoes for cooking are plum tomatoes, which hold their shape well and should have a fine flavor. Tomatoes will only ripen properly if left for long enough on the vine, so try to buy "vine-ripened" varieties. If you can find only unripe tomatoes, you can ripen them by putting them in a brown paper bag with a ripe tomato or leaving them in a fruit bowl with a banana; the gases the ripe fruits give off will ripen the tomatoes but, alas, they cannot improve the flavor.

Try to buy tomatoes loose so that you can smell them. They should have a wonderful aroma. If the flavor is not all it should be, add a good pinch of sugar to enhance it. For cooked recipes, if you cannot find really flavorful tomatoes, use canned instead. The best are San Marzano plum tomatoes, which are grown near Salerno. In Italy, you will often find large knobby green tomatoes, which are sold as *pomodori da insalata.* Although you can let them ripen in the usual way, Italians prefer to slice these tomatoes thinly and eat them in their unripe state as a crunchy and refreshing salad.

Large tomatoes
Not always as smooth as these, locally grown Italian tomatoes bought at a market can be very ridged and almost pumpkin-shaped

Vine-ripened tomatoes
Tomatoes sold on the vine are likely to have a far better flavor than those sold loose

Peeling Tomatoes

It is easy to remove the skin from tomatoes. Prick the tomatoes with the point of a sharp knife, plunge them into a bowl of boiling water for about 30 seconds, then refresh in cold water. Peel away the skins, cut the tomatoes into quarters or halves and remove the seeds using a teaspoon.

Vegetables

Spinaci (spinach)

Spinach and its close relatives, *bietola* (Swiss chard) and *biete* (spinach beet), are dark green leafy vegetables, rich in minerals (especially iron) and vitamins. Unlike many other vegetables, they are often served in Italy as side dishes to a main course, although they appear in numerous composite dishes as well. All spinach, whether flat-leafed or curly-leafed, has a distinctive metallic flavor, which people either love or loathe. The latter should avoid dishes *alla fiorentina*, which use spinach in large quantities.

Curly-leaf spinach is a summer variety with very dark green leaves. Winter spinach has flat, smooth leaves, but tastes very similar. Usually, only the leaves are eaten and the stalks are discarded. Spinach has a delicate, melting quality and should be cooked only very briefly.

The coarser *bietola* contains less iron and has a less pronounced flavor than spinach. The leaves have broad, tender creamy or pale green midribs, and both the leaves and stalks are eaten, but are cooked in different ways. *Bietola* is available all year round, but is particularly popular in autumn and winter, when more delicate spinach is not available. No one is quite sure why it is called Swiss chard; the Swiss certainly eat it, but in much smaller quantities than the French or Italians.

Biete (spinach beet) has a much smaller stalk and more closely resembles spinach. The stalks are usually left attached to the leaves for cooking. The coarser texture of *biete* makes it more suitable than spinach for recipes that require more than the briefest cooking. Balls of ready-cooked *biete* are often sold in Italian delicatessens.

HISTORY

Spinach was originally cultivated in Persia in the sixth century and was brought to Europe by Arab traders some thousand years later. It had become very popular in France, Spain and England by the sixteenth century, when it was used for both sweet and savory dishes, but it did not reach Italy until the eighteenth century.

CULINARY USES

Tender young spinach leaves can be eaten raw in salads or cooked and served cold with a dressing of olive oil and lemon. Cooked spinach is used to make gnocchi and is often combined with ricotta to make fillings for pasta and *crespoline* (pancakes). Florentine-style recipes usually contain spinach, and it is a classic partner for eggs, fish, poultry and white meats. Spinach, *biete* and *bietola* are all used in savory tarts, such as *torta alla pasqualina*, an Easter speciality. They make excellent soups and soufflés. *Bietola* stalks are delicious sautéed in butter and baked in a white sauce sprinkled with Parmesan.

Spinach
The tender young leaves can be eaten raw; larger leaves need to be cooked

Spinach beet
The coarse texture of biete *makes it more suitable than spinach for slower-cooked recipes*

Buying and Storing

All types of spinach should look very fresh and green, with no signs of wilting. The leaves should be unblemished and the stalks crisp. Spinach and spinach beets contain a very high proportion of water and wilt down to about half their weight during cooking, so always buy far more than you think you will need—at least 9 oz per serving. Loose spinach should be used as soon as possible after buying. Packed loosely into a plastic bag, it will keep in the refrigerator for a couple of days. Unopened bags of pre-packaged spinach will keep for up to a week.

Bietola (Swiss chard)

Pull off the green leaves from the stems. Snap the veins and leafstalks and remove the stringy parts (do not cut with a knife, or the strings will not come off). Wash as you would spinach and cut the stalks into 2½–3½ in lengths.

Swiss chard
Available all year round, this vegetable is particularly popular in winter when the more tender spinach is not available

Preparing and Cooking Spinach and Swiss Chard

Spinach and spinach beet: Carefully pick over the spinach, discarding any withered or damaged leaves and tough stalks. Wash thoroughly in several changes of water until no signs of earth or grit remain. Spinach should be cooked with only the water that clings to the leaves after washing. Sauté it in butter with a clove of chopped garlic for about 5 minutes; overcooked spinach will be unpleasantly watery. To stew spinach, put it in a large saucepan, cover and cook gently until wilted, turning it over halfway through cooking. Drain and gently squeeze out the excess moisture with your hands. Toss in butter or olive oil, season with freshly grated nutmeg or chop finely and use for gnocchi and pasta fillings.

Swiss chard leaves can be cooked exactly like spinach. The prepared stalks should be blanched until tender in salted water or vegetable stock, then baked in a sauce or tart, sautéed in butter or used as a stuffing. A popular bietola *dish is a* sformato, *a savory, molded, baked custard.*

Vegetables

Zucca (squash) and zucchini

Squashes and zucchini are widely used in northern Italian cooking. Both have large, open, deep-yellow flowers, which are considered a great delicacy. Squashes come in a variety of shapes and sizes, from huge orange pumpkins to small, pale butternut squashes and green acorn squashes. They all have dense, sweet-tasting flesh. Zucchini are especially versatile, with shiny green skin and a sweet, delicate flavor. In Italy, tiny specimens are often sold with their flowers attached.

CULINARY USES

The pumpkin is the symbol of Mantua and recipes *alla mantovana* use the flesh a multitude of ways, from *tortelli alla zucca* (pumpkin-filled tortelli) to risotti, soups and sweet dessert tarts. Pumpkin flowers can be coated in batter and deep-fried, stuffed with a filling of ricotta, or chopped and added to risotti for extra color and flavor.

Zucchini combine well with other Mediterranean vegetables, like tomatoes and eggplants. They can be dipped in batter and deep-fried, made into fritters or served with a white sauce seasoned with Parmesan or nutmeg. Served cold with a mint-flavored vinaigrette (*zucchini a scapece*) or tomato sauce, they can be part of an *antipasto*. They can be halved and stuffed with a meat or vegetable filling. Young zucchini can also be thinly sliced or grated and eaten raw in a salad.

BUYING AND STORING

Zucchini are available almost all year round, but are at their best in spring and summer. The smaller and skinnier zucchini are, the better they taste. They should have very glossy green skins and feel very firm. Do not buy flabby zucchini or those with blemished skins. Larger specimens are useful for stuffing.

Zucchini
These familiar vegetables combine well with other Mediterranean vegetables

Pumpkins
Italians use the flesh of these large vegetables in a multitude of ways

Small pumpkins
Like their larger cousins, these small pumpkins have dense, sweet-tasting flesh

If you can find them in markets, buy tiny zucchini with their flowers attached. Allow 9 oz zucchini per serving. They will keep in the vegetable compartment of the refrigerator for up to a week.

Squashes should feel firm and heavy for their size. It is not worth buying enormous pumpkins (other than for decorative purposes), as their flesh tends to be stringy and flavorless. All whole squashes keep well, but once they are opened, they should be wrapped in plastic wrap and kept in the refrigerator for no more than three days.

If you are lucky enough to find squash or zucchini flowers (the best way is to grow your own), they must be cooked immediately, as they are extremely perishable.

Preparing Zucchini, Squashes and Pumpkins

Zucchini should be trimmed, then sliced, diced, cut into batons or grated as appropriate. They do not need peeling.

Flowers may contain small insects, so wash them quickly under cold running water and gently pat dry with paper towels. Cut off all but 1 in of the stems. Zucchini are best sautéed in butter or olive oil flavored with plenty of chopped garlic and parsley. Zucchini deep fried in a light batter are a favorite appetizer or side dish in Italy. The flowers can be prepared in the same way. To make zucchini a scapece, *slice 2¼ lb zucchini and brown in hot olive oil. Place in a dish and scatter on about 20 torn mint leaves and 1 finely chopped garlic clove. Season and dress with one part red wine vinegar and two parts olive oil. Mix well and let the flavors develop for 2 hours before serving.*

Squashes and pumpkins should be peeled and the seeds and fibrous parts removed. Cut the flesh into chunks or slices. The skin of large pumpkins may be too hard to peel; if so, break open the pumpkin with a hammer or drop it on the floor, and scoop out the flesh, discarding the seeds.

Pumpkin and squash should be blanched in boiling salted water, then sweated in butter until soft and made into soup or stuffing, cooked au gratin or grated raw and added to a risotto. Pumpkin can also be sweetened and used as a pie filling.

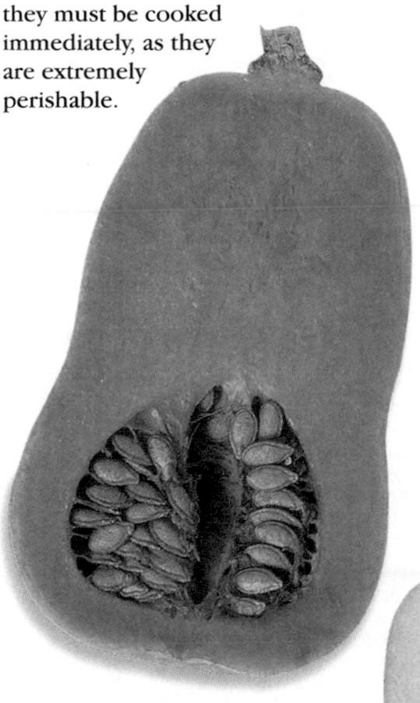

Butternut squash
The brightly colored flesh of butternut squashes is widely used in northern Italian cooking

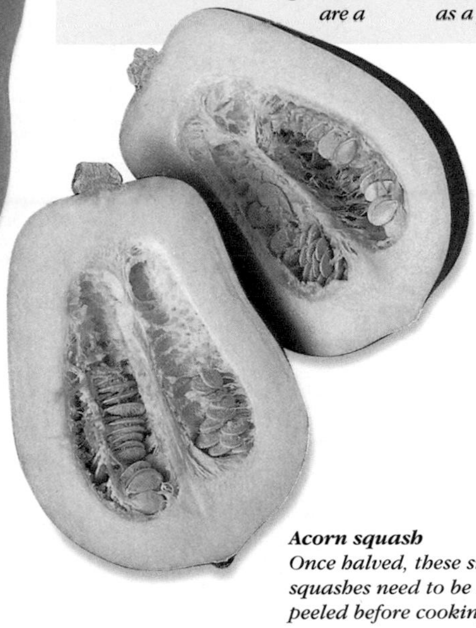

Acorn squash
Once halved, these small squashes need to be seeded and peeled before cooking

Salad Greens

Italians grow salad greens in profusion and gather them from the wild to create inventive and interesting combinations, such as *misticanza*, a potpourri of wild greens and cultivated leaves. In high season, you will find at least a dozen different salad greens at an Italian market, ranging from fresh green round garden lettuces to bitter dark green grass-like leaves and purplish-red radicchio. Such salads are served after the main course, simply dressed with olive oil and vinegar to cleanse the palate.

Cicoria di campo or dente di leone (dandelion)

Dandelion leaves are rich in iron and vitamins, and are also reputed to be a powerful diuretic. They have a pungent, peppery taste and long, fresh green indented leaves (hence the name "lion's tooth"). They can be picked in the wild before the plant has flowered, but only the young leaves should be eaten. Cultivated dandelion leaves are available. They are more tender than wild leaves, but have a less intense flavor.

Culinary Uses

Young dandelion leaves are usually served raw in salads together with other leaves; they are particularly good with crisply cooked bacon and hard-cooked eggs. They can also be cooked like spinach.

Radicchio

This variety of red-leafed chicory comes originally from Treviso. *Radicchio di Treviso* has elongated purplish-red leaves with pronounced cream-colored veins. The more familiar round variety is known as *radicchio di Verona*. Both types of red-leafed chicory have a bitter taste, and for salads are best used in small quantities together with other leaves. They look particularly attractive when combined with frilly-leafed curly endive, pale whitish-green chicory leaves, or the darker arugula.

Dandelion leaves
Pick these peppery-tasting leaves from the wild before the plant has flowered

Radicchio di Verona
The more familiar round red-leafed chicory

Radicchio di Treviso
This elongated variety is delicious grilled with olive oil

Culinary Uses

Radicchio can also be eaten as a hot vegetable, either quartered and grilled with olive oil, or stuffed with a mixture of bread crumbs, anchovies, capers and olives and baked—but it loses its beautiful color when cooked. A little radicchio added to a risotto made with red wine will add to the pretty pink color.

Buying and Storing

Radicchio leaves should be fresh-looking with no trace of brown at the edges. *Radicchio di Verona* should be firm with tightly packed leaves. Both types will keep in the refrigerator for up to a week.

Rucola (arugula)

Arugula has dark green elongated, indented leaves and a hot, pungent flavor and aroma. Like dandelions, it grows wild in the Italian countryside, but it is also cultivated commercially. Home-grown arugula has a much better flavor than the immature leaves usually found in supermarkets, but it bolts easily and should be picked as soon as the leaves are large enough.

CULINARY USES

Arugula adds zest to any green salad and can be eaten on its own with a dressing of olive oil and lemon juice or balsamic vinegar. Combined with radicchio, lamb's lettuce and fresh herbs, arugula makes a good substitute for *misticanza*. It can be added to pasta sauces and risotto, or cooked like spinach, but cooking does diminish the pungent flavor.

BUYING AND STORING

In Italy, arugula is always sold in small bunches. The leaves should look very fresh with no sign of wilting. Arugula does not keep well unless it has been pre-packaged. To keep it for a day or two, wrap it in damp newspaper or damp paper towels and store in the refrigerator.

Arugula
This hot, pungent salad leaf grows wild in the Italian countryside, but it is also cultivated commercially

Valeriana (lamb's lettuce)

This delicate salad plant, called lamb's lettuce, has tender green rounded leaves bunched together in a rosette shape. It grows wild in fields in Italy, but is also cultivated and is an essential ingredient of *misticanza*. It has a delicate but distinctive flavor, which adds interest to winter salads.

CULINARY USES

Lamb's lettuce is usually served by itself or in a mixed green salad, but it can also be cooked like spinach. The tender leaves will blacken if damaged, so take care when tossing a salad not to bruise them.

BUYING AND STORING

Lamb's lettuce should look fresh and green, with no drooping leaves. The smaller and rounder the leaves, the better the flavor. It will keep in the salad compartment of the refrigerator for several days, but take care not to squash it.

Lamb's Lettuce
The delicate but distinctive flavor of this salad plant adds interest to winter salads

PREPARING LAMB'S LETTUCE

Lamb's Lettuce is sold with the root attached, so it must be washed before use. Dunk it in several changes of cold water to remove all the grit, then dab the leaves dry with paper towels, handling them very gently.

Mushrooms

Italian country-dwellers have always been passionate collectors of edible wild mushrooms; in spring and autumn, the woods and fields are alive with furtive fungi hunters in search of these flavorful delicacies. Cultivated button mushrooms are rarely eaten in Italy, even when fresh wild varieties are out of season; Italians prefer to use dried or preserved wild fungi with their robust, earthy taste.

The most prized mushroom for use in Italian cooking is the *porcino* (cepe). Since these are extremely expensive, they are most often dried and used in small quantities to add flavor to field or other wild mushrooms. Drying actually intensifies the flavor of *porcini*, so they are not regarded as inferior to the fresh mushrooms—quite the reverse. Other popular wild fungi include *gallinacci* (chanterelles), *prataioli* (field mushrooooms) and *ovoli* (Caesar's mushrooms).

History

From earliest times, man gathered and ate wild mushrooms. The Greeks and Romans enjoyed many fungi, including *amanita caesarea* (Caesar's mushroom), which was popular with the Emperor Claudius and ultimately his downfall; his wife Agrippina poisoned him by adding deadly *amanita phalloides* (the aptly named deathcap) to a dish of his favorite fungi. The Romans succeeded in cultivating several types of mushrooms, but cultivation on a large scale really began in the seventeenth century, when a French botanist discovered how to grow mushrooms in compost all year round.

Storing

Never store mushrooms in a plastic bag, as they will sweat and turn mushy. Put them into a paper bag and keep in the vegetable compartment of the refrigerator for no more than two days.

Preparing and Cooking Mushrooms

Mushrooms should never be washed or they will become waterlogged and mushy. To clean them, cut off the earthy base of the stalk and lightly brush the caps with a soft brush or wipe them clean with a slightly damp cloth.

With very few exceptions (including cepes and Caesar's mushrooms, which can be eaten raw), wild mushrooms should be cooked to destroy any mild toxins they may contain. All mushrooms can be sliced and sauteéd in hot olive oil or a mixture of butter and olive oil with finely chopped garlic or shallots, a little red chili and herbs (parsley, marjoram, thyme or mint are particularly good).

Chanterelles
These orangey-yellow mushrooms have a delicious, delicate flavor and a distinct apricot aroma

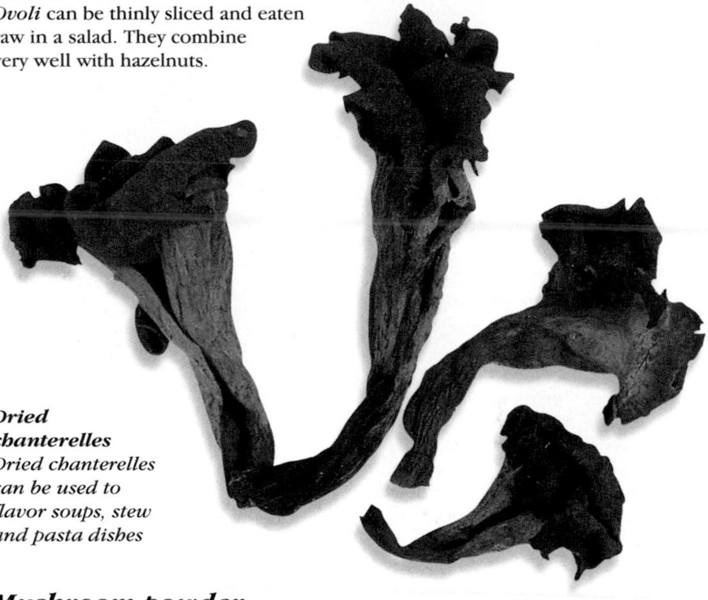

COOKING CHANTERELLES

Chanterelles have a delicious, delicate flavor and a slightly chewy texture; they should be cooked slowly or they may become hard. Fry them gently in butter with chopped garlic or shallots for about 10 minutes, adding some finely chopped parsley, marjoram or thyme toward the end of the cooking time. Serve them on hot buttered toast, or add to omelets or scrambled eggs. They are particularly good with poultry, rabbit or veal and can also be dressed with a herb-flavored vinaigrette and served warm in a salad.

CULINARY USES

Ovoli can be thinly sliced and eaten raw in a salad. They combine very well with hazelnuts.

Dried chanterelles
Dried chanterelles can be used to flavor soups, stew and pasta dishes

Ovoli (Caesar's mushrooms; Latin name amanita caesarea)

These large mushrooms with an orangey-yellow cap have an excellent flavor and were a favorite of the Roman emperors. They are still found in Italy, but are very rare elsewhere.

Mushroom powder

Well-flavored dried mushrooms can be crushed to a powder and used to flavor sauces, soups and stews. Some Italian delicatessens stock mushroom powder. If you make your own, store it in an airtight container.

DRYING CHANTERELLES

Leave the chanterelles whole, or halve them if they are large.

Lay them on a double thickness of newspaper and let sit in a very warm, airy place (above the heater is ideal), turning them over every few hours until they have become completely dry and brittle. Alternatively, string them like necklaces and hang them up to dry, or place in a very cool convection oven (maximum 250°F), leaving the door ajar. When the chanterelles are completely dry, store them in jars or paper bags. All mushrooms can be dried in this way; slice them thinly before drying. It is only worth drying perfect specimens.

RECONSTITUTING DRIED MUSHROOMS

Soak 1 oz dried mushrooms in 1 cup hot water for about 20 minutes until soft, then drain and use like fresh mushrooms. Keep the soaking water to use in sauces, stocks or soups; it will have an intense mushroom flavor.

Mushrooms

Porcini (cepes)

These are the king of mushrooms in Italian cooking. Their Italian name means "little piglets," which aptly describes their bulbous stalks and rounded brown caps. In autumn, they are found in woodlands, where they can grow to an enormous size, weighing more than $1\frac{1}{4}$ lb each (although mushroom-hunters rarely leave them for long enough to grow to these proportions). There are many different varities of *porcini*, all of which have a fine flavor and meaty texture.

Culinary Uses

All cepes can be cooked in the same way as other mushrooms. Young ones can be thinly sliced and eaten raw, dressed with extra virgin olive oil. Larger caps are delicious brushed with olive oil, grilled and served with a grinding of salt and pepper. Don't discard the stalks, which have an excellent flavor; chop them and cook with the caps, or use them for sauces, stocks and soups; just trim off the earthy bits from the base.

Drying

Cepes can be thinly sliced and dried in the same way as *gallinacci*. Dried *porcini* are commercially available. They are very expensive, but a little goes a long way. Just 1 oz dried porcini, soaked and drained, will enhance the flavor of $1\frac{1}{4}$ lb cultivated mushrooms beyond recognition. Don't be tempted to buy cheap packages of dried *porcini*, which may contain a high proportion of inferior dried mushrooms and bits of twig from the forest floor.

Storing

Fresh *porcini* can be kept in the vegetable compartment of the refrigerator for up to two days. Dried mushrooms will keep in an airtight container for at least a year.

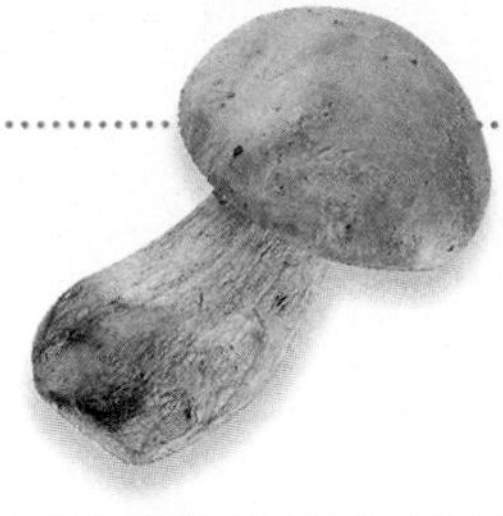

Porcini *(cepes)*
Italian cooks consider these to be the king of mushrooms

Freezing

Small *porcini* in perfect condition can be frozen whole. Large or blemished specimens should be sliced and lightly sautéed in butter, then drained and frozen. Do not defrost before use, or they will become mushy. Simply cook the frozen mushrooms in hot olive oil or butter. Frozen mushrooms will only keep for about one month.

Pickling *Porcini*

Unblemished fresh porcini *can be preserved by pickling. Choose unblemished fungi (if you don't have enough* porcini*, use a mixture of mushrooms), leaving small ones whole and slicing or quartering large ones.*

$2\frac{1}{4}$ lb mushrooms
generous 2 cups white wine vinegar
generous 2 cups water
2 tsp salt
1 tsp peppercorns, lightly crushed
2 bay leaves
2 tsp coriander seeds
2 garlic cloves, peeled and halved
4 small dried red chilies
olive oil

***1** Put the mushrooms in a saucepan with all the ingredients except the olive oil. Bring to a boil and simmer for 5–10 minutes, until the mushrooms are tender but still firm. Drain them, reserving the pickling aromatics, and let cool completely.*

***2** Spoon the mushrooms and aromatics into a sterilized preserving jar and fill up the jar with olive oil. Seal and let sit for at least a month. Pickled mushrooms will keep for at least six months.*

Dried* porcini *(cepes)
These dried porcini *are expensive to buy, but since drying actually accentuates their flavor, a little goes a long way*

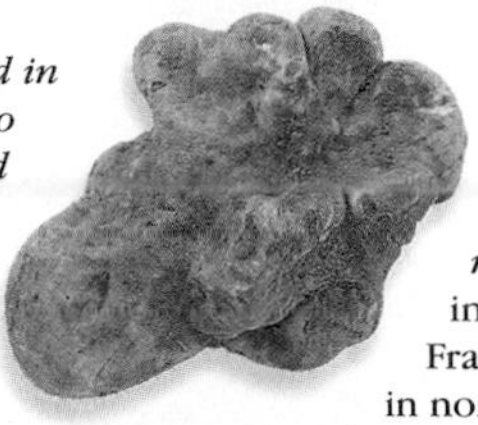

Black truffles
No one has succeeded in cultivating truffles, so they remain rare and expensive—the black variety is more highly prized than the white

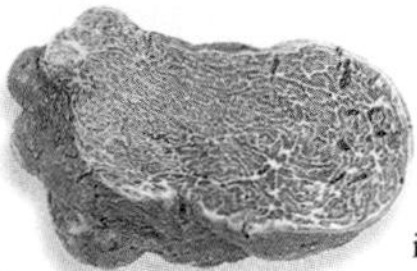

White truffles
Found in Piedmont, northern Italy, these delicately flavored truffles are usually served raw

Chiodini (honey fungus; Latin name armillaria mellea)

No gardener welcomes the sight of honey fungus (the Italian name means "little nails"), as it is a parasitic fungus that destroys the trees on whose roots it grows. However, the caps of these small golden mushrooms are good to eat (the fibrous stalks should be discarded). In their raw state they are mildly toxic, but once they have been blanched in very hot oil or boiling water, then stewed in butter with a little garlic, seasoning and parsley, they make good eating.

Culinary Uses

Honey fungus makes a good filling for a *frittata* (Italian omelet). Allow 5 oz *chiodini* caps and 4 large eggs for two people. Season the eggs and beat them lightly with 1 oz grated Parmesan. Heat 2 tbsp olive oil in a frying pan and sauté the blanched mushroom caps with 1 chopped garlic clove and 1 tbsp chopped parsley for about 3 minutes. Season with salt and pepper, pour in the eggs and stir well. Cook the *frittata* until set on the bottom, then sprinkle with a little more Parmesan and place under a hot grill until golden brown. Cut into wedges and serve hot or cold.

Tartufi (truffles)

Truffles grow 8 in underground, usually near oak trees. They are in season from October to late December. Their irregular, knobby, round shape conceals a pungent, earthy and delicious aroma and flavor. There are two main varieties, black and white. The more highly prized black truffles (*tuber melanosporum*) grow mostly in the Périgord region of France, but they are also found in northern Italy, in Tuscany and Piedmont. The more common Piedmont truffle is the white variety (*tuber magnatum*), which has a more delicate flavor.

No one has yet succeeded in cultivating truffles commercially, so they remain rare and expensive. They are sniffed out by trained pigs or dogs, who can detect their subterranean scent. In order to develop their full aroma and flavor, the truffles must be left to mature, so truffle-hunters often cover up those that the animals have unearthed (praying that nobody else will find their buried treasure) until they reach full maturity.

History

Truffles have been eaten since ancient times. They were a favorite dish of the ancient Egyptians. The Greeks and Romans believed them to have aphrodisiac properties, but in the Middle Ages they were thought to be manifestations of the devil. Louis XIV of France, however, subscribed to the earlier theory, and from his reign on truffles were enthusiastically consumed by all those rich enough to afford this luxury food.

Culinary Uses

Truffles can be eaten raw or cooked. White Piedmont truffles are usually served raw, shaved very thinly over fresh pasta, a *fonduta* or eggs. They can be heated briefly in butter and seasoned with salt, white pepper and nutmeg. Black or white truffles are delicious with all poultry and white meat. A few slivers of truffle will add a touch of luxury to almost any savory sauce. A classic rich Italian dish using truffles is *vincisgrassi*, sheets of fresh pasta layered with butter, cream, slivers of truffle, ham and chicken livers. It is a speciality of the Marches and the Abruzzi.

Buying and Storing

If you are lucky enough to find a fresh truffle, use it as soon as possible, as the flavor is volatile. Brush off the earth from the skin and peel the truffle (keep the peelings to use in a sauce). To give whole fresh eggs the most wonderful flavor, put them in a bowl with the truffle, cover and let sit overnight; they will absorb the superb musty aroma.

You are more likely to buy canned or bottled truffles than fresh. Whole ones are extremely expensive, but cheaper pieces and even peelings are available. The most economical way to enjoy the flavor of truffles is to buy Italian oil scented with white truffles. A drop or two of this added to a dish will transform it into something really special.

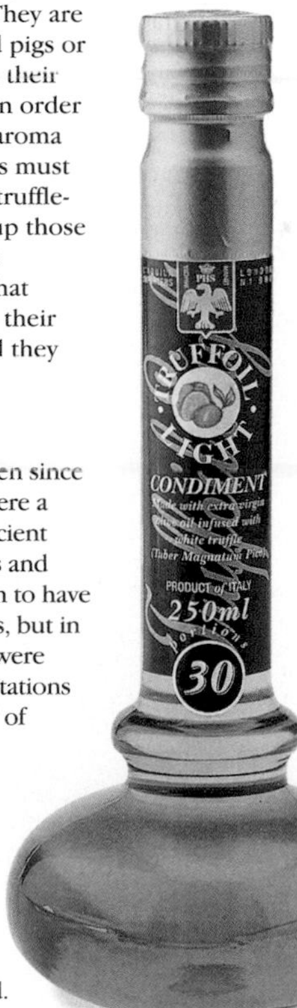

Truffle oil
The most economical way to enjoy the flavor of truffles—a drop or two of this scented oil will enhance sauces, pastas and salads

Fruits & Nuts

Italians prefer to buy only those fruits and nuts that are in season, and who can blame them? Italy produces an abundance of berries, pitted fruits and citrus fruits, all bursting with flavor and often available fresh from the tree. There are apples and pears from the orchards of the northern regions; nuts, peaches, plums and figs from the central plains; while the south and Sicily produce almost every kind of fruit—grapes, cherries, oranges and lemons—as well as pistachios and almonds. Many of these fruits are indigenous to Italy and have been grown there since time immemorial.

After a full meal of *antipasto*, pasta and a *secondo* (main course), it is hardly surprising that Italian desserts very often consist of nothing but a bowl of seasonal fresh fruit served on its own or made into a refreshing *macedonia* (fruit salad). Berries form the basis of ice creams, sorbets, *granite* and *frullati* (fresh fruit milkshakes), while nuts and winter fruits (often dried or candied) are baked into tarts and pastries.

Amarena (Morello cherry)

Although Italy does produce sweet dessert cherries, it is best known for the bitter Morello variety, which are preserved in syrup or brandy, or made into ice cream and Maraschino liqueur. These cherries are small, with dark red skins and firm flesh. They are in season from late June to early July, and can be eaten raw, although they have quite a sharp flavor.

Culinary Uses

Morello cherries can be poached in sugar syrup and served whole, or puréed and made into a rich, dark, cherry syrup. Pit the cherries and purée them. Strain the cherries through a fine sieve and let the juice sit at room temperature for about 24 hours. Strain through muslin and add 1 lb, 10 oz sugar per generous 2 cups cherry juice. Heat gently. When the sugar has dissolved, bring the cherry syrup to a boil, strain again and pour into airtight bottles or containers. These cherries also make excellent jam. A popular Venetian dish is Morello cherries poached in a red wine syrup flavored with cinnamon. Bottled cherries in vinegar can be used in sauces for meat, duck and game.

Buying and Storing

Choose fresh cherries with unwrinkled and unblemished skins, which look shiny and feel firm. Stored in a plastic bag, they will keep in the refrigerator for up to a week.

Morello cherries
These dark red cherries are usually preserved in syrup and used for desserts. Those bottled in vinegar can be used for savory recipes

Arancia (orange)

Many varieties of oranges are grown in Sicily and southern Italy. The best-known Sicilian oranges are the small blood oranges with their bright ruby-red flesh. Other types of sweet oranges include seedless navels, which take their name from the umbilical-like end which contains an embryonic orange, and seeded late oranges, which have paler flesh and are available throughout the winter. Bitter oranges (*arance amare*) are also grown; these rough-skinned varieties are made into preserves (although rarely marmalade in Italy), candied peel and *liquore all'arancia* (orange liqueur).

History

Oranges originated in China, but bitter oranges may possibly have been known in Ancient Greece; the mythical "golden apples of the Hesperides" are said by some to have been Seville oranges, although this seems historically far-fetched. They were certainly brought to Italy by Arab traders during the Roman Empire and over the centuries became a symbol of wealth and opulence—so much so that the Medici family incorporated them into their coat of arms as five golden balls. Sweet oranges did not arrive in Italy until the seventeenth century.

Oranges
Sweet varieties are used for both sweet and savory recipes—they are a favorite addition to salads

Bitter oranges
This rough-skinned variety can be used to add zest to savory dishes—it combines well with white fish, liver, duck and game—and is used for preserves

CULINARY USES

A favorite Sicilian recipe is *insalata di arance alla siciliana*, a salad of thinly sliced oranges and red onion rings dressed with black olives and their oil. Oranges also combine well with raw fennel and chicory. They can be sliced and served *alla veneziana*, coated with caramel, or simply macerated in a little lemon juice with a sliver of lemon peel for a refreshing dessert. They can be squeezed for juice, or made into sorbet and *granita*. Bitter oranges combine well with white fish, calf's liver, duck or game, and add zest to a tomato sauce.

BUYING AND STORING

Oranges are available all year round, but are at their best in winter. They should have unblemished shiny skins and feel heavy for their size (this indicates that they contain plenty of juice and that the flesh is not dry). If you intend to candy the peel or incorporate it into a recipe, choose unwaxed oranges. Oranges will keep at room temperature for a week and for at least two weeks in the refrigerator. Bring them back to room temperature or warm them slightly before eating them.

Preparing Fresh Oranges

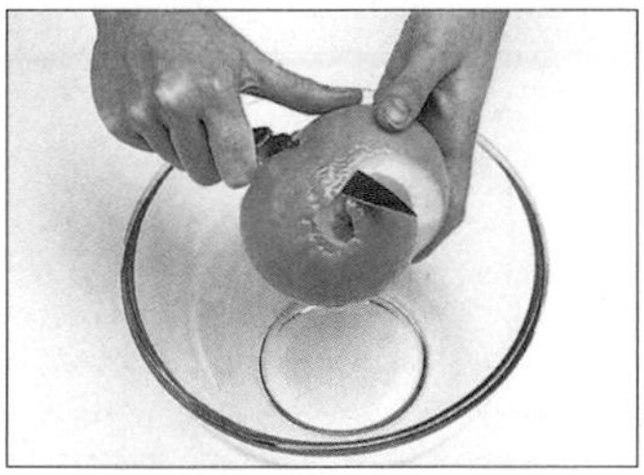

1 When peeling an orange it is important to remove all the bitter white pith and membrane. Hold the orange over a bowl to catch the juice and use a very sharp knife to cut off the peel, pith and the membrane enclosing the flesh.

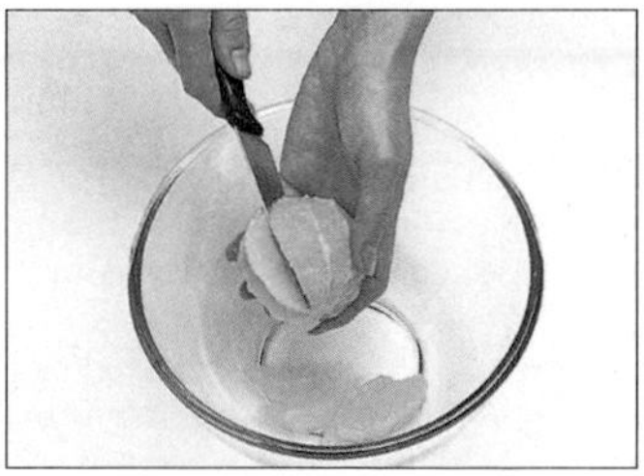

2 To segment the orange, cut down between the membranes of the segments and ease out the flesh. Squeeze the membranes into the bowl to extract the juice.

3 To remove strips of orange rind, run a paring knife down the orange, or use a zester for finer shreds. If you cannot find unwaxed fruit, wash the oranges in warm water, rinse and dry well before removing strips of rind.

Fruit

Fico (fig)

Figs are grown all over Italy, but thanks to the hot climate Sicilian figs are perhaps the most luscious of all. During the summer months you will often find Italian farmers at the roadside selling containers of ripe figs from their own trees. There are two types of Italian figs, green and purple. Both have thin, tender skins and very sweet, succulent, red flesh, and are rich in Vitamins A, B and C. They are in season from July to October and are best eaten straight off the tree when they are perfectly ripe.

Purple figs
The sweet succulent flesh of this variety makes a perfect partner to nuts of all kinds

History

Figs were said to grow in the Garden of Eden, where Adam and Eve used the leaves to cover their nakedness. In fact they probably originated in Asia Minor, although the oldest fig tree in the world is reputed to be growing in a garden in Palermo in Sicily. The Greeks and Romans certainly enjoyed figs, which are still as highly prized today.

Green figs
Delicious served raw with prosciutto or salami as an antipasto

Culinary Uses

Fresh figs are delicious served on their own, but they have an affinity with nuts such as walnuts, pistachios and almonds. They can be served raw with prosciutto or salami as an *antipasto*, or stuffed with raspberry coulis or mascarpone as a dessert. Poached in a little water or wine flavored with cinnamon or nutmeg, they make an excellent accompaniment to duck, game or lamb.

Buying and Storing

Ripe figs are extremely delicate and do not travel well, so it is hard to find imported fruit at a perfect stage of maturity. In season in Italy, however, you can find local figs that are just ripe for eating; they should be soft and yielding, but not squashy. Sometimes the skin may have split, revealing the luscious red or pink flesh. As long as you are going to eat the fig immediately, this does not matter. Take great care not to squash the figs on your way home, or you will end up with a squishy, inedible mess.

Under-ripe figs can be kept at room temperature for a day or two until the skin softens, but they will never develop the fine flavor of tree-ripened figs. Ripe figs should be eaten on the day they are bought.

Preparing and Cooking Figs

Wash the figs briefly and gently pat dry. Discard the stalk and peel the figs, if desired.

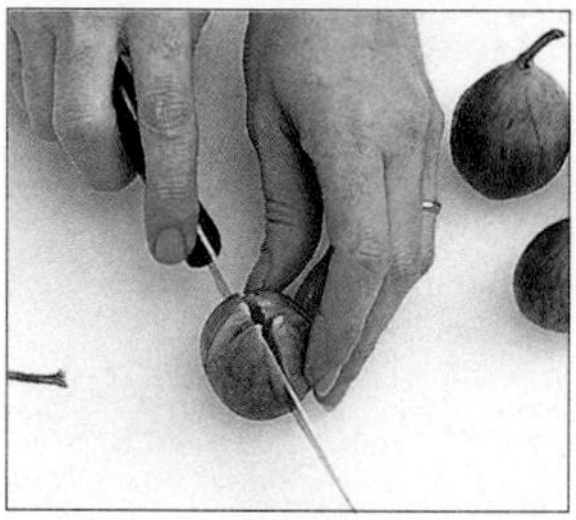

To serve as an antipasto *or dessert, cut them downward from the stalk end into quarters, leaving them attached at the base. Open them out like flowers.*

Perfectly ripe figs are best eaten raw, but less perfect specimens can be improved by cooking. They can be gently poached in syrup or red wine flavored with a cinnamon stick or vanilla pod, or rolled in sugar and baked in the oven until caramelized. Barely ripe figs also make excellent jam.

Limone (lemon)

Lemons are grown all over Italy, even in the northern regions. Lake Garda even boasts a town called Limone, named for its abundance of lemon trees. But the most famous Italian lemons come from the Amalfi coast, where they grow to an extraordinary size and have such a sweet flavor that they can almost be eaten as a dessert fruit. Their aromatic flavor enhances almost any dish, and they have the added advantage of being rich in Vitamin C.

History

Lemons originated in India or Malaysia and were brought by the Assyrians to Greece, which in turn took them to Italy. The Greeks and Romans greatly appreciated their culinary and medicinal qualities. Later seafarers ate them in large quantities to protect against scurvy, and society ladies used them as a beauty treatment to whiten their skin, bleach their hair and redden their lips.

Culinary Uses

Lemons are extraordinarily versatile. The juice can be squeezed to make a refreshing *spremuta di limone*, or it can be added to other cold drinks or tea. It is an antioxidant, which prevents discoloration when applied to other fruits and vegetables. The juice is used for dressings and for flavoring all sorts of drinks and sauces. A squeeze of lemon juice adds a different dimension to intrinsically bland foods, such as fish, poultry, veal or certain vegetables. Its acidity also helps to bring out the flavor of other fruits. The zest makes a wonderfully aromatic flavoring for cakes and pastries, and is an essential ingredient of *gremolata*, a topping of grated zest, garlic and parsley for *osso buco*. Quartered lemons are always served with *fritto misto di mare* (mixed fried fish) and other foods fried in batter.

Preparing Lemons

Before squeezing a lemon, warm it gently: Either put it in a bowl, pour boiling water over the top and let stand for about 5 minutes or, if you prefer, microwave the lemon on full power for about 30 seconds—this will significantly increase the quantity of juice you will obtain.

For sweet dishes, when you want to add the flavor of lemons, but not the grated rind, rub a sugar lump over the skin of the lemon to absorb the oil, then use the sugar as part of the recipe.

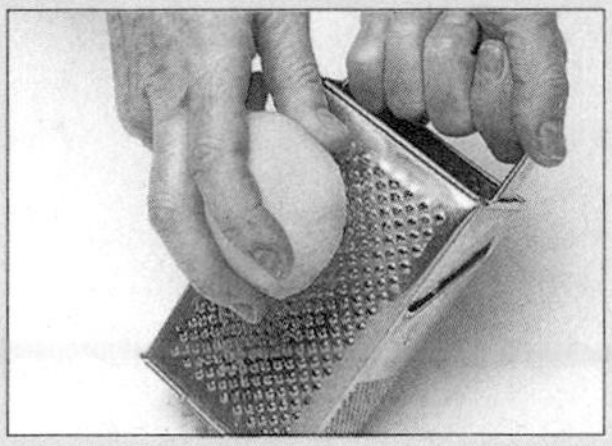

To prepare grated lemon rind, thoroughly wash and dry unwaxed lemons. Grate the rind or peel it off with a zester, taking care not to include any white pith.

Buying and Storing

Depending on the variety, lemons may have thick indented skin, or be perfectly smooth. Their appearance does not affect the flavor, but they should feel heavy for their size. If you intend to use the zest, buy unwaxed lemons. Lemons will keep in the refrigerator for up to two weeks.

Lemons
Lemons are grown all over Italy—their aromatic flavor enhances almost any dish

Fruits

Melone (melon)

Many different varieties of sweet, aromatic melons are grown in Italy, and each has its own regional name. *Napoletano* melons have a smooth pale green rind and delicately scented orange flesh. *Cantalupo* (cantaloupe) melons have a warty skin, which is conveniently marked into segments, and highly scented deep yellow flesh. A similar Tuscan melon with gray-green rind and orange flesh is called *popone*. These melons are all perfect for eating with Prosciutto or salami as an *antipasto*.

Watermelons (*anguria* or *cocomero*) are grown in Tuscany. These huge green melons with their refreshing bright pink or red flesh and edible brown seeds can be round or sausage-shaped. In Florence, the feast of San Lorenzo, the patron saint of cooks, is celebrated with an orgy of watermelons on August 10th. During this season, roadside stalls groan under the weight of hundreds of these gigantic fruits.

Culinary Uses

Italians eat melon as an appetizer, usually accompanied by wafer-thin *prosciutto crudo* or cured meats. Melons and watermelons are occasionally served as a dessert fruit on their own, but more often appear in a *macedonia* (fruit salad).

Buying and Storing

The best way to tell whether a melon is ripe is to smell it; it should have a mild, sweet scent. If it smells highly perfumed and musky, it will be over-ripe. The fruit should feel heavy for its size and the skin should not be bruised or damaged. Gently press the rind with your thumbs at the stalk end; it should give a little. Melons will ripen quickly at room temperature and should be eaten within two or three days. Wrap cut melon tightly in plastic wrap before storing in the refrigerator, or its scent may permeate other foods.

Preparing Melon

For serving as an antipasto, *cut the melon into wedges, scoop out the seeds and run a flexible knife between the rind and flesh. Remove the rind before serving.*

Napoletano melon
The sweet scented flesh of this and the similar cantaloupe melon is perfect for eating with prosciutto as an antipasto

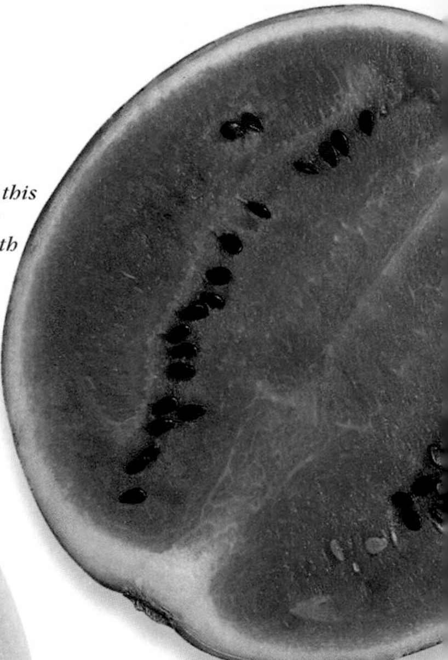

Pesche (peaches) and pesche noci (nectarines)

Peaches, with their velvety skin and sweet, juicy flesh, are a summer fruit grown in central and southern Italy. The most common variety is the *pesca gialla* (yellow peach), which has succulent, yellow flesh. More highly prized are the *pesche bianche* (white peaches), whose pink-tinted flesh is full of juice and flavor.

Nectarines have smooth plum-like skins and taste very similar to peaches. They also come in yellow and white varieties and, like peaches, the white nectarines have a finer flavor. Some people prefer nectarines as a dessert fruit because they do not require peeling. Peaches and nectarines are interchangeable in cooked dishes.

Culinary Uses

Peaches and nectarines are delicious served as a dessert fruit, but can also be macerated in fortified wine or spirits or poached in white wine and syrup. They have a particular affinity with almonds; a favorite Italian dessert is *pesche ripiene alla piemontese*, halved peaches stuffed with crumbled almond-flavored amaretti cookies and baked in white wine. They are also delicious served with raspberries, or made into fruit drinks (the famous Bellini cocktail is made with fresh peach juice) and ice creams and sorbets.

Buying and Storing

Peaches are in season from June to September. Make sure they are ripe, but not too soft, with unwrinkled and unblemished skins. They should have a sweet, intense scent. Peaches and nectarines bruise very easily, so try to buy those that have been kept in compartmented trays rather than piled into crates.

Do not keep peaches and nectarines for more than a day or two. If they are very ripe, store them in the refrigerator; underripe fruit will ripen in a couple of days if kept in a brown paper bag at room temperature.

Preparing Peaches

To peel peaches, place them in a heatproof bowl and pour boiling water over them. Let sit for 15–30 seconds (depending on how ripe they are), then refresh in very cold water; the skins will slip off easily.

Peaches
This summer fruit is grown in central and southern Italy

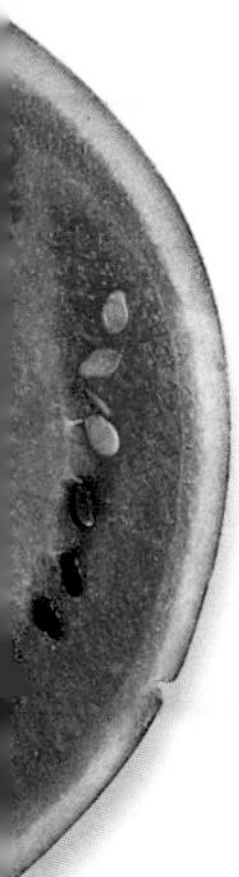

Watermelon
Occasionally served on its own in wedges as a dessert, this vibrant red fruit is more usually chopped and added to a fruit salad

Nectarines
These smooth-skinned fruits are delicious served as a dessert fruit

Fruits

Uva (grapes)

Italy is the world's largest producer of grapes of all kinds. Almost every rural property boasts an expanse of vineyards, some producing wine-making grapes intended only for home consumption. Others (particularly in Chianti and the south) are destined for the enormous Italian wine-making industry. But Apulia, Abruzzo and Sicily produce sweet dessert grapes on a vast commercial scale, from large luscious Italia, with their fine muscat flavor, to Cardinal, named for its deep red color, purple Alphonse Lavallé, and various small seedless varieties.

Despite their high caloric value, grapes are extremely good for you, since they are rich in potassium, iron and vitamins.

History

Wild grapes grew in the Caucasus as early as the Stone Age, and early man soon discovered the secret of cultivating vineyards and making wine. The Greeks and Romans discovered that drying grapes transformed them into sweet raisins. The Gauls invented the wooden wine cask, and from that time on wine production became a major industry.

Culinary Uses

Dessert grapes are best eaten on their own or as an accompaniment to cheese, but they can be used in pastries or as a garnish for cooked quails, guinea fowl or other poultry. The seeds are pressed into grapeseed oil, which has a neutral taste and is high in polyunsaturated fatty acids.

Buying and Storing

Choosing white, black or red grapes is a matter of preference; beneath the skin, the flesh is always pale green and juicy. Buy bunches of grapes with fruit which is of equal size and not too densely packed on the stalk. Check that none is withered or rotten. The skin should have a delicate bloom and be firm to the touch. Try to eat one grape from a bunch to see how they taste. The flesh should be firm and very juicy and refreshing.

Grapes should be washed immediately after purchase, then placed in a bowl and kept in the refrigerator for up to three days. Keeping them in a plastic bag causes them to become overripe very quickly.

Preparing Grapes

Grapes used for cooking should be peeled and deseeded. Put them in a bowl, pour in boiling water and let sit for 10–20 seconds, depending on the ripeness of the grapes. Peel off the skin. To remove the seeds, halve the grapes and scoop out the seeds with the tip of a pointed knife.

Italia grapes
These luscious red and white grapes have a wonderful Muscat flavor

Nuts

Many different kinds of nuts are grown in Italy—chestnuts and hazelnuts in the north, pine nuts in the coastal regions, and almonds, pistachios and walnuts in the south. They are used in a wide variety of savory dishes, cakes and pastries, or served as a dessert with a glass of *vin santo* (sweet white wine).

Castagne (chestnuts)

These are a mainstay of Tuscan and Sardinian cooking, dating back to the days when the peasants could not afford wheat to make flour, so they ground up the chestnuts that grow in abundance throughout the region instead. Most varieties of sweet chestnut contain two or three separate nuts inside the spiky green husk, but commercially grown varieties contain a single, large nut, which is easier to peel and better for serving whole.

Chestnuts
A mainstay of Tuscan and Sardinian cooking

Chestnuts have shiny, rich reddish-brown shells with a wrinkled, thin skin beneath, which can be very hard to remove. They cannot be eaten raw, but once cooked, the starchy nuts are highly nutritious and very sustaining.

Culinary Uses

Chestnuts roasted over an open fire conjure up the spirit of autumn. Peeled chestnuts can be boiled, poached in red wine or milk or fried in butter as a garnish. They make hearty soups, or can be puréed into sauces for game. In Piedmont, they are candied to make *marrons glacés*, and a favorite Italian dessert is *monte bianco*, a rich concoction of puréed chestnuts and cream.

Chestnut flour is still widely used in Tuscany and Liguria, where it is baked into cakes and pastries, such as *castagnaccio*, a confection with pine nuts and herbs.

Buying and Storing

The nicest chestnuts are those you gather yourself, but if you are buying them, look for large, shiny specimens, with no tiny holes in the shells. The chestnuts should feel heavy for their size and not rattle when you shake them. They will keep in a cool place for at least two weeks. If any holes appear in the shells, discard the nut immediately, or you will very soon have an infestation of maggots.

Mandorle (almonds)

Two varieties of almonds are grown in central and southern Italy. *Mandorle dolci* (sweet almonds) are eaten as a dessert or used in cooking and baking, while *mandorle amare* (bitter almonds) are used to flavor liqueurs such as amaretto or bittersweet confections such as amaretti cookies. These almonds are not edible in their raw state; in fact, they are poisonous if consumed in large quantities. Both types of almonds have a velvety pale green outer casing; the hard light brown shell within encloses one or two oval nuts.

Culinary Uses

Early in the season (late May), sweet almonds can be eaten raw as a dessert. They have a delicious fresh flavor and the brown skin is still soft enough to be palatable. Later, dried sweet almonds are blanched, slivered or ground to be used for cakes, pastries and all sorts of confectionery, including *marzapane* (marzipan) and *croccante* (almond brittle). They can be devilled or salted as an appetizing snack with an *aperitivo*. Toasted almonds are the classic garnish for trout, and go well with chicken or rabbit. Dried bitter almonds are used in small quantities to add a more intense flavor to cookies and cakes.

Preparing Chestnuts

There are three possible ways to peel chestnuts.

Slit the domed side of the shells with a very sharp knife, then drop them into boiling water for 5 minutes, or put them in a roasting pan with a little hot water and cook in a very hot oven for about 10 minutes. Shell and skin the chestnuts as soon as they are cool enough to handle. Alternatively, shell the raw chestnuts and boil them in their skins for about 20 minutes, then peel off the skins.

Almonds
In Italy in late spring, fresh almonds are eaten raw as a dessert

Nuts

BUYING AND STORING
Fresh almonds in the shell are available from late May to late June. They are difficult to crack, so you may prefer to buy shelled nuts. They should look plump, and the skins should not feel too dry. Pre-blanched almonds can often be a disappointment; buy the nuts with their skins on and blanch them yourself. Store shelled almonds in an airtight container for no longer than a month.

Shelled almonds
These dried almonds are used for cakes, pastries and candies

Nocciole (hazelnuts)

Fresh hazelnuts are harvested in August and September and during these months are always sold in their frilled green husks. The small round nuts have a very sweet flavor and a milky texture when fresh. In Italy, they are generally dried and used in candy and cakes.

CULINARY USES
Hazelnuts are used in all sorts of confectionery, including *torrone* (a sort of nougat) and *gianduiotti*, a delicious fondant chocolate from Piedmont. The famous chocolate *baci* ("kisses") from Perugia contain a whole hazelnut in the center. Hazelnuts are finely ground to make cakes and cookies, and are excellent in stuffings for poultry and game.

BUYING AND STORING
If hazelnuts are sold in their fresh green husks, you can be sure they are fresh and juicy. Otherwise, look for shiny unblemished shells that are not too thick; cracked shells will cause the nut to shrivel and dry out. Shelled hazelnuts should be kept in an airtight container for no longer than one month.

Shelled hazelnuts
These dried nuts are used for candies and cakes

Hazelnuts
When fresh, these small nuts have a very sweet flavor

Noci (walnuts)

Walnuts grow in abundance throughout central and southern Italy. The kernels, shaped like the two halves of a brain, grow inside a pale brown, heavily indented shell enclosed by a smooth green fleshy husk or "shuck." Fresh walnuts have a delicious milky sweetness and a soft texture, which hardens as the nuts mature. Walnuts do not need to be skinned before eating.

Walnuts
In Italy, fresh walnuts are very often eaten straight from the shell as a dessert.

PREPARING ALMONDS

To blanch almonds, place them in a strainer and plunge into boiling water for a few seconds. As soon as the skin begins to loosen, transfer the almonds to a bowl of cold water and slip off the skins. Dry thoroughly before storing.

Culinary Uses

Fresh walnuts are usually eaten straight from the shell as a dessert. They can be ground or chopped and used in cakes and desserts, or halved and used for decoration. They are used to make savory sauces for pasta, such as *salsa di noci*, a rich combination of ground walnuts, butter and cream. Walnut oil has a distinctive flavor and, used sparingly, makes an excellent salad dressing. Unripe walnuts can be pickled, and they are used to make sweet, sticky liqueurs.

Buying and Storing

Fresh "wet" walnuts are available from late September to late October. They should be kept in a wicker basket and eaten within a week. Dried walnuts should not have cracked or broken shells. They will keep for at least two months. Never store walnuts in the refrigerator, as the oil they contain will harden and ruin the flavor. Dried walnut kernels will have the flavor and texture of fresh nuts if they are soaked in milk for at least 4 hours.

Pinoli (pine nuts)

Pine nuts (more accurately known as pine kernels) are actually the seeds from the stone pine trees that grow in profusion along the Adriatic and Mediterranean coasts of Italy. The small, oblong, cream-colored seeds grow inside a hard husk and are extracted from between the scales of the pine cones. The soft-textured kernels, which have an oily, slightly resinous flavor, are always sold de-husked. They can be eaten raw, but are usually toasted before use to bring out the flavor.

Culinary Uses

Pine nuts are used in many Italian dishes, both sweet and savory, but they are best known as an essential ingredient of pesto. They go well with meat and game, and make exceptionally delicious cookies and tarts.

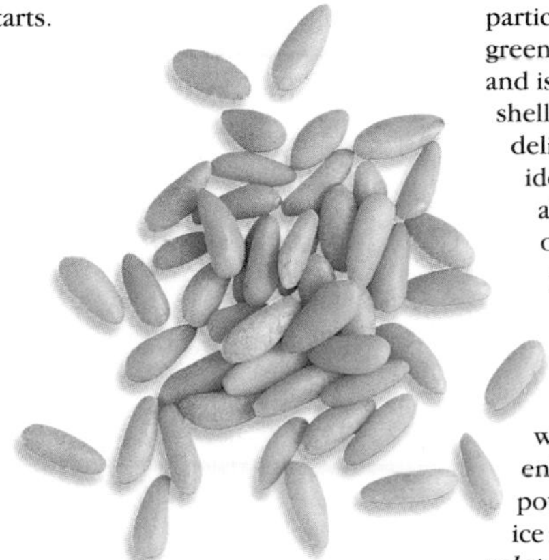

Pine nuts
The oily, slightly resinous flavor is accentuated by toasting

Pistachio nuts
Grown in southern Italy, these sweet, delicately flavored nuts are used in mortadella

Preparing Pine Nuts

For most recipes and when used as a garnish, they should be lightly toasted. Heat a dry, heavy frying pan, put in the pine nuts and toss quickly until they turn pale golden. Do not let them brown, or they will taste unpleasant.

Buying and Storing

Pine nuts are always sold out of the husk. Because they are very oily, they go rancid quite quickly, so buy only as much as you need at any one time. Store them in an airtight container in the fridge for not more than a week.

Pistacchi (pistachios)

Pistachios are native to the Near East, but are grown in southern Italy, particularly Sicily. The small, bright green nut has a yellowish-red skin and is enclosed in a smooth, pale shell. Pistachios have a sweet, delicate flavor, which makes them ideal for desserts, but they are also used to stud mortadella and other pale cooked meat products.

Culinary Uses

Pistachios can be eaten raw or roasted and salted as a snack with an *aperitivo*. Their color enhances most white meats and poultry. They make deliciously rich ice cream and are used in *cassata gelata*, the famous Sicilian dessert.

Buying and Storing

If possible, buy pistachios still in their shells. These will be easier to open if they are already slightly ajar; once open, the nut is very easy to remove. Shelled, blanched pistachios are also available. They are useful for cooking, but lack the fine flavor of whole nuts. Store blanched pistachios in an airtight container for up to two weeks. Whole nuts will keep for well over a month.

Herbs & Seasonings

Herbs are vital to Italian cooking. Their aromatic flavor adds depth and interest to what is essentially plain cooking, based on fine, fresh ingredients. It is impossible to imagine roast chicken or veal without rosemary or sage, or tomatoes or pesto without basil. Many wild herbs grow in the Italian countryside, and these are often incorporated into Italian recipes. One of the most popular is mentuccia, *a wild mint with tiny leaves and the delicate favor of marjoram. If a recipe specifies* mentuccia *or its close relative* nepitella, *substitute a smaller quantity of mint.*

Basil
More than any other, this pungent, intensely flavored herb is associated with Italian cooking—it is an essential ingredient in many dishes, including pesto

Always use fresh herbs whenever you can; the dried varieties have a stronger and often quite different taste, and lack the subtlety of fresh herbs. If you must use dried herbs, try to buy them freeze-dried; these taste much closer to the real thing. As a general rule, you will need only about one-third as much dried herb as fresh—in other words, allow about 1 tsp dried herbs for every 1 tbsp fresh.

Basilico (basil)

Basil, with its intense aroma and fresh, pungently sweet flavor, is associated with Italian cooking more than any other herb. It is an essential ingredient of pesto, but it also finds its way into soups, salads and almost all dishes based on tomatoes, with which it has an extraordinary affinity. There are over 50 varieties of this annual herb, but the one most commonly used in Italy is sweet basil, with its fresh broad green leaves and wonderfully spicy aroma.

Culinary Uses

Basil has a volatile flavor, so it is best added to dishes at the end of cooking. It can be used in any dish that contains tomatoes and is delicious sprinkled on a pizza. It adds a pungent, sweet note to almost all salads and is particularly good with white fish and seafood. It makes an excellent flavoring for omelets and is often added to minestrone. The most famous of all basil dishes is pesto, the fragrant Genovese sauce made by pounding together fresh basil, garlic, Parmesan, pine nuts and olive oil.

Buying and Storing

In sunny climates, such as southern Italy, basil grows outdoors all through the summer. In other places it is available cut or growing in pots all year round, so there really is no reason to use dried basil. Look for sweet basil with bright green leaves—the larger the better. If you have grown your own and have a glut, you can freeze basil leaves to preserve the flavor, but they lose their fresh texture and darken in color. Alternatively, put a bunch of basil in a jar and fill up with olive oil for a fragrant flavored oil for dressings. To store fresh cut basil, wrap it in damp paper towels and keep in the vegetable compartment of the refrigerator for up to two days.

Preparing Basil

Basil leaves are tender and bruise easily, so never chop them with a knife, but tear them lightly with your fingers immediately before using.

Pesto

To make enough pesto for 4–6 servings of pasta, put 2 cups basil leaves in a mortar with ½ cup pine nuts, 2 fat peeled garlic cloves and a large pinch of coarse salt, and crush to a paste with a pestle. Work in ½ cup freshly grated Parmesan. Gradually add about ½ cup extra virgin olive oil, working it in thoroughly with a wooden spoon to make a thick, creamy sauce. Put the pesto in a screwtop jar; it will keep for several weeks in the refrigerator.

Maggiorana (sweet marjoram) **and origano** *(oregano)*

These two highly aromatic herbs are closely related (oregano is the wild variety), but marjoram has a much milder flavor. Marjoram is more commonly used in northern Italy, while oregano is widely used in the south to flavor tomato dishes, vegetables and pizzas. Drying greatly intensifies the flavor of both herbs, so they should be used very sparingly.

Culinary Uses

In northern Italy, sweet marjoram is used to flavor meat, poultry, vegetables and soups; the flavor goes particularly well with carrots and cucumber. Despite its rather pungent aroma, marjoram has a delicate flavor, so it should be added to long-cooked foods toward the end of cooking.

Oregano is used exclusively in southern Italian cooking, especially in tomato-based dishes. It is a classic flavoring for pizza, but should always be used in moderation.

Buying and Storing

Marjoram and oregano are in season throughout the summer, but cut fresh herbs are available all year round at supermarkets. The leaves dry out quickly, so store them in plastic bags in the refrigerator; they will keep for up to a week. Dried oregano should be stored in small airtight jars away from the light. It loses its pungent flavor after a few months, so only buy a little at a time.

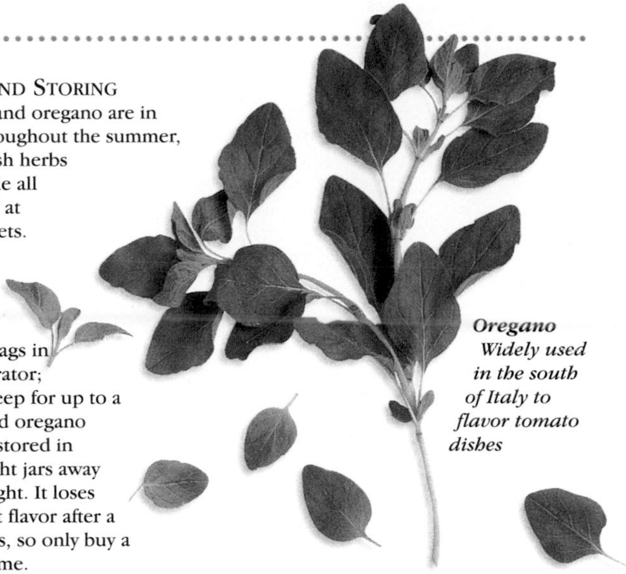

Oregano
Widely used in the south of Italy to flavor tomato dishes

Prezzemolo (parsley)

Italian parsley is the flat leaf variety, which has a more robust flavor than curly parsley. It has attractive dark green leaves, which resemble cilantro. It is used as a flavoring in innumerable cooked dishes, but rarely as a garnish. If flat leaf parsley is not available, curly parsley makes a perfectly adequate substitute. Parsley is an extremely nutritious herb, rich in iron and potassium and Vitamin C.

Marjoram
The aromatic flavor of this herb is very similar to that of oregano, but much milder

Parsley
Italian parsley is the flat leafed variety. It has a strong, robust flavor

Herbs & Seasonings

CULINARY USES
Parsley can be used to flavor innumerable savory dishes. It adds color and flavor to sauces, soups and risotto. The stalks can be used to flavor stocks and stews. Chopped parsley can be sprinkled over cooked savory dishes; whole leaves are rarely used as a garnish in Italy.

BUYING AND STORING
Parsley is available all year round, so it should never be necessary to use the dried variety. A large bunch of parsley will keep for up to a week in the fridge if washed and wrapped in damp paper towels. Chopped parsley freezes very well and can be added to cooked dishes straight from the freezer.

Rosmarino (rosemary)

Spiky evergreen rosemary bushes, with their attractive blue flowers, grow wild all over Italy. The herb has a delicious, highly aromatic flavor, which is intensifed when it is dried. The texture of rosemary leaves is quite hard and the flavor very pungent, so it is never used raw, but only in cooking. It can easily overpower a dish, so only a few leaves should be used in a dish.

CULINARY USES
Rosemary combines extremely well with roast or grilled lamb, veal and chicken. A few needles will enhance the flavor of baked fish or any tomato dish, and it adds a wonderful flavor to roast potatoes and onions. Some rosemary branches added to the charcoal on a barbecue impart a superb flavor to whatever is being cooked. Dried rosemary can always be substituted for fresh; it is extremely pungent, so should be used very sparingly.

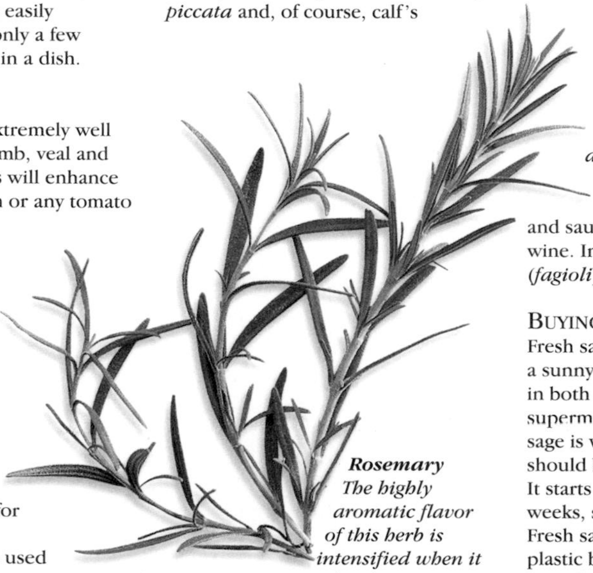

Rosemary *The highly aromatic flavor of this herb is intensified when it is dried*

Salvia (sage)

Wild sage grows in profusion in the Italian countryside. There are several varieties, including the common garden sage, with furry silvery-gray leaves and spiky purple flowers, and clary sage, with hairy curly leaves, which is used to make dry vermouth. All sages have a slightly bitter aromatic flavor, which contrasts well with fatty meats such as pork. In northern Italy, particularly Tuscany, it is used to flavor veal and chicken. It is an excellent medicinal herb (the Latin name means "good health"); an infusion of sage leaves makes a good gargle for a sore throat.

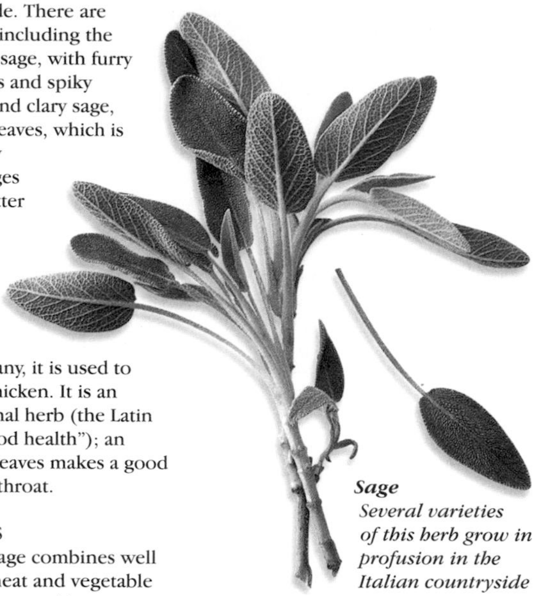

Sage *Several varieties of this herb grow in profusion in the Italian countryside*

CULINARY USES
Used sparingly, sage combines well with almost all meat and vegetable dishes and is often used in minestrone. It has a particular affinity with veal (such as *osso buco*, *piccata* and, of course, calf's liver) and is an essential ingredient of *saltimbocca alla romana*, veal scallops and *prosciutto crudo* topped with sage leaves and sautéed in butter and white wine. In Tuscany, white beans (*fagioli*) are often flavored with sage.

BUYING AND STORING
Fresh sage is very easy to grow on a sunny windowsill. It is available in both fresh and dried forms at supermarkets all year round. Dried sage is very strongly flavored, so should be used in tiny quantities. It starts to taste musty after a few weeks, so replace it fairly frequently. Fresh sage should be stored in a plastic bag in the refrigerator; it will keep for up to a week.

Aceto (vinegar)

Like all wine-making countries, Italy produces excellent red and white wine vinegar as a byproduct. The best vinegar is made from good wines, which are fermented in oak casks to give a depth of flavor. Good vinegar should be clean-tasting and aromatic, with no trace of bitterness, and it should be transparent, not cloudy. White wine vinegar is pale golden with a pinkish tinge; red wine vinegar ranges from deep pink to dark red.

Aceto balsamico (balsamic vinegar)

Balsamic vinegar is the king of vinegars. Its name means "balm-like," reflecting its digestive qualities. Indeed, the best has a flavor so mellow and sweet that it can be drunk on its own as a *digestivo*. Balsamic vinegar is made in the area around Modena; the boiled and concentrated juice of local *trebbiano* grapes is aged in a series of barrels of decreasing size and different woods over a long period—sometimes as long as 50 years—which gives it a slightly syrupy texture and a rich, deep mahogany color. Like Parmigiano Reggiano and prosciutto, genuine balsamic vinegar *(aceto balsamico tradizionale di Modena)* is strictly controlled by law; it must have been aged in the wood for at least 12 years. Vinegar aged 20 years or more is called *stravecchio*.

Culinary Uses

Red and white wine vinegars are principally used to make salad dressings and marinades, or to preserve vegetables *sott'aceto* for *antipasti*. They also add the requisite sharpness to sauces such as *agrodolce* (sweet-and-sour). Good balsamic vinegar is also used as a dressing, sometimes on its own. It can be used to finish a delicate sauce for white fish, poultry or calf's liver. A few drops sprinkled over ripe strawberries will enhance their flavor.

Buying and Storing

Price is usually an indication of quality where vinegar is concerned, so always buy the best you can afford. Genuine balsamic vinegar must be labeled *aceto balsamico tradizionale di Modena*; products that purport to be the real thing but are not labeled as such have either not been aged for long enough or, worse, are just red wine vinegar colored and flavored with caramel. Proper balsamic vinegar is expensive, but the flavor is so concentrated that a little goes a long way, and it is worth paying more for the genuine article. Vinegar will keep in a cool dark place for many months.

Balsamic vinegar
This is the king of vinegars and has a wonderfully sweet and mellow flavor

Red and white wine vinegars
These vinegars have a sharp flavor and are used primarily for salad dressings

Herbs & Seasonings

Aglio (garlic)

Garlic is not, as you might suppose, a type of onion, but is a member of the lily family. The bulb or "head" is a collection of cloves held together by a papery white or purplish skin. When crushed or chopped it releases a pungent, slightly acrid oil with a very distinctive flavor and smell. Freshly picked garlic is milder than older, dried garlic, and the large, mauve-tinged variety has a more delicate flavor than the smaller white variety.

Garlic finds its way into many Italian dishes, but it is generally used with discretion so as not to flavor the food too aggressively. It is indispensable to certain dishes such as *bagna cauda* (hot anchovy and garlic dip), *spaghetti all'aglio e olio* (garlic and olive oil) and pesto. In the south, garlic is used to flavor tomato sauces and fish soups.

Culinary Uses

Used in small quantities, garlic enlivens almost any sauce, soup or stew. It can be roasted with lamb and potatoes, or baked in its skin for a mellower flavor. Blanched, crushed garlic will aromatize olive oil to make an excellent dressing for salads or to use in cooking where only a hint of garlic flavor is required. Raw, skinned garlic cloves can be rubbed over toasted croutons to make flavorful *bruschetta* bases.

Buying and Storing

Garlic sold loose by the head is usually fresher and better than pre-packaged varieties. The heads should feel firm and the skin should not be too papery. Do not buy garlic that is sprouting green shoots; the cloves will be soft and of no culinary value.

Stored in a cool dry place, garlic will keep for many months. If possible, hang the heads in bunches to keep them aerated. Once garlic has become soft or withered, it is useless, so throw it away.

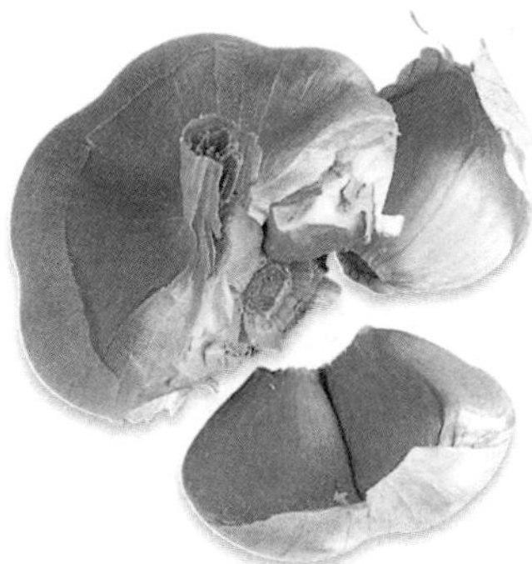

Garlic
Italian cooks prefer to use garlic with discretion, but it is indispensable to many dishes. The purple-skinned variety has a more delicate flavor than the white variety

Preparing and Cooking Garlic

To peel garlic, cut off the root end with a small sharp knife and peel the skin upward.

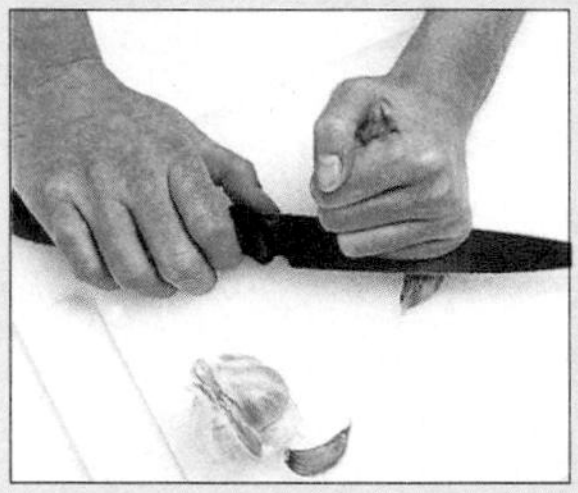

Alternatively, lay a garlic clove on the work surface, place the flat side of a heavy knife blade on top and bring the side of your fist sharply down on to the blade. This will flatten the garlic and split the skin.

To chop garlic, halve the clove and remove the bitter-tasting green shoot. Chop the garlic as finely as possible.

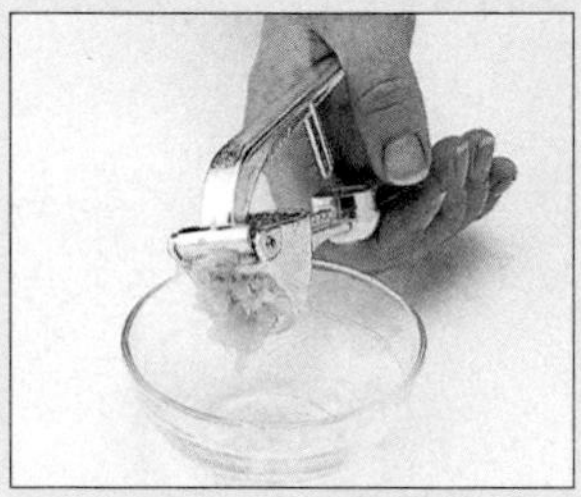

For very fine garlic, crush it in a garlic press.

Garlic should be softened gently in oil or butter; it will become very bitter if allowed to brown. For a subtle flavor, heat a whole clove of garlic in the oil, then remove it before adding the other ingredients. The flavor of garlic dissipates quite quickly during cooking, so for long-cooked dishes add it toward the end of the cooking time.

Olive (olives)

A wide variety of olives is cultivated all over Italy. Most are destined to be pressed into oil (nearly 20 percent of their weight is oil), but some are kept as table olives to be salted, pickled or marinated, and served as part of an *antipasto* or used in cooking. There are two main types of olive, green (immature) and black (mature); both are bitter and inedible in their natural state. All olives have a high caloric content and are rich in iron, potassium and vitamins.

Green olives are the unripe fruit, which are picked in October or November. They have a sharper flavor and crunchier texture than black olives, which continue to ripen on the tree and are not harvested until December. Among the best Italian table olives are the small, shiny black Gaeta olives from Liguria. Wrinkled black olives from Lazio have a strong, salty flavor, while Sardinian olives are semi-ripened and are brown or purplish in color. The largest olives come from Apulia and Sicily, where giant, green specimens are grown. These are sometimes pitted and stuffed with pimento, anchovy or almonds. Cured olives can be flavored with all sorts of aromatics, such as garlic, local herbs, orange or lemon zest and dried chilies.

Black olives
Olives are among the oldest fruits known to man. They are grown all over Italy

History

Olive trees have been grown in the Mediterranean since Biblical times, when they were brought there from the East by the Romans. Ancient civilizations venerated the olive tree; the Egyptians believed that the goddess Isis discovered the secret of extracting oil from the fruit.

Culinary Uses

Olives can be served on their own or as a garnish or topping for pizza. They are used as an ingredient in many Italian recipes, such as *caponata*. Sicilian *caponata* is a dome-shaped salad of fried eggplants with celery, onions, tomatoes, capers and green olives, while the Ligurian dish of the same name consists of stale crackers or bread soaked in olive oil and topped with a mixture of chopped olives, garlic, anchovies and oregano. Olives combine well with Mediterranean ingredients such as tomatoes, eggplants, anchovies and capers and are used in sauces for rabbit, chicken and firm-fleshed fish. Made into a paste with red wine vinegar, garlic and olive oil, they make an excellent topping for *crostini*.

Buying and Storing

Cured olives vary enormously in flavor, so ask to taste one before making your selection. Loose olives can be kept in an airtight container in the refrigerator for up to a week.

Green olives
These unripe olives have a sharper flavor than black olives

Capperi (capers)

Capers are the immature flower buds of a wild Mediterranean shrub. They are pickled in white wine vinegar or preserved in brine, which gives them a piquant, peppery flavor. Sicilian capers are packed in whole salt, which should be rinsed off before using the capers. Bottled nasturtium flower buds are sometimes sold as a cheaper alternative to true capers. Caper berries look like large, fat capers on a long stalk, but they are actually the fruit of the caper shrub. They can be served as an hors d'oeuvre or in a salad.

Caper berries
The pickled fruit of the caper shrub can be served as an hors d'oeuvre.

Herbs & Seasonings

Culinary Uses

Capers are mainly used as a condiment or garnish, but they also add zest to seafood and fish dishes, salads, pizzas and pasta sauces such as the famous Sicilian *pasta colle sarde*, a mixture of sardines, parsley, tomatoes, pine nuts and raisins.

Buying and Storing

Choosing pickled or brined capers is a matter of taste, as is whether or not you should rinse them before use. Large capers are usually cheaper than small ones; there is no difference in flavor, but small capers make a more attractive garnish. Salt-packed capers are always sold loose by the *etto* ($3\frac{1}{2}$ oz); they should be used as soon as possible. Once opened, jars of capers should be kept in the refrigerator. Make sure any capers left in the jar are covered with the preserving liquid.

Pickled capers
Rinsing these capers before use softens their sharp, piquant flavor

Olio di oliva (olive oil)

Unlike other oils, which are extracted from the seeds or dried fruits of plants, olive oil is pressed from the pulp of ripe olives, which gives it an inimitable richness and flavor. Different regions of Italy produce distinctively different olive oils; Tuscan oil (considered the best) is pungent and peppery, Ligurian oil is lighter and sweeter, while the oils from the south and Sicily are powerful and nutty.

The best olive oil is *extra vergine*, which is strictly controlled and regulated like wine. This is made simply by pressing the olives to extract the oil, with no further processing. Extra virgin olive oil must have an acidity level of less than 1 percent. The distinctive fruity flavor of this oil makes it ideal for dressings and using raw. Virgin olive oil is pressed in the same way, but has a higher acidity level and a less refined flavor. It, too, can be used as a condiment, but is also suitable for cooking. Unclassified olive oil is refined, then blended with virgin oil to add flavor. It has an undistinguished taste, but is ideal for cooking; it should not be used as a condiment.

Buying and Storing

The best olive oil comes from Lucca in Tuscany and is very expensive. It is made with slightly under-ripe olives, which give it a luminous green color. If your budget does not stretch to this, buy the best extra virgin oil you can afford to use "neat" or in dressings. Experiment with small bottles of different extra virgin oils to see which you prefer. For cooking, pure olive oil is fine. Once opened, olive oil should be kept in a cool place away from the light. The best oil will soon lose its savor, so use it within six months.

Cooking with Olive Oil

Olive oil can be heated to very high temperatures without burning or smoking, which makes it ideal for frying, sauce-making and other cooking. Extra virgin olive oil should be saved for dressing fish, vegetables and salads.

Extra virgin olive oil
The distinctive fruity flavor makes this oil ideal for salad dressings

Peperoncini (dried red chilies)

Hot flakes of dried chilies are added to many southern Italian dishes, such as *arrabbiata* sauce and the famous *pasta all'aglio, olio e peperoncino* (dressed with garlic, oil and chilies). Chilies are unusual in that their "hotness" is usually in inverse proportion to their size, so larger dried varieties are generally milder than the smaller ones. In summer, bunches of tiny fresh red chilies can be bought in Italian markets. These can be used fresh, preserved in olive oil to make a spicy dressing or to drizzle over a pizza, or hung up to dry and crumbled to add "oomph" to a dish. Crushed chili flakes are available in jars.

Culinary Uses

A small pinch of dried chili flakes spices up stews and sauces, particularly those made with tomatoes. For a really hot pizza, crumble a few flakes over the top. Dried chilies are extremely fiery and should be used very sparingly.

Buying and Storing

Dried chilies will last for years, but they do lose their savor over a period of time, so buy only small quantities. Whole *peperoncini* should be hung up in bunches and crumbled directly into the dish you are cooking.

Dried red chili flakes
Just a small pinch of these fiery flakes spices up stews and sauces

Zafferano (saffron)

Saffron consists of the dried stigmas of the saffron crocus. It takes about 80,000 crocuses to produce about 1¼ lb of spice and these have to be hand-picked, so it is hardly surprising that saffron is the world's most expensive spice. Saffron stigmas or threads are a vivid orangey-red color with a pungent aroma. They are also sold ground into powder. Saffron has a highly aromatic flavor and will impart a wonderful, rich golden color to risotti and sauces.

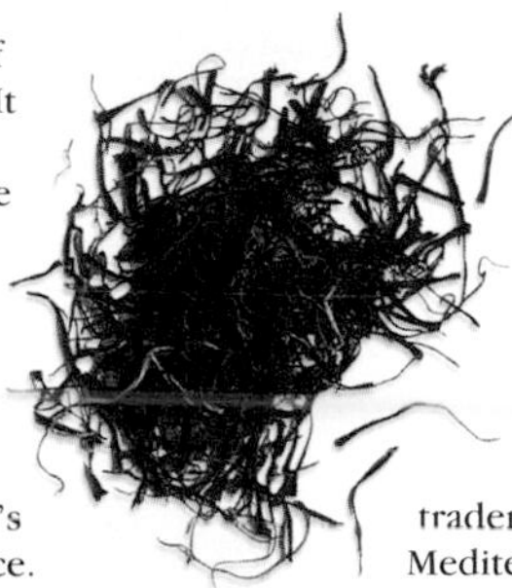

Saffron threads
Used to flavor and color the classic risotto alla milanese

Dried chilies
These are often used in fiery southern Italian dishes, such as arrabbiata *sauce*

History

Saffron originated in Asia Minor, where it was used by ancient civilizations as a flavoring, as a dye, in perfumery and for medicinal purposes. Arab traders brought the spice to the Mediterranean in the tenth century; for centuries it was so highly prized that stealing or adulterating it was punishable by death. The best saffron is nowadays cultivated in Spain, but it is also grown in Italy.

Culinary Uses

In Italy, saffron is mainly used to flavor and color risotti, such as the classic *risotto alla milanese*. It is excellent in sauces for fish and poultry and can be used to flavor cookies and cakes.

Buying and Storing

Saffron threads are sold in small boxes or jars containing only a few strands. The wiry threads should be a deep orangey-red in color; paler yellowish-orange threads are probably the much cheaper and less desirable safflower, which will add color but not flavor to a dish. Powdered saffron is convenient to use, but less reliable, as it may have been adulterated with safflower. Stored in small, airtight containers, saffron will keep for months.

Cooking with Saffron

Do not add saffron directly to a dish. Infuse threads in a little hot water for at least 5 minutes before blending into a dish to bring out the flavor and ensure even coloring. Add the soaking water together with the threads. Never fry saffron in hot oil or butter; this will ruin the flavor.

Cakes, Cookies & Breads

In Italy it is perfectly normal and acceptable for a hostess to buy a dolce *(cake or dessert) to serve at the end of a meal, rather than make it herself. Pastry shops and bakeries sell a wide variety of traditional tarts, spiced yeast cakes and cookies to be enjoyed with coffee or a glass of vin santo, sweet dessert wine or a liqueur. Some of these, such as* panettone *and* colomba, *are reserved for special occasions like Christmas and Easter, and almost every town has its own specialty for its local saint's day.*

Panettone
This light-textured yeast cake is a specialty of Milan

Amaretti *(macaroons)*

Amaretti cookies are made from ground almonds, egg whites and sugar. They have a distinctive flavor, which comes from the addition of bitter almonds. They originated in Venice during the Renaissance and their English name of macaroons comes from the Venetian *macerone*, meaning "fine paste." They come in dozens of different forms, from the famous crunchy sugar-encrusted cookies wrapped in pairs in twists of crisp white paper to soft-centered macaroons wrapped in brightly-colored foil. Amaretti are delicious dipped into hot coffee. They can also be crumbled to make a stuffing for baked peaches or apricots.

Amaretti
These crunchy sugar-encrusted cookies are delicious dipped into hot coffee

Cantucci

These hard, high-baked lozenge-shaped cookies from Tuscany are designed to be dipped into *espresso* coffee or vin santo. When moistened, they become deliciously soft and crumbly. They are usually studded with almonds or other nuts and flavored with aniseed or vanilla.

Cantucci

Panettone

Literally meaning "big bread," *panettone* is a light-textured spiced yeast bread containing raisins and candied fruit. Originally a specialty of Milan, it is now sold all over Italy as a Christmas delicacy and is traditionally given as a gift. *Panettoni* can vary in size from small to enormous. They are sometimes sold in pastel-colored dome-shaped boxes, which are often hung from the ceiling of bakeries and delicatessens, and look very festive. At Easter, they are baked into the shape of a lamb (*agnello*) or a dove (*colomba*). *Panettone* is sliced into wedges and eaten like cake.

Crumiri

These sweet elbow-shaped cookies are a speciality of Piedmont. The rich golden brown dough is made with polenta and honey and piped through a fluted nozzle to give the cookies their characteristic ridged texture. Although the cookies seem hard on the outside, the polenta flour gives the *crumiri* a pleasantly crunchy texture. *Crumiri* are good snack cookies, but they are also excellent dipped in hot coffee.

Panforte

Somewhat resembling a Christmas pudding in flavor, but shaped like a flat disc, *panforte* is a rich, dark spiced cake crammed with dried fruit and toasted nuts. It is a speciality of Siena and is sold in a colorful glossy wrapping, often depicting Sienese scenes. It is extremely rich, so can only be eaten in small quantities, which is just as well, since it is also quite expensive.

Panettone
The characteristic box often hangs from the ceiling in Italian delicatessens

Panforte
This Italian spice cake is packed full of fruit and nuts

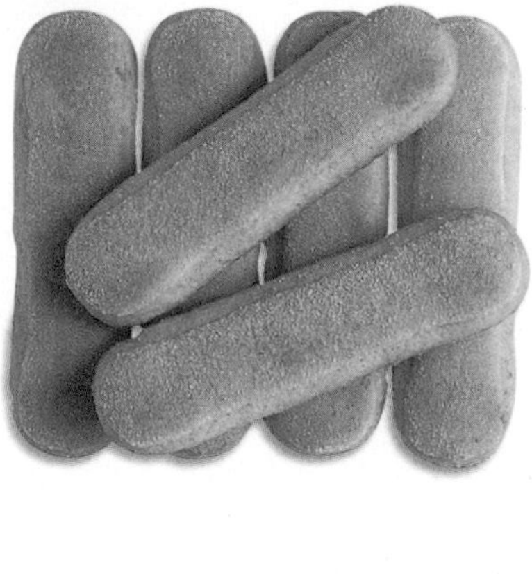

Savoiardi
These soft-textured, Italian sponge finger cookies are used as a base for tiramisù

Savoiardi (sponge cookies)

As their name suggests, *savoiardi* come from the Savoy region of Piedmont. They are plumper and wider than sponge fingers and have a softer texture. They are excellent dunked into tea or coffee, and are traditionally served with *zabaglione*; but they are best of all used as a base for tiramisù, the wickedly rich Italian coffee and mascarpone dessert.

Pane (Bread)

No Italian meal is ever served without bread to accompany the food. Indeed, it often constitutes one of the dishes in a meal in the form of *crostini* and *bruschetta* (toasted canapés), soups such as *pancotto*, *panzanella* (bread salad) or pizza. In Tuscany, bread plays a more important part in the food of the region than pasta. A favorite antipasto is *fettunta*, toasted or grilled bread rubbed with garlic, anointed with plenty of olive oil and sprinkled with coarse salt. When a topping is added, it becomes *bruschetta*.

Italians buy or make fresh bread every day, but stale or leftover loaves are never wasted. Instead they are made into bread crumbs and used for thickening sauces and stews, or for stuffings, salads or wonderfully sustaining soups.

There are hundreds of different types of Italian bread with many regional variations to suit the local food. Traditional Tuscan country bread is made without salt, since it is designed to be served with salty cured meats such as salami and *prosciutto crudo*. (If you prefer salted bread, ask for *pane salato*.) Southern Italian breads often contain olive oil, which goes well with tomatoes. *Pane integrale* (whole-wheat bread) is traditionally baked in a wood oven. The texture and flavor of the bread depends on the type of flour used and the amount of seasoning, but nearly all Italian breads are firm-textured with substantial crusts. You will never find flabby damp white sandwich loaves in an Italian bakery, although the inside of traditional white *panini* (bread rolls) can sometimes resemble cotton balls.

Ciabatta

These flattish, slipper-shaped loaves with squared or rounded ends are made with olive oil and are often flavored with fresh or dried herbs, olives or sun-dried tomatoes. They have an airy texture inside and a pale, crisp crust. *Ciabatta* is delicious served warm, and is excellent for sandwiches.

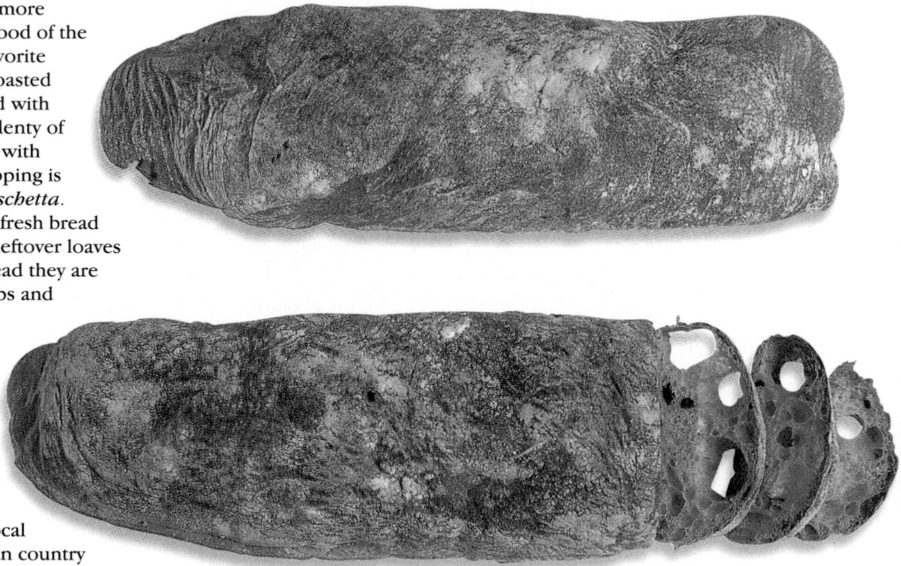

Ciabatta
These popular loaves are available plain or flavored with olives or sun-dried tomatoes

Whole-wheat bread
In Italy this bread is traditionally baked in a wooden oven

Focaccia

A dimpled flat bread similar to pizza dough, *focaccia* is traditionally oiled and baked in a wood oven. A whole *focaccia* from a bakery weighs several pounds and is sold by weight, cut into manageable pieces. A variety of ingredients can be worked into the dough or serve as a topping—onions, *pancetta*, rosemary or oregano, ham, cheese or olives. *Focaccine* are small versions, which are split and served with fillings like a sandwich. In Apulia, *focaccia del Venerdì Santo*, with its topping of fennel, chicory, anchovies, olives and capers, is traditionally served on Good Friday.

Focaccia
In Italy these large flat breads are sold by weight, cut into manageable pieces. It can be plain, as here, or flavored with herbs, sun-dried tomatoes or olives

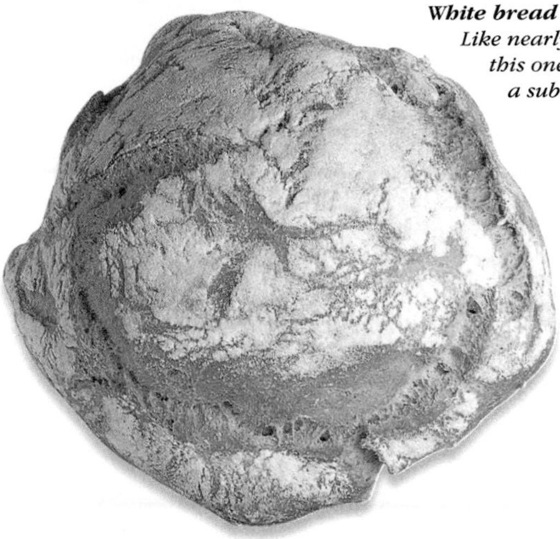

White bread
Like nearly all Italian breads, this one is firm-textured, with a substantial crust

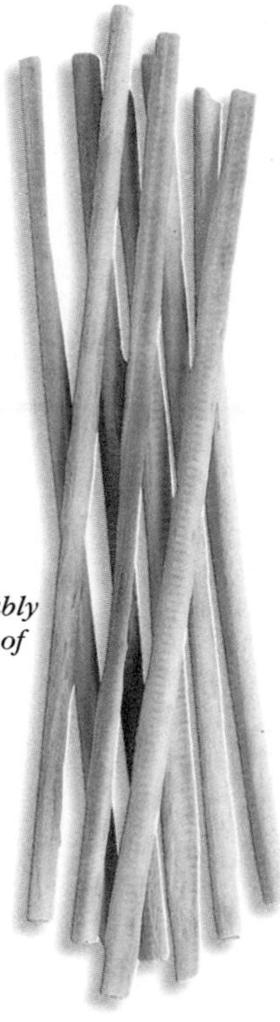

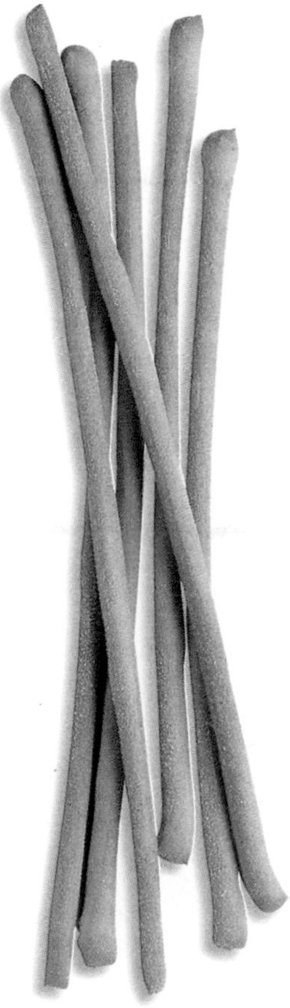

Grissini
The cover charge in every Italian restaurant invariably includes packages of bread sticks

Grissini

These crisp golden bread sticks originated in Turin, but are now found in almost every Italian restaurant, packaged in long envelopes. They range in size from matchstick-thin to hefty, knobby, homemade batons. Italian bakers often use up any leftover dough to make *grissini*, which are sold loose by weight. They can be rolled in sesame or poppy seeds for extra flavor.

Pantry

One of the great joys of Italian food is that you can create a delicious meal almost instantly using ingredients from your pantry. Rice and pasta can be combined with any number of jarred or canned vegetables, seafood or sauces to make a speedy and nutritious meal. Unopened jars and cans last for months, if not years, so it is worth keeping a selection in your pantry for an impromptu meal that you can create in moments.

Pesto

Although nothing is as good as homemade pesto, there are some excellent jarred varieties of this fragrant green basil sauce. Traditional pesto is made with basil, pine nuts, Parmesan or Pecorino cheese and olive oil, but you may also find a red version based on red bell peppers.

Culinary Uses

Pesto can be used as an instant dressing for any type of pasta or potato gnocchi. It gives a lift to risotti and tomato sauces, and is delicious stirred into minestrone or tomato-based soups. A spoonful of pesto will add a new dimension to bottled mayonnaise, creating a rich, pungent *maionese verde*. For a quick, attractive hors d'oeuvre, halve some cherry tomatoes, scoop out the seeds and fill the tomatoes with pesto.

Pesto
Both the traditional green version shown here and a red type based on red bell peppers are used to flavor sauces and pasta

Pomodori secchi (sun-dried tomatoes)

Sun-drying tomatoes intensifies their flavor to an astonishing sweetness and pungency and allows you to enjoy the full savor of tomatoes even in winter. If you are extremely lucky, you may still find in markets in southern Italy locally grown tomatoes that have been spread out to dry in the sun, but the commercially produced "sun-dried" tomatoes are actually air-dried by machine. Wrinkled red dried tomatoes are available dry in packages or preserved in olive oil. Dry tomatoes are brick-red in color and have a chewy texture. They can be eaten on their own as a snack, but for cooking they should be soaked in hot water until soft (the tomato-flavored soaking water can be used for a soup or sauce). Jarred sun-dried tomatoes are sold in chunky pieces or as a paste.

Dried tomatoes
Dried tomatoes should always be softened in water before use

Sun-dried tomatoes
These strong-flavored tomatoes add extra piquancy to dishes

Culinary Uses

Sun-dried tomatoes add piquancy to vegetable dishes, soups or sauces. They can be chopped and added to a simple *sugo di pomodoro* or a meaty *ragù* for extra flavor. They make an excellent *antipasto* combined with sliced fresh tomatoes, mozzarella and basil or with other preserved or pickled vegetables. They go well with fresh Mediterranean vegetables like fennel, eggplants and zucchini, and add a special something to egg dishes, such as *frittata*. Use the oil in which the tomatoes are preserved for salad dressings or for sweating vegetables for a soup or sauce.

The paste can be used in small quantities for sauces and soups, or used on its own or with a little butter as a dressing for pasta.

Passata
This rich tomato pureé varies in fineness from the ultra-smooth to the chunkier sugocasa

Passata (tomato pulp)

Rich red passata is simply sieved ripe tomatoes, a wonderfully convenient shortcut whenever tomato pulp is required. Depending on the degree of sieving, it can be perfectly smooth or slightly chunky (*polpa di pomodoro* or *passata rustica*: "rustic passata"). The chunky variety is sold in tall jars, while the smoothest type is available in cartons or jars. More highly concentrated tomato paste (*concentrato di pomodoro*) is packed in small cans or tubes. This product is extremely strong and should only be used in small quantities.

Culinary Uses

Passata can be used as a basis for soups and sauces, and as a substitute for fresh tomatoes in all recipes where they require long cooking. For a very quick pasta sauce, sweat some finely chopped onion and garlic in olive oil, add a jar of passata and bubble the sauce while the pasta is cooking. Flavor with fresh basil, oregano, parsley or some chopped olives, capers and/or anchovies. For more body and depth and a richer color, stir in a spoonful or two of tomato concentrate.

Black olive paste

Green olive paste

Pasta di olive (olive paste)

Green or, more usually, black olives are pounded to a paste with salt and olive oil and packed in small jars. Olive paste tends to be very salty and rich, so a little goes a long way.

Culinary Uses

Olive paste can be spread very thinly over pizza bases, or scraped onto toasted croutons and topped with tomatoes or mushrooms to make *crostini*. Mixed with olive oil and a little lemon juice, it can be a dip for raw vegetables. For an interesting *antipasto*, mash a little olive paste into the yolks of halved hard-cooked eggs, spoon the mixture back into the cavity and top with a few capers.

A little olive paste adds a rich flavor to a tomato sauce, while a spoonful stirred into a vinaigrette makes a good dressing for a robust salad. If you are a real olive lover, stir a small amount into hot pasta for the simplest of dressings.

Legumi sott'olio (vegetables preserved in oil)

Italians produce a wide variety of vegetables preserved in olive or sunflower oil, or a mixture of both. The choicest are often cooked *alla brace* (grilled) before being packed in the best olive oil—tiny *carciofini* (artichokes), *funghi* and *porcini* (button and wild mushrooms), *peperoni* (red and yellow bell peppers) and *melanzane* (eggplants)—and look as beautiful as they taste. You will sometimes find large bulbous jars containing colorful layers of different vegetables in oil; these are packed by hand and are extremely expensive.

Culinary Uses

A mixture of oil-preserved vegetables combined with a selection of cured meats makes a wonderful *antipasto*. They can also be chopped or sliced and used to dress hot or cold pasta, or stirred into rice for a substantial cold salad. They make a delicious topping for *crostini* or pizza.

Artichoke hearts
These olive oil-packed vegetables are often combined with sliced cured meats to make an antipasto

Pantry

Giardiniera (pickled vegetables)

Mixed pickled vegetables are sold packed *in agrodolce* (vinegar and oil). Single varieties such as peeled or unpeeled eggplants and zucchini are available, but a mixture of these vegetables along with artichokes, baby onions, carrots, celery and peppers is more colorful. These vegetables are sometimes described as *alla contadina* (peasant-style).

Culinary Uses

Pickled vegetables can be served with salami and ham as an *antipasto*, or drained and mixed with raw vegetables and mayonnaise for a piquant version of *insalata russa* (Russian salad). Their vinegary taste makes an excellent counterpoint to plain cold roast meats or poultry.

Peppers
The vinegary flavor of these pickled vegetables goes well with cold roast meats

Filetti di acciughe (anchovy fillets)

Anchovy fillets are available preserved in salt or oil. The salted fillets have a superior flavor, but they are are only available in catering tins to be sold by the *etto* ($3^1/_2$ oz) at delicatessens. You can buy these and soak them for 30 minutes, then dry them thoroughly and pack them in olive oil, but it is more practical to buy canned or jarred anchovies.

Culinary Uses

Anchovies can be chopped and added to tomato sauces and salad dressings. They can be stirred into a fish risotto, or mixed with tomatoes and capers for a topping for pizzas or *crostini*. They are best of all made into *bagna cauda*, a delicious and quick hot dip for raw vegetables. For six people, heat $^2/_3$ cup olive oil with 4 tbsp unsalted butter. As soon as it begins to foam, add 3 finely chopped garlic cloves and soften but do not brown. Drain and roughly chop a 2-oz can of anchovy fillets, add to the pan and stir over low heat until they have disintegrated to a paste. Keep the sauce hot and dip in the vegetables.

Anchovy fillets
Usually chopped and added to sauces or salads for extra flavor. These are available packed in oil or salt—the salted variety have a better flavor

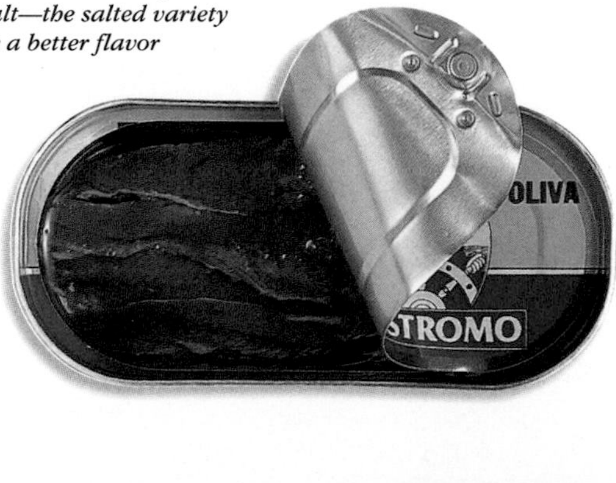

Bottarga (salted roe)

The pressed, salted and dried roe of the gray mullet or tuna, also known as *buttariga, butarega* and *ovotarica*, is a speciality of Sardinia, Sicily and the Veneto, where it is regarded as a great delicacy. It is usually packed in a sausage shape inside a skin that should be removed before preparing. Wrapped in plastic wrap, it will keep for several months.

Culinary Uses

Bottarga can be served as an *antipasto* thinly sliced and dressed with a little extra virgin olive oil and lemon juice. In Sicily, it is served with *caponata*, a dome-shaped salad of fried eggplant and celery. It is delicious simply grated over hot pasta with a pat of unsalted butter and a little chopped fresh parsley or dried chili flakes.

Baccalà *(salted dried cod)*

Air-drying is the oldest known method of preserving fish. Before the days of deep-freezing, dried fish was invaluable for people who wished to observe meatless days, but who lived far from the sea, because the salting and drying process ensures that it remains edible for many months. The most popular dried fish in Italy is salt cod, which is traditionally eaten on Good Friday. It is sometimes known confusingly as *stoccafisso* (although true stockfish is unsalted). It looks rather unappealing, like a flat, grayish board, but once it has been soaked and reconstituted it is absolutely delicious. Unlike other pantry ingredients, *baccalà* must be prepared a day in advance, but it is worth the effort.

Clams in brine

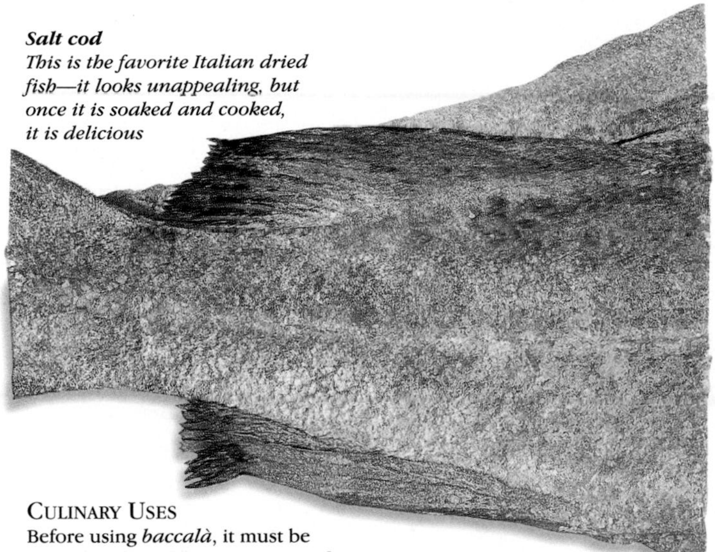

Salt cod
This is the favorite Italian dried fish—it looks unappealing, but once it is soaked and cooked, it is delicious

Culinary Uses

Before using *baccalà*, it must be soaked under cold running water for at least 8 hours to rehydrate it and remove the excess salt. Once this has been done, it can be creamed with olive oil, garlic, cream and parsley to make *baccalà mantecato*, a famous Venetian dish, which is served on fried polenta. In the Florentine version, the salt cod is cut into chunks, coated with flour and fried with tomatoes and onions. *Baccalà* combines well with all Mediterranean flavors and can be stewed or baked with red bell peppers, potatoes, fennel or celery, capers, olives and anchovies. Many recipes also include pine nuts and raisins. For a simple pasta sauce, mix some flaked salt cod with cream and chopped herbs and stir it into the hot pasta.

Vongole (clams)

Tiny clams are sold packed in brine in glass jars. These miniature golden nuggets need no further cooking and can be simply heated through and tossed into hot pasta or risotto, or combined with tomato sauce. If you have time, drain the clams and reduce the juice in which they are packed with finely chopped garlic and a few dried chili flakes to make a more intense sauce.

Mostarda di Cremona *(mustard fruit chutney)*

This sweet crystallized fruit chutney with its piquant undertone of the mustard was first produced over a hundred years ago in Cremona and Venice. Its vibrant colors come from the assortment of candied fruits from which it is made—cherries, pears, melons, figs, apricots and clementines, infused in mustard seed oil. Also known as *mostarda di frutta*, the chutney is traditionally served with sausages such as zampone and cotechino, or roast and boiled beef, veal and pork. For an unusual and delicious dessert, serve the chutney as a topping for creamy mascarpone.

Mustard fruit chutney

Aperitifs & Liqueurs

Behind every bar in Italy is displayed row upon row of bottles containing dozens of different aperitivi *and* digestivi*, many of them never found outside Italy. They are consumed at any hour of the day; a favorite Italian morning drink is* caffè corretto, espresso *coffee laced with grappa or* Stock *(Italian brandy). Many of the vermouths and spirits are made from local ingredients, including herbs, nuts, lemons, artichokes or regional wines. The Italians have an unshakeable belief in the digestive properties of such drinks, many of which are so bitter that most non-Italians find them completely unpalatable. At the end of a restaurant meal, you will always find the men clustered around the bar aiding their digestion with a small glass of spirit or liqueur.*

Amaro

A very bitter *aperitivo* much beloved by the Italians, *amaro* is flavored with gentian, herbs and orange peel and contains quinine and iron. Marginally less bitter than straight *amaro* are the wine-based *amari* such as Campari, which is usually mixed with soda water and drunk before a meal to stimulate the appetite and cleanse the palate. Others, such as Fernet-Branca, are served as a pick-me-up and cure for stomach aches. *Amaro* is reputed to have excellent digestive and tonic properties, to cure hangovers and to have aphrodisiac qualities, which probably explains its popularity in Italy.

Campari

A bright crimson *aperitivo* from the *amaro* family, wine-based Campari has a bitter, astringent flavor. It was first produced in the nineteenth century by the Campari brothers from Milan, and has been produced by the same family ever since. Campari is sold in triangular single-portion bottles ready-mixed with soda (Campari soda). The neat bitters are an essential ingredient of cocktails such as *Negroni* and *Americano*.

Campari soda

Amaro

Fernet-Branca

Cynar

This dark brown, intensely bitter, aperitif with an alcoholic content of 17 percent is made from artichokes. Too bitter to swallow on its own, it is usually served as a long drink with ice and soda water.

Punt e Mes

The name of this intensely bitter red *aperitivo* means "point and a half." It is said to have been created by the Carpano distillery when customers ordered their drinks to be mixed according to their own specification. Punt e Mes is usually drunk on its own, but can be served with ice and soda.

Vermouth

All vermouths, both white and red, are made from white wine flavored with aromatic herbal extracts and spices. The first vermouth was made in Turin in the eighteenth century, and vermouth is still produced there. Red vermouths, such as Cinzano and sweet Martini, are sweetened with sugar and tinted with caramel to give them a deep red color. These sweet red varieties are generically called "Italian" vermouth—the "it" in gin and it. Dry vermouth is white and contains less sugar. It is known as "French," but is also produced in Italy by companies such as Martini and Rossi. Other well-known brands include Riccadonna and Gancia.

Culinary Uses

Although the Italians tend to use white wine rather than vermouth in their cooking, dry white vermouth can be substituted in sauces and veal, rabbit or poultry dishes. It adds a touch of dryness and intensity.

Cynar

Punt e Mes

Extra-dry white vermouth

Fortified Wines

Marsala

This rich brown fortified wine has a sweet, musky flavor and an alcoholic content of about 18 percent. It is made in the west of Sicily, near the town from which it takes its name. The best Marsala (*vergine*) has been matured for at least five years to give an intensity of flavor and color. Although sweet Marsala is better known, dry varieties (*ambra secco*) are also produced; their flavor is reminiscent of medium sherry. The sweetest version is *Marsala all'uovo*, an intensely rich and sticky dessert wine enriched with egg yolks, which can only be drunk in tiny quantities. Dry Marsala is generally served as an *aperitivo*, while the sweet version is served after a meal, usually with little cookies to dip into the wine. Unlike sherry, sweet Marsala does not deteriorate once the bottle is opened, so it makes a very useful standby in the kitchen.

Vin santo

This "holy wine" from Tuscany is made from semi-dried grapes with a long slow fermentation, followed by many years of aging to produce a syrupy golden wine. Although not a fortified wine, its intense flavor has some similarity to sherry and it is drunk in much the same way. Vin santo can be dry or sweet, but the sweet version is more common. It is generally served with a plate of *cantucci* or *biscotti di Prato*, hard slipper-shaped cookies studded with nuts. These are dunked into the wine to make a delicious dessert.

Vin santo

Culinary Uses

Sweet Marsala is probably best known as an essential ingredient of *zabaglione*, a light frothy dessert made from whisked egg yolks, sugar and Marsala. It is used in *zuppa inglese* (trifle) and many other desserts. Dry Marsala is widely used in Italian cooking, particularly in veal dishes such as *scaloppina* and *piccata al Marsala* and sautéed chicken livers. A few spoonfuls of Marsala added to the pan in which veal or poultry has been sautéed will mingle with the pan juices to make a delicious syrupy sauce. It adds extra flavor to wild mushrooms or a mushroom risotto.

Marsala
The sweet variety is used to flavor zabaglione

Marsala
Widely used by Italian cooks for flavoring veal and poultry dishes

Liqueurs & Digestivi

Amaretto

This sweet liqueur is made from apricot pits and flavored with almonds and aromatic extracts. There are several brands produced, but the best is Disaronno Amaretto, which comes in a distinctive squarish rippled glass bottle with a square cap.

Culinary Uses

The distinctive almond flavor of Amaretto enhances many desserts, such as *macedonia* (fruit salad), *zuppa inglese* (trifle) and *panna* (whipped cream).

Galliano

A bright yellow liqueur from Lombardy, Galliano is flavored with herbs and spices and tastes a little like a bittersweet Chartreuse. It is occasionally drunk on its own as a *digestivo*, but is best known as an ingredient for cocktails such as Harvey Wallbanger and Golden Cadillac.

Galliano

Amaretto

Liqueurs & Digestivi

Grappa

A pungent colorless brandy with an alcoholic content of about 40 percent, distilled from the pressed skins and seeds of the grapes left after wine-making. At its crudest, grappa tastes of raw spirit, but after maturing the taste becomes refined and the best grappa can be as good as a fine French *marc*. Grappa is made in many regions, usually from local grapes, which lend each variety its characteristic flavor. On the whole, you get what you pay for; cheap grappa is fiery and pungent, while expensive, well-matured varieties can be very smooth. The very best grappa often comes in exquisite hand-blown bottles. The spirit can be flavored with various aromatics, including rose petals and lemon peel.

Culinary Uses

Grappa is not used in Italian cooking, except in *capretto alla piemontese* (braised goat). It can be used for flambéeing and for preserving berries. The spirit takes on the flavor of the berries and can be drunk as a *digestivo* after the berries have been eaten.

Grappa

Liquore al limone or *Cedro*

This sticky sweet liqueur is made from the peel of the lemons that grow in profusion around the Amalfi coast. Almost every delicatessen in the region sells a homemade version of this opaque yellow drink, whose sweetness is tempered by the tangy citrus fruit. It should be served ice-cold straight from the refrigerator or freezer and makes a refreshing *aperitivo* or *digestivo*.

Liquore al limone

Maraschino

This sweet, colorless cherry liqueur is made from fermented bitter Maraschino cherries. It can be drunk on its own as a *digestivo*, but is more commonly used for flavoring cocktails or sweet dishes.

Maraschino

Nocino

This sticky, dark brown liqueur from Emilia-Romagna is made from unripe green walnuts steeped in spirit. It has an aromatic but bittersweet flavor.

Sambuca

The colorless liqueur has a strong taste of aniseed, although it is actually distilled from witch elder. Traditionally it is served in a schooner-shaped glass, flambéed and with a coffee bean floating on top. The coffee bean is crunched as the Sambuca is drunk, so that its bitterness counteracts the intense sweetness of the liqueur. This method of serving Sambuca is known as *colla mosca* ("with the fly"), the "fly" being the coffee bean.

Strega

A bright yellow liqueur made from herbs and flowers, strega (meaning "witch"), has a bittersweet flavor and is definitely an acquired taste.

Nocino

Sambuca

Strega

ACETO
BALSAMICO
di Modena
Mazzetti
6% Acidity
250 ml
0586
Bottle N°
LANGLICHE SARDELLENFILETS
IN OLIVENÖL

The Recipes

The recipes in this collection cover a range of styles, from regional specialities to popular modern classics. More unusual, innovative offerings are here too, destined to become future favorites. All of the recipes use ingredients that can be found easily outside Italy, and all are as delicious to eat as they are easy to make.

Buon Appetito!

Antipasti

Antipasto means "before the meal," and no respectable Italian meal would start without it. The recipes in this chapter are typical of Italian antipasti—appetizing and easy on the eye, light and tasty. Vegetables, fish and salads are the mainstay, not only for their lightness and freshness, but also for their color.

Roast Bell Pepper Terrine

Torta di peperoni al forno

This terrine is perfect for a dinner party because it tastes better if made ahead. Prepare the salsa on the day of serving. Serve with hot Italian bread.

Ingredients

8 bell peppers (red, yellow and orange)
3 cups mascarpone cheese
3 eggs, separated
2 tbsp each roughly chopped flat-leaf parsley and shredded basil
2 large garlic cloves, roughly chopped
2 red, yellow or orange bell peppers, seeded and roughly chopped
2 tbsp extra virgin olive oil
2 tsp balsamic vinegar
a few basil sprigs
pinch of sugar
salt and freshly ground black pepper
serves 8

1 Place the peppers under a hot broiler for 8–10 minutes, turning them frequently until the skins are charred and blistered on all sides. Put the hot peppers in ziplock bags, seal and set aside until cold.

2 ▲ Rub off the pepper skins under cold running water. Break open the flesh and rub out the cores and seeds. Drain the peppers, dry them on paper towels, then cut seven of them lengthwise into thin, even-size strips. Reserve the remaining pepper for the salsa.

Variation

For a low-fat version of this terrine, use ricotta cheese instead of the mascarpone.

3 Put the mascarpone cheese in a bowl with the egg yolks, herbs and half the garlic. Add salt and pepper to taste. Beat well. In a separate bowl, whisk the egg whites to a soft peak, then fold into the cheese mixture until evenly incorporated.

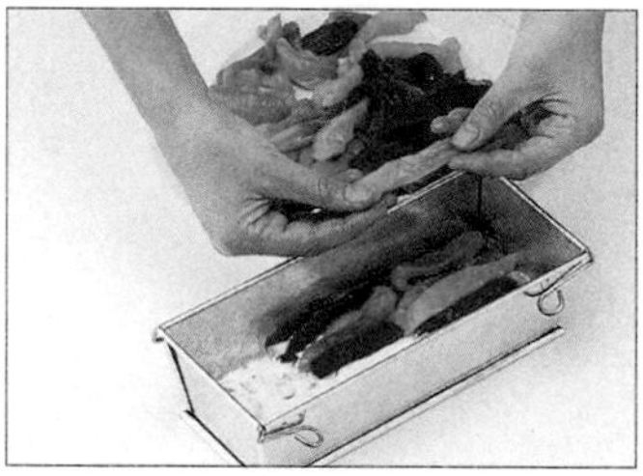

4 ▲ Preheat the oven to 350°F. Line the base of a lightly oiled 2-pound loaf pan. Put one-third of the cheese mixture in the pan and spread level. Arrange half the pepper strips on top in an even layer. Repeat until all the cheese and peppers are used.

5 Cover the pan with foil and place in a roasting pan. Pour in boiling water to come halfway up the sides of the pan. Bake for 1 hour. Let cool in the water bath, then lift out and chill overnight.

6 A few hours before serving, make the salsa. Place the remaining roast pepper and fresh peppers in a food processor. Add the remaining garlic, oil and vinegar. Set aside a few basil leaves for garnishing and add the rest to the processor. Process until finely chopped. Transfer the mixture to a bowl, add sugar and salt and pepper to taste and mix well. Cover and chill until ready to serve.

7 Turn out the terrine, peel off the paper and slice thickly. Garnish with the basil leaves and serve cold, with the sweet pepper salsa.

Pan-fried Chicken Liver Salad

Insalata di fegatini

This Florentine salad uses vin santo, a sweet dessert wine from Tuscany, but this is not essential—any dessert wine will do, or a sweet or cream sherry.

Ingredients
3 oz fresh baby spinach leaves
3 oz lollo rosso or red leaf lettuce
5 tbsp olive oil
1 tbsp butter
8 oz chicken livers, trimmed and thinly sliced
3 tbsp vin santo
2–3 oz fresh Parmesan cheese, shaved into curls
salt and freshly ground black pepper
serves 4

1 ▲ Wash and dry the spinach and lollo rosso. Tear the leaves into a large bowl, season with salt and pepper to taste and toss gently to mix.

2 ▲ Heat 2 tablespoons of the oil with the butter in a large heavy frying pan. When foaming, add the chicken livers and toss over medium to high heat for 5 minutes or until the livers are browned on the outside but still pink in the center. Remove from the heat.

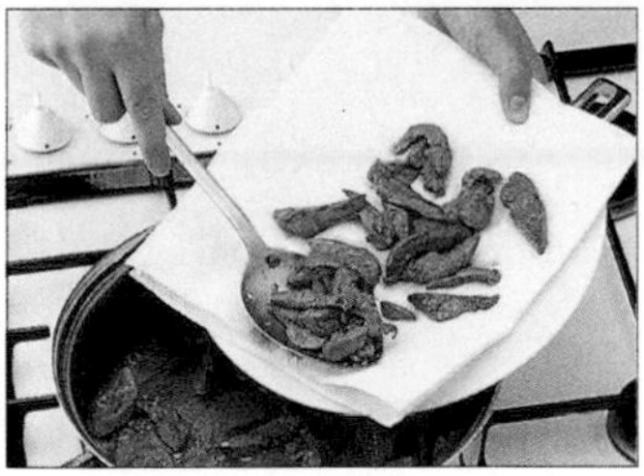

3 ▲ Remove the livers from the pan with a slotted spoon, drain them on paper towels, then place on top of the spinach.

4 ▲ Return the pan to medium heat, add the remaining oil and the vin santo and stir until sizzling.

5 Pour the hot dressing over the spinach and livers and toss to coat. Put the salad in a serving bowl and sprinkle the Parmesan shavings on top. Serve immediately.

Salad Leaves with Gorgonzola

Insalata verde con gorgonzola

Crispy fried pancetta makes tasty croutons, which contrast well in texture and flavor with the softness of mixed salad greens and the sharp taste of Gorgonzola.

Ingredients
8 oz pancetta strips, any rinds removed, coarsely chopped
2 large garlic cloves, roughly chopped
3 oz arugula leaves
3 oz radicchio leaves
1/2 cup walnuts, roughly chopped
4 oz Gorgonzola cheese
4 tbsp olive oil
1 tbsp balsamic vinegar
salt and freshly ground black pepper
serves 4

Variation
Use walnut oil instead of olive oil, or hazelnuts and hazelnut oil instead of walnuts and olive oil.

1 ▲ Put the chopped pancetta and garlic in a non-stick or heavy frying pan and heat gently, stirring constantly, until the pancetta fat runs. Increase the heat and fry until the pancetta and garlic are crisp. Remove with a slotted spoon and drain on paper towels. Leave the pancetta fat in the pan, off the heat.

2 ▲ Tear the arugula and radicchio leaves into a large salad bowl. Sprinkle on the walnuts, pancetta and garlic. Add salt and pepper to taste and toss to mix. Crumble the Gorgonzola over the top.
3 Return the frying pan to medium heat and add the oil and balsamic vinegar to the pancetta fat. Stir until sizzling, then pour over the salad. Serve immediately, toss at the table.

Tomato and Mozzarella Toasts

Bruschetta casalinga

These resemble mini pizzas and are good with drinks before a dinner party. Prepare them several hours in advance and pop them in the oven just as your guests arrive.

Ingredients
3 *sfilatini* (thin ciabatta)
about 1 cup sun-dried tomato paste
3 5-oz packages mozzarella cheese, drained
about 2 tsp dried oregano or mixed herbs
2–3 tbsp olive oil
freshly ground black pepper
serves 6–8

Variations
Use red or green pesto instead of the sun-dried tomato paste—a combination of colors is especially effective if the toasts are served on a large platter. Halved olives or criss-crossed strips of anchovy can be pressed into the cheese.

1 ▲ Cut each *sfilatino* on the diagonal into 12–15 slices, discarding the ends. Toast lightly on both sides.

2 Preheat the oven to 425°F. Spread sun-dried tomato paste on one side of each slice of toast. Cut the mozzarella into small pieces and arrange over the tomato paste.

3 ▲ Put the toasts on baking sheets, sprinkle with herbs and pepper to taste and drizzle with oil. Bake for 5 minutes or until the mozzarella has melted and is bubbling. Let the toasts settle for a few minutes before serving.

Genoese Squid Salad

Calamari in insalata alla genovese

This is a good salad for summer, when green beans and new potatoes are at their best. Serve it for a first course or light lunch.

Ingredients

1 lb prepared squid, cut into rings
4 garlic cloves, roughly chopped
1¼ cups Italian red wine
1 lb waxy new potatoes, scrubbed clean
8 oz green beans, trimmed and cut into short lengths
2–3 drained sun-dried tomatoes in oil, thinly sliced lengthwise
4 tbsp extra virgin olive oil
1 tbsp red wine vinegar
salt and freshly ground black pepper
serves 4–6

Cook's Tip

The French potato called Charlotte is perfect for this type of salad because it retains its shape and does not break up when boiled. Prepared squid can be bought at supermarkets with fresh fish counters, and at fishmongers.

1 ▲ Preheat the oven to 350°F. Put the squid rings in an earthenware dish with half the garlic, the wine and pepper to taste. Cover and cook for 45 minutes or until the squid is tender.

2 Put the potatoes in a saucepan, cover with cold water and add a good pinch of salt. Bring to a boil, cover and simmer for 15–20 minutes or until tender. Using a slotted spoon, lift out the potatoes and set aside. Add the beans to the boiling water and cook for 3 minutes. Drain.

3 ▲ When the potatoes are cool enough to handle, slice them thickly on the diagonal and place them in a bowl with the warm beans and sun-dried tomatoes. Whisk the oil, wine vinegar and the remaining garlic in a pitcher and add salt and pepper to taste. Pour over the potato mixture.

4 Drain the squid and discard the wine and garlic. Add the squid to the potato mixture and fold very gently to mix. Arrange the salad on individual plates and grind pepper liberally all over. Serve warm.

Tuna Carpaccio

Carpaccio di tonno

Fillet of beef is most often used for carpaccio, but meaty fish such as tuna—and swordfish —make an unusual change. The secret is to slice the fish wafer thin, made possible by freezing the fish first, a technique used by the Japanese for making sashimi.

Ingredients

2 fresh tuna steaks, about 1 pound total weight
4 tbsp extra virgin olive oil
1 tbsp balsamic vinegar
1 tsp superfine sugar
2 tbsp drained bottled green peppercorns or capers
salt and freshly ground black pepper
lemon wedges and green salad, to serve

serves 4

Cook's Tip

Raw fish is safe to eat as long as it is very fresh, so check with your fishmonger before purchase, and make and serve carpaccio on the same day. Do not buy fish that has been frozen and thawed.

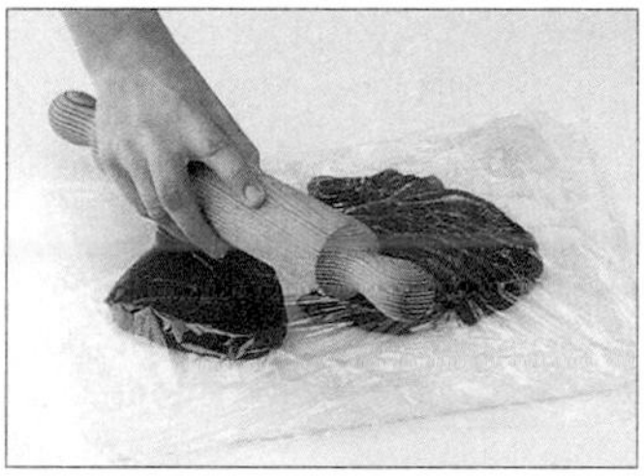

1 ▲ Remove the skin from each tuna steak and place each steak between two sheets of plastic wrap or waxed paper. Pound with a rolling pin until flattened slightly.

2 Roll up the tuna as tightly as possible, then wrap tightly in plastic wrap and place in the freezer for 4 hours or until firm.

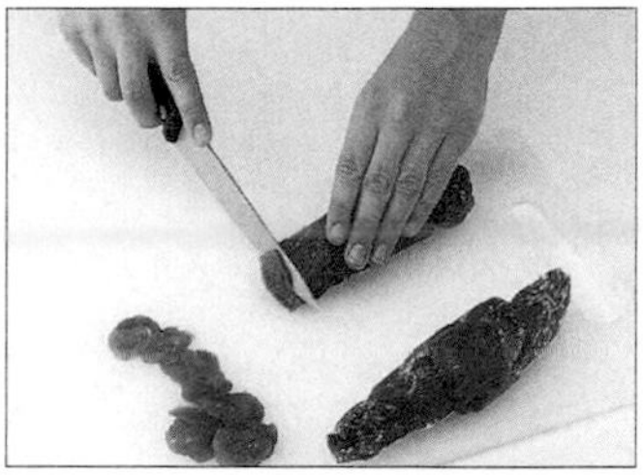

3 ▲ Unwrap the tuna and cut vertically into the thinnest possible slices. Arrange on individual plates.

4 Whisk together the remaining ingredients, season and pour over the tuna. Cover and let come to room temperature for 30 minutes before serving with lemon wedges and green salad.

Marinated Vegetable Antipasto

Verdura marinata per antipasto

Antipasto means "before the meal" and traditionally consists of a selection of marinated vegetable dishes served with good Italian salami and thin slices of prosciutto. Serve in attractive bowls, with plenty of fresh crusty bread.

Ingredients

For the peppers

3 red bell peppers
3 yellow bell peppers
4 garlic cloves, sliced
handful fresh basil, plus extra to garnish
extra virgin olive oil
salt and freshly ground black pepper

For the mushrooms

1 lb open cap mushrooms
4 tbsp extra virgin olive oil
1 large garlic clove, crushed
1 tbsp chopped fresh rosemary
1 cup dry white wine
fresh rosemary sprigs, to garnish

For the olives

1 dried red chili, crushed
grated rind of 1 lemon
1/2 cup extra virgin olive oil
1 1/3 cups Italian black olives
2 tbsp chopped fresh flat-leaf parsley
1 lemon wedge, to serve

serves 4

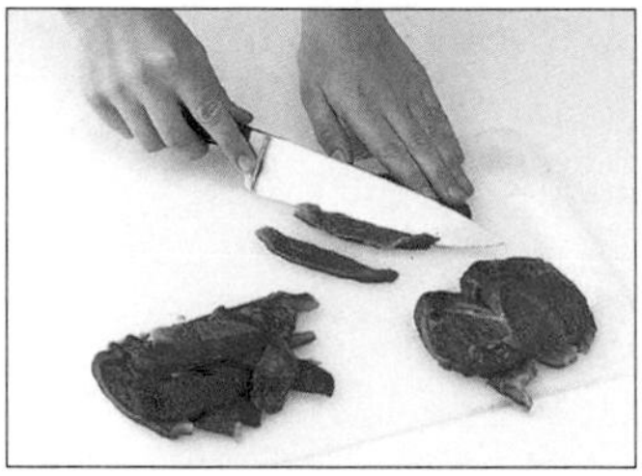

1 ▲ Place the peppers under a hot broiler. Turn occasionally until they are blackened and blistered all over. Remove from the heat and place in a large plastic bag. When cool, remove the skin, halve the peppers and remove the seeds. Cut the flesh into strips lengthwise and place them in a bowl with the sliced garlic and basil leaves. Add salt, to taste, cover with oil and marinate for 3–4 hours before serving, tossing occasionally. When serving, garnish with more basil leaves.

2 Thickly slice the mushrooms and place in a large bowl. Heat the oil in a small pan and add the garlic and rosemary. Pour in the wine. Bring the mixture to a boil, then lower the heat and simmer for 3 minutes. Add salt and pepper to taste.

3 ▲ Pour the mixture over the mushrooms. Mix well and let cool, stirring occasionally. Cover and marinate overnight. Serve at room temperature, garnished with rosemary sprigs.

4 ▲ Prepare the olives. Place the chili and lemon rind in a small pan with the oil. Heat gently for about 3 minutes. Add the olives and heat for 1 more minute. Pour into a bowl and let cool. Marinate overnight. Sprinkle on the parsley just before serving with the lemon wedge.

Cook's Tip

The pepper antipasto can be stored in the refrigerator for up to 2 weeks covered in olive oil in an airtight jar.

Stuffed Roast Peppers with Pesto

Peperoni arrostiti con pesto

Serve these scallop- and pesto-filled red bell peppers with Italian bread, such as ciabatta or focaccia, to mop up the garlicky juices.

Ingredients
4 squat red bell peppers
2 large garlic cloves, cut into thin slivers
4 tbsp olive oil
4 shelled scallops
3 tbsp pesto
salt and freshly ground black pepper
freshly grated Parmesan cheese, to serve
salad leaves and fresh basil sprigs, to garnish
serves 4

Cook's Tip
Scallops are available at most fishmongers and supermarkets with fresh fish counters. Never cook scallops for longer than the time stated in the recipe or they will be tough and rubbery.

1 Preheat the oven to 350°F. Cut the peppers in half lengthwise, through their stalks. Scrape out and discard the cores and seeds. Wash the pepper shells and pat dry.

2 ▲ Put the peppers, cut-side up, in an oiled roasting pan. Divide the slivers of garlic equally among them and sprinkle with salt and pepper to taste. Spoon the oil into the peppers, then roast for 40 minutes.

3 ▲ Cut each of the shelled scallops in half to make two flat discs. Remove the peppers from the oven and place a scallop half in each pepper half. Top with pesto.

4 Return the pan to the oven and roast for 10 more minutes. Transfer the peppers to individual serving plates, sprinkle with grated Parmesan and garnish each plate with a few salad leaves and fresh basil sprigs. Serve warm.

Mozzarella Skewers

Spiedini alla romana

Stacks of flavor—layers of oven-baked mozzarella, tomatoes, basil and bread.

Ingredients
12 slices white country bread, each about 1/2 inch thick
3 tbsp olive oil
8 oz mozzarella cheese, cut into 1/4-inch slices
3 plum tomatoes, cut into 1/4-inch slices
1/2 cup fresh basil leaves, plus extra to garnish
salt and freshly ground black pepper
2 tbsp chopped fresh flat-leaf parsley, to garnish
serves 4

Cook's Tip
If you use wooden skewers, soak them in water first, to prevent scorching.

1 ▲ Preheat the oven to 425°F. Trim the crusts from the bread and cut each slice into four equal squares. Arrange on a baking sheet and brush on one side (or both sides) with half the olive oil. Bake for 3–5 minutes, until the squares are pale gold.

2 Remove from the oven and place the bread squares on a board with the other ingredients.

3 ▲ Make 16 stacks, each starting with a square of bread, then a slice of mozzarella topped with a slice of tomato and a basil leaf. Sprinkle with salt and pepper, then repeat, ending with the bread. Push a skewer through each stack and place on the baking sheet. Drizzle with the remaining oil and bake for 10–15 minutes, until the cheese begins to melt. Garnish with fresh basil leaves and serve scattered with chopped fresh flat leaf parsley.

Eggplant Fritters

Frittelle di melanzane

These simply delicious fritters make a superb appetizer or vegetarian supper dish.

Ingredients
1 large eggplant, about 1 1/2 lb, cut into 1/2 inch thick slices
2 tbsp olive oil
1 egg, lightly beaten
2 garlic cloves, crushed
4 tbsp chopped fresh parsley
2 1/4 cups fresh white bread crumbs
generous 1 cup grated Parmesan cheese
generous 1 cup feta cheese, crumbled
3 tbsp flour
sunflower oil, for shallow frying
salt and freshly ground black pepper

To serve
plain yogurt, flavored with fried red chilies and cumin seeds
lime wedges
serves 4

1 ▲ Preheat the oven to 375°F. Brush the eggplant slices with the olive oil, then place them on a baking sheet and bake for about 20 minutes until golden and tender. Chop the slices finely and place them in a bowl with the egg, garlic, parsley, bread crumbs, Parmesan and feta. Add salt and pepper to taste, and mix well. Let the mixture rest for about 20 minutes. If the mixture looks very sloppy, add more bread crumbs.

2 ▲ Divide the mixture into eight balls and flatten them slightly. Place the flour on a plate and season with salt and pepper. Coat the fritters in the flour, shaking off any excess.

3 Shallow fry the fritters in batches for 1 minute on each side, until golden brown. Drain on paper towels and serve with the flavored yogurt and lime wedges.

Soups

The Italians are avid soup eaters, and some of the best soups in the world come from Italy. Clear broth, brodo, *and delicate puréed soups are served as a first course before a main meal. More substantial chunky soups,* minestre, *are often main meals in themselves, usually served in the evening if the main meal of the day has been at lunchtime.*

Onion Soup

La cipollata

This warming winter soup comes from Umbria, where it is sometimes thickened with beaten eggs and lots of grated Parmesan cheese. It is then served on top of hot toasted croutons—rather like savory scrambled eggs.

Ingredients
- 4 oz pancetta slices, any rinds removed, roughly chopped
- 2 tbsp olive oil
- 1 tbsp butter
- 1½ lb onions, thinly sliced
- 2 tsp sugar
- about 5 cups chicken stock
- 12 oz ripe Italian plum tomatoes, peeled and roughly chopped
- a few basil leaves, shredded
- salt and freshly ground black pepper
- freshly grated Parmesan cheese, to serve

serves 4

1 ▲ Put the chopped pancetta in a large saucepan and heat gently, stirring constantly, until the fat runs. Increase the heat to medium, add the oil, butter, onions and sugar and stir well to mix.

2 ▲ Half cover the pan and cook the onions gently for about 20 minutes, until golden. Stir frequently and lower the heat if necessary.

3 ▲ Add the stock, tomatoes and salt and pepper and bring to a boil, stirring. Lower the heat, half cover the pan and simmer, stirring occasionally, for about 30 minutes.

4 Check the consistency of the soup and add a little more stock or water if it is too thick.

5 Just before serving, stir in most of the basil and taste for seasoning. Serve hot, garnished with the remaining shredded basil. Serve the freshly grated Parmesan separately.

Cook's Tip
Look for Vidalia onions to make this soup. They are available at large supermarkets, and have a very sweet flavor and attractive yellowish flesh.

Cream of Zucchini Soup

Vellutata di zucchini

The beauty of this soup is its delicate color, rich and creamy texture and subtle taste. If you prefer a more pronounced cheese flavor, use Gorgonzola instead of Dolcelatte.

Ingredients
2 tbsp olive oil
1 tbsp butter
1 medium onion, roughly chopped
2 pounds zucchini, trimmed and sliced
1 tsp dried oregano
about 2½ cups vegetable or chicken stock
4 oz mild blue cheese (such as Dolcelatte), rind removed, diced
1¼ cups light cream or half-and-half
salt and freshly ground black pepper
fresh oregano and extra cheese, to garnish
serves 4–6

1 ▲ Heat the oil and butter in a large saucepan until foaming. Add the onion and cook gently for about 5 minutes, stirring frequently, until softened but not brown.

2 ▲ Add the zucchini and oregano, with salt and pepper to taste. Cook over medium heat for 10 minutes, stirring frequently.

3 ▲ Pour in the stock and bring to a boil, stirring. Lower the heat, half cover the pan and simmer gently, stirring occasionally, for about 30 minutes. Stir in the diced Dolcelatte until melted.

Cook's Tip
To save time, trim off and discard the ends of the zucchini, cut them into thirds, then chop in a food processor fitted with the metal blade.

4 ▲ Process the soup in a blender or food processor until smooth, then press through a sieve into a clean pan.

5 Add two-thirds of the cream and stir over low heat until hot, but not boiling. Check the consistency and add more stock if the soup is too thick. Taste for seasoning, then pour into heated bowls. Swirl in the remaining cream. Garnish with oregano and extra cheese and serve.

Wild Mushroom Soup

Zuppa di porcini

Wild mushrooms are expensive. Dried porcini have an intense flavor, so only a small quantity is needed. The beef stock may seem unusual in a vegetable soup, but it helps to strengthen the earthy flavor of the mushrooms.

Ingredients
2 cups dried porcini mushrooms
2 tbsp olive oil
1 tbsp butter
2 leeks, thinly sliced
2 shallots, roughly chopped
1 garlic clove, roughly chopped
3 cups fresh wild mushrooms
5 cups beef stock
½ tsp dried thyme
⅔ cup heavy cream
salt and freshly ground black pepper
fresh thyme sprigs, to garnish
serves 4

Cook's Tip
Porcini are cepes. Italian cooks would make this soup with a combination of fresh and dried cepes, but if fresh cepes are difficult to obtain, you can use other wild mushrooms, such as chanterelles.

1 ▲ Put the dried porcini in a bowl, add 1 cup warm water and let soak for 20–30 minutes. Lift them out of the liquid and squeeze over the bowl to remove as much of the soaking liquid as possible. Strain all the liquid and reserve to use later. Finely chop the porcini.

2 Heat the oil and butter in a large saucepan until foaming. Add the sliced leeks, chopped shallots and garlic and cook gently for about 5 minutes, stirring frequently, until softened but not colored.

3 ▲ Chop or slice the fresh mushrooms and add to the pan. Stir over medium heat for a few minutes until they begin to soften. Pour in the stock and bring to a boil. Add the porcini, soaking liquid, dried thyme and salt and pepper. Lower the heat, half cover the pan and simmer gently for 30 minutes, stirring occasionally.

4 ▲ Pour about three-quarters of the soup into a blender or food processor and process until smooth. Return to the soup remaining in the pan, stir in the cream and heat through. Check the consistency and add more stock if the soup is too thick. Taste for seasoning. Serve hot, garnished with thyme sprigs.

Tomato and Fresh Basil Soup

Crema di pomodori al basilico

A soup for late summer when fresh tomatoes are at their most flavorful.

Ingredients
1 tbsp olive oil
2 tbsp butter
1 medium onion, finely chopped
2 pounds ripe Italian plum tomatoes, roughly chopped
1 garlic clove, roughly chopped
about 3 cups chicken or vegetable stock
½ cup dry white wine
2 tbsp sun-dried tomato paste
2 tbsp shredded fresh basil, plus a few whole leaves, to garnish
⅔ cup heavy cream
salt and freshly ground black pepper
serves 4–6

1 ▲ Heat the oil and butter in a large saucepan until foaming. Add the onion and cook gently for about 5 minutes, stirring frequently, until softened but not brown.

2 ▲ Stir in the chopped tomatoes and garlic, then add the stock, white wine and sun-dried tomato paste, with salt and pepper to taste. Bring to a boil, then lower the heat, half cover the pan and simmer gently for 20 minutes, stirring occasionally to prevent the tomatoes from sticking to the base of the pan.

3 ▲ Process the soup with the shredded basil in a blender or food processor, then press through a sieve into a clean pan.

4 ▲ Add the heavy cream and heat through, stirring. Do not let the soup approach the boiling point. Check the consistency and add more stock if necessary and then taste for seasoning. Pour into heated bowls and garnish with basil. Serve immediately.

Variation
The soup can also be served chilled. Pour it into a container after straining and chill for at least 4 hours. Serve in chilled bowls.

Minestrone with Pasta and Beans

Minestrone alla milanese

This classic minestrone from Lombardy includes pancetta for a pleasant touch of saltiness. Milanese cooks vary the recipe according to what is at hand, and you can do the same.

Ingredients
3 tbsp olive oil
4 oz pancetta, any rinds removed, roughly chopped
2–3 celery stalks, finely chopped
3 medium carrots, finely chopped
1 medium onion, finely chopped
1–2 garlic cloves, crushed
2 cans (14 oz each) chopped tomatoes
about 4 cups chicken stock
1 can (14 oz) cannellini beans, drained and rinsed
1/2 cup macaroni
2–4 tbsp chopped flat-leaf parsley, to taste
salt and freshly ground black pepper
shaved Parmesan cheese, to serve
serves 4

Variation
Use long-grain rice instead of the pasta, and borlotti beans instead of cannellini.

1 ▲ Heat the oil in a large saucepan. Add the pancetta, celery, carrots and onion and cook over low heat for 5 minutes, stirring constantly, until the vegetables are softened.

2 Add the garlic and tomatoes, breaking them up well with a wooden spoon. Pour in the stock. Add salt and pepper to taste and bring to a boil. Half cover the pan, lower the heat and simmer gently for about 20 minutes, until the vegetables are soft.

3 ▲ Drain the beans and add them to the pan with the macaroni. Bring to a boil again. Cover, lower the heat and continue to simmer for about 20 more minutes. Check the consistency and add more stock if necessary. Stir in the parsley and taste for seasoning.

4 Serve hot, sprinkled with plenty of Parmesan cheese. This makes a meal in itself if served with chunks of crusty Italian bread.

Summer Minestrone

Minestrone estivo

This brightly colored, fresh-tasting soup makes the most of summer vegetables.

Ingredients
3 tbsp olive oil
1 large onion, finely chopped
1 tbsp sun-dried tomato paste
1 lb ripe Italian plum tomatoes, peeled and finely chopped
8 oz green zucchini, trimmed and roughly chopped
8 oz yellow summer squash, trimmed and roughly chopped
3 waxy new potatoes, diced
2 garlic cloves, crushed
about 5 cups chicken stock or water
1/4 cup shredded fresh basil
2/3 cup grated Parmesan cheese
salt and freshly ground black pepper
serves 4

1 ▲ Heat the oil in a large saucepan, add the onion and cook gently for about 5 minutes, stirring constantly, until softened. Stir in the sun-dried tomato paste, chopped tomatoes, zucchini, squash, diced potatoes and garlic. Mix well and cook gently for 10 minutes, uncovered, shaking the pan frequently to prevent the vegetables from sticking to the base.

2 ▲ Pour in the stock. Bring to a boil, lower the heat, half cover the pan and simmer gently for 15 minutes or until the vegetables are just tender. Add more stock if necessary.

3 Remove the pan from the heat and stir in the basil and half the cheese. Taste for seasoning. Serve hot, sprinkled with the remaining cheese.

Clam and Pasta Soup

Zuppa alle vongole

This soup is a play on a popular pasta dish—spaghetti alle vongole—using pantry ingredients. Serve it with hot focaccia or ciabatta for an informal supper with friends.

Ingredients

2 tbsp olive oil
1 large onion, finely chopped
2 garlic cloves, crushed
1 can (14 oz) chopped tomatoes
1 tbsp sun-dried tomato paste
1 tsp sugar
1 tsp dried mixed herbs
about 3 cups fish or vegetable stock
$^2/_3$ cup red wine
$^1/_2$ cup small pasta shapes
1 jar or can (5 oz) clams in natural juice
2 tbsp finely chopped flat-leaf parsley, plus a few whole leaves, to garnish
salt and freshly ground black pepper

serves 4

1 ▲ Heat the oil in a large saucepan. Cook the onion gently for 5 minutes, stirring frequently, until softened.

2 ▲ Add the garlic, tomatoes, tomato paste, sugar, herbs, stock and wine, with salt and pepper to taste. Bring to a boil. Lower the heat, half cover the pan and simmer for 10 minutes, stirring occasionally.

3 ▲ Add the pasta and continue simmering, uncovered, for about 10 minutes or until *al dente*. Stir occasionally, to prevent the pasta shapes from sticking together.

Cook's Tip

This soup has a fuller flavor if it is made the day before and reheated.

4 ▲ Add the clams and their juice to the soup and heat through for 3–4 minutes, adding more stock if required. Do not let it boil or the clams will be tough. Remove from the heat, stir in the parsley and taste the soup for seasoning. Serve hot, sprinkled with coarsely ground black pepper and parsley leaves.

Tuscan Bean Soup

Zuppa di fagioli alla toscana

There are lots of versions of this wonderful soup. This one uses cannellini beans, leeks, cabbage and good olive oil—and tastes even better reheated.

Ingredients
3 tbsp extra virgin olive oil
1 onion, roughly chopped
2 leeks, roughly chopped
1 large potato, peeled and diced
2 garlic cloves, finely chopped
5 cups vegetable stock
1 can (14 oz) cannellini beans, drained, liquid reserved
1/2 (6 oz) Savoy cabbage, shredded
3 tbsp chopped fresh flat-leaf parsley
2 tbsp chopped fresh oregano
1 cup Parmesan cheese, shaved
salt and freshly ground black pepper

For the garlic toasts
2–3 tbsp extra virgin olive oil
6 thick slices country bread
1 garlic clove, peeled and bruised
serves 4

1 ▲ Heat the oil in a large saucepan and gently cook the onion, leeks, potato and garlic for 4–5 minutes.

2 ▲ Pour in the stock and liquid from the beans. Cover and simmer for 15 minutes.

3 ▲ Stir in the cabbage and beans, with half the herbs, season and cook for 10 more minutes. Spoon about one-third of the soup into a food processor or blender and process until fairly smooth. Return to the soup in the pan, taste for seasoning and heat through for 5 minutes.

4 ▲ Meanwhile, make the garlic toasts. Drizzle a little oil over the slices of bread, then rub both sides of each slice with the garlic. Toast until browned on both sides. Ladle the soup into bowls. Sprinkle with the remaining herbs and the Parmesan shavings. Add a drizzle of olive oil and serve with the toasts.

Lentil Soup with Tomatoes

Minestra di lenticchie

A classic rustic Italian soup flavored with rosemary, delicious served with garlic bread.

Ingredients
1 cup dried green or brown lentils
3 tbsp extra virgin olive oil
3 strips bacon, diced
1 onion, finely chopped
2 celery stalks, finely chopped
2 carrots, finely diced
2 rosemary sprigs, finely chopped
2 bay leaves
1 can (14 oz) chopped plum tomatoes
8 cups vegetable stock
salt and freshly ground black pepper
bay leaves and rosemary sprigs, to garnish
serves 4

Cook's Tip
Look for the small green lentils sold at Italian groceries or delicatessens.

1 Place the lentils in a bowl and cover with cold water. Let soak for 2 hours. Rinse and drain well.

2 ▲ Heat the oil in a large saucepan. Add the bacon and cook for about 3 minutes, then stir in the onion and cook for 5 minutes, until softened. Stir in the celery, carrots, rosemary, bay leaves and lentils. Toss over the heat for 1 minute until thoroughly coated in the oil.

3 ▲ Pour in the tomatoes and stock and bring to a boil. Lower the heat, half cover the pan, and simmer for about 1 hour or until the lentils are perfectly tender.

4 Remove the bay leaves, add salt and pepper to taste and serve with a garnish of fresh bay leaves and rosemary sprigs.

Spinach and Rice Soup

Minestra di riso e spinaci

Use very fresh, young spinach leaves to prepare this light and fresh-tasting soup.

Ingredients
1½ lb fresh spinach, washed
3 tbsp extra virgin olive oil
1 small onion, finely chopped
2 garlic cloves, finely chopped
1 small fresh red chili, seeded and finely chopped
generous 1 cup risotto rice
5 cups vegetable stock
¼ cup grated Pecorino cheese
salt and freshly ground black pepper
serves 4

1 Place the spinach in a large pan with just the water that clings to its leaves after washing. Add a large pinch of salt. Heat gently until the spinach has wilted, then remove from the heat and drain, reserving any liquid.

2 ▲ Either chop the spinach finely using a large knife or place in a food processor and process to a fairly coarse purée.

3 ▲ Heat the oil in a large saucepan and gently cook the onion, garlic and chili for 4–5 minutes until softened. Stir in the rice until well coated, then pour in the stock and reserved spinach liquid. Bring to a boil, lower the heat and simmer for 10 minutes. Add the spinach, with salt and pepper to taste. Cook for 5–7 more minutes, until the rice is tender. Check the seasoning and serve with the Pecorino cheese.

Pasta & Gnocchi

In Italy, pasta and gnocchi are traditionally served as a first course after the antipasto and before the second course of fish or meat. Everyday dishes are often simple, served with nothing more than olive oil or butter, grated Parmesan and basil. Outside of Italy there are no hard-and-fast rules, and nowadays people eat pasta and gnocchi whenever they like.

Cannelloni with Tuna

Cannelloni sorpresa

Children love this pasta dish. Fontina cheese has a sweet, nutty flavor and melts perfectly. Look for it at large supermarkets and Italian delicatessens.

Ingredients
¹/₄ cup butter
¹/₂ cup flour
about 3 ³/₄ cups hot milk
2 cans (7 oz each) tuna, drained
1 cup Fontina cheese, grated
¹/₄ tsp grated nutmeg
12 cannelloni tubes
²/₃ cup grated Parmesan cheese
salt and freshly ground black pepper
fresh herbs, to garnish
serves 4–6

1 ▲ Melt the butter in a heavy saucepan, add the flour and stir over low heat for 1–2 minutes. Remove the pan from the heat and gradually add 1¹/₂ cups of the milk, beating vigorously after each addition. Return the pan to the heat and whisk for 1–2 minutes, until the sauce is very thick and smooth. Remove from the heat.

2 ▲ Mix the drained tuna with about ¹/₂ cup of the warm white sauce in a bowl. Add salt and black pepper to taste. Preheat the oven to 350°F.

3 ▲ Gradually whisk the remaining milk into the rest of the sauce, then return to the heat and simmer, whisking constantly, until thickened. Add the grated Fontina and nutmeg, with salt and pepper to taste. Simmer for a few more minutes, stirring frequently. Pour about one-third of the sauce into a baking dish and spread to the corners.

4 ▲ Fill the cannelloni tubes with the tuna mixture, pushing it in with the handle of a teaspoon. Place the cannelloni in a single layer in the dish. Thin the remaining sauce with a little more milk if necessary, then pour it over the cannelloni. Sprinkle with Parmesan cheese and bake for 30 minutes or until golden. Serve hot, garnished with herbs.

Seafood Lasagne

Lasagne alla marinara

Rich and creamy, this flavorful lasagne makes a good dinner party dish.

Ingredients
5 tbsp butter
1 lb monkfish fillets, skinned and diced small
8 oz large shrimp, shelled, deveined and roughly chopped
3 cups button mushrooms, chopped
3 tbsp flour
2 1/2 cups hot milk
1 1/4 cups heavy cream
1 can (14 oz) chopped tomatoes
2 tbsp shredded fresh basil
8 sheets no-cook lasagne
1 cup grated Parmesan cheese
salt and freshly ground black pepper
fresh herbs, to garnish
serves 6

1 ▲ Melt 1 tbsp of the butter in a large, deep sauté pan, add the monkfish and shrimp and sauté over medium to high heat for 2–3 minutes. As soon as the shrimp turn pink, remove them with a slotted spoon and place in a bowl.

2 Add the mushrooms to the pan and sauté for about 5 minutes, until the juices run and the mushrooms are soft. Remove with a slotted spoon and add to the fish in the bowl.

3 Melt the remaining butter in a saucepan, add the flour and stir over low heat for 1–2 minutes. Remove the pan from the heat and gradually whisk in the milk. Return to the heat and bring to a boil, whisking. Lower the heat and simmer for 2–3 minutes, whisking occasionally, until thick. Whisk in the cream and cook over low heat for 2 more minutes.

4 ▲ Remove the sauce from the heat and stir in the fish and mushroom mixture with all the juices that have collected in the bowl. Add salt to taste, and plenty of pepper. Preheat the oven to 375°F.

5 Spread half the chopped tomatoes over the bottom of a baking dish. Sprinkle with half the basil and add salt and pepper to taste. Ladle one-third of the sauce over the tomatoes.

6 ▲ Cover the sauce with four lasagne sheets. Spread the remaining tomatoes over the lasagne and sprinkle with the basil and salt and pepper to taste. Ladle half the sauce over. Arrange the remaining lasagne sheets on top, top with the remaining sauce and cover with the cheese. Bake for 30–40 minutes until golden and bubbling. Serve hot, garnished with fresh herbs.

Spaghetti with Clams and White Wine *Spaghetti alle vongole*

Raid the pantry to make this quick and easy pasta dish with an intense flavor.

Ingredients
2 tbsp olive oil
1 onion, very finely chopped
2 garlic cloves, crushed
1 can (14 oz) chopped tomatoes
⅔ cup dry white wine
1 jar or can (5 oz) clams in natural juice, drained with juice reserved
12 oz dried spaghetti
2 tbsp finely chopped fresh flat-leaf parsley, plus extra to garnish
salt and freshly ground black pepper
serves 4

Cook's Tip
The tomato sauce can be made several days ahead of time and kept in the refrigerator. Add the clams and heat them through at the last minute—but don't let the sauce boil or they will toughen.

1 Heat the oil in a saucepan, add the onion and cook gently, stirring frequently for about 5 minutes, until softened, but not brown.

2 ▲ Stir in the garlic, tomatoes, wine and reserved clam juice, with salt to taste. Add a generous grinding of black pepper. Bring to a boil, stirring, then lower the heat. Cover the pan and simmer the sauce gently for about 20 minutes, stirring occasionally.

3 ▲ Meanwhile, coil the spaghetti into a large saucepan of rapidly boiling salted water and cook for 12 minutes or until it is *al dente*.

4 Drain the spaghetti. Add the clams and finely chopped parsley to the tomato sauce and heat through, then taste for seasoning. Pour the drained spaghetti into a warmed serving bowl, pour on the tomato sauce and toss to mix. Serve immediately, sprinkled with more parsley.

Pasta with Cream and Parmesan *Pasta Alfredo*

This popular classic originated in Rome. It is incredibly quick and simple, perfect for a midweek supper.

Ingredients
12 oz dried fettuccine
2 tbsp butter
1¼ cups heavy cream
⅔ cup grated Parmesan cheese, plus extra to serve
2 tbsp finely chopped fresh flat-leaf parsley, plus extra to garnish
salt and freshly ground black pepper
serves 3–4

Variation
In Rome, fettuccine would traditionally be served with this sauce, but tagliatelle can be used if you prefer. Pasta shapes, such as penne, rigatoni or farfalle, are also suitable.

1 Cook the fettuccine in a large pan of rapidly boiling salted water for 8–10 minutes or until *al dente*.

2 ▲ Meanwhile, melt the butter in a large flameproof casserole and add the cream and Parmesan, with salt and pepper to taste. Stir over medium heat until the cheese has melted and the sauce has thickened.

3 ▲ Drain the fettuccine and add it to the sauce with the chopped parsley. Fold the pasta and sauce together over medium heat until the strands of pasta are generously coated. Grind more black pepper over the pasta and garnish with the extra chopped parsley. Serve immediately, with a bowl of grated Parmesan served separately.

Tagliatelle with Bolognese Sauce

Tagliatelle alla bolognese

Most people think of bolognese sauce, the famous ragù from Bologna, as being served with spaghetti. Traditionally, it is served with tagliatelle.

Ingredients

2 tbsp olive oil
1 onion, finely chopped
1 carrot, finely chopped
1 celery stick, finely chopped
1 garlic clove, crushed
12 oz ground beef
⅔ cup red wine
1 cup milk
1 can (14 oz) chopped tomatoes
1 tbsp sun-dried tomato paste
12 oz dried tagliatelle
salt and freshly ground black pepper
shredded fresh basil, to garnish
grated Parmesan cheese, to serve

serves 4

1 ▲ Heat the oil in a large saucepan. Add the onion, carrot, celery and garlic and cook gently, stirring frequently, for about 10 minutes, until softened. Do not let the vegetables color.

2 ▲ Add the ground beef to the pan with the vegetables and cook over medium heat until the meat changes color, stirring constantly and breaking up any lumps with a wooden spoon.

3 ▲ Pour in the wine. Stir frequently until it has evaporated, then add the milk and continue cooking and stirring until this has evaporated, too.

Cook's Tip

Don't skimp on the cooking time—it is essential for a full-flavored bolognese sauce. Some Italian cooks insist on cooking it for 3–4 hours, so the longer the better.

4 ▲ Stir in the tomatoes and tomato paste, with salt and pepper to taste. Simmer the sauce uncovered, over the lowest possible heat for at least 45 minutes.

5 Cook the tagliatelle in a large pan of rapidly boiling salted water for 8–10 minutes or until *al dente*. Drain thoroughly and pour into a warmed large bowl. Pour on the sauce and toss to combine. Garnish with basil and serve immediately, with Parmesan cheese served separately.

Penne with Pancetta and Cream

Penne alla carbonara

This makes a gloriously rich supper dish. Follow it with a simple salad.

Ingredients

12 oz dried penne
2 tbsp olive oil
1 small onion, finely chopped
6 oz pancetta slices, any rinds removed, cut into bite-size strips
1–2 garlic cloves, crushed
5 egg yolks
¾ cup heavy cream
1⅓ cups grated Parmesan cheese, plus extra to serve
salt and freshly ground black pepper

serves 3–4

1 ▲ Cook the penne in a large pan of rapidly boiling salted water for about 10 minutes or until *al dente*.

2 Meanwhile, heat the oil in a large flameproof casserole. Add the onion and cook gently for about 5 minutes, stirring frequently, until softened. Add the pancetta and garlic. Cook over medium heat until the pancetta is cooked but not crisp. Remove the pan from the heat and set aside.

3 ▲ Put the egg yolks in a bowl and add the cream and Parmesan cheese. Grind in plenty of black pepper. Beat well to mix.

4 ▲ Drain the penne thoroughly, pour into the casserole and toss over medium to high heat until the pancetta mixture is evenly mixed with the pasta.

5 Remove from the heat, pour in the egg yolk mixture and toss well to combine. Spoon into a large shallow serving dish, grind a little black pepper on top and sprinkle with some of the extra Parmesan. Serve the rest of the Parmesan separately.

Cook's Tip

Serve this dish the moment it is ready or it will not be hot enough. Having added the egg yolks, don't return the pan to the heat or attempt to reheat the pasta and sauce together or the egg yolks will scramble and give the pasta a curdled appearance.

Farfalle with Mushrooms and Cheese

Farfalle boscaiole

Fresh wild mushrooms are very good in this sauce, but they are expensive. To cut the cost, use half wild and half cultivated, or as many wild as you can afford—even a small handful will intensify the mushroom flavor.

Ingredients

1 cup dried porcini mushrooms
2 tbsp butter
1 small onion, finely chopped
1 garlic clove, crushed
3 cups fresh mushrooms, thinly sliced
a few fresh sage leaves, very finely chopped, plus a few whole leaves, to garnish
⅔ cup dry white wine
2 cups dried farfalle
½ cup mascarpone cheese
1 cup Gorgonzola or torta di Gorgonzola cheese, crumbled
salt and freshly ground black pepper
serves 4

1 ▲ Put the dried porcini in a small bowl with 1 cup warm water and let soak for 20–30 minutes. Remove from the liquid and squeeze the porcini over the bowl to extract as much liquid as possible. Strain the liquid and set it aside. Finely chop the porcini.

2 Melt the butter in a large saucepan, add the onion and chopped porcini and cook gently, stirring for about 3 minutes, until the onion is soft. Add the garlic and fresh mushrooms, chopped sage, salt and plenty of black pepper. Cook over medium heat, stirring frequently, for about 5 minutes or until the mushrooms are soft and juicy. Stir in the soaking liquid and the wine and simmer.

3 ▲ Cook the farfalle in a large saucepan of rapidly boiling salted water, for about 10 minutes or until *al dente*.

Variation

For a lighter sauce, use crème fraîche instead of mascarpone.

4 ▲ Meanwhile, stir the mascarpone and Gorgonzola into the mushroom sauce. Heat through, stirring, until melted. Taste for seasoning. Drain the pasta thoroughly, add to the sauce and toss to mix. Serve immediately, with black pepper ground liberally on top. Garnish with sage leaves.

Pasta with Tomato and Chili Sauce

Pasta all'arrabbiata

This is a speciality of Lazio—the word arrabbiata means rabid or angry, and describes the heat that comes from the chili. This quick version is made with jarred sugocasa.

Ingredients

1 lb sugocasa (see Cook's Tip)
2 garlic cloves, crushed
$^2/_3$ cup dry white wine
1 tbsp sun-dried tomato purée
1 fresh red chili
12 oz penne or tortiglioni
$^1/_4$ cup finely chopped fresh flat-leaf parsley
salt and freshly ground black pepper
freshly grated Pecorino cheese, to serve

serves 4

1 ▲ Put the sugocasa, garlic, wine, tomato paste and whole chili in a saucepan and bring to a boil. Cover and simmer gently.

2 ▲ Drop the pasta into a large saucepan of rapidly boiling salted water and simmer for 10–12 minutes or until *al dente*.

Cook's Tip

Sugocasa is sold in jars sometimes labeled "crushed Italian tomatoes." It is finer than canned chopped tomatoes and coarser than passata, and so is ideal for pasta sauces, soups and stews.

3 ▲ Remove the chili from the sauce and add half the parsley. Taste for seasoning. If you prefer a hotter taste, chop some or all of the chili and return it to the sauce.

4 ▲ Drain the pasta and pour into a warmed large bowl. Pour the sauce over the pasta and toss to mix. Serve immediately, sprinkled with grated Pecorino and the remaining parsley.

Three-cheese Lasagne

Lasagne ai tre formaggi

The cheese makes this lasagne quite expensive, so reserve it for a special occasion.

Ingredients
2 tbsp olive oil
1 onion, finely chopped
1 carrot, finely chopped
1 celery stalk, finely chopped
1 garlic clove, crushed
1½ lb ground beef
1 can (14 oz) chopped tomatoes
1¼ cups beef stock
1¼ cups red wine
2 tbsp sun-dried tomato paste
2 tsp dried oregano
9 sheets no-cook lasagne
3 5-oz packages mozzarella cheese, thinly sliced
2 cups ricotta cheese
4 ounces Parmesan cheese, grated
salt and freshly ground black pepper
serves 6–8

1 Heat the oil and gently cook the onion, carrot, celery and garlic, stirring for 10 minutes until softened.

2 Add the beef and cook until it changes color, stirring constantly and breaking up the meat.

3 ▲ Add the tomatoes, stock, wine, tomato paste, oregano and salt and pepper and bring to a boil, stirring. Cover, lower the heat and simmer gently for 1 hour, stirring occasionally.

4 ▲ Preheat the oven to 375°F. Check for seasoning, then ladle one-third of the meat sauce into a 9 x 13 in baking dish and cover with 3 sheets of lasagne. Arrange one-third of the mozzarella slices over the top, dot with one-third of the ricotta, then sprinkle with one-third of the Parmesan.

5 Repeat these layers twice, then bake for 40 minutes. Let cool for 10 minutes before serving.

Tortiglioni with Spicy Sausage Sauce

Tortiglioni alla siciliana

This heady pasta dish is not for the faint-hearted. Serve it with a robust Sicilian red wine.

Ingredients
2 tbsp olive oil
1 onion, finely chopped
1 celery stalk, finely chopped
2 large garlic cloves, crushed
1 fresh red chili, seeded and chopped
1 lb ripe Italian plum tomatoes, peeled and finely chopped
2 tbsp tomato paste
⅔ cup red wine
1 tsp sugar
12 oz dried tortiglioni
6 oz spicy salami, rind removed
salt and freshly ground black pepper
2 tbsp chopped fresh parsley, to garnish
grated Parmesan cheese, to serve
serves 4

Cook's Tip
Buy the salami for this dish in one piece so that you can chop it into large chunks.

1 ▲ Heat the oil, then add the onion, celery, garlic and chili and cook gently, stirring frequently, for about 10 minutes, until softened.

2 Add the tomatoes, tomato paste, wine, sugar and salt and pepper to taste and bring to a boil, stirring. Lower the heat, cover and simmer gently, stirring occasionally, for about 20 minutes. Add a few spoonfuls of water occasionally if the sauce becomes too thick.

3 ▲ Meanwhile, drop the pasta into a large saucepan of rapidly boiling salted water and simmer, uncovered, for 10–12 minutes.

4 Chop the salami into bite-size chunks and add to the sauce. Heat through, then taste for seasoning.

5 Drain the pasta, tip it into a large bowl, then pour on the sauce and toss to mix. Scatter over the parsley and serve with grated Parmesan.

Pasta and Bolognese Casserole

Pasticcio

Pasticcio is Italian for pie, and in some regions this is made with a pastry topping. This simple version makes a great family supper because it's such a favorite with children.

Ingredients

8 oz dried conchiglie
1 quantity hot Bolognese Sauce (see Tagliatelle with Bolognese Sauce, page 158)
salt and freshly ground black pepper

For the white sauce

4 tbsp butter
½ cup flour
3 cups milk
1 cup grated Parmesan cheese
1 egg, beaten
good pinch of grated nutmeg
mixed salad leaves, to serve
serves 4

1 Cook the conchiglie in a large pan of rapidly boiling salted water for 10–12 minutes or until *al dente*.

2 Meanwhile, make the white sauce. Melt the butter in a saucepan until foaming, add the flour and stir over low heat for 1–2 minutes. Remove the pan from the heat and gradually whisk in the milk. Return the pan to the heat and bring to a boil, whisking constantly. Lower the heat and simmer for 2–3 minutes, whisking occasionally, until the sauce thickens. Remove the pan from the heat.

3 ▲ Preheat the oven to 375°F. Drain the pasta thoroughly, pour it into a 8 x 12-in baking dish and mix in the hot bolognese sauce. Level the surface.

4 ▲ Stir about two-thirds of the Parmesan into the white sauce, then stir in the beaten egg and nutmeg, with salt and pepper to taste. Pour on top of the pasta and sauce and sprinkle with the remaining Parmesan. Bake for 20 minutes or until golden and bubbling. Serve hot, straight from the dish. Add a salad garnish to each plate.

Cook's Tip

This is a good way of using up leftover bolognese sauce and cooked pasta—the quantities do not need to be exact.

Pasta with Eggplants

Pasta alla Norma

This Sicilian recipe is traditionally made from fried eggplants. This version is lighter.

Ingredients
2 medium eggplants, about 8 ounces each, diced small
3 tbsp olive oil
10 oz dried macaroni or fusilli
⅔ cup grated Pecorino cheese
salt and freshly ground black pepper
shredded fresh basil leaves, to garnish
crusty bread, to serve

For the tomato sauce
2 tbsp olive oil
1 onion, finely chopped
1 can (14 oz) chopped tomatoes or 1 jar (14 oz) passata
serves 4

Cook's Tip
In Sicily, a cheese called ricotta salata is used for this recipe. This is a matured salted ricotta that is grated like Pecorino and Parmesan. It is unlikely that you will find ricotta salata outside Sicily; Pecorino is the best substitute because it tastes slightly saltier than Parmesan.

1 Soak the diced eggplant in a bowl of cold salted water for 30 minutes.

2 Meanwhile, preheat the oven to 425°F. Make the sauce. Heat the oil in a large saucepan, add the onion and cook gently for about 3 minutes, until softened. Add the tomatoes, with salt and pepper to taste. Bring to a boil, lower the heat, cover and simmer for 20 minutes. Stir the sauce and add a few spoonfuls of water occasionally, to prevent it from becoming too thick. Remove from the heat.

3 ▲ Drain the eggplants and pat dry. Spread the pieces out in a roasting pan, add the oil and toss to coat. Bake for 20–25 minutes, turning the eggplants every 4–5 minutes with a spatula so that they brown evenly.

4 Cook the pasta in a large pan of rapidly boiling salted water for 10–12 minutes or until *al dente*. Reheat the tomato sauce.

5 ▲ Drain the pasta thoroughly and add it to the tomato sauce, with half the roasted eggplant and half the Pecorino. Toss to mix, then taste for seasoning.

6 Spoon the pasta and sauce mixture into a warmed large serving dish and top with the remaining roasted eggplant. Scatter the shredded fresh basil leaves on top, followed by the remaining Pecorino. Serve immediately, with generous chunks of crusty bread.

Spinach and Ricotta Gnocchi

Gnocchi di spinaci e ricotta

The mixture for these tasty little herb dumplings needs to be handled very carefully to achieve light and fluffy results. Serve with sage butter and grated Parmesan.

Ingredients
6 garlic cloves, unpeeled
1 oz mixed fresh herbs, such as parsley, basil, thyme, coriander and chives, finely chopped
8 oz fresh spinach leaves
generous 1 cup ricotta cheese
1 egg yolk
2/3 cup grated Parmesan cheese
2/3 cup flour
1/4 cup butter
2 tbsp fresh sage, chopped
salt and freshly ground black pepper
serves 4

1 Cook the garlic cloves in boiling water for 4 minutes. Drain and pop out of the skins. Place in a food processor with the herbs and blend to a purée or mash the garlic with a fork and add the herbs to mix well.

2 ▲ Place the spinach in a large pan with just the water that clings to the leaves and cook gently until wilted. Let cool, then squeeze out as much liquid as possible. Chop finely.

3 Place the ricotta in a bowl and beat in the egg yolk, spinach, herbs and garlic. Stir in half the Parmesan, sift in the flour and mix well.

Cook's Tip
Squeeze the spinach dry to ensure the gnocchi are not wet and to give a lighter result. The mixture should be fairly soft and will be easier to handle if chilled for an hour before preparing the dumplings.

4 ▲ Using floured hands, break off pieces of the mixture slightly smaller than a walnut and roll into small dumplings.

5 Bring a large pan of salted water to a boil and carefully add the gnocchi. When they rise to the top of the pan they are cooked, this should take about 3 minutes.

6 ▲ The gnocchi should be light and fluffy all the way through. If not, simmer for another minute. Drain well. Meanwhile, melt the butter in a frying pan and add the sage. Simmer gently for 1 minute. Add the gnocchi to the frying pan and toss in the butter over gentle heat for 1 minute, then serve sprinkled with the remaining Parmesan.

Gnocchi with Gorgonzola Sauce

Gnocchi al gorgonzola

Gnocchi are prepared all over Italy with different ingredients used in different regions. These are gnocchi di patate, *potato dumplings.*

Ingredients
1 lb potatoes, unpeeled
1 large egg
1 cup flour
salt and freshly ground black pepper
fresh thyme sprigs, to garnish

For the sauce
4 oz Gorgonzola cheese
1/4 cup heavy cream
1 tbsp fresh thyme, chopped
1/4 cup freshly grated Parmesan cheese, to serve
serves 4

1 Cook the potatoes in boiling salted water for about 20 minutes until they are tender. Drain and, when cool enough to handle, remove the skins.

2 ▲ Force the potatoes through a sieve, pressing through using the back of a spoon, into a mixing bowl. Add plenty of seasoning and then beat in the egg until completely incorporated. Add the flour a little at a time, stirring well with a wooden spoon after each addition until you have a smooth dough. (You may not need all the flour.)

3 Turn the dough out onto a floured surface and knead for about 3 minutes, adding more flour if necessary, until it is smooth and soft and not sticky to the touch.

Cook's Tips
Choose dry, floury potatoes. Avoid new or red-skinned potatoes, which do not have the right dry texture.

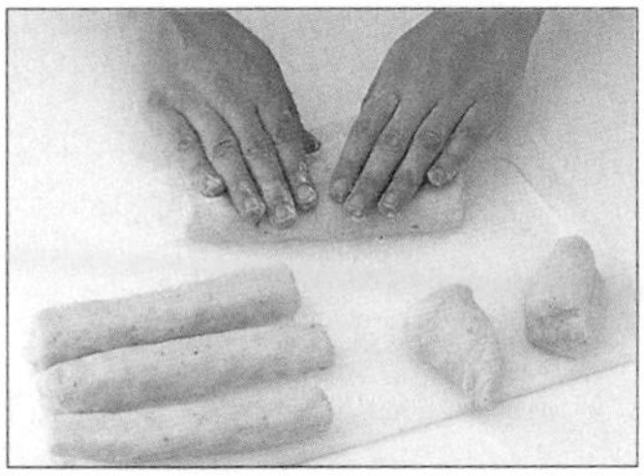

4 ▲ Divide the dough into 6 equal pieces. Flour your hands and gently roll each piece between your hands into a log shape measuring 6–8 in long and 1 in around. Cut each log into 6–8 pieces, about 1 in long, then gently roll each piece in the flour. Form into gnocchi by gently pressing each piece on to the floured surface with the tines of a fork to leave ridges in the dough.

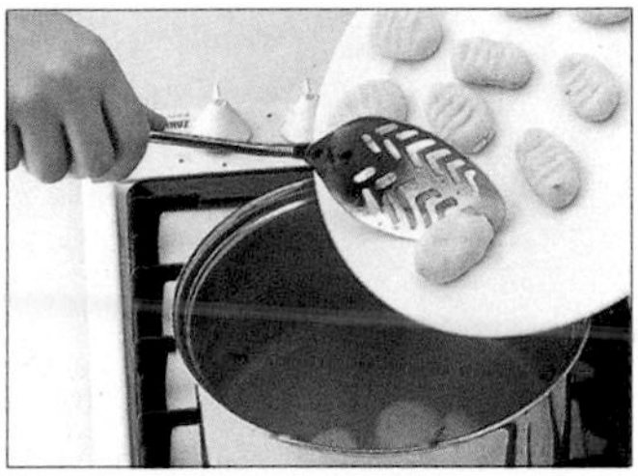

5 ▲ To cook, drop the gnocchi into a pan of boiling water about 12 at a time. Once they rise to the surface, after about 2 minutes, cook for 4–5 more minutes. Remove and drain.

6 Place the Gorgonzola, cream and thyme in a large frying pan and heat gently until the cheese melts to form a thick, creamy consistency. Add the drained gnocchi and toss well to combine. Serve with Parmesan and garnish with thyme.

Rice, Polenta & Pizzas

In the north of Italy, rice is served as a first course, as a creamy risotto, but you can serve it as a main dish, with a salad and Italian bread. Polenta, also from the north of Italy, is most often served with the main course, especially with meaty casseroles. Pizzas hail from the south, where they are eaten at any time of day, the ultimate convenience food.

Risotto with Spring Vegetables

Risotto primavera

This is one of the prettiest risottos, especially when made with yellow summer squash.

Ingredients
1 cup shelled fresh peas
1 cup green beans, cut into short lengths
2 tbsps olive oil
6 tbsp butter
2 small yellow summer squash, cut into matchsticks
1 onion, finely chopped
1½ cups risotto rice
½ cup Italian dry white vermouth
about 4 cups boiling chicken stock
1 cup grated Parmesan cheese
a small handful of fresh basil leaves, finely shredded, plus a few whole leaves, to garnish
salt and freshly ground black pepper
serves 4

1 Blanch the peas and beans in a large saucepan of lightly salted boiling water for 2–3 minutes, until just tender. Drain, refresh under cold running water, drain again and set aside for later.

2 ▲ Heat the oil and 2 tbsp of the butter in a medium saucepan until foaming. Add the squash and cook gently for 2–3 minutes or until just softened. Remove with a slotted spoon and set aside. Add the onion to the pan and cook gently for about 3 minutes, stirring frequently, until softened.

3 ▲ Stir in the rice until the grains start to swell and burst, then add the vermouth. Stir until the vermouth stops sizzling and most of it has been absorbed by the rice, then add a few ladlefuls of the stock, with salt and pepper to taste. Stir over low heat until the stock has been absorbed.

4 Continue cooking and stirring for 20–25 minutes, adding the remaining stock a few ladlefuls at a time. The rice should be *al dente* and the risotto should have a moist and creamy appearance.

5 ▲ Gently stir in the vegetables, the remaining butter and about half the grated Parmesan. Heat through, then stir in the shredded basil and taste for seasoning. Garnish with a few whole basil leaves and serve hot, with the remaining grated Parmesan served separately.

Variations
Shelled fava beans can be used instead of the peas, and asparagus tips instead of the green beans. Use green zucchini if yellow summer squash are unavailable.

Rice with Peas, Ham and Cheese

Risi e bisi

A classic risotto from the Veneto. Although it is traditionally served as an appetizer in Italy, risi e bisi makes an excellent supper dish with hot crusty bread.

Ingredients
6 tbsp butter
1 small onion, finely chopped
about 4 cups boiling chicken stock
$1\frac{1}{2}$ cups risotto rice
$\frac{2}{3}$ cup dry white wine
2 cups frozen peas, thawed
4 oz cooked ham, diced
salt and freshly ground black pepper
$\frac{2}{3}$ cup Parmesan cheese, to serve
serves 4

1 ▲ Melt 4 tbsp of the butter in a saucepan until foaming. Add the onion and cook gently for about 3 minutes, stirring frequently, until softened. Have the hot stock ready in an adjacent pan.

2 ▲ Add the rice to the onion mixture. Stir until the grains start to burst, then pour in the wine. Stir until it stops sizzling and most of it has been absorbed, then pour in a little hot stock, with salt and pepper to taste. Stir over low heat until the stock has been absorbed.

3 ▲ Add the remaining stock, a little at a time, allowing the rice to absorb all the liquid before adding more, and stirring constantly. Add the peas toward the end. After 20–25 minutes, the rice should be *al dente* and the risotto moist and creamy.

4 ▲ Gently stir in the diced cooked ham and the remaining butter. Heat through until the butter has melted, then taste for seasoning. Transfer to a warmed serving bowl. Grate or shave a little Parmesan over the top and serve the rest separately.

Saffron Risotto

Risotto alla milanese

This classic risotto is always served with osso buco, but makes a delicious first course or light supper dish in its own right.

Ingredients
about 5 cups beef or chicken stock
good pinch of saffron threads or
1 envelope of saffron powder
6 tbsp butter
1 onion, finely chopped
1½ cups risotto rice
1 cup grated Parmesan cheese
salt and freshly ground black pepper
serves 4

1 Bring the stock to a boil, then reduce to a low simmer. Ladle a little stock into a small bowl. Add the saffron threads or powder and set aside to infuse.

2 Melt 4 tbsp of the butter in a large saucepan until foaming. Add the onion and cook gently for about 3 minutes, stirring frequently, until softened.

3 Add the rice. Stir until the grains start to swell and burst, then add a few ladlefuls of the stock, with the saffron liquid and salt and pepper to taste. Stir over low heat until the stock is absorbed. Add the remaining stock, a few ladlefuls at a time, allowing the rice to absorb all the liquid before adding more, and stirring constantly. After 20–25 minutes, the rice should be *al dente* and the risotto golden yellow, moist and creamy.

4 ▲ Gently stir in about two-thirds of the grated Parmesan and the remaining butter. Heat through until the butter has melted, then taste for seasoning. Transfer the risotto to a warmed serving bowl or platter and serve hot, with the remaining grated Parmesan sprinkled on top.

Polenta Elisa

Polenta Elisa

This dish comes from the valley around Lake Como. Serve it solo as an appetizer, or with a mixed salad and some sliced salami or prosciutto for a midweek supper.

Ingredients
1 cup milk
2 cups pre-cooked polenta
1 cup grated Gruyère cheese
1 cup torta di Dolcelatte cheese, crumbled
4 tbsp butter
2 garlic cloves, roughly chopped
a few fresh sage leaves, chopped
salt and freshly ground black pepper
prosciutto, to serve
serves 4

1 Preheat the oven to 400°F. Lightly butter an 8–10-in glass baking dish.

Cook's Tip
Pour the polenta into the boiling liquid in a continuous stream, stirring constantly with a wooden spoon or balloon whisk. If using a whisk, change to a wooden spoon once the polenta thickens.

2 ▲ Bring the milk and 3 cups water to a boil in a large saucepan, add 1 tsp salt, then pour in the polenta. Cook for about 8 minutes or according to the instructions on the package.

3 Spoon half the polenta into the baking dish and level. Cover with half the grated Gruyère and crumbled Dolcelatte. Spoon the remaining polenta evenly over the top and sprinkle with the remaining cheeses.

4 Melt the butter in a small saucepan until foaming, add the garlic and sage and fry, stirring, until the butter turns golden brown.

5 ▲ Drizzle the butter mixture over the polenta and cheese and grind black pepper liberally over the top. Bake for 5 minutes. Serve hot, with slices of prosciutto.

Risotto with Four Cheeses

Risotto ai quattro formaggi

This is a very rich dish. Serve it for a dinner-party first course, with sparkling white wine.

Ingredients
3 tbsp butter
1 small onion, finely chopped
4 cups boiling chicken stock
1¾ cups risotto rice
scant 1 cup sparkling dry white wine
½ cup grated Gruyère cheese
½ cup Fontina cheese, diced small
½ cup Gorgonzola cheese, crumbled
⅔ cup grated Parmesan cheese
salt and freshly ground black pepper
fresh flat-leaf parsley, to garnish
serves 6

Cook's Tip
If you're feeling extravagant you can use Champagne for this risotto, although Asti spumante works quite well.

1 Melt the butter in a saucepan until foaming. Add the onion and cook gently, stirring frequently for about 3 minutes, until softened. Have the hot stock ready in an adjacent pan.

2 ▲ Add the rice and stir until the grains start to swell and burst, then add the sparkling wine. Stir until it stops sizzling and most of it has been absorbed by the rice, then pour in a little of the hot stock. Add salt and pepper to taste. Stir over low heat until the stock has been absorbed.

3 Add more stock, a little at a time, allowing the rice to absorb it before adding more, and stirring constantly. After 20–25 minutes the rice will be *al dente* and the risotto creamy.

4 ▲ Turn off the heat under the pan, then add the Gruyère, Fontina, Gorgonzola and 2 tbsp of the Parmesan. Stir gently until the cheeses have melted, then taste for seasoning. Pour into a serving bowl and garnish with parsley. Serve the remaining Parmesan separately.

Polenta with Mushroom Sauce

Polenta con salsa di funghi

Polenta, made from maize flour, fulfills the same function as rice, bread or potatoes in forming the starchy base for a meal. Here, it is cooked until it forms a soft dough, then flavored with Parmesan. Its subtle taste works well with the rich mushroom sauce.

Ingredients
5 cups vegetable stock
3 cups polenta
⅔ cup grated Parmesan cheese
salt and freshly ground black pepper

For the sauce
1 cup dried porcini mushrooms
1 tbsp olive oil
4 tbsp butter
1 onion, finely chopped
1 carrot, finely chopped
1 celery stalk, finely chopped
2 garlic cloves, crushed
6 cups mixed chestnut and large flat mushrooms, roughly chopped
½ cup red wine
1 can (14 oz) chopped tomatoes
1 tsp tomato paste
1 tbsp chopped fresh thyme leaves
serves 4

1 ▲ Make the sauce. Put the dried mushrooms in a bowl, add ⅔ cup of hot water and soak for 20 minutes. Drain the mushrooms, reserving the liquid, and chop them roughly.

2 Heat the oil and butter in a saucepan and add the onion, carrot, celery and garlic. Cook over low heat for about 5 minutes, until the vegetables are beginning to soften, then raise the heat and add the fresh and soaked dried mushrooms to the pan of vegetables. Cook for 8–10 minutes, until the mushrooms are softened and golden.

3 ▲ Pour in the wine and cook rapidly for 2–3 minutes, until reduced, then pour in the tomatoes and reserved mushroom liquid. Stir in the tomato paste with the thyme and plenty of salt and pepper. Lower the heat and simmer for 20 minutes, until the sauce is rich and thick.

Cook's Tip
The polenta will spit during cooking, so use a long-handled spoon and wrap a towel around your hand to protect it while stirring.

4 ▲ Meanwhile, heat the stock in a large heavy saucepan. Add a generous pinch of salt. As soon as it simmers, pour in the polenta in a fine stream, whisking until the mixture is smooth. Cook for 30 minutes, stirring constantly, until the polenta comes away from the pan. Remove from the heat and stir in half the Parmesan and some black pepper.

5 Divide among four heated bowls and top each with sauce. Sprinkle with the remaining Parmesan.

Butternut Squash and Sage Pizza

Pizza con zucca e salvia

The combination of the sweet butternut squash, sage and sharp goat cheese works wonderfully on this pizza. Pumpkin and winter squashes are popular in northern Italy.

Ingredients
1 tbsp butter
2 tbsp olive oil
2 shallots, finely chopped
1 butternut squash, peeled, seeded and cubed, about 1 pound prepared weight
16 sage leaves
1 recipe risen Pizza Dough
1 recipe Tomato Sauce
1 cup mozzarella cheese, sliced
½ cup firm goat cheese
salt and freshly ground black pepper
serves 4

1 ▲ Preheat the oven to 400°F. Oil four baking sheets. Put the butter and oil in a roasting pan and heat in the oven for a few minutes. Add the shallots, squash and half the sage leaves. Toss to coat. Roast for 15–20 minutes, until tender.

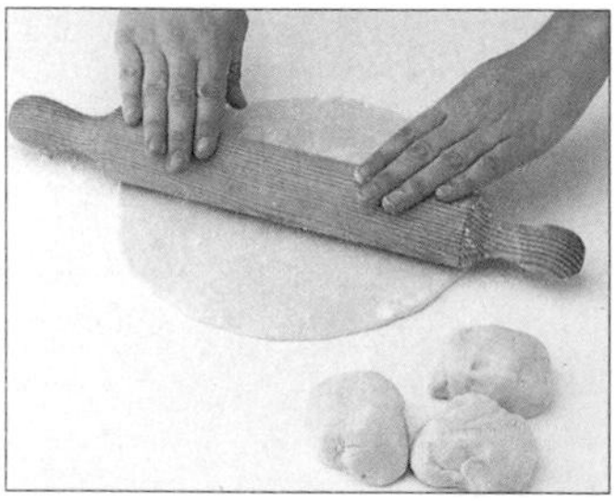

2 ▲ Raise the oven temperature to 425°F. Divide the pizza dough into four equal pieces and roll out each piece on a lightly floured surface to a 10-in round.

3 ▲ Transfer each round to a baking sheet and spread with the tomato sauce, leaving a ½-in border all around. Spoon the squash and shallot mixture over the crust.

4 ▲ Arrange the slices of mozzarella over the squash mixture and crumble the goat cheese on top. Scatter the remaining sage leaves on top and season with plenty of salt and pepper. Bake for 15–20 minutes, until the cheese has melted and the crust on each pizza is golden.

Ricotta and Fontina Pizza

Pizza con ricotta e fontina

The flavor of the earthy mixed mushrooms is delicious with the creamy cheeses.

Ingredients

For the pizza dough

1/2 tsp active dried yeast
pinch of sugar
4 cups flour
1 tsp salt
2 tbsp olive oil

For the tomato sauce

1 can (14 oz) chopped tomatoes
2/3 cup passata
1 large garlic clove, finely chopped
1 tsp dried oregano
1 bay leaf
2 tsp malt vinegar
salt and freshly ground black pepper

For the topping

2 tbsp olive oil
1 garlic clove, finely chopped
4 cups mixed mushrooms (chestnut, flat or button), sliced
2 tbsp chopped fresh oregano, plus whole leaves, to garnish
generous 1 cup ricotta cheese
8 oz Fontina cheese, sliced

makes 4 10-in thin crust pizzas

1 ▲ Make the dough. Put 1¼ cups warm water in a measuring cup. Add the yeast and sugar and set aside for 5–10 minutes until frothy. Sift the flour and salt into a large bowl and make a well in the center. Gradually pour in the yeast mixture and the olive oil. Mix to make a smooth dough. Knead on a lightly floured surface for about 10 minutes until smooth, springy and elastic. Place the dough in a floured bowl, cover and let rise in a warm place for 1½ hours.

2 Meanwhile, make the tomato sauce. Place all the ingredients in a saucepan, cover and bring to a boil. Lower the heat, remove the lid and simmer for 20 minutes, stirring occasionally, until reduced.

3 ▲ Make the topping. Heat the oil in a frying pan. Add the garlic and mushrooms, with salt and pepper to taste. Cook, stirring, for about 5 minutes or until the mushrooms are tender and golden. Set aside.

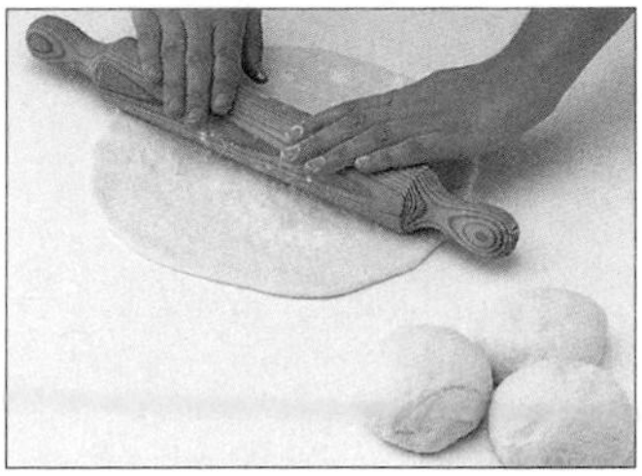

4 ▲ Preheat the oven to 425°F. Brush four baking sheets with oil. Knead the dough for 2 minutes, then divide into four equal pieces. Roll out each piece to a 10-in round and place on a baking sheet.

5 Spoon the tomato sauce over each dough round. Brush the edge with a little olive oil. Add the mushrooms, oregano and cheese. Bake for about 15 minutes until golden brown. Scatter the oregano leaves on top.

Fried Pizza Pasties

Panzerotti

These tasty little morsels are served all over central and southern Italy as a snack food or as part of a hot antipasto. Although similar to calzone, they are fried instead of baked.

Ingredients
½ recipe Pizza Dough
½ recipe Tomato Sauce
8 oz mozzarella cheese, chopped
4 oz Italian salami, thinly sliced
handful of fresh basil leaves, roughly torn
sunflower oil, for deep frying
salt and freshly ground black pepper
serves 4

Cook's Tip
To test that the oil is ready, carefully drop a piece of bread into the oil. If it sizzles instantly, the oil is ready.

1 Preheat the oven to 400°F. Brush two baking sheets with oil. Divide the dough into 12 pieces and roll out each piece on a lightly floured surface to a 4-in round.

2 ▲ Spread the center of each round with a little of the tomato sauce, leaving a sufficient border all around for sealing the pasty, then top with a few pieces of mozzarella and salami slices. Sprinkle with salt and freshly ground black pepper and add a few fresh basil leaves to each round.

3 ▲ Brush the edges of the dough rounds with a little water, then fold over and press together to seal.

4 Heat oil to a depth of about 4 in in a heavy pan. When hot, deep-fry the pasties, a few at a time, for 8–10 minutes until golden. Drain on paper towels and serve hot.

Sicilian Pizza

Pizza alla siciliana

This robust-flavored pizza is topped with mozzarella and Pecorino cheeses.

Ingredients
1 small eggplant, cut into thin rounds
2 tbsp olive oil
½ recipe risen Pizza Dough
½ recipe Tomato Sauce
6 oz mozzarella cheese, sliced
½ cup pitted black olives
1 tbsp drained capers
¼ cup grated Pecorino cheese
salt and freshly ground black pepper
serves 2

Cook's Tip
For best results choose olives that have been marinated in extra virgin olive oil and flavored with herbs and garlic.

1 ▲ Preheat the oven to 400°F. Brush one or two baking sheets with oil. Brush the eggplant rounds with olive oil and arrange them on the baking sheet(s). Bake for 10–15 minutes, turning once, until browned and tender. Remove the eggplant slices from the baking sheet(s) and drain on paper towels.

2 Raise the oven temperature to 425°F. Roll out the pizza dough into two 10-in rounds. Transfer to baking sheets and spread with the tomato sauce.

3 ▲ Pile the eggplant slices on top of the tomato sauce and cover with the mozzarella. Dot with the black olives and capers. Sprinkle the Pecorino cheese liberally over the top, and season with plenty of salt and pepper. Bake for 15–20 minutes, until the crust on each pizza is golden.

Fish & Shellfish

Italy has such an extensive coastline—and so many lakes, rivers and streams—that it is no wonder that fish and shellfish are so popular. Of course there are many different types that are unique to the country itself, but the most common varieties are available outside Italy. Cooking methods are very simple and quick, and any accompanying sauces light and fresh.

Monkfish with Tomato and Olive Sauce *Pesce alla calabrese*

This dish comes from the coast of Calabria in southern Italy. Garlic-flavored mashed potatoes are delicious with its robust sauce.

Ingredients
1 lb fresh mussels, scrubbed
a few fresh basil sprigs
2 garlic cloves, roughly chopped
1¼ cups dry white wine
2 tbsp olive oil
1 tbsp butter
2 lb monkfish fillets, skinned and cut into large chunks
1 onion, finely chopped
1¼ lb jar sugocasa or passata
1 tbsp sun-dried tomato paste
1 cup pitted black olives
salt and freshly ground black pepper
extra fresh basil leaves, to garnish
serves 4

1 ▲ Put the mussels in a flameproof casserole with some basil leaves, the garlic and the wine. Cover and bring to a boil. Lower the heat and simmer for 5 minutes, shaking the pan frequently. Remove the mussels, discarding any that fail to open. Strain the cooking liquid and reserve.

2 ▲ Heat the oil and butter until foaming, add the monkfish pieces and sauté over a medium heat until they just change color. Remove.

3 ▲ Add the onion to the juices in the casserole and cook gently for about 5 minutes, stirring frequently, until softened. Add the sugocasa or passata, the reserved cooking liquid from the mussels and the tomato paste. Season with salt and pepper to taste. Bring to a boil, stirring, then lower the heat, cover and simmer for 20 minutes, stirring occasionally.

4 ▲ Pull off and discard the top shells from the mussels. Add the monkfish pieces to the tomato sauce and cook gently for 5 minutes. Gently stir in the olives and remaining basil, then taste for seasoning. Place the mussels in their half shells on top of the sauce, cover the pan and heat the mussels through for 1–2 minutes. Serve immediately, garnished with basil.

Char-grilled Squid

Grigliata di calamari

If you like your food hot, chop some—or all—of the chili seeds with the flesh. If not, cut the chilies in half lengthwise, scrape out the seeds and discard them before chopping the flesh.

Ingredients
2 whole prepared squid, with tentacles
5 tbsp olive oil
2 tbsp balsamic vinegar
2 fresh red chilies, finely chopped
¼ cup dry white wine
salt and freshly ground black pepper
hot cooked risotto rice, to serve
sprigs of fresh parsley, to garnish
serves 2

1 ▲ Make a lengthwise cut down the body of each squid, then open out the body flat. Score the flesh on both sides of the bodies in a criss-cross pattern with the tip of a sharp knife. Chop the tentacles. Place all the squid in a china or glass dish. Whisk the oil and vinegar in a small bowl. Add salt and pepper to taste and pour over the squid. Cover and let marinate for about 1 hour.

2 ▲ Heat a ridged cast-iron pan until hot. Add the body of one of the squid. Cook over medium heat for 2–3 minutes, pressing the squid with a spatula to keep it flat. Repeat on the other side. Cook the other squid body in the same way.

3 ▲ Cut the squid bodies into diagonal strips. Pile the hot risotto rice in the center of heated soup plates and top with the strips of squid, arranging them in criss-cross fashion. Keep hot.

4 ▲ Add the chopped tentacles and chilies to the pan and toss over medium heat for 2 minutes. Stir in the wine, then drizzle over the squid and rice. Garnish with the parsley and serve immediately.

Pan-fried Shrimp in their Shells

Gamberi fritti in padella

Although expensive, this is a very quick and simple dish, ideal for an impromptu supper with friends. Serve with hot crusty Italian bread to scoop up the juices.

Ingredients

¼ cup extra virgin olive oil
32 large fresh shrimp, in their shells
4 garlic cloves, finely chopped
½ cup Italian dry white vermouth
3 tbsp passata
salt and freshly ground black pepper
chopped fresh flat-leaf parsley, to garnish
crusty bread, to serve
serves 4

Cook's Tip

Shrimp in their shells are sweet and juicy, and fun to eat with your fingers. They can be quite messy though, so provide guests with finger bowls and napkins.

1 ▲ Heat the olive oil in a large heavy frying pan until just sizzling. Add the shrimp and toss over medium to high heat until their shells just begin to turn pink. Sprinkle the garlic over the shrimp in the pan and toss again, then add the vermouth and let it bubble, tossing the shrimp constantly so that they cook evenly and absorb the flavors of the garlic and vermouth.

2 ▲ Keeping the pan on the heat, add the passata, with salt and pepper to taste. Stir until the shrimp are thoroughly coated in the sauce. Serve immediately, sprinkled with the parsley and accompanied by plenty of hot crusty bread.

Broiled Red Mullet with Rosemary

Triglie al rosmarino

This recipe is very simple—the taste of broiled red mullet is so good in itself that it needs very little to bring out the flavor.

Ingredients

4 red mullet, cleaned, about 10 ounces each
4 garlic cloves, cut lengthwise into thin slivers
5 tbsp olive oil
2 tbsp balsamic vinegar
2 tsp very finely chopped fresh rosemary or 1 tsp dried rosemary
freshly ground black pepper
coarse sea salt, to serve
fresh rosemary sprigs and lemon wedges, to garnish
serves 4

Variation

Red mullet are extra delicious cooked on the barbecue. If possible, enclose them in a basket grill so that they are easy to turn over.

1 ▲ Cut three diagonal slits in both sides of each fish. Push the garlic slivers into the slits. Place the fish in a single layer in a shallow dish. Whisk the oil, vinegar and rosemary, with ground black pepper to taste.

2 ▲ Pour the marinade over the fish, cover with plastic wrap and let marinate in a cool place for 1 hour. Put the fish on the rack of a broiler pan and broil for 5–6 minutes on each side, turning once and brushing with the marinade. Serve hot, sprinkled with coarse sea salt and garnished with fresh rosemary sprigs and lemon wedges.

Pan-fried Sole with Lemon

Sogliole al limone

The delicate flavor and texture of sole is brought out in this simple, classic recipe. Lemon sole is used here because it is easier to obtain—and less expensive—than Dover sole.

Ingredients

2–3 tbsp flour
4 lemon sole fillets
3 tbsp olive oil
4 tbsp butter
¼ cup lemon juice
2 tbsp rinsed bottled capers
salt and freshly ground black pepper
fresh flat-leaf parsley and lemon wedges, to garnish

serves 2

Cook's Tip

It is important to cook the pan juices to the right color after removing the fish. Too pale, and they will taste insipid, too dark, and they may taste bitter. Take great care not to be distracted at this point so that you can watch the color of the juices change to a golden brown.

1 ▲ Season the flour with salt and black pepper. Coat the sole fillets evenly on both sides. Heat the oil with half the butter in a large shallow pan until foaming. Add two sole fillets and fry over medium heat for 2–3 minutes on each side.

2 Lift out the sole fillets with a spatula and place on a warmed serving platter. Keep hot. Fry the remaining sole fillets.

3 ▲ Remove the pan from the heat and add the lemon juice and remaining butter. Return the pan to high heat and stir vigorously until the pan juices are sizzling and beginning to turn golden brown. Remove from the heat and stir in the capers.

4 Pour the pan juices over the sole, sprinkle with salt and pepper to taste and garnish with the parsley. Add the lemon wedges and serve immediately.

Three-color Fish Kebabs

Spiedini tricolori

Don't let the fish marinate for more than an hour. The lemon juice will start to break down the fibers of the fish after this time and it will be difficult not to overcook it.

Ingredients
½ cup olive oil
finely grated rind and juice of 1 large lemon
1 tsp crushed chili flakes
12 oz monkfish fillet, cubed
12 oz swordfish fillet, cubed
12 oz thick salmon fillet or steak, cubed
2 red, yellow or orange bell peppers, cored, seeded and cut into squares
2 tbsp finely chopped fresh flat-leaf parsley
salt and freshly ground black pepper

For the sweet tomato and chili salsa
8 oz ripe tomatoes, finely chopped
1 garlic clove, crushed
1 fresh red chili, seeded and chopped
3 tbsp extra virgin olive oil
1 tbsp lemon juice
1 tbsp finely chopped fresh flat-leaf parsley
pinch of sugar
serves 4

1 ▲ Put the oil in a shallow glass or china bowl and add the lemon rind and juice, the chili flakes and pepper to taste. Whisk to combine, then add the fish chunks. Turn to coat evenly.

2 Add the pepper squares, stir, then cover and marinate in a cool place for 1 hour, turning occasionally.

Variation
Use tuna instead of swordfish. It has a similar meaty texture.

3 ▲ Thread the fish and peppers onto eight oiled metal skewers, reserving the marinade. Barbecue or grill the skewered fish for 5–8 minutes, turning once.

4 Meanwhile, make the salsa by mixing all the ingredients in a bowl, and seasoning to taste with salt and pepper. Heat the reserved marinade in a small pan, remove from the heat and stir in the parsley, with salt and pepper to taste. Serve the kebabs hot, with the marinade spooned over, accompanied by the salsa.

Roast Sea Bass

Branzino al forno

Sea bass has meaty flesh. It is an expensive fish, best cooked as simply as possible. Avoid elaborate sauces, which would mask its delicate flavor.

Ingredients

1 fennel bulb with fronds, about 10 oz
2 lemons
$^1/_2$ cup olive oil
1 small red onion, diced
2 sea bass, about 1$^1/_4$ lb each, cleaned with heads left on
$^1/_2$ cup dry white wine
salt and freshly ground black pepper
lemon slices, to garnish
serves 4

1 ▲ Preheat the oven to 375°F. Cut the fronds off the top of the fennel and reserve for the garnish. Cut the fennel bulb lengthwise into thin wedges, then into dice. Cut one half lemon into four slices. Squeeze the juice from the remaining lemon half and the other lemon.

2 ▲ Heat 2 tbsp of the oil in a frying pan, add the diced fennel and onion and cook gently, stirring frequently, for about 5 minutes, until softened. Remove from the heat.

3 ▲ Make three diagonal slashes on both sides of each sea bass with a sharp knife. Brush a roasting pan generously with oil, add the fish and tuck two lemon slices in each cavity. Scatter the softened fennel and onion over the fish.

Cook's Tip

Farmed or wild sea bass are available year round from the fishmonger. They are expensive, but well worth buying for a special main course. Sizes vary from the ones used here, which are a very good size for two servings, to 3–4$^1/_2$ lb, which take up to 50 minutes to cook.

4 ▲ Whisk the remaining oil, the lemon juice and salt and pepper to taste and pour over the fish. Cover with foil and roast for 30 minutes or until the flesh flakes, removing the foil for the last 10 minutes. Discard the lemon slices, transfer the fish to a heated serving platter and keep hot.

5 Put the roasting pan on top of the stove. Add the wine and stir over medium heat to incorporate all the pan juices. Bring to a boil, then spoon the juices over the fish. Garnish with the reserved fennel fronds and lemon slices and serve immediately.

Stuffed Swordfish Rolls

Involtini di pesce spada

This is a very tasty dish, with strong flavors from the tomato, olive and caper sauce—and from the salty Pecorino cheese. If desired, substitute Parmesan cheese, which is milder.

Ingredients

2 tbsp olive oil
1 small onion, finely chopped
1 celery stalk, finely chopped
1 lb ripe Italian plum tomatoes, chopped
4 oz pitted green olives, half roughly chopped, half left whole
3 tbsp drained bottled capers
4 large swordfish steaks, each about ½ inch thick and 4 ounces in weight
1 egg
⅔ cup grated Pecorino cheese
½ cup fresh white bread crumbs
salt and freshly ground black pepper
sprigs of fresh parsley, to garnish
serves 4

Cook's Tip

This dish is not for the inexperienced cook because the pounding, stuffing and rolling of the fish is quite tricky. If you prefer, you can omit the stuffing and simply cook the swordfish steaks in the sauce.

1 ▲ Heat the oil in a large heavy frying pan. Add the onion and celery and cook gently for about 3 minutes, stirring frequently. Stir in the tomatoes, olives and capers, with salt and pepper to taste. Bring to a boil, then lower the heat, cover and simmer for about 15 minutes. Stir occasionally and add a little water if the sauce becomes too thick.

2 Remove the fish skin and place each steak between two sheets of plastic wrap. Pound lightly with a rolling pin until each steak is reduced to about ¼ in thick.

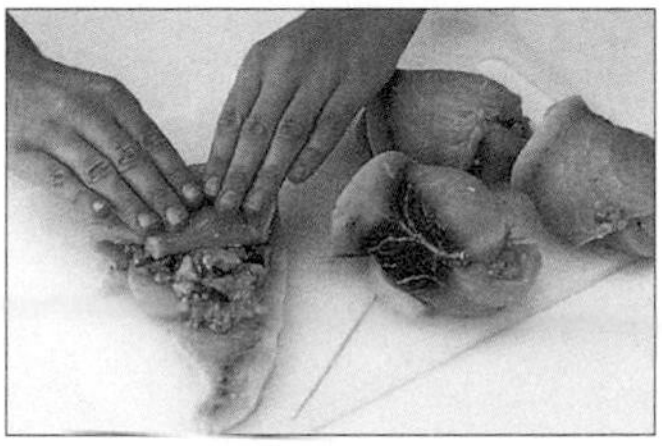

3 ▲ Beat the egg in a bowl and add the cheese, bread crumbs and a few spoonfuls of the sauce. Stir well to mix to a moist stuffing. Spread one-quarter of the stuffing over each swordfish steak, then roll up into a sausage shape. Secure with wooden toothpicks.

4 ▲ Add the rolls to the sauce in the pan and bring to a boil. Lower the heat, cover and simmer for about 30 minutes, turning once. Add a little water as the sauce reduces.

5 Remove the rolls from the sauce and discard the toothpicks. Place on warmed dinner plates and spoon the sauce over and around. Garnish with the parsley and serve hot.

Poultry & Meat

*The Italians eat a wide variety of different meats, and tastes vary according to region. Veal, pork and poultry are popular all over the country, while beef is farmed and eaten more in the north, and lamb is a great Roman speciality. All meats are eaten as a second course—*secondo piatto*—usually simple and served solo, with vegetables to follow.*

Beef Stew with Tomatoes, Wine and Peas *Spezzatino*

It seems there are as many spezzatino recipes as there are Italian cooks. This one is very traditional, perfect for a winter lunch or dinner. Serve it with boiled or mashed potatoes to soak up the deliciously rich sauce.

Ingredients
2 tbsp flour
2 tsp chopped fresh thyme or
1 tsp dried thyme
$2^1/_4$ lb braising or stewing steak, cut into large cubes
3 tbsp olive oil
1 medium onion, roughly chopped
1 jar (1 lb) sugocasa or passata
1 cup beef stock
1 cup red wine
2 garlic cloves, crushed
2 tbsp tomato paste
2 cups shelled fresh peas
1 tsp sugar
salt and freshly ground black pepper
fresh thyme, to garnish
serves 4

1 ▲ Preheat the oven to 325°F. Put the flour in a shallow dish and season with the thyme and salt and pepper. Add the beef cubes and coat evenly.

2 ▲ Heat the oil in a large flameproof casserole, add the beef and brown on all sides over medium to high heat. Remove with a slotted spoon and drain on paper towels.

3 ▲ Add the onion to the pan, scraping the base of the pan to mix in any sediment. Cook gently for about 3 minutes, stirring frequently, until softened, then stir in the sugocasa, stock, wine, garlic and tomato paste. Bring to a boil, stirring. Return the beef to the pan and stir well to coat with the sauce. Cover and cook in the oven for $1^1/_2$ hours.

4 ▲ Stir in the peas and sugar. Return the casserole to the oven and cook for 30 more minutes, or until the beef is tender. Taste for seasoning. Garnish with fresh thyme before serving.

Variation
Use thawed frozen peas instead of fresh. Add them 10 minutes before the end of cooking.

Meatballs with Peperonata

Polpette di manzo

These taste very good with creamed potatoes. Use a potato ricer to get them really smooth.

Ingredients
14 oz ground beef
2 cups fresh white bread crumbs
2/3 cup grated Parmesan cheese
2 eggs, beaten
pinch of paprika
pinch of grated nutmeg
1 tsp dried mixed herbs
2 thin slices of mortadella or prosciutto (total weight about 2 ounces), chopped
vegetable oil, for shallow frying
salt and freshly ground black pepper
snipped fresh basil leaves, to garnish

For the peperonata
2 tbsp olive oil
1 small onion, thinly sliced
2 yellow bell peppers, cored, seeded and cut lengthwise into thin strips
2 red bell peppers, cored, seeded and cut lengthwise into thin strips
1 1/4 cups finely chopped tomatoes or passata
1 tablespoon chopped fresh parsley
serves 4

1 ▲ Put the ground beef in a bowl. Add half the bread crumbs and all the remaining ingredients, including salt and ground black pepper to taste. Mix well with clean wet hands. Divide the mixture into 12 equal portions and roll each into a ball. Flatten the meat balls slightly so they are about 1/2 in thick.

2 Put the remaining bread crumbs on a plate and roll the meatballs in them, a few at a time, until they are evenly coated. Place on a plate, cover with plastic wrap and chill for about 30 minutes to firm up.

3 ▲ Meanwhile, make the peperonata. Heat the oil in a medium saucepan, add the onion and cook gently for about 3 minutes, stirring frequently, until softened. Add the pepper strips and cook for 3 minutes, stirring constantly. Stir in the tomatoes and parsley, with salt and pepper to taste. Bring to a boil, stirring. Cover and cook for 15 minutes, then remove the lid and continue to cook, stirring frequently, for 10 more minutes, or until reduced and thick. Taste for seasoning. Keep hot.

4 ▲ Pour oil into a frying pan to a depth of about 1 in. When hot but not smoking, shallow fry the meatballs for 10–12 minutes, turning them 3–4 times and pressing them flat with a spatula. Remove and drain on paper towels. Serve hot, with the peperonata alongside. Garnish with the basil.

Variation
Instead of ground beef, used half ground pork and half ground veal.

Veal Shanks with Tomatoes and White Wine *Osso buco*

This famous Milanese dish is rich and hearty. It is traditionally served with risotto alla milanese, but plain boiled rice goes equally well. The lemony gremolata garnish helps to cut the richness of the dish, as does a crisp green salad—serve it after the osso buco and before the dessert, to refresh the palate.

Ingredients
2 tbsp flour
4 pieces of osso buco
2 small onions
2 tbsp olive oil
1 large celery stalk, finely chopped
1 medium carrot, finely chopped
2 garlic cloves, finely chopped
1 can (14 ounces) chopped tomatoes
1¼ cups dry white wine
1¼ cups chicken or veal stock
1 strip of thinly pared lemon rind
2 bay leaves, plus extra for garnishing (optional)
salt and freshly ground black pepper

For the gremolata
2 tbsp finely chopped fresh flat-leaf parsley
finely grated rind of 1 lemon
1 garlic clove, finely chopped
serves 4

1 ▲ Preheat the oven to 325°F. Season the flour with salt and pepper and spread it out in a shallow bowl. Add the pieces of veal and turn them in the flour until evenly coated. Shake off any excess flour.

2 ▲ Slice one of the onions and separate it into rings. Heat the oil in a large flameproof casserole, then add the veal, with the onion rings, and brown the veal on both sides over medium heat. Remove the veal shanks with tongs and set aside on paper towels to drain.

3 ▲ Chop the remaining onion and add it to the pan with the celery, carrot and garlic. Stir the bottom of the pan to incorporate the pan juices and sediment. Cook gently, stirring frequently, for about 5 minutes, until the vegetables soften slightly.

4 ▲ Add the chopped tomatoes, wine, stock, lemon rind and bay leaves, then season to taste with salt and pepper. Bring to a boil, stirring. Return the veal to the pan and coat with the sauce. Cover and cook in the oven for 2 hours or until the veal feels tender when pierced with a fork.

5 Meanwhile, make the gremolata. In a small bowl, combine the chopped parsley, lemon rind and chopped garlic. Remove the casserole from the oven and lift out and discard the strip of lemon rind and the bay leaves. Taste the sauce for seasoning. Serve the osso buco hot, sprinkled with the gremolata and garnished with extra bay leaves, if desired.

Cook's Tip
Osso buco is available at large supermarkets and good butchers. Choose pieces about ¾ in thick.

Calf's Liver with Balsamic Vinegar

Fegato all'aceto balsamico

This sweet-and-sour liver dish is a speciality of Venice. Serve it very simply, with green beans sprinkled with browned bread crumbs.

Ingredients

1 tbsp flour
1/2 tsp finely chopped fresh sage
4 thin slices of calf's liver, cut into serving pieces
3 tbsp olive oil
2 tbsp butter
2 small red onions, sliced and separated into rings
2/3 cup dry white wine
3 tbsp balsamic vinegar
pinch of sugar
salt and freshly ground black pepper
fresh sprigs of sage, to garnish
green beans sprinkled with browned bread crumbs, to serve

serves 2

Cook's Tip

Never overcook calf's liver, because it quickly turns tough. Its delicate flesh is at its most tender when it is served slightly underdone and pink—like a rare steak.

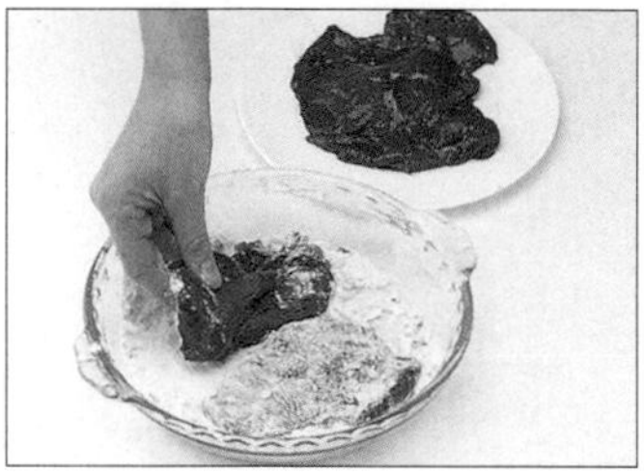

1 ▲ Spread out the flour in a shallow bowl. Season it with the sage and plenty of salt and pepper. Turn the liver in the flour until well coated.

2 Heat 2 tbsp of the oil with half of the butter in a wide heavy saucepan or frying pan until foaming. Add the onion rings and cook gently, stirring frequently, for about 5 minutes, until softened but not colored. Remove with a spatula and set aside.

3 ▲ Heat the remaining oil and butter in the pan until foaming, add the liver and cook over medium heat for 2–3 minutes on each side. Transfer to heated dinner plates and keep hot.

4 Add the wine and vinegar to the pan, then stir to mix with the pan juices and any sediment. Add the onions and sugar and heat through, stirring. Spoon the sauce over the liver, garnish with sage sprigs and serve immediately with the green beans.

Veal Cutlets with Lemon

Scaloppine al limone

Popular in Italian restaurants, this dish is very easy to make at home.

Ingredients
4 veal cutlets
2–3 tbsp flour
4 tbsp butter
¼ cup olive oil
¼ cup Italian dry white vermouth or dry white wine
3 tbsp lemon juice
salt and freshly ground black pepper
lemon wedges and fresh parsley, to garnish
green beans and peperonata, to serve
serves 4

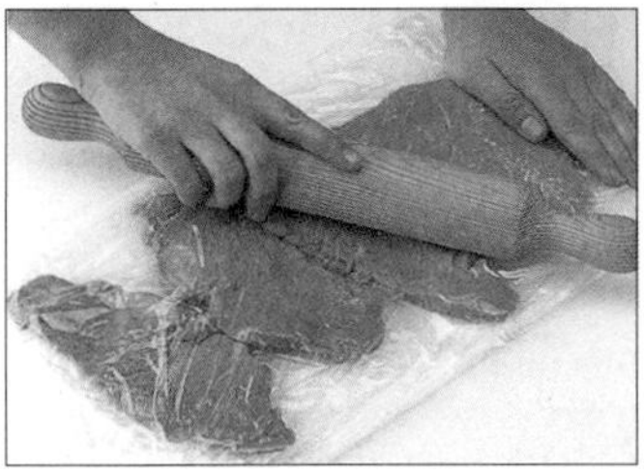

1 ▲ Put each cutlet between two sheets of plastic wrap and pound until very thin.

2 Cut the pounded cutlets in halves or quarters, and coat in the flour, seasoned with salt and pepper.

3 ▲ Melt the butter with half the oil in a large, heavy frying pan until sizzling. Add as many cutlets as the pan will hold. Fry over medium to high heat for 1–2 minutes on each side, until lightly colored. Remove with a spatula and keep hot. Add the remaining oil and cook the remaining cutlets in the same way.

4 Remove the pan from the heat and add the vermouth and the lemon juice. Stir vigorously to mix with the pan juices, then return to the heat and return all the veal to the pan. Spoon the sauce over the veal. Shake the pan over medium heat until all of the cutlets are coated in the sauce and heated through.

5 Serve immediately, garnished with lemon wedges and parsley. Lightly cooked green beans and peperonata make a delicious accompaniment.

Variation
Use skinless boneless chicken breasts instead of the veal. If they are thick, cut them in half before pounding.

Roast Lamb with Rosemary

Agnello al rosmarino

In Italy, lamb is traditionally served at Easter. This simple roast with potatoes owes its wonderful flavor to the fresh rosemary and garlic. It makes the perfect Sunday lunch at any time of year, served with one or two lightly cooked fresh vegetables, such as broccoli, spinach or baby carrots.

Ingredients

1/2 leg of lamb, about 3 lb
2 garlic cloves, cut lengthwise into thin slivers
7 tbsp olive oil
leaves from 4 sprigs of fresh rosemary, finely chopped
about 1 cup lamb or vegetable stock
1 1/2 pounds potatoes, cut into 1-in cubes
a few fresh sage leaves, chopped
salt and freshly ground black pepper
lightly cooked baby carrots, to serve

serves 4

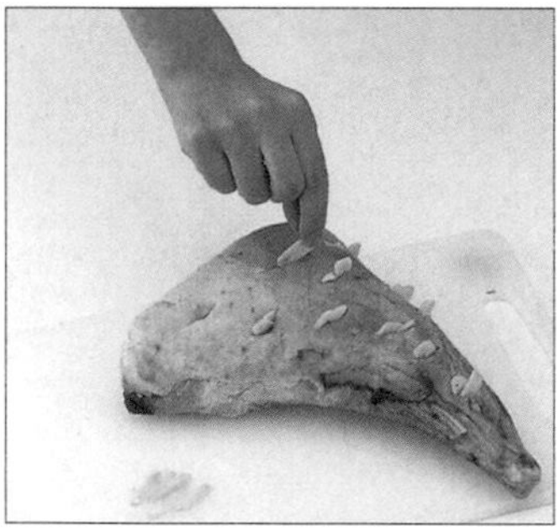

1 ▲ Preheat the oven to 450°F. Using the point of a sharp knife, make deep incisions in the lamb, especially near the bone, and insert the slivers of garlic.

2 ▲ Put the lamb in a roasting pan and rub it all over with 3 tbsp of the oil. Sprinkle on about half of the chopped rosemary, patting it on firmly, and season with plenty of salt and pepper. Roast for 30 minutes, turning once.

3 ▲ Lower the oven temperature to 375°F. Turn the lamb over again and add 1/2 cup of the stock.

4 Roast for 1 1/4 –1 1/2 hours longer until the lamb is tender, turning the joint two or three times more and adding the rest of the stock in two or three batches. Baste the lamb each time it is turned.

5 ▲ Meanwhile, put the potatoes in a separate roasting pan and toss with the remaining oil and rosemary and the sage. Roast, on the same shelf as the lamb if possible, for 45 minutes, turning the potatoes several times until they are golden and tender.

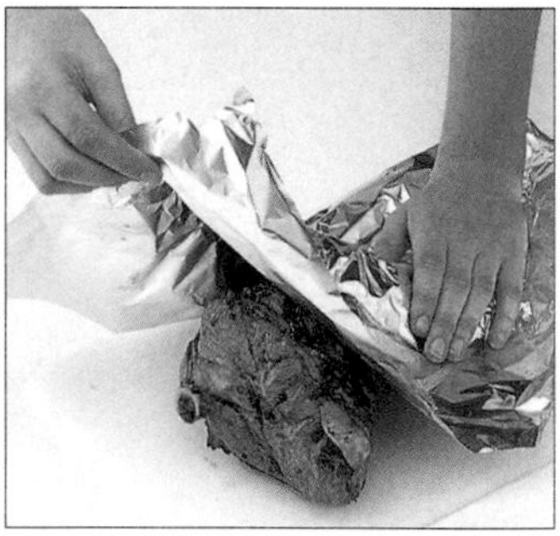

6 ▲ Transfer the lamb to a carving board, tent with foil and set aside in a warm place for 10 minutes so that the flesh firms for easier carving. Serve whole or carved into thin slices, surrounded by the potatoes and accompanied by baby carrots.

Cook's Tip

If desired, the cooking juices can be strained and used to make a thin gravy with stock and red wine.

INOX

Pork in Sweet-and-Sour Sauce

Scaloppine di maiale in agrodolce

The combination of sweet and sour flavors is popular in Venetian cooking, especially with meat and liver. This recipe is given extra bite with the addition of crushed mixed peppercorns. Served with shelled fava beans tossed with grilled bacon—it is delectable.

Ingredients

1 whole pork fillet, about 12 oz
$1\frac{1}{2}$ tbsp flour
2–3 tbsp olive oil
1 cup dry white wine
2 tbsp white wine vinegar
2 tsp sugar
1 tbsp mixed peppercorns, coarsely ground
salt and freshly ground black pepper
fava beans tossed with grilled bacon, to serve

serves 2

1 ▲ Cut the pork diagonally into thin slices. Place between two sheets of plastic wrap and pound lightly with a rolling pin to flatten them evenly.

2 ▲ Spread out the flour in a shallow bowl. Season well and coat the meat.

Cook's Tip

Grind the peppercorns in a pepper grinder, or crush them with a mortar and pestle.

3 ▲ Heat 1 tbsp of the oil in a wide heavy saucepan or frying pan and add as many slices of pork as the pan will hold. Fry over medium to high heat for 2–3 minutes on each side, until crispy and tender. Remove with a spatula and set aside. Repeat with the remaining pork, adding more oil as necessary.

4 ▲ Mix the wine, wine vinegar and sugar in a bowl. Pour into the pan and stir vigorously over high heat until reduced, scraping the pan to incorporate the sediment. Stir in the peppercorns and return the pork to the pan. Spoon the sauce over the pork until it is evenly coated and heated through.

Chicken with Tomatoes and Shrimp

Pollo alla marengo

This Piedmontese dish was created especially for Napoleon after the battle of Marengo. Versions of it appear in both Italian and French recipe books.

Ingredients
1/2 cup olive oil
8 chicken thighs on the bone, skinned
1 onion, finely chopped
1 celery stalk, finely chopped
1 garlic clove, crushed
12 oz ripe Italian plum tomatoes, peeled and roughly chopped
1 cup dry white wine
1/2 tsp finely chopped fresh rosemary
1 tbsp butter
8 small triangles of thinly sliced white bread, without crusts
20 large shrimp, shelled
salt and freshly ground black pepper
finely chopped flat-leaf parsley, to garnish
serves 4

1 ▲ Heat about 2 tbsp of the oil in a frying pan, add the chicken thighs and sauté over medium heat for about 5 minutes, until they have changed color on all sides. Transfer to a flameproof casserole.

2 ▲ Add the onion and celery to the frying pan and cook gently, stirring frequently, for about 3 minutes, until softened. Add the garlic, tomatoes, wine, rosemary and salt and pepper to taste. Bring to a boil, stirring.

3 Pour the tomato sauce over the chicken. Cover and cook gently for 40 minutes or until the chicken is tender when pierced.

4 ▲ About 10 minutes before serving, add the remaining oil and the butter to the frying pan and heat until hot but not smoking. Add the triangles of bread and shallow fry until crisp and golden on each side. Drain on paper towles.

5 ▲ Add the shrimp to the tomato sauce and heat until the shrimp are cooked. Taste the sauce for seasoning. Dip one of the tips of each fried bread triangle in parsley. Serve the dish hot, garnished with the bread triangles.

Variation
To make the dish look more like its original, authentic version, garnish it with a few large crayfish or shrimp in their shells.

Chicken with Chianti

Pollo al chianti

Together the robust, full-flavored red wine and red pesto give this sauce a rich color and almost spicy flavor, while the grapes add a delicious sweetness. Serve the stew with grilled polenta or warm crusty bread, and accompany with piquant greens, such as arugula or watercress, tossed with a tasty dressing.

Ingredients

3 tbsp olive oil
4 part-boned chicken breasts, skinned
1 medium red onion
2 tbsp red pesto
1¼ cups Chianti
1¼ cups water
4 oz red grapes, halved lengthwise and seeded if necessary
salt and freshly ground black pepper
fresh basil leaves, to garnish
arugula salad, to serve
serves 4

1 ▲ Heat 2 tbsp of the oil in a large frying pan, add the chicken breasts and sauté over medium heat for about 5 minutes until they have changed color on all sides. Remove with a slotted spoon and drain on paper towels.

Cook's Tip

Use part-boned chicken breasts, if you can get them, in preference to boneless chicken for this dish, as they have a better flavor. Chicken thighs or drumsticks could also be cooked in this way.

2 Cut the onion in half, through the root. Trim off the root, then slice the onion halves lengthwise to create thin wedges.

3 ▲ Heat the remaining oil in the pan, add the onion wedges and red pesto and cook gently, stirring constantly, for about 3 minutes, until the onion is softened, but not browned.

4 ▲ Add the Chianti and water to the pan and bring to a boil, stirring, then return the chicken to the pan and add salt and pepper to taste.

5 Reduce the heat, then cover the pan and simmer gently for about 20 minutes or until the chicken is tender, stirring occasionally.

6 ▲ Add the grapes to the pan and cook over low to medium heat until heated through, then taste the sauce for seasoning. Serve the chicken hot, garnished with basil and accompanied by the arugula salad.

Variations

Use green pesto instead of red, and substitute a dry white wine such as pinot grigio for the Chianti, then finish with seedless green grapes. A few spoonfuls of mascarpone cheese can be added at the end if desired, to enrich the sauce.

Hunter's Chicken

Pollo alla cacciatora

This traditional dish sometimes has strips of green bell pepper in the sauce for extra color and flavor instead of the fresh mushrooms.

Ingredients

1 cup dried porcini mushrooms
2 tbsp olive oil
1 tbsp butter
4 chicken pieces, on the bone, skinned
1 large onion, thinly sliced
1 can (14 oz) chopped tomatoes
$^{2}/_{3}$ cup red wine
1 garlic clove, crushed
leaves of 1 sprig of fresh rosemary, finely chopped
1$^{3}/_{4}$ cups fresh field mushrooms, thinly sliced
salt and freshly ground black pepper
fresh rosemary sprigs, to garnish

serves 4

1 ▲ Put the porcini in a bowl, add 1 cup warm water and soak for 20–30 minutes. Remove from the liquid and squeeze the porcini over the bowl. Strain the liquid and reserve. Finely chop the porcini.

2 ▲ Heat the oil and butter in a large flameproof casserole until foaming. Add the chicken. Sauté over medium heat for 5 minutes or until golden. Remove and drain on paper towels.

3 ▲ Add the onion and chopped mushrooms to the pan. Cook gently, stirring frequently, for about 3 minutes, until the onion has softened but not browned. Stir in the chopped tomatoes, wine and reserved mushroom soaking liquid, then add the crushed garlic and chopped rosemary, with salt and pepper to taste. Bring to a boil, stirring all the time.

4 ▲ Return the chicken to the pan and coat with the sauce. Cover and simmer gently for 30 minutes.

5 Add the fresh mushrooms and stir well to mix into the sauce. Continue simmering gently for 10 minutes or until the chicken is tender. Taste for seasoning. Serve hot, with creamed potato or polenta, if desired. Garnish with rosemary.

Turkey with Marsala Cream Sauce

Tacchino al marsala

Marsala makes a very rich and tasty sauce. The addition of lemon juice gives it a sharp edge, which helps to offset the richness.

Ingredients

6 turkey breasts
3 tbsp flour
2 tbsp olive oil
2 tbsp butter
¾ cup dry Marsala
¼ cup lemon juice
¾ cup heavy cream
salt and freshly ground black pepper
lemon wedges and chopped fresh parsley, to garnish
snow peas and green beans, to serve

serves 6

1 ▲ Put each turkey breast between two sheets of plastic wrap and pound with a rolling pin to flatten and stretch. Cut each breast in half or into quarters, cutting away and discarding any sinew.

2 ▲ Spread out the flour in a shallow bowl. Season well and coat the meat.

Variation

Veal or pork cutlets or chicken breasts can be used instead of the turkey, and ¼ cup mascarpone cheese can be substituted for the heavy cream.

3 ▲ Heat the oil and butter in a wide heavy saucepan or frying pan until sizzling. Add as many pieces of turkey as the pan will hold and sauté over medium heat for about 3 minutes on each side, until crispy and tender. Transfer to a warmed serving dish with tongs and keep hot. Repeat with the remaining turkey.

4 ▲ Lower the heat. Mix the Marsala and lemon juice in a bowl, add to the pan and raise the heat. Bring to a boil, stirring in the sediment, then add the cream. Simmer, stirring constantly, until the sauce is reduced and glossy. Taste for seasoning. Spoon the sauce over the turkey, garnish with the lemon wedges and parsley and serve immediately with the snow peas and green beans.

Chicken with Prosciutto and Cheese

Pollo alla valdostana

The name Valdostana is derived from Val d'Aosta, home of the Fontina cheese used here.

Ingredients
2 thin slices of prosciutto
2 thin slices of Fontina cheese
4 part-boned chicken breasts
4 sprigs of basil
2 tbsp olive oil
1 tbsp butter
½ cup dry white wine
salt and freshly ground black pepper
tender young salad greens, to serve
serves 4

Cook's Tip
There is nothing quite like the buttery texture and nutty flavor of Fontina cheese, and it also has superb melting qualities, but you could use a Swiss or French mountain cheese, such as Gruyère or Emmental. Ask for the cheese to be sliced thinly on the machine slicer, as you will find it difficult to slice it thinly yourself.

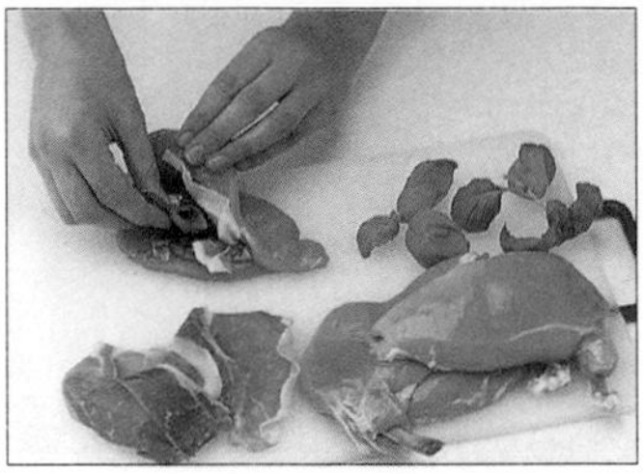

1 ▲ Preheat the oven to 400°F. Lightly oil a baking dish. Cut the prosciutto and Fontina slices in half crosswise. Skin the chicken breasts, open out the slit in the center of each one, and fill each cavity with half a ham slice and a basil sprig.

2 ▲ Heat the oil and butter in a wide heavy frying pan until foaming. Cook the chicken breasts over medium heat for 1–2 minutes on each side, until they change color. Transfer to the baking dish. Add the wine to the pan juices, stir until sizzling, then pour over the chicken and season to taste.

3 Top each chicken breast with a slice of Fontina. Bake for 20 minutes or until the chicken is tender. Serve hot, with tender young salad greens.

Deviled Chicken

Pollo alla diavola

You can tell this spicy, barbecued chicken dish comes from southern Italy because it has dried red chilies in the marinade. Versions without the chilies are just as good.

Ingredients
½ cup olive oil
finely grated rind and juice of 1 large lemon
2 garlic cloves, finely chopped
2 tsp finely chopped or crumbled dried red chilies
12 skinless, boneless chicken thighs, each cut into 3 or 4 pieces
salt and freshly ground black pepper
flat-leaf parsley leaves, to garnish
lemon wedges, to serve
serves 4

Cook's Tip
Thread the chicken pieces spiral-fashion on the skewers so they do not fall off during cooking.

1 ▲ Make a marinade by mixing the oil, lemon rind and juice, garlic and chilies in a large, shallow glass or china dish. Add salt and pepper to taste. Whisk well, then add the chicken pieces, turning to coat with the marinade. Cover and marinate in the refrigerator for at least 4 hours or, preferably, overnight.

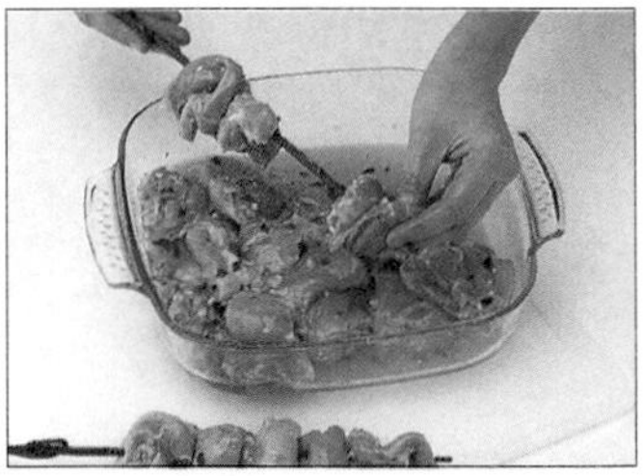

2 ▲ When ready to cook, prepare the barbecue or preheat the broiler and thread the chicken pieces onto eight oiled metal skewers. Cook on the barbecue or under a hot broiler for 6–8 minutes, turning frequently, until tender. Garnish with parsley leaves and serve hot, with lemon wedges.

Vegetables & Salads

There is no shortage of fresh and delicious vegetables in Italy, and the dishes are imaginative and varied. Most Italian cooks buy only when the vegetables are in season and at their best, so you will rarely find winter and summer vegetables together in one dish. The list of irresistible salad combinations, however, is endless, often with roasted ingredients stirred into crisp green leaves.

Roasted Plum Tomatoes and Garlic

Pomodori al forno

These are so simple to prepare, yet taste absolutely wonderful. Use a large, shallow earthenware dish that will allow the tomatoes to sear and char in a hot oven.

Ingredients
8 plum tomatoes, halved
12 garlic cloves
¼ cup extra virgin olive oil
3 bay leaves
salt and freshly ground black pepper
3 tbsp fresh oregano leaves, to garnish
serves 4

Cook's Tip
Use ripe plum tomatoes for this recipe, as they keep their shape and do not fall apart when roasted at such a high temperature. Leave the stalks on, if possible.

1 ▲ Preheat the oven to 450°F. Select an ovenproof dish that will hold all the tomatoes snugly in a single layer. Place the tomatoes in the dish and push the whole, unpeeled garlic cloves between them.

2 ▲ Brush the tomatoes with the oil, add the bay leaves and sprinkle black pepper over the top. Bake for about 45 minutes, until the tomatoes have softened and are sizzling in the pan. They should be charred around the edges. Season with salt and a little more black pepper, if needed. Garnish with oregano and serve.

Green Beans with Tomatoes

Fagiolini al pomodoro

This is a real summer favorite using the best ripe plum tomatoes and green beans.

Ingredients
2 tbsp olive oil
1 large onion, finely sliced
2 garlic cloves, finely chopped
6 large ripe plum tomatoes, peeled, seeded and coarsely chopped
$^2/_3$ cup dry white wine
1 lb green beans, sliced in half lengthwise
16 pitted black olives
2 tsp lemon juice
salt and freshly ground black pepper
serves 4

Cook's Tip
Green beans need little preparation and now that they are grown without the string, you simply trim the ends. When choosing make sure that the beans snap easily—this is a good sign of freshness.

1 ▲ Heat the oil in a large frying pan. Add the onion and garlic and cook for about 5 minutes, until the onion is softened but not brown.

2 ▲ Add the chopped tomatoes, white wine, beans, olives and lemon juice and cook over low heat for 20 more minutes, stirring occasionally, until the sauce is thickened and the beans are tender. Season with salt and pepper to taste and serve immediately.

Fennel Gratin

Finocchi gratinati

This is one of the best ways to eat fresh fennel. The fennel takes on a delicious, almost creamy, flavor, which contrasts beautifully with the sharp, strong Gruyère.

Ingredients
2 fennel bulbs, about 1½ lb total weight
1¼ cups milk
1 tbsp butter, plus extra for greasing
1 tbsp flour
scant ½ cup dry white bread crumbs
3 oz Gruyère cheese, grated
salt and freshly ground black pepper
serves 4

Cook's Tip
Instead of the Gruyère, Parmesan, Pecorino or any other strong cheese would work perfectly.

1 ▲ Preheat the oven to 475°F. Discard the stalks and root ends from the fennel. Slice into quarters and place in a large saucepan. Pour in the milk and simmer for 10–15 minutes until tender. Butter a baking dish.

2 Remove the fennel pieces with a slotted spoon, reserving the milk, and arrange the fennel pieces in the dish.

3 ▲ Melt the butter in a small saucepan and add the flour, stir well, then gradually whisk in the reserved milk. Stir the sauce until thickened.

4 Pour the sauce over the fennel pieces, and sprinkle with the bread crumbs and grated Gruyère. Season with salt and black pepper and bake for about 20 minutes, until browned.

Sweet-and-Sour Onions

Cipolline in agrodolce

Onions are naturally sweet, and when they are cooked at a high temperature the sweetness intensifies. Serve with roasts and meat dishes or as part of an antipasto.

Ingredients
4 tbsp butter
5 tbsp sugar
½ cup white wine vinegar
2 tbsp balsamic vinegar
1½ lb small pickling onions, peeled
salt and freshly ground black pepper
serves 4

Cook's Tips
This recipe also looks and tastes delicious when made with either yellow or red onions, which are cut into either thin slices or chunks. Cooking times will vary, depending on the size of the onion pieces.

1 ▲ Heat the butter in a large saucepan over low heat. Add the sugar and heat until dissolved, stirring constantly.

2 ▲ Add the vinegars to the pan with the onions and combine well. Season with salt and pepper and cover and cook over medium heat for 20–25 minutes, until the onions are a golden color and soft when pierced with a knife. Serve hot.

Roasted Potatoes with Red Onions

Patate al forno

These mouth-watering potatoes are a fine accompaniment to just about anything. The key is to use small firm potatoes; the smaller they are cut, the quicker they will cook.

Ingredients

1 1/2 lb small firm potatoes
2 tbsp butter
2 tbsp olive oil
2 red onions, cut into chunks
8 garlic cloves, unpeeled
2 tbsp chopped fresh rosemary
salt and freshly ground black pepper
serves 4

Cook's Tip

To ensure that the potatoes are crisp, make sure they are completely dry before cooking. Resist the urge to turn the potatoes too often. Let them brown on one side before turning. Do not salt the potatoes until the end of cooking—salting beforehand encourages them to release their liquid, making them limp.

1 ▲ Preheat the oven to 450°F. Peel and quarter the potatoes, rinse them well and pat thoroughly dry with paper towels. Place the butter and oil in a roasting pan and place in the oven to heat.

2 ▲ When the butter has melted and is foaming, add the potatoes, red onions, garlic and rosemary. Toss well, then spread out in one layer.

3 Place the pan in the oven and roast for about 25 minutes, until the potatoes are golden and tender when tested with a fork. Shake the pan occasionally to redistribute the potatoes. When cooked, season with salt and pepper.

Radicchio and Chicory Gratin

Radicchio e indivia gratinati

Vegetables such as radicchio and chicory take on a different flavor when cooked in this way. The creamy béchamel combines wonderfully with the bitter leaves.

Ingredients
2 heads radicchio, quartered lengthwise
2 heads chicory, quartered lengthwise
½ cup drained sun-dried tomatoes in oil, chopped roughly
2 tbsp butter
1 tbsp flour
1 cup milk
pinch grated nutmeg
½ cup grated Emmenthal cheese
salt and freshly ground black pepper
chopped fresh parsley, to garnish
serves 4

1 ▲ Preheat the oven to 350°F. Grease a 5-cup baking dish. Trim the radicchio and chicory and separate the leaves, discarding any that are damaged or wilted. Quarter them lengthwise and arrange in the baking dish. Scatter on the sun-dried tomatoes, and brush the leaves liberally with the oil from the jar. Sprinkle with salt and pepper and cover with foil. Bake for 15 minutes, then remove the foil and bake for another 10 minutes, until the vegetables are softened.

Cook's Tip
In Italy radicchio and chicory are often grilled outdoors on a barbecue. To do this, simply prepare the vegetables as above and brush with olive oil. Place cut-side down on the grill for 7–10 minutes until browned. Turn and grill until the other side is browned, about 5 minutes longer.

2 ▲ Make the sauce. Place the butter in a small saucepan and melt over medium heat. When the butter is foaming, add the flour and cook for 1 minute, stirring. Remove from the heat and gradually add the milk, whisking constantly. Return to the heat and bring to a boil, them simmer for 2–3 minutes to thicken. Season to taste and add the nutmeg.

3 Pour the sauce over the vegetables and sprinkle with the grated cheese. Bake for about 20 minutes, until golden. Serve immediately, garnished with parsley.

Potato and Pumpkin Pudding

Tortino di patate e zucca

Serve this savory pudding with any rich meat dish or simply with a mixed salad.

Ingredients
3 tbsp olive oil
1 garlic clove, sliced
large wedge ($1\frac{1}{2}$ lb) pumpkin, cut into $\frac{3}{4}$-inch chunks
12 oz potatoes, unpeeled
2 tbsp butter
scant $\frac{1}{2}$ cup ricotta cheese
$\frac{2}{3}$ cup grated Parmesan cheese
pinch grated nutmeg
4 eggs, separated
salt and freshly ground black pepper
chopped fresh parsley, to garnish
serves 4

1 Preheat the oven to 400°F. Grease an 8-cup, shallow, oval baking dish.

Cook's Tip
You may process the vegetables in a food processor for a few seconds, but be careful not to overprocess, as they will become very gluey.

2 ▲ Heat the oil in a large frying pan, add the garlic and pumpkin and cook, stirring often to prevent sticking, for 15–20 minutes or until the pumpkin is tender. Meanwhile, cook the potatoes in boiling salted water for 20 minutes, until tender. Drain, leave until cool enough to handle, then peel off the skins. Place the potatoes and pumpkin in a large bowl and mash together well with the butter.

3 Mash the ricotta with a fork until smooth and add to the potato and pumpkin mixture, mixing well.

4 ▲ Stir the Parmesan, nutmeg and plenty of seasoning into the ricotta mixture—it should be smooth and creamy.

5 Add the egg yolks one at a time until mixed in thoroughly.

6 Whisk the egg whites with an electric whisk until they form stiff peaks, then fold gently into the mixture. Spoon into the prepared baking dish and bake for 30 minutes, until golden and firm. Serve hot, garnished with parsley.

Fried Spring Greens

Cavolo fritto

This dish can be served as a vegetable side dish, or it can be enjoyed simply on its own, with some warm crusty bread.

Ingredients
2 tbsp olive oil
2 tbsp butter
4 strips bacon, chopped
1 large onion, thinly sliced
1 cup dry white wine
2 garlic cloves, finely chopped
2 pounds spring greens, shredded
salt and freshly ground black pepper
serves 4

Cook's Tips
This dish would work just as well using shredded red cabbage and red wine. Let simmer for 10 minutes longer, as red cabbage leaves are slightly tougher than the spring greens.

1 In a large frying pan, heat the oil and butter and add the bacon. Fry for 2 minutes, then add the onions and fry for another 3 minutes, until the onion is beginning to soften.

2 Add the wine and simmer vigorously for 2 minutes to reduce.

3 Reduce the heat and add the garlic, spring greens and salt and pepper. Cook over low heat for about 15 minutes, until the greens are tender. (Cover the pan so that the greens retain their color.) Serve hot.

Fennel, Orange and Arugula Salad

Insalata di finocchio

This light and refreshing salad is ideal to serve with spicy or rich foods.

Ingredients
2 oranges
1 fennel bulb
4 oz arugula leaves
$^1/_3$ cup black olives

For the dressing
2 tbsp extra virgin olive oil
1 tbsp balsamic vinegar
1 small garlic clove, crushed
salt and freshly ground black pepper
serves 4

1 With a vegetable peeler, cut strips of rind from the oranges, leaving the pith behind, and cut into thin julienne strips. Cook in boiling water for a few minutes. Drain. Peel the oranges, removing all the white pith. Slice them into thin rounds and discard any seeds.

2 Cut the fennel bulb in half lengthwise and slice across the bulb as thinly as possible, preferably in a food processor fitted with a slicing disc or using a mandoline.

3 ▲ Combine the oranges and fennel in a serving bowl and toss with the arugula leaves.

4 ▲ Combine the oil, vinegar, garlic and seasoning and pour over the salad, toss together well and let stand for a few minutes. Sprinkle with the black olives and julienne strips of orange.

Eggplant, Lemon and Caper Salad

Caponata

This cooked vegetable relish is a classic Sicilian dish, which is delicious served as an accompaniment to cold meats, with pasta or simply on its own with some good crusty bread. Make sure the eggplant is well cooked until it is meltingly soft.

Ingredients
1 large eggplant, about $1^1/_2$ lb
$^1/_4$ cup olive oil
grated rind and juice of 1 lemon
2 tbsp capers, rinsed
12 pitted green olives
2 tbsp chopped fresh flat-leaf parsley
salt and freshly ground black pepper
serves 4

Cook's Tips
This will taste even better when made the day before. Serve at room temperature. It will keep, covered in the refrigerator, for up to 4 days. To enrich this dish to serve it on its own as a main course, add toasted pine nuts and shavings of Parmesan cheese. Serve with crusty bread.

1 ▲ Cut the eggplant into 1-in cubes. Heat the olive oil in a large frying pan and cook the eggplant cubes over medium heat for about 10 minutes, tossing regularly, until golden and softened. You may need to do this in two batches. Drain on paper towels and sprinkle with a little salt.

2 ▲ Place the eggplant cubes in a large serving bowl, toss with the lemon rind and juice, capers, olives and chopped parsley and season well with salt and pepper. Serve at room temperature.

Spinach and Roast Garlic Salad *Insalata di spinaci con aglio arrosto*

Don't worry about the amount of garlic in this salad. During roasting, the garlic becomes sweet and subtle and loses its pungent taste.

Ingredients
12 garlic cloves, unpeeled
1/4 cup extra virgin olive oil
1 lb baby spinach leaves
1/2 cup pine nuts, lightly toasted
juice of 1/2 lemon
salt and freshly ground black pepper
serves 4

Cook's Tip
If spinach is to be served raw in a salad, the leaves need to be young and tender. Wash them well, drain and pat dry with paper towels.

1 ▲ Preheat the oven to 375°F. Place the garlic in a small roasting dish, toss in 2 tbsp of the olive oil and bake for about 15 minutes, until the garlic cloves are slightly charred around the edges.

2 ▲ While still warm, pour the garlic into a salad bowl. Add the spinach, pine nuts, lemon juice, remaining olive oil and a little salt. Toss well and add black pepper to taste. Serve immediately, inviting guests to squeeze the softened garlic purée out of the skin to eat.

Sweet-and-Sour Artichoke Salad

Carciofi in salsa agrodolce

Agrodolce is a sweet-and-sour sauce that works perfectly in this salad.

Ingredients
6 small artichokes
juice of 1 lemon
2 tbsp olive oil
2 medium onions, roughly chopped
1 cup fresh or frozen fava beans
1½ cups fresh or frozen peas (shelled)
salt and freshly ground black pepper
fresh mint leaves, to garnish

For the salsa agrodolce
½ cup white wine vinegar
1 tbsp superfine sugar
handful fresh mint leaves, roughly torn
serves 4

1 ▲ Peel the outer leaves from the artichokes and cut into quarters. Place the artichokes in a bowl of water with the lemon juice.

2 ▲ Heat the oil in a large saucepan and add the onions. Cook until the onions are golden. Add the beans and stir, then drain the artichokes and add to the pan. Pour in about 1¼ cups of water and cook, covered, for 10–15 minutes.

3 ▲ Add the peas, season with salt and pepper and cook for 5 more minutes, stirring occasionally, until the vegetables are tender. Strain through a sieve and place all the vegetables in a bowl, let cool, then cover and chill.

4 ▲ To make the salsa agrodolce, mix all the ingredients in a small pan. Heat gently for 2–3 minutes, until the sugar has dissolved. Simmer gently for about 5 minutes, stirring occasionally. Let cool. To serve, drizzle the salsa over the vegetables and garnish with mint leaves.

Bell Pepper and Tomato Salad

Peperoni arrostiti con pomodori

This is one of those lovely recipes that brings together perfectly the colors, flavors and textures of southern Italian food. Eat this dish at room temperature with a green salad.

Ingredients

3 red bell peppers
6 large plum tomatoes
½ tsp dried red chili flakes
1 red onion, finely sliced
3 garlic cloves, finely chopped
grated rind and juice of 1 lemon
3 tbsp chopped fresh flat-leaf parsley
2 tbsp extra virgin olive oil
salt and freshly ground black pepper
black and green olives and extra chopped flat-leaf parsley, to garnish

serves 4

Cook's Tip

Peppers roasted this way will keep for several weeks. After peeling off the skins, place the pepper pieces in a jar with a tight-fitting lid. Pour enough olive oil over them to cover completely. Store in the refrigerator.

1 ▲ Preheat the oven to 425°F. Place the peppers on a baking sheet and roast, turning occasionally, for 10 minutes or until the skins are almost blackened. Add the tomatoes to the baking sheet and bake for 5 more minutes.

2 Place the peppers in a plastic bag, close the top loosely, trapping in the steam, and then set them aside, with the tomatoes, until they are cool enough to handle.

3 ▲ Carefully pull off the skin from the peppers. Remove the seeds, then chop the peppers and tomatoes roughly and place in a mixing bowl.

4 Add the chili flakes, onion, garlic, lemon rind and juice. Sprinkle on the parsley. Mix well, then transfer to a serving dish. Sprinkle with a little salt, drizzle on the olive oil and scatter olives and extra parsley over the top. Serve at room temperature.

Marinated Zucchini

Zucchini a scapece

This is a simple vegetable dish that is prepared all over Italy using the best of the season's zucchini. It can be eaten hot or cold.

Ingredients

4 zucchini
¼ cup extra virgin olive oil
2 tbsp chopped fresh mint, plus whole leaves, to garnish
2 tbsp white wine vinegar
salt and freshly ground black pepper
whole-wheat Italian bread and green olives, to serve

serves 4

Cook's Tip

Carrots, green beans, and onions can also be prepared in this way.

1 ▲ Cut the zucchini into thin slices. Heat 2 tbsp of the oil in a wide heavy saucepan. Fry the zucchini in batches, for 4–6 minutes, until tender and brown around the edges. Transfer the zucchini to a bowl. Season well.

2 ▲ Heat the remaining oil in the pan, then add the mint and vinegar and let it bubble for a few seconds. Pour the marinade over the zucchini. Marinate for 1 hour, then serve garnished with mint and accompanied by bread and olives.

Stuffed Eggplants

Melanzane alla ligure

This typical Ligurian dish is spiked with paprika and allspice, a legacy from the days when spices from the East came into northern Italy via the port of Genoa.

Ingredients
2 eggplants, about 8 oz each, stalks removed
10 oz potatoes, peeled and diced
2 tbsp olive oil
1 small onion, finely chopped
1 garlic clove, finely chopped
good pinch of ground allspice and paprika
1 egg, beaten
½ cup grated Parmesan cheese
1 tbsp fresh white bread crumbs
salt and freshly ground black pepper
fresh mint sprigs, to garnish
salad greens, to serve
serves 4

1 Bring a large saucepan of lightly salted water to a boil. Add the whole eggplant and cook for 5 minutes, turning frequently. Remove with a slotted spoon and set aside. Add the potatoes to the pan and cook for 20 minutes until soft.

2 ▲ Meanwhile, cut the eggplants in half lengthwise and gently scoop out the flesh with a small sharp knife and a spoon, leaving ¼ in of the shell intact. Select a baking dish that will hold the eggplant shells snugly in a single layer. Brush it lightly with oil. Put the shells in the baking dish and chop the eggplant flesh roughly.

Cook's Tip
The eggplants can be filled in advance, then covered with foil and kept in the refrigerator. Add the crumb topping just before baking.

3 ▲ Heat the oil in a frying pan, add the onion and cook gently, stirring frequently, until softened. Add the chopped eggplant flesh and the garlic. Cook, stirring frequently, for 6–8 minutes. Pour into a bowl. Preheat the oven to 375°F.

4 Drain and mash the potatoes. Add the spices and beaten egg to the eggplant mixture. Set aside 1 tbsp of the Parmesan and add the rest to the eggplant mixture, stir in salt and pepper to taste.

5 ▲ Spoon the mixture into the eggplant shells. Mix the bread crumbs with the reserved Parmesan cheese and sprinkle the mixture onto the eggplants. Bake for 40–45 minutes, until the topping is crisp. Garnish with mint and serve with salad greens.

Bell Pepper Gratin

Peperoni gratinati

Serve this simple but delicious dish as an appetizer with a small mixed leaf or arugula salad and some good crusty bread to mop up the juices from the peppers.

Ingredients
2 red bell peppers
2 tbsp extra virgin olive oil
¼ cup fresh white bread crumbs
1 garlic clove, finely chopped
1 tsp drained bottled capers
8 pitted black olives, roughly chopped
1 tbsp chopped fresh oregano
1 tbsp chopped fresh flat-leaf parsley
salt and freshly ground black pepper
fresh herbs, to garnish
serves 4

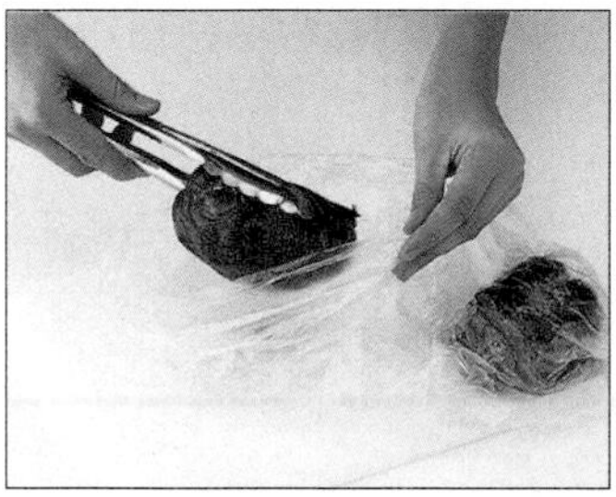

1 ▲ Preheat the oven to 400°F. Place the peppers under a hot broiler. Turn occasionally until they are blackened and blistered all over. Remove from the heat and place in a plastic bag. Seal and let cool.

2 ▲ When cool, peel the peppers. (Don't skin them under the tap, as the water would wash away some of the delicious smoky flavor.) Halve and remove the seeds, then cut the flesh into large strips.

3 ▲ Use a little of the olive oil to grease a small baking dish. Arrange the pepper strips in the dish.

4 ▲ Scatter the remaining ingredients on top, drizzle with the remaining olive oil and add salt and pepper to taste. Bake for about 20 minutes, until the bread crumbs have browned. Garnish with fresh herbs and serve immediately.

Desserts

An everyday Italian meal usually concludes with fresh fruit. Desserts are reserved for special occasions, and are often bought at the local pasticceria or gelateria. This is not to say that sweet things are unpopular, but they are usually eaten with a cup of espresso coffee at other times of the day.

Tiramisù

Tiramisù

The name of this popular dessert translates as "pick me up," which is said to derive from the fact that it is so good that it literally makes you swoon when you eat it. There are many, many versions, and the recipe can be adapted to suit your own taste—you can vary the amount of mascarpone, eggs, ladyfingers, coffee and liqueur.

Ingredients

3 eggs, separated
2 cups mascarpone cheese, at room temperature
1 tbsp vanilla sugar
3/4 cup cold, very strong, black coffee
1/2 cup Kahlúa or other coffee-flavored liqueur
18 savoiardi (Italian ladyfingers)
sifted cocoa powder and grated bittersweet chocolate, to finish

serves 6–8

1 ▲ Put the egg whites in a grease-free bowl and whisk with an electric mixer until stiff and in peaks.

2 ▲ Mix the mascarpone, vanilla sugar and egg yolks in a separate large bowl and whisk with the electric mixer until evenly combined. Fold in the egg whites, then put a few spoonfuls of the mixture in the bottom of a large serving bowl and spread it out evenly.

3 ▲ Combine the coffee and liqueur in a shallow dish. Dip a ladyfinger in the mixture, turn it quickly so that it becomes saturated but does not disintegrate, and place it on top of the mascarpone in the bowl. Add five more dipped ladyfingers, placing them side by side.

4 ▲ Spoon in about one-third of the remaining mixture and spread it out. Make more layers in the same way, ending with mascarpone. Level the surface, then sift cocoa powder all over. Cover and chill overnight. Before serving, sprinkle with cocoa and grated chocolate.

Stuffed Peaches with Amaretto

Pesche ripiene

Together amaretti cookies and amaretto liqueur have an intense almond flavor, and they make a natural partner for peaches.

Ingredients
4 ripe but firm peaches
2 oz amaretti cookies
2 tbsp butter, softened
2 tbsp confectioners' sugar
1 egg yolk
¼ cup amaretto liqueur
1 cup dry white wine
8 tiny sprigs of basil, to decorate
ice cream or heavy cream, to serve
serves 4

1 ▲ Preheat the oven to 350°F. Following the natural indentation line on each peach, cut in half down to the central pit, then twist the halves in opposite directions to separate them. Remove the peach pits, then cut out a little of the central flesh to make a larger hole for the stuffing. Chop this flesh finely and set aside.

2 ▲ Put the amaretti cookies in a bowl and crush them finely with the end of a rolling pin.

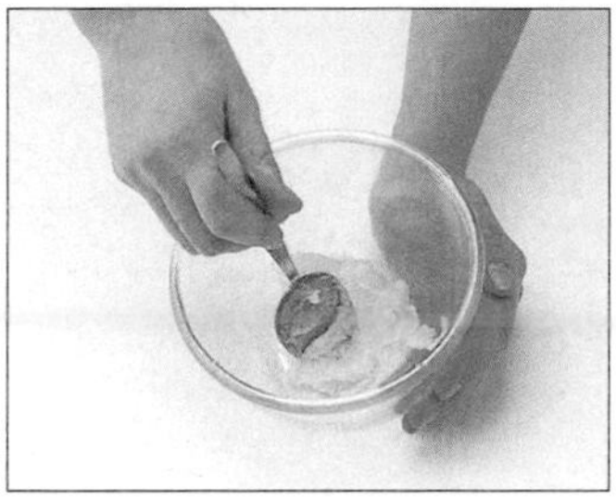

3 ▲ Cream the butter and sugar in a separate bowl until smooth. Stir in the reserved chopped peach flesh, the egg yolk and half the amaretto liqueur with the amaretti crumbs. Lightly butter a baking dish that is just large enough to hold the peach halves in a single layer.

4 ▲ Spoon the stuffing into the peaches, then stand them in the dish. Mix the remaining liqueur with the wine, pour over the peaches and bake for 25 minutes or until the peaches feel tender when tested with a skewer. Decorate with basil and serve immediately, with ice cream or cream.

Zabaglione

Zabaglione

This sumptuous warm dessert is very quick and easy to make, but it does need to be served immediately. For a dinner party, assemble all the ingredients and equipment ahead of time so that all you have to do is quickly combine everything once the main course is over.

Ingredients
4 egg yolks
1/3 cup confectioners' sugar
1/2 cup dry Marsala
savoiardi (Italian ladyfingers), to serve
serves 6

Cook's Tip
When whisking the egg yolks, make sure that the bottom of the bowl does not touch the water or the egg yolks will scramble.

1 ▲ Half fill a pan with water and bring it to the simmering point. Put the egg yolks and sugar in a large heatproof bowl and beat with a hand-held electric mixer until pale and creamy.

2 ▲ Put the bowl over the pan and gradually pour in the Marsala, whisking the mixture until it is very thick and has increased in volume.

3 Remove the bowl from the water and pour the zabaglione into six heatproof, long-stemmed glasses. Serve immediately, with ladyfingers.

Lovers' Knots

Cenci

The literal translation of cenci is "rags and tatters," but they are often referred to by the more endearing term of lovers' knots. They are eaten at carnival time in February.

Ingredients
1 1/4 cups flour
1/2 tsp baking powder
pinch of salt
2 tbsp confectioners' sugar, plus extra for dusting
1 egg, beaten
about 1 1/2 tbsp rum
vegetable oil, for deep-frying
makes 24

Cook's Tip
If you do not have a deep-fat fryer with a built-in thermostat, or a deep-fat thermometer, test the temperature of the oil before deep-frying by dropping in a scrap of the dough trimmings—it should turn crisp and golden in about 30 seconds.

1 ▲ Sift the flour, baking powder and salt into a bowl, then stir in the sugar. Add the egg. Stir with a fork until it is evenly mixed with the flour, then add the rum gradually and continue mixing until the dough draws together. Knead the dough on a lightly floured surface until it is smooth. Divide the dough into quarters.

2 ▲ Roll each piece out to a 6 x 3-in rectangle and trim to make them straight. Cut each rectangle lengthwise into six strips, 1/2 in wide, and tie into a simple knot.

3 Heat the oil in a deep-fat fryer to a temperature of 375°F. Deep-fry the knots in batches for 1–2 minutes, until crisp and golden. Transfer to paper towels with a slotted spoon. Serve warm, dusted with sugar.

Fresh Orange Granita

Granita all'arancia

A granita is like a sorbet, but coarser and quite grainy in texture, hence its name. It makes a refreshing dessert after a rich main course, or a cooling treat on a hot summer's day.

Ingredients
4 large oranges
1 large lemon
$^3/_4$ cup sugar
2 cups water
blanched pared strips of orange and lemon rind, to decorate
cookies, to serve
serves 6

1 ▲ Thinly pare the rind from the oranges and lemon, taking care to avoid the bitter white pith, and set aside for the decoration. Cut the fruit in half and squeeze the juice into a bowl. Set aside.

2 Heat the sugar and water in a heavy saucepan, stirring over low heat until the sugar dissolves. Bring to a boil, then boil without stirring for about 10 minutes, until a syrup forms.

3 ▲ Remove the syrup from the heat, add the pieces of orange and lemon rind and shake the pan. Cover and let cool.

4 ▲ Strain the sugar syrup into a shallow freezer container and add the fruit juice. Stir well to mix, then freeze, uncovered, for about 4 hours, until slushy.

Cook's Tip
To make the decoration, slice extra orange and lemon rind into thin strips. Blanch for 2 minutes, refresh under cold water and dry before use.

5 ▲ Remove the half-frozen mixture from the freezer and mix with a fork, then return to the freezer and freeze again for 4 more hours or until frozen hard. To serve, pour into a bowl and let soften for about 10 minutes, then break up with a fork again and pile into long-stemmed glasses. Decorate with the strips of orange and lemon rind and serve with cookies.

Apple Cake

Torta di mele

This moist cake is best served warm. It comes from Genoa, home of the whisked sponge. When whipping the cream, add grated lemon rind—it tastes delicious.

Ingredients
1½ lb Golden Delicious apples
finely grated rind and juice of 1 large lemon
4 eggs
¾ cup confectioners' sugar
1¼ cups flour
1 tsp baking powder
pinch of salt
8 tbsp butter, melted and cooled, plus extra for greasing
1 tbsp vanilla sugar, for sprinkling
very finely pared strips of citrus rind, to decorate
whipped cream, to serve
serves 6

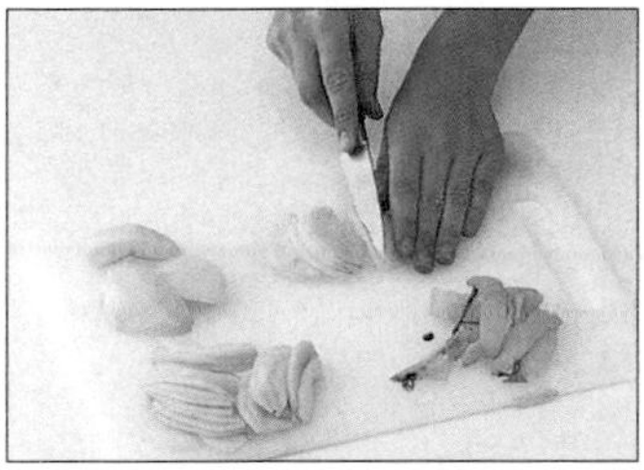

1 ▲ Preheat the oven to 350°F. Brush a 9-in springform pan with melted butter and line the base with parchment paper. Quarter, core and peel the apples, then slice thinly. Put the slices in a bowl and pour in the lemon juice.

2 ▲ Put the eggs, sugar and lemon rind in a bowl and whisk with a hand-held electric mixer until the mixture is thick and mousse-like. The whisks should leave a trail.

3 ▲ Sift half the flour, all the baking powder and the salt over the egg mousse, then fold in gently with a large metal spoon. Slowly drizzle in the melted butter from the side of the bowl and fold it in gently with the spoon. Sift in the remaining flour, fold it in gently, then add the apples and fold these in equally gently.

4 ▲ Spoon into the prepared pan and level the surface. Bake for 40 minutes or until a skewer comes out clean. Let settle in the pan for about 10 minutes, then invert on a wire rack. Turn the cake the right way up and sprinkle the vanilla sugar on top. Decorate with the citrus rind. Serve warm, with whipped cream.

Sicilian Ricotta Cake

Cassata siciliana

The word cassata is often used to describe a layered ice cream cake. In Sicily, however, it is a traditional cake made of layers of sponge, ricotta cheese and candied peel, imbibed with alcohol, and it looks and tastes truly delicious.

Ingredients
3 cups ricotta cheese
finely grated rind of 1 orange
2 tbsp vanilla sugar
5 tbsp orange-flavored liqueur
4 oz candied peel
8 trifle sponge cakes
¼ cup freshly squeezed orange juice
extra candied peel, to decorate
serves 8–10

1 ▲ Push the ricotta cheese through a sieve into a bowl, add the orange rind, vanilla sugar and 1 tbsp of the liqueur and beat well to mix. Transfer about one-third of the mixture to another bowl, cover and chill until serving time.

2 ▲ Finely chop the candied peel and beat into the remaining ricotta cheese mixture until evenly mixed. Set aside while you prepare the pan.

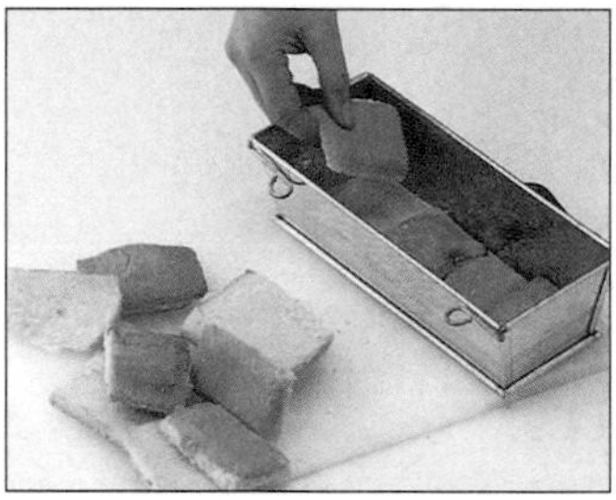

3 ▲ Line the base of a 5-cup loaf pan with non-stick baking paper. Cut the trifle sponges in half through their thickness. Arrange four pieces of sponge side by side in the bottom of the loaf pan and sprinkle with 1 tbsp each of liqueur and orange juice.

4 ▲ Put one-third of the ricotta and fruit mixture in the pan and spread it out evenly. Cover with four more pieces of sponge and sprinkle with another 1 tbsp each liqueur and orange juice as before.

5 Repeat the alternate layers of ricotta mixture and sponge until all the ingredients are used, soaking the sponge pieces with liqueur and orange juice each time, and ending with soaked sponge. Cover with a piece of parchment paper.

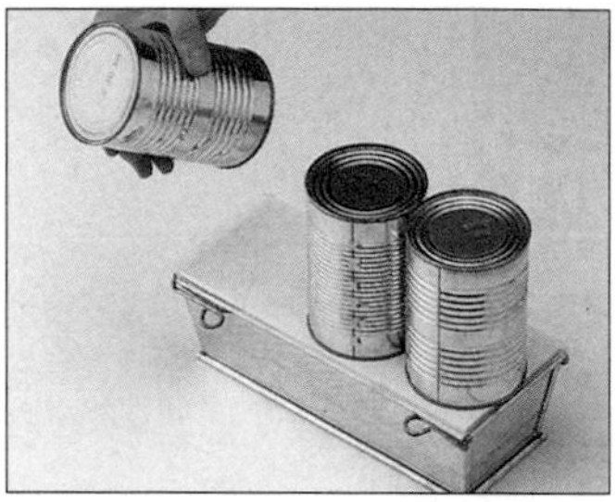

6 ▲ Cut a piece of cardboard to fit inside the pan, place on top of the parchment paper and weight down evenly. Chill for 24 hours.

7 Remove the weights, cardboard and paper and run a spatula between the sides of the cassata and the pan. Invert a serving plate on top of the cassata, then invert the two so that the cassata is upside down on the plate. Peel off the lining paper.

8 Spread the chilled ricotta mixture over the cassata to cover it completely, then decorate the top with candied peel, cut into fancy shapes. Serve chilled.

Cook's Tip
Don't worry if the cassata has pressed into an uneven shape when turned out. This will be disguised when the cake is covered in the chilled ricotta mixture.

Coffee and Chocolate Bombe

Zuccotto

In Italy the commercial ice cream is so good that no one would dream of making their own ice cream for this dessert. Assembling the zuccotto is impressive enough in itself.

Ingredients

15–18 savoiardi (Italian ladyfingers)
about ¾ cup sweet Marsala
3 oz amaretti cookies
about 2 cups coffee ice cream, softened
about 2 cups vanilla ice cream, softened
2 oz bittersweet or plain chocolate, grated
chocolate curls and sifted cocoa powder or confectioners' sugar, to decorate

serves 6–8

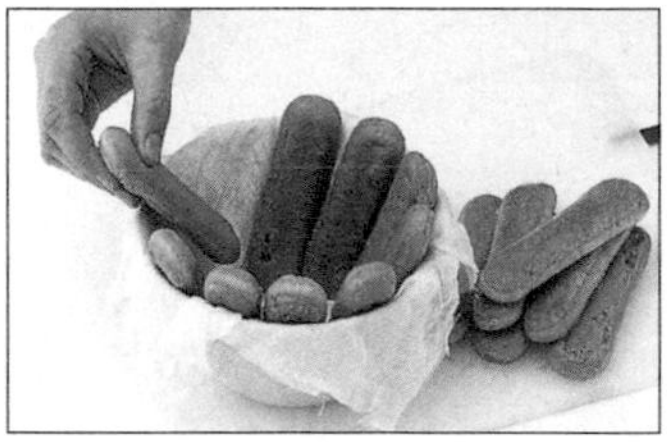

1 ▲ Line a 4-cup souffle dish with a large piece of damp muslin, letting it hang over the top edge. Trim the ladyfingers to fit the basin, if necessary. Pour the Marsala into a shallow dish. Dip a ladyfinger in the Marsala, turning it quickly so that it becomes saturated but does not disintegrate. Stand it against the side of the basin, sugared-side out. Repeat with the remaining sponge fingers to line the basin fully.

2 Fill in the base and any gaps around the side with any trimmings and savoiardi cut to fit. Chill for about 30 minutes.

Cook's Tip

In Italy there are special dome-shaped molds for making this dessert, the name for which comes from the Italian word zucca, meaning pumpkin. The shape will not be quite the same when it is made in a souffle dish.

3 ▲ Put the amaretti cookies in a large bowl and crush them with a rolling pin. Add the coffee ice cream and any remaining Marsala and beat until mixed. Spoon into the ladyfinger-lined dish.

4 Press the ice cream against the sponge to form an even layer with a hollow. Freeze for 2 hours.

5 Put the vanilla ice cream and grated chocolate in a bowl and beat together until evenly mixed. Spoon into the hollow in the center of the mold. Smooth the top, then cover with the overhanging muslin. Place in the freezer overnight.

6 To serve, run a spatula between the muslin and the basin, then unfold the top of the muslin. Invert a chilled serving plate on top of the zuccotto, then invert the two so that the zuccotto is upside down on the plate. Carefully peel off the muslin. Decorate the zuccotto with the chocolate curls, then sift cocoa powder or confectioners' sugar over. Serve immediately.

Ricotta Pudding

Budino di ricotta

This creamy, rich dessert is very easy to make and, as it can be made up to 24 hours ahead, it is ideal for a dinner party. The combination of ricotta cheese and candied fruits is very popular in Sicily, where this recipe originated.

Ingredients
1 cup ricotta cheese
1/3 cup candied fruits
1/4 cup sweet Marsala
1 cup heavy cream
1/4 cup confectioners' sugar, plus extra to serve
finely grated rind of 1 orange
2 cups fresh raspberries
strips of thinly pared orange rind, to decorate
serves 4–6

Cook's Tip
Buy candied fruits in large pieces at a good gourmet food store—the chopped candied peel in tubs is too tough to eat raw, and should only be used in baking.

1 ▲ Press the ricotta through a sieve into a bowl. Finely chop the candied fruits and stir into the sieved ricotta with half of the Marsala. Put the cream, sugar and orange rind in another bowl and whip until the cream is standing in soft peaks.

2 ▲ Fold the whipped cream into the ricotta mixture. Spoon into individual glass serving bowls and top with the raspberries. Chill until serving time. Sprinkle with the remaining Marsala and dust the top of each bowl liberally with confectioners' sugar just before serving. Decorate with the orange rind.

Chocolate Roll

Salame al cioccolato

This after-dinner treat resembles a salami in shape, hence its curious name. It is very rich and will serve a lot of people. Slice it very thinly and serve with espresso coffee and amaretto liqueur.

Ingredients
24 butter cookies, broken
12 oz bittersweet or plain chocolate, broken into squares
2 sticks unsalted butter, softened
1/4 cup amaretto liqueur
2 egg yolks
1/2 cup slivered almonds, lightly toasted
1/4 cup ground almonds
serves 8–12

1 ▲ Place the cookies in a food processor fitted with a metal blade and process until coarsely crushed.

2 Place the chocolate in a large heatproof bowl. Place the bowl over a saucepan of barely simmering water, add a small chunk of the butter and all the liqueur and heat until the chocolate melts, stirring occasionally.

Cook's Tip
Take care when melting chocolate that it does not overheat, or it will form a hard lump. The base of the bowl containing the chocolate must not touch the water, and the chocolate must be melted very slowly and gently. If you think the water is getting too hot, remove the pan from the heat.

3 ▲ Remove the bowl from the heat, let the chocolate cool for a minute or two, then stir in the egg yolks followed by the remaining butter, a little at a time. Pour in most of the crushed cookies, leaving behind a good handful, and stir well to mix. Stir in the almonds. Set aside the mixture in a cold place for about 1 hour, until it begins to stiffen.

4 ▲ Process the remaining crushed cookies in the food processor until they are very finely ground. Pour into a bowl and mix with the ground almonds. Cover and set aside until serving time.

5 ▲ Transfer the chocolate and cookie mixture to a sheet of lightly oiled waxed paper, then shape into a 14-in sausage with a spatula, tapering the ends slightly so that the roll looks like a salami. Wrap in the paper and freeze for at least 4 hours, until solid.

6 To serve, unwrap the "salami." Spread the ground cookies and almonds out on a clean sheet of waxed paper and roll the "salami" in them until evenly coated. Transfer to a board and let stand for about 1 hour before serving in slices.

Baking

The Italian tradition of baking dates back to Roman times, and Italian bakers and pastry chefs today take enormous pride in their art. Baking at home is generally simple—rustic breads, pies and tarts, the occasional cheesecake or batch of cookies. Elaborate confections are usually left to the professionals.

Raisin and Walnut Bread

Pane di uva con noci

This bread is delicious with soup for a first course, or with salami, cheese and salad for lunch. It tastes good with jam and toasts extremely well when it is a day or two old.

Ingredients
2¾ cups flour
½ tsp salt
1 tbsp butter
1½ tsp active dry yeast
scant 1 cup golden raisins
½ cup walnuts, roughly chopped
melted butter, for brushing
makes 1 loaf

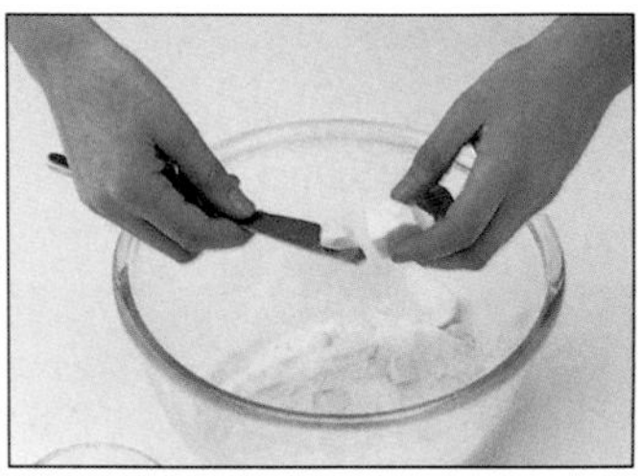

1 ▲ Sift the flour and salt into a bowl, cut in the butter with a knife, then stir in the yeast.

2 ▲ Gradually add ¾ cup tepid water to the flour mixture, stirring with a spoon at first, then gathering the dough together with your hands.

3 Turn the dough out onto a floured surface and knead for about 10 minutes, until smooth and elastic.

Cook's Tip
Active dried yeast is sold in envelopes at most supermarkets. It is a real boon for the busy cook because it eliminates the need to let the dough rise before shaping.

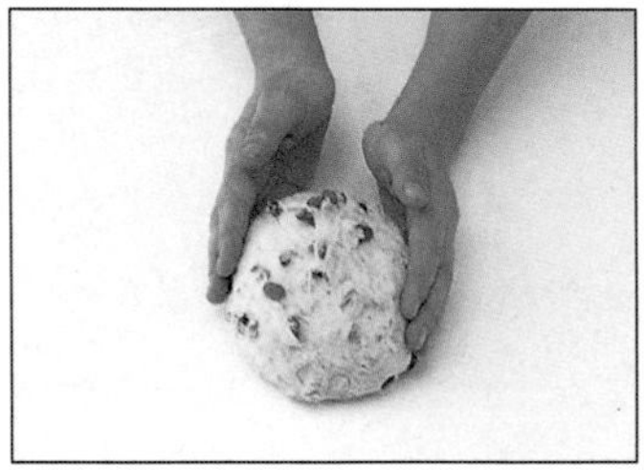

4 ▲ Knead the raisins and walnuts into the dough until they are evenly distributed. Shape into a rough oval, place on a lightly oiled baking sheet and cover with oiled plastic wrap. Let rise in a warm place for 1–2 hours, until doubled in bulk. Preheat the oven to 425°F.

5 Uncover the loaf and bake for 10 minutes, then reduce the oven temperature to 375°F and bake for 20–25 more minutes.

6 ▲ Transfer to a wire rack, brush with melted butter and cover with a dish towel. Cool before slicing.

Chocolate Bread

Pane al cioccolato

In Italy it is the custom to serve this dessert bread as a snack with mascarpone or Gorgonzola cheese and a glass of red wine. Although this combination may sound unusual, it is really delicious. Chocolate bread also tastes good spread with butter, and is excellent toasted the next day for breakfast and served with butter and jam.

Ingredients
4 cups flour
½ tsp salt
2 tbsp butter
2 tbsp confectioners' sugar
2 tsp active dry yeast
2 tbsp cocoa powder
½ cup chocolate chips
melted butter, for brushing
makes 2 loaves

1 ▲ Sift the flour and salt into a bowl, cut in the butter with a knife, then stir in the sugar, yeast and cocoa powder.

2 Gradually add 1¼ cups of tepid water to the flour mixture, stirring with a spoon at first, then gathering the dough together with your hands.

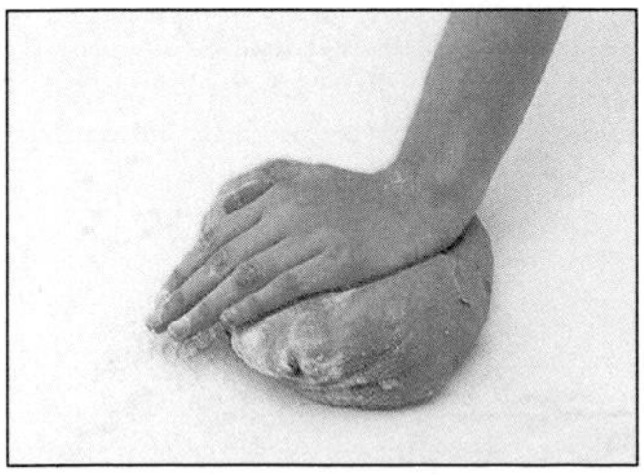

3 ▲ Turn the dough out onto a floured surface and knead for about 10 minutes, until smooth and elastic.

4 ▲ Cut the dough in half and knead half the chocolate chips into each piece of dough until they are evenly distributed. Shape into rounds, place on lightly oiled baking sheets and cover with oiled plastic wrap. Let rise in a warm place for 1–2 hours, until the dough has doubled in bulk.

5 Preheat the oven to 425°F. Uncover the loaves and bake for 10 minutes, then reduce the oven temperature to 375°F and bake for 15–20 more minutes.

6 ▲ Place the loaves on a wire rack and brush liberally with butter. Cover with a dish towel and let cool.

Ricotta Cheesecake

Crostata di ricotta

Low-fat ricotta cheese is excellent for cheesecake fillings because it has a good, firm texture. Here it is enriched with eggs and cream and enlivened with tangy orange and lemon rind to make a Sicilian-style dessert.

Ingredients
2 cups low-fat ricotta cheese
½ cup heavy cream
2 eggs
1 egg yolk
⅓ cup confectioners' sugar
finely grated rind of 1 orange
finely grated rind of 1 lemon

For the pastry
1½ cups flour
3 tbsp sugar
pinch of salt
8 tbsp chilled butter, diced
1 egg yolk
serves 8

1 ▲ Make the pastry. Sift the flour, sugar and salt onto a cold work surface. Make a well in the center and put in the diced butter and egg yolk. Gradually work the flour into the diced butter and egg yolk, using your fingertips.

Variations
Add ⅓–⅔ cup finely chopped candied peel to the filling in step 3 (or use ⅓ cup chocolate chips). For a really rich dessert, you can add both candied peel and some grated plain chocolate.

2 ▲ Gather the dough together, reserve about a quarter for the lattice, then press the rest into a 9-in fluted tart pan with a removable base. Chill the pastry shell for 30 minutes.

3 ▲ Meanwhile, preheat the oven to 375°F and make the filling. Put all the ricotta, cream, eggs, egg yolk, sugar and orange and lemon rinds in a large bowl and beat until evenly mixed.

4 ▲ Prick the bottom of the pastry shell, then line with foil and fill with baking beans. Bake blind for 15 minutes, then transfer to a wire rack, remove the foil and beans and allow the tart shell to cool in the pan.

5 ▲ Spoon the cheese and cream filling into the pastry case and level the surface. Roll out the reserved dough and cut into strips. Arrange the strips on the top of the filling in a lattice pattern, sticking them in place with water.

6 Bake for 30–35 minutes, until golden and set. Transfer to a wire rack and let cool, then carefully remove the side of the pan, leaving the cheesecake on the pan base.

Pine Nut Tart

Pinolata

Strange though it may seem, this traditional tart is an Italian version of the rustic Bakewell tart from Derbyshire in England.

Ingredients
8 tbsp butter, softened
generous 1/2 cup confectioners' sugar
1 egg
2 egg yolks
1 1/4 cups ground almonds
1 cup pine nuts
1/4 cup seedless raspberry jam
confectioners' sugar, for dusting
whipped cream, to serve (optional)

For the pastry
1 1/2 cups flour
1/3 cup confectioners' sugar
1/4 tsp baking powder
pinch of salt
8 tbsp chilled butter, diced
1 egg yolk
serves 8

1 ▲ Make the pastry. Sift the flour, sugar, baking powder and salt onto a cold work surface. Make a well in the center and put in the diced butter and egg yolk. Gradually work the flour into the butter and egg yolk, using your fingertips.

2 ▲ Gather the dough together, then press it into a 9-in fluted tart pan with a removable base. Chill for 30 minutes.

3 ▲ Meanwhile, make the filling. Cream the butter and sugar with an electric mixer until light and fluffy, then beat in the egg and egg yolks a little at a time, alternating them with the ground almonds. Beat in the pine nuts.

Cook's Tip
This pastry is too sticky to roll out, so simply mold it into the bottom and sides of the pan with your fingertips.

4 ▲ Preheat the oven to 325°F. Spread the jam over the pastry shell, then spoon in the filling. Bake for 30–35 minutes or until a skewer inserted in the center of the tart comes out clean.

5 Transfer to a wire rack and let cool, then carefully remove the side of the pan, leaving the tart on the pan base. Dust with confectioners' sugar and serve with whipped cream, if desired.

Baked Sweet Ravioli

Ravioli dolci al forno

These delicious sweet ravioli are made with a rich pastry flavored with lemon and filled with the traditional ingredients used in Sicilian cassata.

Ingredients

2 cups flour
1/3 cup superfine sugar
8 tbsp butter
1 egg
1 tsp finely grated lemon rind
confectioners' sugar and grated chocolate, for sprinkling

For the filling

3/4 cup ricotta cheese
1/4 cup confectioners' sugar
3/4 tsp vanilla extract
1 medium egg yolk
1 tbsp mixed candied fruits or mixed citrus peel
1 oz dark chocolate, finely chopped or grated
1 small egg, beaten

serves 4

1 Put the flour and sugar into a food processor and, working on full speed, add the butter in pieces until fully worked into the mixture. With the food processor still running, add the egg and lemon rind. The mixture should form a dough that just holds together. Scrape the dough onto a sheet of plastic wrap, cover with another sheet, flatten and chill until needed.

2 ▲ To make the filling, push the ricotta through a sieve into a bowl. Stir in the sugar, vanilla extract, egg yolk, peel and chocolate until combined.

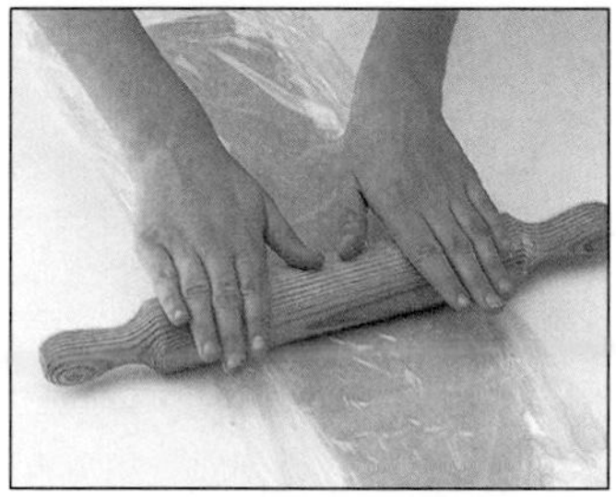

3 ▲ Remove the pastry from the refrigerator and let it come to room temperature. Divide the pastry in half and roll each half between sheets of plastic wrap to make strips, measuring 6 x 22 in. Preheat the oven to 350°F.

4 Arrange heaping spoonfuls of the filling in two rows along one of the pastry strips, ensuring there is at least 1 in clear space around each spoonful. Brush the pastry between the dollops of filling with beaten egg. Place the second strip of pastry on top and press down between each mound of filling to seal.

5 Using a 2 1/2-in plain cookie cutter, cut around each mound of filling to make circular ravioli. Lift each one and, with your fingertips, seal the edges. Place the ravioli on a greased baking sheet and bake for 15 minutes, until golden brown. Serve warm sprinkled with confectioners' sugar and grated chocolate.

Spicy Fruit Cake from Siena

Panforte di Siena

This is a delicious flat cake with a wonderful spicy flavor. Panforte is very rich, so should be cut into small wedges—offer a glass of sparkling wine to go with it.

Ingredients
butter for greasing
1 cup hazelnuts, roughly chopped
½ cup whole almonds, roughly chopped
1⅓ cups mixed candied fruits, diced
¼ tsp ground coriander
¾ tsp ground cinnamon
¼ tsp ground cloves
¼ tsp grated nutmeg
½ cup flour
½ cup honey
generous 1 cup sugar
confectioners' sugar, for dusting
serves 12–14

1 Preheat the oven to 350°F. Grease an 8-in round cake pan with the butter. Line the base of the pan with parchment paper.

2 ▲ Spread the nuts on a baking tray and place in the oven for about 10 minutes, until lightly toasted. Remove and set aside. Lower the oven temperature to 300°F.

3 In a large mixing bowl combine the candied fruits, all the spices and the flour and stir together with a wooden spoon. Add the nuts and stir in thoroughly.

Cook's Tip
This will store in an airtight container for up to 2 weeks.

4 ▲ In a small heavy saucepan, stir together the honey and sugar and bring to a boil. Cook the mixture until it reaches 280°F on a sugar thermometer or when a small bit forms a hard ball when pressed between fingertips in ice water. Take care when doing this and use a spoon to remove a little mixture out of the pan for testing.

5 ▲ At this stage, immediately pour the sugar syrup into the dry ingredients and stir in well until evenly coated. Pour into the prepared pan. Dip a spoon into water and use the back of the spoon to press the mixture into the pan. Bake for 1 hour.

6 When ready, it will still feel quite soft but will harden as it cools. Cool completely in the pan and then turn out onto a serving plate. Dust with confectioners' sugar before serving.

Hazelnut Bites

Nocciolini

Serve these sweet little nut cookies as petits fours with after-dinner coffee.

Ingredients
8 tbsp butter, softened
3/4 cup confectioners' sugar, sifted
1 cup flour
3/4 cup ground hazelnuts
1 egg yolk
blanched whole hazelnuts, to decorate
confectioners' sugar, to finish
makes about 26

1 ▲ Preheat the oven to 350°F. Line 3–4 baking sheets with parchment paper. Cream the butter and sugar with an electric mixer until light and fluffy.

2 ▲ Beat in the flour, ground hazelnuts and egg yolk until evenly mixed.

Cook's Tip
Don't worry that the cookies are still soft at the end of the baking time—they will harden as they cool.

3 ▲ Take a teaspoonful of the mixture at a time and shape it into a round with your fingers. Place the rounds well apart on the baking paper and press a whole hazelnut into the center of each one.

4 ▲ Bake the cookies, one tray at a time, for about 10 minutes or until golden brown, then transfer to a wire rack and sift over confectioners' sugar over them to cover. Let cool.

Ladies' Kisses

Baci di dama

These old-fashioned Piedmontese cookies make pretty petits fours.

Ingredients
10 tbsp butter, softened
1/2 cup confectioners' sugar
1 egg yolk
1/2 tsp almond extract
1 cup ground almonds
1 1/2 cups flour
2 ounces chocolate
makes 20

1 Cream the butter and sugar with an electric mixer until light and fluffy, then beat in the egg yolk, almond extract, ground almonds and flour until evenly mixed. Chill until firm, about 2 hours.

2 Preheat the oven to 325°F. Line 3–4 baking sheets with parchment paper.

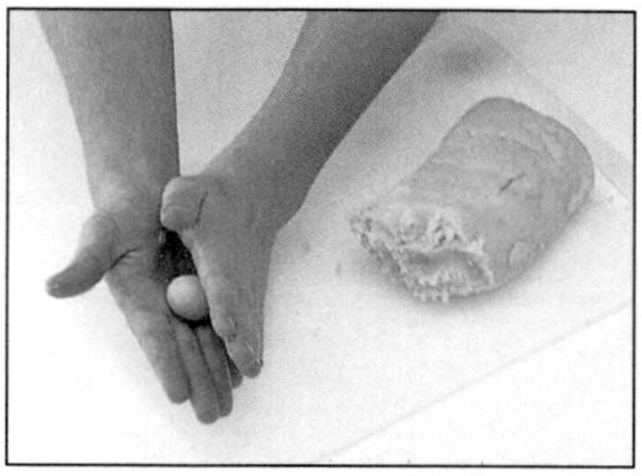

3 ▲ Break off small pieces of dough and roll into balls with your hands, making 40 altogether. Place the balls on the baking sheets, spacing them out, as they will spread in the oven.

Cook's Tip
These cookies look extra dainty served in frilly petit four cases.

4 Bake the cookies for 20 minutes or until golden. Remove the baking sheets from the oven, lift off the paper with the cookies on, then place on wire racks. Let the cookies cool on the paper. Repeat with the remaining mixture.

5 ▲ When the cookies are cold, lift them off the paper. Melt the chocolate in a bowl over a pan of hot water. Sandwich the cookies in pairs, with the melted chocolate. Let cool and set before serving.

Tea Cookies

Pastine da the

These cookies are very quick and easy to make. If you don't want to pipe the mixture, simply spoon it onto the baking paper and press it down with a fork.

Ingredients
10 tbsp butter, softened
3/4 cup confectioners' sugar, sifted
1 egg, beaten
a few drops of almond extract
2 cups flour
2–3 large pieces of candied peel
makes 20

Variation
Use 10 candied cherries instead of the candied peel. Cut them in half and press one half, cut-side down, into the center of each cookie.

1 Preheat the oven to 450°F. Line two baking sheets with non-stick baking paper.

2 Cream the butter and sugar with an electric mixer until light and fluffy, then beat in the egg, almond extract and flour until evenly mixed.

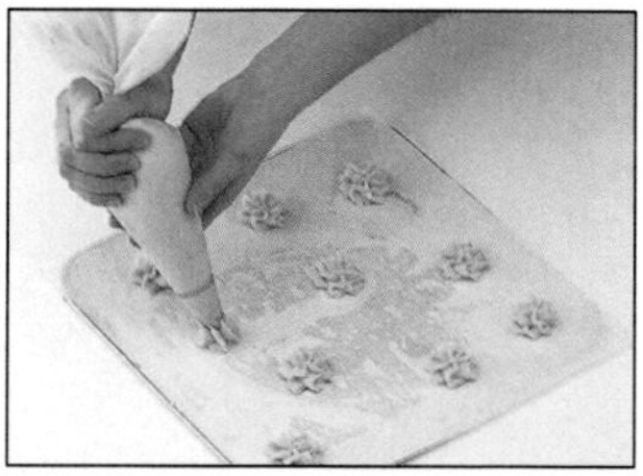

3 ▲ Spoon the mixture into a piping bag fitted with a star nozzle and pipe 10 rosette shapes on each of the baking sheets.

4 ▲ Cut the candied peel into small diamond shapes and press one diamond into the center of each cookie, to decorate. Bake for 5 minutes or until golden. Transfer the cookies on the baking paper to a wire rack and let cool. Lift the cookies off the paper when cool.

Index

Index

Index

Notes

Notes

NOTES

Notes